Learning Together

Teachers have long understood that the best way to learn is to teach. This is equally true for students. This book explores student learning within the context of peer tutoring and offers a practical guide to activities. Focusing on peer tutoring in higher education, the book contains chapters on:

- promoting and planning peer tutoring;
- preparing students for learning in this way;
- theoretical frameworks underlying the practice;
- beneficial effects associated with peer tutoring.

This book also contains contributions from practitioners who reflect on the problems they have encountered and the solutions they have tried.

With useful summaries at the end of every chapter, and clear, helpful tables to aid the practitioner, *Learning Together* will be a valuable resource to teachers and staff developers in higher education, as well as teacher trainers and education researchers.

Nancy Falchikov has worked as a teacher in higher education for many years, and has been researching ways of improving learning and teaching since the mid-1980s. Until recently she was a senior lecturer in psychology at Napier University, Edinburgh. She is now a member of the Educational Developments Service at Napier and a research fellow in the Department of Higher and Further Education, the University of Edinburgh.

Learning Together

Peer tutoring in higher education

Nancy Falchikov

With contributions by
Margo Blythman, David Boud, Rebecca Brent, Ruth Cohen, Donald F. Dansereau, Richard M. Felder, Sinclair Goodlad, Daphne Hampton, Melissa Highton, Deborah Laurs, Barbara McCombs, Robert Neale, Dianna Newbern, Jane Sampson, Nils Tomes, Neal Whitman, Erin Wilson, Jim Wood

London and New York

First published 2001
by RoutledgeFalmer
11 New Fetter Lane, London EC4P 4EE

Simultaneously published in the USA and Canada
by RoutledgeFalmer
29 West 35th Street, New York, NY 10001

RoutledgeFalmer is an imprint of the Taylor & Francis Group

Typeset in Goudy by The Midlands Book Typesetting Co., Leicestershire
Printed and bound in Great Britain by St Edmundsbury Press,
Bury St Edmonds, Suffork

British Library Cataloguing in Publication Data
A catalogue record for this book is available from the British Library

Library of Congress Cataloging in Publication Data
Falchikov, Nancy, 1939–
    Learning together : peer tutoring in higher education/Nancy Falchikov.
        p. cm.
    Includes bibliographical references (p.) and index.
        1. Peer-group tutoring of students.   2. College teaching.   I. Title.
LB1031.5 .F35 2001
378.1'794–dc21
                                                                    00-051775

ISBN 0–415–18261–1 (pbk.)
        0–415–18260–3 (hbk.)

Contents

Tables and figures

Tables

Figures

List of contributors

Margo Blythman is the teaching and learning co-ordinator at The London College of Printing. She has wide experience in the area of study support and tutorial development in both FE and HE. Her current post also includes responsibility for retention strategy, student feedback and staff development in relation to teaching, learning and assessment.

Communication should be directed to: London College of Printing, Elephant and Castle, London SE1 6SB, UK; Telephone +44 171 514 6698; Fax +44 171 514 6535; E-mail **m.blythman@lcp.linst.ac.uk**

David Boud is Professor of Adult Education and Associate Dean of Research in the Faculty of Education, University of Technology, Sydney (UTS). He has written extensively on teaching and learning in higher education.

Communication should be directed to: PO Box 123, Broadway, NSW 2007, Australia; Telephone: +61 2 9514 3945; Fax: +61 2 9514 3933; E-mail **David.Boud@uts.edu.au   http://www.education.uts.   edu.au/staff/ boud.html; http://www.ravl.uts.edu.au**

Rebecca Brent is an educational consultant, faculty development co-director of the SUCCEED Engineering Education Coalition, and Adjunct Professor of Education at East Carolina University, Greenville, North Carolina. She has taught undergraduate and graduate courses in classroom organization and management, instructional planning, and language arts methods, and published articles on co-operative learning, uses of writing in undergraduate courses, classroom and computer-based simulations in teacher education, and the promotion of listening skills in students. She was formerly an Associate Professor of Education at East Carolina University, where she won the University Outstanding Teacher Award.

Communication should be directed to: College of Engineering, North Carolina State University, Raleigh, NC 27695-7904, USA; Telephone +1 919 851-5374; Fax: +1 919 852-5338; E-mail: **rbrent@mindspring.com**

Ruth Cohen is a Senior Lecturer in the Faculty of Education, University of Technology, Sydney. She is well known for her work on the recognition of prior learning and experiential learning. Recent work has been in the development of a national programme for technical education in Mexico, and currently Ruth is managing an English Language Training project for Japanese teachers of English in Japan.

Communication should be directed to: PO Box 7425, Bondi Beach, NSW 2026, Australia; Telephone and fax +61 2 9130 3133; E-mail **Ruth.Cohen@uts.edu.au**

Donald F. Dansereau has been on the faculty at Texas Christian University since 1969, where he is now Professor of Psychology and Senior Research Scientist in the Institute of Behavioral Research. He teaches graduate statistics and cognitive psychology, and his research focuses on cognitive approaches for improving education, and drug-abuse prevention and treatment. His interests include the development of theoretical models on how individuals acquire and use complex information. His publications include over 120 papers.

Communication should be directed to: Cognitive Psychology, Carnegie-Mellon University, 1969, USA, E-mail; **d.dansereau@tcu.edu**

Nancy Falchikov has worked as a teacher in higher education for many years, and has been researching ways of improving learning and teaching since the mid-1980s. She has always linked her discipline, psychology, with her practice. She has published widely on aspects of peer learning such as self- and peer assessment, group process analysis and student approaches to learning, in addition to her work on peer tutoring.

Communication should be directed to: Educational Developments Service, Napier University, Craighouse Campus, Craighouse Road, Edinburgh, EH10 5LG, UK; Telephone +44 131 455 6108; Fax +44 131 455 6191; E-mail **n.falchikov@napier.ac.uk**

Richard M. Felder is Celanese Acetate Professor Emeritus of Chemical Engineering at North Carolina State University, Raleigh, North Carolina, and faculty development co-director of the SUCCEED Engineering Education Coalition. He has authored or co-authored over 150 papers on chemical process engineering and engineering education. His honours include the R. J. Reynolds Award for Excellence in Teaching, Research, and Extension in 1982, the Chemical Manufacturers Association National Catalyst Award in 1989, and the American Society for Engineering Education Chester F. Carlson Award for Innovation in Engineering Education in 1997. He was selected as one of five Outstanding Engineering Educators of the Century by the Southeastern Section of the ASEE in 1993.

Communication should be directed to: Department of Chemical Engineering, North Carolina State University, Raleigh, NC 27695-7905, USA; Telephone +1 919 515-2327; Fax +1 919 852-5338; E-mail **rmfelder@mindspring.com**
Web site: **http://www2.ncsu.edu/effective_teaching/**

Sinclair Goodlad is Professor and Director of the Humanities Programme at the Imperial College of Science, Technology and Medicine, University of London. He has taught in India and at MIT and has been visiting associate at the University of California Berkeley. He has written and edited a number of books about tutoring including, *Students as tutors and mentors* (1995a) and *Mentoring and tutoring by students* (1998). One of his recent books, *The quest for quality: sixteen forms of heresy in higher education* (1995b), locates tutoring in the wider context of a systematic philosophy of higher education. With Stephanie McIvor, he recently published a study extending the 'tutoring' idea to museum interpretation – *Museum volunteers* (1998).

Communication should be directed to: Director of the Humanities Programme, Imperial College of Science, Technology & Medicine, Exhibition Road, London SW7 2BX, UK; Telephone +44 171 594 8752; Fax +44 171 594 8759; E-mail **s.goodlad@ic.ac.uk**

Daphne Hampton is a learning development tutor in the study support team at the London College of Printing. She has worked in HE for many years, during which time she has been a tutor/counsellor for the Open University and taught interpersonal behaviour, personal effectiveness and communication studies to students from a wide range of backgrounds, including business, the arts and printing and publishing. As well as study support, she has a particular interest in tutorial provision and supporting autonomous student learning.

Communication should be directed to: London College of Printing, Elephant and Castle, London SE1 6SB, UK; Telephone +44 171 514 6648; Fax +44 171 514 6535; E-mail **d.hampton@lcp.linst.ac.uk**

Melissa Highton was until recently Academic Development Officer at Napier University. Her role was to investigate and develop opportunities for students to gain academic credit for the learning achieved through activities they become involved in alongside their other studies. She now works in the Educational Development Centre at Royal Holloway University of London.

Communication should be directed to: Educational Development Centre, Bedford Library, Royal Holloway University of London, Egham, Surrey, TW20 0EX; Telephone +44 (0) 1784 41 4371

Deborah Laurs is a Senior Tutor in the School of English and Media Studies at Massey University, Palmerston North, New Zealand. She taught alongside Robert Neale in his very successful course, 'Writing: Theory and Practice', for ten years. She also contributes to the teaching of courses in Written Communication (i.e. academic writing), Performance Drama, Media Studies and runs a team-taught paper, 'Survey of English Literature: six hundred years of poetry in 12 weeks'! Currently, she is undertaking doctoral research on the representation of adolescence in New Zealand children's fiction.

Communication should be directed to: Senior Tutor, School of English and Media Studies, Massey University, Private Bag 11 222, Palmerston North, New

Zealand; Telephone direct dial: +64 6 350 5799 ext 7276 or +64 9 443 9799 ext 7276; School fax: +64 350 5672; E-mail: **D.E.Laurs@massey.ac.nz**

Barbara McCombs received her PhD in Educational Psychology from Florida State University and has spent more than 25 years directing research and development efforts in the area of motivational and self-development training programmes for empowering youth and adults. She currently directs the Human Motivation, Learning, and Development Center at the University of Denver Research Institute. In this position, she leads a variety of applied research projects that focus on ways in which to best apply research-validated learner-centred psychological principles to the design, implementation, and evaluation of K-12, undergraduate, graduate, and adult learning and training programmes and environments. Topics on which Center activities focus include professional development, school violence prevention, systemic educational reform, and personal and educational systems change. Learner- and person-centred models for addressing human motivation, learning, and development needs are applied to research, development, and evaluation activities within a living systems framework.

Communication should be directed to: Senior Research Scientist, Human Motivation, Learning, and Development Center, University of Denver Research Institute, Boettcher East – Room 218, 2050 E. Iliff Ave., Denver, CO 80208, USA; Telephone +1 303 871-4245; Fax +1 303 871-2716; E-mail **bmccombs@du.edu**

Robert Neale was educated at Balliol College, Oxford, became Head of English at Sherborne School and taught at the University of Michigan. He spent most of his working life, however, at New Zealand's Massey University, specializing in medieval literature (English and Latin) and establishing New Zealand's first university course in Writing. He served for twenty years as University Public Orator, and retired in 1999.

Communication should be directed to: 111 Manawatu Street, Palmerston North, New Zealand; Telephone +64 6 358 4717; E-mail **R.A.Neale@massey.ac.nz**

Dianna Newbern is a Lecturer in the Department of Psychology, Texas Christian University, Fort Worth, TX, where she teaches cognitive psychology, organizational psychology, and human relations. She also participates in research projects in the Center for Productive Communication, M. J. Neeley School of Business and at the Institute of Behavioral Research; both are also part of Texas Christian University. Dianna's research is directed towards understanding cognitive, emotional, and interpersonal factors that affect academic learning outcomes and workplace performance. This work involves the development and implementation of practical strategies to boost performance in educational, organizational, and drug-abuse treatment settings. She presents research findings at scientific meetings and conducts business management training workshops.

Communication should be directed to: Department of Psychology, Texas Christian University, TCU Box 298920, Fort Worth, TX 76129, USA. Telephone +1 61 817 257-6438; Fax +1 61 817 257-7681; E-mail: **d.newbern@tcu.edu**

Jane Sampson is a lecturer in the Faculty of Education at the University of Technology, Sydney with a particular focus on community and Aboriginal education and the professional development of adult educators.

Communication should be directed to: Faculty of Education, University of Technology, Sydney, PO Box 123, Broadway, NSW 2007, Australia; E-mail **Jane.Sampson@uts.edu.au**

Nils Tomes is Manager of the Learning Technology Centre at Heriot-Watt University, Edinburgh, a centre of expertise within the UK in the application and evaluation of educational technologies. The Learning Technology Centre designs and integrates educationally focused systems, bringing together collaborative and interactive technologies.

Communication should be directed to: The Learning Technology Centre, Heriot-Watt University, Edinburgh EH14 4AS, UK; Telephone: +44 131 451 3282; Fax: +44 131 451 3283: E-mail: **N.Tomes@hw.ac.uk**

Neal Whitman is a doctor of education who teaches doctors of medicine how to teach more effectively. He is a professor in the Department of Family and Preventive Medicine at the University of Utah School of Medicine and the School's Director of Educational Development. He has been teaching and writing about medical education since 1971 and has been on the faculty of the University of Utah School of Medicine since 1981. In 1999, he won the Gender Equity Award from the Utah Chapter of the American Medical Women's Assocation.

Communication should be directed to: Department of Family and Preventive Medicine, University of Utah School of Medicine, 50 North Medical Drive, University of Utah, Salt Lake City, Utah 84132, USA; Telephone +1 801 581-7234; Fax +1 801 581-2759; E-mail **nwhitman@dfpm.utah.edu**

Erin Wilson is a lecturer at La Trobe University in Melbourne, Australia. She has spent much of the past thirteen years working in Indigenous adult education, mostly in remote areas of Australia, and most recently with the Centre for Aboriginal Studies at Curtin University in Western Australia. She has research interests in this area and is currently concluding a Doctorate on the subject of 'agency' in education and research in postcolonial contexts.

Communication should be directed to: Flexible Teaching and Learning, Academic Development Unit, La Trobe University, Bundoora, Victoria 3083, Australia; Telephone: +61 3 9479 3528; Fax +61 3 9479 2996; E-mail **e.wilson@latrobe.edu.au**

Jim Wood, a qualified National Vocational Qualifications (NVQ) Assessor, is Co-ordinator of the National Mentoring Pilot Project at Universities of Newcastle and Northumbria and Project Manager of the Tyneside and Northumberland Students into Schools Project. The project recruits, trains, places, supports and evaluates the work of over 400 undergraduate student tutors each year. Over 70 per cent of the students can achieve degree course credit by choosing a tutoring module or unit in which they develop a portfolio of evidence which demonstrates their competence in key skills. Jim presented a seminar at the 2nd BP International Student Tutoring and Mentoring Conference and also contributed a chapter to the book of the conference.

Communication should be directed to: Project Manager, Tyneside and Northumberland Students into Schools Project, Joseph Cowan House, St Thomas St, Newcastle, NE1 7RU, UK; Telephone +44 191 222 8677; E-mail **j.wood@newcastle.ac.uk; http://www.ncl.ac.uk/sis**

Preface

WHO IS THIS BOOK FOR?

This book explores student learning in the context of peer tutoring. It provides a practical guide to activities, a theoretical framework in which to situate peer tutoring and reviews of relevant empirical work on the subject. It also contains contributions by practitioners which illuminate a variety of issues and problems. It is hoped that teachers in further and higher education, researchers and staff developers may find the book a valuable resource.

HOW TO READ THIS BOOK

The book is concerned with the design, delivery and evaluation of peer tutoring and with the context in which it operates. There are two main strands to the book: the first situates peer tutoring in context and the second provides a practical guide to the development of peer-tutoring schemes. Both strands develop out of the introduction and first two chapters. In the introduction, I define key terms and explore issues surrounding the concept of 'peer'. Chapter 1, 'What is peer tutoring?', provides an introduction to many useful methods arranged in a taxonomy, and includes tables and 'How to do' sheets containing information necessary for implementation of each approach to peer tutoring. This chapter is designed as a practical resource to help readers. It is long, but is the core of the book for those interested in practical methods. Chapter 2, 'Beneficial effects: why teachers use peer tutoring', investigates the reasons why teachers have introduced peer tutoring into their programmes and explores its effects and benefits.

There are then three possible ways of proceeding though the book. It is, of course, possible to read straight through the chapters in the order in which they are presented. This route will provide the reader with information about peer tutoring in a theoretical and research context, and with practical advice about the practice. However, those whose interest is primarily in the practical might wish to move straight on to Chapters 5, 6, 7, 8 and 9. This I have named the 'practical' route. An alternative route takes the reader to Chapters 3 and 4 which investigate how knowledge and use of the theoretical underpinnings of peer tutoring may increase our understanding of the processes involved in the practice. This is the 'processes' route. Both of these routes conclude with Chapters 10 and 11 which contain reflections from practitioners and my personal reflections and suggestions for ways forward, respectively.

The 'processes' route through the book starts with Chapter 3, 'Theoretical frameworks for peer tutoring'. In this chapter, I stress the value and importance of theoretical approaches to study design and evaluation which will help readers continue to develop new approaches to their own teaching.

In Chapter 4, 'How theory can inform practice', we investigate how theory may be used to help shed light on problems encountered in peer tutoring. I revisit data from an early implementation of peer tutoring by myself and Carol Fitz-Gibbon (Falchikov and Fitz-Gibbon, 1989) which had pointed to tutor–tutee differences, and formulate questions and predictions derived from various social-psychological theoretical standpoints. I then re-analyse the data in order to test predictions and obtain answers. In this way, we see how theory can increase understanding and, thus, inform practice.

The 'practical' route moves to Chapters 5 and 6 which are designed to help teachers introduce peer tutoring into their programmes. Chapter 5, 'Planning and promoting peer tutoring', focuses on issues from a teacher's perspective, and includes a set of 'golden rules' for setting up schemes contributed by Sinclair Goodlad. It also includes a training workshop for use by staff developers. Some responses to frequently asked questions bring the chapter to a close. Chapter 6, 'Helping students become peer tutors', consists of a review of different ways of training and supporting students in their efforts to become good peer tutors.

In Chapter 7, 'Evaluation of peer tutoring schemes', I argue, along with Congos and Schoeps (1997: 24) among others, that, 'in today's higher education climate – one stressing outcome measurement and cost effectiveness – program evaluation is essential'. The chapter focuses on qualitative and quantitative evaluation methods, providing examples of each.

I believe that problems present us with opportunities for learning more about events and Chapter 8, 'Problems associated with peer tutoring', looks at difficulties that practitioners may encounter. It also provides answers to four frequently asked questions. In addition, the chapter includes a contribution from Richard Felder and Rebecca Brent on group composition.

In Chapter 9, 'Technology-supported collaborative learning', Nils Tomes discusses some issues relating to the ways that collaborative learning and peer tutoring may be supported by technology, particularly computer-based approaches.

Chapters 10 and 11 are important concluding chapters for all routes through the book. They contain reflections on practice and are also concerned with aspects of problems associated with peer tutoring.

Chapter 10, 'Benefiting from hindsight: practitioners reflect on peer tutoring', contains nine contributions from practitioners who reflect on problems they have encountered in their own work and offer advice based on their experiences. The chapter starts with reflections from Melissa Highton and Jim Wood on issues associated with the accreditation of undergraduate peer tutoring in schools. Next, Barbara McCombs discusses motivation in the context of peer learning, and Daphne Hampton and Margo Blythman describe their scheme of informal peer tutoring in study support networks, designed to encourage attendance. Problems encountered in the assessment of peer learning are then discussed by Ruth Cohen, David Boud and Jane Sampson. Next, Erin Wilson reflects on some problems of peer learning at a distance. Dianna Newbern and Donald Dansereau's contribution follows. In this, they explain the origins of the Scripted Co-operative Dyad (SCD) technique and outline key steps in the development of their work. The development of the studies that make up this corpus is particularly interesting, as it resembles a good detective story in many respects. Unanswered questions and problems that arise during studies are followed up, and new studies designed to test new hypotheses. In this way, understanding of the phenomenon of the SCD technique grows. Chapter 10 concludes with two case studies of peer teaching and collaborative learning in contrasting contexts. Robert Neale and Deborah Laurs describe co-operative learning in the teaching of writing, and Neal Whitman reflects on peer teaching in a medical school.

In the final chapter, Chapter 11, 'Reflections and prospects', I summarize the key issues that have arisen in the book, and reflect on the development of my own practice and research. I also suggest some interesting directions for future action research.

The structure of the book is summarized in Figure 0.1.

ACKNOWLEDGEMENTS

I would like to express particular thanks to all the contributors whose additions to the book have greatly enriched it. I feel, also, that in collaborating with them I have enlarged my circle of colleagues and friends. I wish also to thank students and colleagues who have provided me with not only a rich source of research data but also many stimulating discussions and ideas. I hope they have benefited as much as I have.

I wish to acknowledge the help and support given to me by Greg Michaelson who, after reading and commenting on all chapters, sometimes more than once, knows more about peer tutoring than is probably good for him. I also thank George Brown for very helpful feedback and encouragement during the process of writing. Thanks, too, are due to Anna Clarkson at RoutledgeFalmer, for very constructive suggestions about improving the manuscript.

Richard Felder and Rebecca Brent's contribution to Chapter 8 is an extract from ERIC document 377 038, October 1994, 'Co-operative learning in technical courses: procedures, pitfalls and payoffs', 6–9, reprinted with permission of the authors.

Sinclair Goodlad's contribution is an extract from his keynote address to the 2nd BP Regional Conference on Tutoring and Mentoring at Murdoch University, Western Australia, September 1999, reprinted with the author's permission.

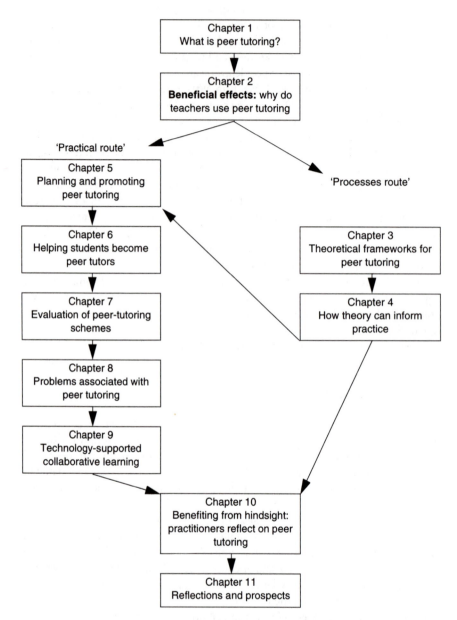

Figure 0.1 Structure of the book and possible routes through it

Finally, I wish to thank Melissa Highton for her permission to use support materials from her tutoring module in Tables 6.1, 'Setting personal goals', 6.2, 'Instructions for completing diary sheets' and Table 7.1, 'A sample module evaluation form', Nils Tomes for permission to include Figure 9.1, 'The learning cycle' and the American Psychological Association for permission to reprint Table 10.1, 'The APA learner-centred principles'.

Note

Some website addresses have been included in the book. While these are active at the time of writing, their existence in the future cannot be guaranteed. I apologize to readers for any frustration caused should websites cease to be.

Introduction

Students co-operate to learn

There are many confusing terms in the context of higher education. In the field of peer learning and assessment, for example, the word 'peer' may be found in combination with a variety of nouns: 'peer assessment'; 'peer feedback'; 'peer tutoring'. We can also add to this list 'peer teaching' and 'peer learning'. While all these practices involve some form of student interaction with their peers, and all are designed to aid the process of learning, the activities have distinct characteristics. In order to minimize confusion, I shall describe what I understand by each, starting with a discussion of who is a 'peer'.

WHO MAY BE DESCRIBED AS A 'PEER'?

Most people would share a common-sense understanding of the terms 'peer' and 'peer group'. Broadly, a peer is someone of the same social standing, while a peer group consists of those of the same status with whom one interacts. When teaching by peers was introduced into higher education in 1951 at the Free University of Berlin, use was made of a practical rule-of-thumb definition of 'peer', namely, peers were taken to be students at a similar age and educational level (Goldschmid and Goldschmid, 1976). However, the term 'peer' is now used to describe a variety of relationships in the context of teaching and learning, and the degree to which students are truly 'peers' varies across the range of possible peer tutoring applications. Whitman (1988) classified relationships between tutors and tutees on the basis of the degrees of similarity and difference between partners, and identified several types of peer tutoring used in higher education, some classified as involving 'near-peers', others making use of 'co-peers'. Whitman saw 'near-peer' tutors, such as undergraduate teaching assistants, tutors and counsellors, as being at a more advanced level than the learner, while 'co-peers', such as partners or work group members, are deemed to be at the same level.

Theodore Newcomb (Newcomb and Wilson, 1966) identified the peer group as the single most powerful influence in undergraduate education.

WHAT IS PEER ASSESSMENT?

In peer assessment, members of a class grade the work or performance of their peers using relevant criteria. Peer assessment may also involve students giving feedback to peers. As with self-assessment, in peer assessment, marks may be awarded by students or negotiated with teachers. Marks may or may not be used for formal grading purposes. For most practitioners, a key aim of peer assessment is to enhance learning.

Student involvement in assessment can be peripheral or extensive. It can vary from a single simple decision taken by students, such as determining the submission date of assignments, or ascertaining preferred modes of assessment, to involvement in the entire process. Where students are involved in all stages of assessment, the first thing that needs to be done is for teachers and learners to agree on the criteria by which work or performance will be judged. Sometimes, these criteria are supplied by the teacher. Very infrequently, students supply their own criteria in the absence of the teacher. Once criteria have been identified, self- or peer assessment may then follow.

For some time, I have been collecting papers on peer assessment for a study which synthesizes results from investigations involving statistical comparisons (Falchikov and Goldfinch, 2000). Quantitative peer assessment studies which compared peer and teacher marks were subjected to meta-analysis, a technique which allows results collected in a wide variety of contexts to be compared. The analysis suggested that peer assessments more closely resemble teacher assessments when students are required to make global judgements based on clear and explicit criteria, and when students are familiar with, and have some degree of ownership of, the criteria, rather than when grading involves assessing several individual dimensions. Assessment of professional practice appears to be more difficult than assessment of academic products and processes. Peer–teacher similarities were greater in well-designed studies than in poorly designed ones.

WHAT IS PEER FEEDBACK?

In peer feedback, students engage in reflective criticism of the work or performance of other students using previously identified criteria and supply feedback to them. This may be a 'one-off' activity or involve a series of meetings during which students supply feedback to peers on increasingly polished versions of a piece of written work.

For me, the practice of peer feedback developed out of my work on peer assessment. My analyses of quantitative and qualitative self- and peer-assessment data had pointed not only to many perceived benefits, but also to some problem areas. Students were reluctant to evaluate their peers, particularly when they were also friends.

> Marking someone else's (essay) is hard as the person may be annoyed if their assessment mark is lowered because of you.
>
> (Falchikov, 1986: 159)

I find it difficult to assess people as fairly as I want to. You may feel obliged to friends – everybody knows everybody's writing.

(Falchikov, 1995: 289)

Thus, it was not too surprising that I found that peer assessments tended to be slightly more generous than either self- or teacher assessments. Students sometimes indicated that they were aware of the dilemma caused by their valuing the experience of being involved in assessment, but being unhappy about the need to award marks.

This problem acted as a spur to the development of a peer feedback scheme. I extended my peer assessment scheme to include the provision of feedback. The scheme, which I called *Peer Feedback Marking* (PFM), can operate in the assessment of both products (e.g. essays) and processes (e.g. oral presentations) (Falchikov, 1995a, 1995b, 1996). As with peer assessment, in PFM, criteria are identified at the outset, and a feedback form designed to reflect these criteria supplied to students. Students are also required to identify at least one strength of the product or process being assessed and to supply at least one suggestion for improvement. In order to do this successfully, students need to develop diplomatic and constructive ways of communicating critical feedback to their peers.

WHAT IS PEER LEARNING?

In peer learning, students learn with and from each other, normally within the same class or cohort. Interaction with peers can result in the development of cognitive or intellectual skills or to an increase in knowledge and understanding. The peer group is widely regarded as an important influence on individuals, as we saw above. As we shall see in Chapter 3, 'Theoretical frameworks for peer tutoring', Piaget (1971) believed that co-operation between peers is likely to encourage real exchange of thought and discussion. He stressed the value of the cognitive conflict that multiple perspectives can bring, and deemed co-operation essential for the development of a critical attitude of mind, objectivity and discursive reflection. Vygotsky (1962), too, valued peer learning. He argued that the range of skills that can be developed with peer collaboration or adult guidance is greater than anything that can be attained alone.

In peer assessment, peer feedback and peer learning, the status of the 'peer' is generally unambiguous. This is not the case when we consider peer tutoring.

WHAT IS PEER TUTORING?

Early manifestations of peer tutoring involved children acting as surrogate teachers whose aim was the transmission of knowledge. In contrast, more modern conceptions of peer tutoring involve 'people from similar social groupings who are not professional teachers helping each other to learn and learning themselves by teaching' (Topping,

1996b: 6). Topping also stressed that peer tutoring is characterized by specific role taking. In other words, someone fulfils the role of tutor while another or others take the role of tutee. Forman and Cazden (1985) argued that, for peer tutoring to occur, there needs to be a difference in knowledge between two individuals, so that the more knowledgeable individual can act as tutor to the less knowledgeable. When knowledge is equal or 'not intentionally unequal' (Forman and Cazden, 1985: 324), equal-status collaboration may be expected.

Bruffee (1993) has argued that the educational benefits of peer tutoring depend on the degree to which tutors and tutees are *real* peers, that is to say, persons of equal standing. Similarly, Hawkins (1982: 29) argued that it is the social dimension of peer tutoring, the 'sharing in the work of the system between two friends who trust each other', the reciprocal relationship between equals, that allows the work to get done. Bruffee (1993) claimed that peer tutoring may be compromised by the nature of the tasks assigned to tutors by lecturers, which often imply or reinforce the authority structure of traditional education. He identified two kinds of peer tutoring: the monitor type, where undergraduates are used as 'institutional manpower for prevailing institutional ends' (Bruffee, 1993: 83), and the collaborative type which mobilizes interdependence and peer influence for educational ends. Most peer tutoring programmes are a mixture of the two, claimed Bruffee, and the degree of peership is governed largely by the way peer tutors are taught to tutor. Thus, student tutors and tutees may both reinforce traditional teaching.

Peer tutoring is not a unitary concept. As we shall see in the first chapter, the label 'peer tutoring' may be applied to a variety of learning situations and the term encompasses a multitude of different ways of constituting learning pairs. Undergraduate students tutor school students, advanced undergraduates tutor less advanced colleagues, or equal-status students work in reciprocal dyadic relationships taking turns to be tutor and tutee.

WHAT DEFINES THE TUTOR'S ROLE?

Defining the role of peer tutor is very difficult, and getting tutors to understand the role themselves is, perhaps, an even more perplexing problem. Peer tutors are often defined by what they are *not*. Peer tutors are not teachers. They do not have a professional qualification. They do not have the power to award final grades. In many traditional educational settings, peer tutors do not have control over the curriculum or over the materials used. It is, therefore, tempting to assume that peer tutors are more or less identical with their tutees. In the higher educational context, the concept of tutor as equal stems from the fact that the near-peer tutor is still an undergraduate, is seen as such (even though the tutor may be a more advanced undergraduate) and is more likely to be able to create an open communicative atmosphere than a teacher. The student tutor's credibility often stems from her/his previous success in 'the system'. The tutee may respond without fear of ridicule or reprisal and may be less reticent about asking 'stupid' questions of a peer tutor than they would of a teacher.

While this equality of status may be the case for same-level peer tutors and tutees, there are clear differences between cross-level peer tutors and the learners for whom they assume some responsibility. Most cross-level peer tutors have been through a selection and training procedure. Many have been selected because of the excellence of their grades. Some have gained some knowledge about theories of learning that their tutees have not. Cross-level tutors are often supplied with support materials which may not be immediately available to tutees. In addition, tutees may be selected because of difficulties they are experiencing. Some peer tutoring schemes make positive use of this difference, applying Vygotsky's concept of the 'zone of proximal development' (Vygotsky, 1962). Potential development may be realized under guidance or in collaboration with more capable peers. In such cases, peer tutors are seen as cognitive facilitators who offer 'cognitive scaffolding' to tutees, thus enabling them to work within their zone of proximal development. We shall return to this issue in Chapter 3.

As I have argued, for me, student involvement in learning, by means of self or peer assessment or peer tutoring, is a way of improving learning, and promoting personal and intellectual development.

WHAT IS PEER TEACHING?

As we shall see in Chapter 1, 'What is peer tutoring?', peer teaching is a variety of peer tutoring in which students take turns in the role of teacher. The kind of activities engaged in during peer teaching can be as varied as the act of teaching itself. Goldschmid and Goldschmid (1976) argued that this method of learning maximizes student responsibility for learning and enhances co-operative and social skills.

SUMMARY

Thus, while there are some differences between the types of student involvement in learning encapsulated in the definitions above, there are also clear similarities. These include:

- all require that criteria and outcomes be made very explicit;
- all require that students take an active part in the process of learning;
- all activities are usually used for formative rather than summative purposes. In addition, involvement in assessment sometimes involves the awarding of marks;
- all activities other than some forms of peer tutoring involve students from the same cohort. Peer tutoring has a greater variety of forms than other peer activities.

In the first chapter, we look at the variety of practices that may be described as 'peer tutoring'.

1   What is peer tutoring?

Peer tutoring can be a great many things, so in this chapter we shall look at a variety of useful techniques organized into a taxonomy. Tables and 'How to do' sheets which illustrate the methods described provide a practical guide to implementation and likely outcomes.

Peer tutoring schemes currently found in higher education may be characterized in a variety of ways. Although there are many features common to all schemes, such as a basic belief in the efficacy of peer learning and benefits of one-to-one or small group experiences, there are also many distinguishing features associated with each. They may differ in terms of their aims and objectives and encompass a variety of group structures to reflect these differences in aims. Different schemes involve different forms of participant interaction.

Thus, a teacher interested in the idea of peer tutoring is faced with what, at first sight, seem to be many pieces of a puzzle with no guiding overall picture to aid understanding of the whole. In addition, the literature on peer tutoring contains a plethora of curiously applied terminology. Interacting pairs of students may be working in 'Scripted Co-operative Dyads' or 'Pairs summarizing/ pairs checking', and their tasks and activities may include 'Dyadic Essay Confrontations', 'Guided Reciprocal Peer Questioning', a 'Three-step interview' or the 'Pair-problem-solving method'. Groups of students co-operating to learn may be using the 'Jigsaw method', 'Roundtable' or 'Peer criticism'. Students may be benefiting from Supplemental Instruction (SI), peer teaching, peer monitoring or peer coaching. We shall look at each of these (and at some other schemes) in this chapter. However, an investigation of the organization of peer tutoring schemes may help us to categorize the large number of peer tutoring varieties.

The question, 'Which variety of peer tutoring is suitable in a given context?', is answered for each group of techniques in summary tables entitled, 'Which technique should I use?' 'How to do' boxes relate information about aims and desired outcomes to specific tutoring methods.

ORGANIZATION OF PEER TUTORING

The organization of peer tutoring involves three key variables:

- the status of participants;
- the location of the activity; and
- the roles undertaken.

Peer tutoring may involve older, more skilled or experienced individuals tutoring younger or less experienced tutees. These individuals may come from the same institution or from a different one. Where two institutions are involved, the tutoring is said to be *both 'cross-level'* and *'cross-institutional'*. Tutoring may also take place between true 'peers', students with similar experiences and achievement levels. When student tutors and tutees are in the same class group, and share similar levels of expertise and are at similar levels of development, the peer tutoring arrangement is referred to as being *'same-level'*.[1] In same-level tutoring, roles of tutor and tutee may be fixed or may change. These distinctions are elaborated in Figure 1.1.

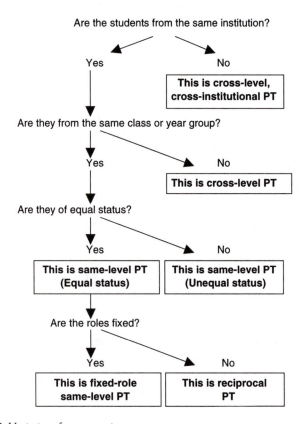

Figure 1.1 Varieties of peer tutoring

At one end of the peer-tutoring continuum we have a clear difference in the status of 'peers'. Students may vary according to age or experience or according to skill level, and may be paired in order to provide support and assistance to the less able partner. Such examples of peer tutoring typically fall into the cross-level peer tutoring category. Typically, in addition to the unequal status of participants, in cross-level peer tutoring, roles within learning pairs are fixed.

VARIETIES OF PEER TUTORING

We shall now look at some examples of the four main categories of peer tutoring that can operate in higher education:

- same-level peer tutoring where participants within a cohort have equal status;
- same-level peer tutoring involving one institution where unequal status is introduced by the co-ordinator;
- cross-level peer tutoring involving one institution where unequal status derives from existing differences between tutors and tutees;
- cross-level peer tutoring involving two institutions.

SAME-LEVEL PEER TUTORING: EQUAL-STATUS PARTICIPANTS WITHIN A DYAD

Simple techniques

Our explorations will include the following varieties of simple techniques designed predominantly to aid interaction and development of skills:

- co-operative note-taking pairs;
- peer coaching;
- peer monitoring;
- three-step interview;
- think-pair-share and think-pair-square;
- flashcard tutoring.

Teachers should choose these techniques according to their desired aims. For example, co-operative note taking might be used when student skills in these areas are deemed inadequate. Peer coaching has particular relevance for trainee teachers or for assisting any student improve an oral presentation or performance skills. Peer monitoring, on the other hand, may be used to help students motivate each other and study together. The three-step interview can act as a simple ice-breaker, while think-pair-share is useful in helping students participate in tutorial discussions. Several examples within this category may be familiar to readers. All are uncomplicated and easily applied.

Co-operative note-taking pairs

In this simple but effective paired learning technique, students are assigned to pairs to compare notes they have taken after a lecture or after reading and making notes from a textual source. This is a technique I use regularly in an informal way during lectures or more formally in tutorials to support other activities. Millis and Cottell (1998) suggested a simple variant. Students are asked to identify three key points and the most surprising thing they heard or read about. In addition, students should take something from their partner to improve their own notes.

Peer coaching

Peer coaching is characterized by members of pairs interacting as equals, by confidentiality, 'non-evaluative' feedback with emphasis on development and the voluntary nature of the scheme (to aid individual ownership). Levene and Frank (1993) described a system of peer coaching developed for academic librarians who are required to teach. Aspects of this technique may also be used in undergraduate teaching and learning. In the original study, librarians formed pairs, selected 'focus areas' and observed each other's classes. They coached each other to develop new skills. It is the coaching aspect of the peer coaching strategy that may be employed to encourage co-operative learning in students in a variety of contexts. Further information about this technique is to be found in 'How to do' box 1.1.

The next technique, peer monitoring, again requires little preparation, but differs from the previous examples in that, in it, students are expected to work together out of class for the duration of a course.

Peer monitoring

Fraser, Beaman, Diener and Kelem (1977) described a study in which students were encouraged and expected to study together in 'learning pairs', preparing and answering each other's questions and motivating each other to study diligently. No special time was allocated for the activity. Students with low Grade Point Averages (GPAs) were 'roughly matched' (Fraser *et al.*, 1977: 102) with students with high averages, though students were not informed of this procedure. Progress of learning pairs was measured by a mid-term multiple-choice test, a final examination, and a paper assignment, and performance compared with that of students taught by means of a traditionally delivered course. At the outset, students in the peer monitoring condition were informed that their grades would be partly determined by averaging the scores of both partners. Further detail of the procedures are contained in 'How to do' box 1.2.

The peer monitoring group outperformed the traditionally taught group, and Fraser *et al.* (1977: 103) concluded that 'the time spent studying with a learning partner was more productive than studying time alone'.

How to do 1.1: Peer coaching

Rationale/objectives

- to formalize and extend the use of spontaneously occurring 'informal coaching that exists among trusted colleagues' (Levene and Frank, 1993: 35);
- to open 'the door to the isolated classroom' (Levene and Frank, 1993: 36);
- to foster individual growth in participants.

Participant characteristics

Participants in Levene and Frank's (1993) study were academic librarians who teach.

How does it work?

1   Participants form pairs (trusted colleagues with similar views).
2   A pre-observation conference takes place. At this meeting, participants

- build trust and rapport;
- share teaching values;
- establish a timetable for observations and future meetings;
- establish ground rules;
- identify points to observe in the classroom;
- agree on ways of collecting data and reporting back.

3   Participants observe one another's classes.
4   A post-observation conference takes place. Very soon after the observation, partners meet privately to discuss the class, and conduct a review of it. A future development plan may be completed.

Outcomes

Participants and authors perceive that peer coaching experiences have benefits. They strengthen collegial relationships, increase participant confidence and encourage 'added instructional innovation'.

Applications

This technique may be of benefit to all trainee (pre-service) teachers during the preparation and delivery of mock lessons/lectures. Students preparing for oral presentations might be encouraged to use the technique (formally or informally). It may also have a use as an in-service staff development activity in any educational setting.

Derived from Levene and Frank (1993)

Other useful references

Levene and Frank's paper includes references to peer coaching in education generally as well as in the context of libraries.

Three-step interview

In the three-step interview (Nattiv, Winitzky and Drickey, 1991), students interview each other in pairs to learn the opinions and ideas of the other on topics introduced by the teacher. They then report their findings back to the group. This technique, which may be familiar to many readers under another name such as 'introduce your partner' (or, indeed, no name at all), is summarized in 'How to do' box 1.3. This exercise may also be used as an 'ice-breaker'.

How to do 1.2: **Peer monitoring**

Rationale/objectives
- to increase level of performance in large classes;
- to investigate the effects of a group contingency procedure on academic performance.

Participant characteristics
Students of introductory social psychology at the University of Washington.

How does it work?

1 Each student is assigned a learning partner (low GPAs roughly matched with high GPAs, though students are not informed of the matching criterion).
2 Students are informed of the 'group contingency procedure', that is to say, they are told that their final grade for the course will be partly determined by averaging the scores of both partners.
3 Partners are encouraged to study together and to monitor each other's work during their own time.

Outcomes
The peer monitoring group outperformed the traditional group. The number of As and Bs awarded increased substantially in the peer monitoring condition, and the number of Cs decreased. No peer monitoring student performed at the D or F level. As the time spent studying was the same for the two groups, the authors concluded that 'the time spent studying with a learning partner was more productive than studying time alone' (Fraser *et al.*, 1977: 103).

Students in the peer monitoring group recorded higher levels of interest in the subject matter and greater liking for the course than control subjects.

Applications
Applications of this technique are potentially very wide, provided that student support for the group contingency procedure is obtained. In my experience, this may be problematic in the current educational climate.

Derived from Fraser *et al.* (1977)

Think-pair-share

In this system, pairs of students discuss their individual responses to a question posed by the teacher (or, sometimes, to a question from another student). Sherman (1991) attributes the discovery of the think-pair-share technique to Lyman, but I predict that this technique, too, will be very familiar to many readers. I have been using it for a very long time, without the benefit of a name, or the realization that such a common-sense activity might have one. I find this technique useful in tutorials for building up student confidence, allowing pairs to rehearse an answer by discussing and agreeing it, so that a greater proportion of students will participate in class discussion. It is equally useful in large lectures where it may provide time for reflection, and opportunity for pairs of students to compare notes, figuratively and practically.

How to do 1.3: **Three-step interview**

Rationale/objectives

Nattiv *et al.*'s (1991) reasons for introducing a variety of co-operative learning methods (including the three-step interview) into their preservice teacher classes:

- classroom research shows co-operative learning to be effective in producing gains in academic achievement and improved social outcomes;
- students are likely to model effective practice, and use methods they have experienced;
- co-operative learning balances individualistic and competitive learning styles and meets the needs of students who prefer co-operation;
- the rationale for co-operative learning rests on the philosophy of Dewey and his belief in the promotion of democracy and good citizenship in students;
- skills developed through co-operation are emphasized and valued by employers.

Participant characteristics

Pre-service teachers (at Utah State University and the University of Utah) studying secondary education courses in general methods and foundations of education.

Undergraduate students of early childhood education and elementary education.

How does it work?

1 Preparation (in common with other forms of co-operative learning). Preparatory work includes the provision of a rationale for the method, an explanation of procedures, demonstrations and guided practice.
2 Students interview each other in pairs to learn the opinions and ideas of their partner on a topic introduced by the teacher.
3 Students report their findings back to the group.
4 Debriefing and evaluation (in common with other forms of co-operative learning).

Outcomes

Nattiv *et al.* (1991) introduced a variety of co-operative methods into their courses. Outcome measures relate to all methods used, and not to the three-step interview per se.

Attitudes to co-operative learning were measured by means of The Co-operative Learning Attitudinal Survey. Most students valued co-operative methods, and stated their intentions to use them in their own classrooms.

Applications

Applications of co-operative learning methods (including the three-step interview) are very wide indeed. The majority of applications to date have been in pre-tertiary education, but use of co-operative methods in higher education is increasing. Such methods may be used in most subject areas.

Derived from Nattiv et al. (1991)

Millis and Cottell (1998) describe a variant to think-pair-share, the *think-pair-square* technique. In this variant, pairs work together solving a problem, but share their responses in structured learning teams rather than in the larger class group.

Flashcard tutoring

Millis and Cottell (1998: 112) described the technique of flashcard tutoring, or 'reinforcing practice', which they deemed particularly suitable for developing relatively low-level cognitive skills such as learning definitions, memorizing concepts or vocabulary building. Students prepare a set of cards, each with one piece of information that they wish to master. On one side of the card is the question, and on the other, the answer. Working in pairs, students take turns in the role of tutor. The tutor takes the partner's cards and shows her/him the question side. If the correct answer is forthcoming, the card is handed over to the tutee. If not, the answer is revealed and studied. The card then goes to the bottom of the pack. When the tutee has earned all her/his cards, the roles are reversed and the process repeated. 'How to do' box 1.4 contains instructions for carrying out this procedure.

How to do 1.4: Flashcard tutoring

Rationale/objectives
- to reinforce practice;
- to aid learning of definitions;
- to aid concept mastery;
- to aid vocabulary building.

Participant characteristics
Any students in higher education.

How does it work?

1   Students prepare a set of cards with questions on one side and answers on the other. Material is chosen to help individuals master areas which they are finding problematic.
2   Students are allocated a partner.
3   One student assumes or is allocated the role of tutor. The other student becomes the tutee.
4   The tutor takes the tutee's cards and holds up the question side of the first of them.
5   If the tutee answers the question correctly, she/he is given the card. If not, the answer side is revealed and studied. The card then goes to the bottom of the pile.
6   The tutoring continues until the tutee has received all her cards.
7   Roles are reversed and the process repeated until all material is mastered.

Outcomes
Mastery of material.

Applications
This technique is appropriate in situations where relatively low-level cognitive skills development is required, or when 'reinforcing practice' (Millis and Cottell, 1998: 112) is needed.

Derived from Millis and Cottell (1998)

These simple techniques are summarized in Table 1.1. Techniques are paired with aims or desired learning outcomes in order to help readers answer the question, 'Which technique should I use?'

More complex techniques

Next we shall look at some more complex peer tutoring techniques designed to develop a variety of lower- and higher-level cognitive skills and meta cognitive skills, to improve problem-solving skills, help students prepare for tests and examinations, encourage co-operative skills and aid acculturation. These techniques involve a greater degree of preparation than those described above.

The techniques are:

- Dyadic Essay Confrontations (DEC);
- the learning cell;
- pair-problem-solving-method;
- Reciprocal Peer Tutoring (RPT);
- reciprocal teaching;
- Scripted Co-operative Dyads (SCD).

Table 1.1 Which technique should I use?
Rationales for using some same-level peer-tutoring techniques which require little preparation

Technique	Aim/desired outcome
Co-operative note-taking pairs	To help improve students' note-taking skills To encourage students to engage with new material
Peer coaching	To strengthen collegial relationships To increase participant confidence To foster individual growth in participants
Peer monitoring	To increase level of performance in large classes To investigate the effects of a group contingency procedure on academic performance
Think-pair-share and Think-pair-square	To encourage students to discuss responses to questions To encourage participation
Three-step interview	To improve academic achievement To encourage modelling of effective practice To provide opportunities for co-operation To improve social outcomes
Flashcard tutoring	To develop relatively low-level cognitive skills such as learning definitions, memorizing concepts or vocabulary building

Dyadic Essay Confrontations (DEC)

In a paper presented at the annual meeting of the American Educational Research Association in 1991, Sherman reviewed some examples of co-operative pedagogical strategies being used in post-secondary education in the United States at the time. Included among the strategies reviewed was Sherman's own initiative, Dyadic Essay Confrontations (DEC) which he had used in the teaching of psychology at college and university level. In carrying out DEC, students are required to compose an essay question along with a model answer to it, based on the comparison of two treatments of the same material, typically a textbook summary and an original source. Questions (but not answers) are distributed randomly to another member of the class whose task it is to write an answer to the essay question. On completion, students must confront the person who composed the question and discuss similarities and differences between the two answers. Questions and answers are evaluated by both students and teacher, using five dimensions supplied by the teacher (general impression, importance, clarity, integration and creativity). Sherman reported that 'this technique is positively accepted by post-graduate students who find it challenging and satisfying' (Sherman, 1991: 33). DEC may be used in almost all disciplines. Millis and Cottell (1998) reviewed a number of higher education applications. For example, Millis, Cottell and Sherman (1993) themselves have used DEC in university classes in English, accounting and psychology.

Implementation details for Dyadic Essay Confrontations are located in 'How to do' box 1.5.

A sample evaluation form for use by partners engaged in Dyadic Essay Confrontations is shown in Table 1.2. Millis and Cottell (1998) provide an alternative version which does not involve self-assessment but which includes instructor evaluation.

Dyadic Essay Confrontation techniques can help develop a wide variety of useful skills, including that of writing itself. (See p.26.)

The learning cell

The 'learning cell' involves co-operative learning in pairs, in which students alternate asking and answering questions on new set readings. Goldschmid and Goldschmid (1976) argued that the learning within a learning cell must be highly structured for it to be effective. Implementation steps are shown in 'How to do' box 1.6.

In a variant of this scheme, partners A and B read different materials. A then teaches B and vice versa. The learning cell has been found to lead to significantly better performance than the traditional system in a large psychology class. Goldschmid and Goldschmid (1976) also found it attracted good student ratings in terms of morale and experiences of the course.

How to do: 1.5 **Dyadic Essay Confrontations**

Rationale/objectives

'It is based on post-modern thought, higher-level thinking processes and the introduction of conceptual conflict, arousal and motivation through integrating the writing process into the psychology curriculum' (Sherman, 1991: 33).

Participant characteristics

Students studying psychological theories of human development.

How does it work?

1　*Outside class*, students read 2 pieces of literature on the same topic: a chapter from a textbook and a primary source.
2　Students compose essay questions, comparing the textbook summary chapter and the original source and identifying important issues common to both.
3　Students prepare a model answer (maximum length, one side, single spaced).
4　Students bring a copy of their question to class.
5　*In class*, each student answers another's question (approximately 25 mins.).
6　Students read each other's answers.
7　'Confrontations' take place. Pairs of students engage in dialogue over ideas encountered in model and peer answers.
8　The class discusses all questions.
9　Peer evaluations of questions and answers are carried out using criteria supplied by the teacher.
10　Instructor evaluation takes place using the same criteria as students.

Outcomes

Postgraduate students find the technique challenging and satisfying.

Applications

May be applied to any discipline or level of study.

Derived from Sherman (1991)

Other useful references

Sherman (1988); Millis and Cottell (1998).

Pair-problem-solving method

This technique involves exactly what it implies: pairs of students work together solving problems set by the teacher. Koch (1992) described a student-centred model of instruction for learning mathematics which made use of a pair-problem-solving methodology (Whimbey and Lochhead, 1982) and/or small co-operative groups.

Participants are shown a video of the pair-problem-solving processes they are to use during the first meeting of the class, which they then discuss. Koch does not supply examples of such processes, but specifies that both 'good' and 'bad' examples were included. Next, students are randomly assigned to pairs and

Table 1.2 Evaluation form for use by students engaged in DEC

Name

Complete this section *before* carrying out the Dyadic Essay Confrontation (DEC) exercise

What are your sources?
1
2

What is your question?

Complete a short **sample answer** to your question on a separate sheet (not more than 1 side of A4).

Complete this section *after* you have completed the DEC exercise

Partner's name

Please rate yourself/your partner on the aspects of performance listed below. Award marks out of 5, where 5 = Very good, 4 = Good, 3 = Adequate, 2 = Poor, 1 = Failure. Briefly justify your rating.

Quality of the question asked by your   Reason for your rating?
partner

Quality of the sample   Reason for your rating?
answer supplied by partner

Quality of *your* answer to   Reason for your rating?
partner's question

Quality of *partner's answer* to *your*   Reason for your rating?
question

Answer the following questions.
What have you learned from this exercise? What would you do differently next time?

How to do 1.6: **The learning cell**

Rationale/objectives

NB These also relate to peer-teaching initiatives other than the learning cell.

- to capitalize on the fact that the reference group is an important influence on students;
- to involve students actively in their learning;
- to improve learning without increasing financial costs to universities;
- to help familiarize students with 'the system';
- to prevent student unrest (for further explanation, see Goldschmid and Goldschmid, 1976: 15).

Participant characteristics

Undergraduate students of psychology.

How does it work?

'The learning cell must be highly structured for success' (Goldschmid and Goldschmid, 1976: 20).

1 Preparation. All students read an assignment and write questions dealing with the major points.
2 In class, students are randomly assigned a partner and one of the pair asks the other a question.
3 After the answer is received, corrected and amplified, the other asks a question, and so on.
4 The instructor moves from dyad to dyad giving feedback, asking and answering questions.

Outcomes

The learning cell has been found to lead to significantly better performance than the traditional system in a large psychology class (n = 250). It also attracted good student ratings in terms of their morale and experiences.

Applications

The system was used in a number of disciplines in a university setting by Goldschmid and Shore (1974). Results 'demonstrated the learning cell's effectiveness and revealed no apparent restrictions on the size of the class, its level, or the nature of the subject matter' (Goldschmid and Goldschmid, 1976: 21).

The system has also been used in pre-tertiary educational settings.

Derived from Goldschmid and Goldschmid (1976)

Other useful references

Goldschmid and Shore (1974).

asked to work on a problem. After a short time, the entire group discusses the experience of working in pairs and the responsibilities associated with it. The instructor and a teaching assistant model the pair-problem-solving method at the next class meeting and ask students to critique the exercise. The student pairs then carry out a pair-problem-solving exercise involving a non-mathematical problem. For the remainder of the course, students are randomly assigned to pairs or small groups at the beginning of each meeting. During meetings they work together on problem solving and participate in class discussion. Students are carefully monitored throughout the course to ensure that all participate.

The methodology was applied to the teaching of mathematics at the University of Minnesota, and affective and performance outcomes compared with those of a traditionally delivered course. Pair-problem-solving students were found to have decreased maths anxiety and improved attitudes towards themselves as students of mathematics. In addition, they outperformed traditionally taught students on post-test (Koch, 1992). Details of the methodology and outcomes are reported in 'How to do' box 1.7.

Reciprocal Peer Tutoring (RPT) (mutual testing)

Reciprocal Peer Tutoring (RPT) in higher education is associated with the work of Fantuzzo and colleagues at California State University and, more recently, at the University of Pennsylvania (e.g. Fantuzzo, Dimeff and Fox, 1989a; Fantuzzo, Riggio, Connelly and Dimeff, 1989b). RPT has been defined as, 'a collaborative learning intervention that was designed to incorporate peer tutoring behaviors .... to contribute to positive academic outcomes' (Ginsburg-Block and Fantuzzo, 1997: 136). In this form of peer tutoring, randomly selected pairs of students test each other in preparation for a class test. RPT enables each student to play the role of tutor and tutee, and thus reap the benefits derived from teaching, and being taught by, another student. Griffin and Griffin (1998) wished to test the generalizability of the beneficial effects of RPT beyond elementary-school and undergraduate psychology students and investigated the effects of the technique on academic achievement, academic self-efficacy and test anxiety of sophomore undergraduate education students. RPT resulted in higher examination scores and lower levels of subjective distress than control conditions. In addition, RPT received higher satisfaction ratings from participants than those in control conditions (Fantuzzo et al., 1989a). 'How to do' box 1.8 supplies instructions on how to carry out this procedure.

Reciprocal teaching

Reciprocal teaching has its origins in pre-tertiary education. Palincsar and Brown (1984) described a series of studies of reciprocal teaching involving teachers and individual seventh grade students whose comprehension skills were poorly developed. Some of the activities used in this study may be readily modified to meet the needs of higher education today. For example, summarizing, questioning, clarifying and predicting encouraged in reciprocal teaching may be applied to good use in any educational context.

More recent reviews of reciprocal teaching in higher education (e.g. Millis and Cottell, 1998) also see this method as being of use when higher education students

How to do 1.7: **Pair-problem-solving**

Rationale/objectives

Hypotheses associated with Koch's evaluative study stated that students learning by means of the pair-problem-solving method would:

- experience a decrease in anxiety levels when studying maths;
- develop more positive attitudes towards themselves as learners of mathematics;
- acquire equal or greater mathematics proficiency than those studying the course delivered traditionally by means of lectures.

Participant characteristics

Undergraduate students enrolled in a developmental arithmetic course.

How does it work?

1　Three *pre-tests* were administered: a maths anxiety rating, attitudes to one self as a learner of mathematics and a test of mathematical skills.
2　Experimental students were shown a video of the pair-problem-solving processes they were to use during the first meeting of the class. This was followed by a discussion on group dynamics.
3　Students were then randomly assigned to pairs and asked to work on a problem. After a short time, the entire group discussed the process and the responsibilities associated with working in pairs.
4　At the next class meeting, the instructor and a teaching assistant model the pair-problem-solving method and ask students to critique the exercise.
5　Randomly assigned student pairs carry out a pair-problem-solving exercise involving a non-mathematical problem.
6　For the remainder of the course, students are randomly assigned to pairs and/or small groups at the beginning of each meeting. Each class period consists of pair or small group work followed by a large class discussion (of the problem just attempted, homework problems or instructor- or student-generated issues).
7　Students are carefully monitored throughout the course to ensure full participation.
8　At the end of the course, *post tests* are administered (identical with the pre-tests).

NB Steps 1 and 8 relate to the evaluation of the initiative.

Outcomes

All hypotheses were supported. Pair-problem-solving students were found to have decreased maths anxiety and improved attitudes towards themselves as students of mathematics. In addition, they outperformed traditionally taught students on post-test.

Applications

Applications of this methodology are very wide. Many courses already use a problem-solving method, and might wish to try the small group or pair-problem-solving variation.

Derived from Koch (1992)

Other useful reference
Boud and Feletti (eds) (1991).

***How to do* 1.8: Reciprocal Peer Tutoring (RPT)**

Rationale/objectives

Several experimental studies were designed

- to determine effects of RPT on academic achievement, student distress and course satisfaction;
- implemented in order;
- to promote mutual tutoring and its benefits.

Participant characteristics

Undergraduates studying abnormal psychology.

How does it work?

The system runs throughout a semester. The following stages are involved:

1   An introductory session takes place in which the benefits of working with peers are discussed with students, and the procedures outlined.
2   Individual participants are assigned randomly to dyads.
3   Each partner prepares 10 multiple-choice questions on assigned readings and lecture material, plus, for each question, a card with correct answer and a reference to the section or sections of text where the material is covered.
4   Tests are administered to each partner under test-like conditions.
5   Subjects switch papers and tests are then marked by authors.
6   Students take turns in giving explanations for questions answered incorrectly.

Outcomes

RPT resulted in higher examination scores and lower levels of subjective distress than control conditions. In addition, RPT received higher satisfaction ratings from participants than control conditions.

Applications

RPT may be incorporated into the structure of any taught undergraduate class. It has also been used in (grade) schools to support low-achieving students.

Derived from Fantuzzo *et al.* (1989a)

Other useful references

Fantuzzo *et al.* (1989b); Sherman (1991); Ginsburg-Block and Fantuzzo (1997); Griffin and Griffin (1998).

---

need to commit information to memory. Moreover, it also aids mastery of learning. It can promote deep learning, too, due to its focus on 'integrating knowledge, active learning, student–student interactions and immediate feedback' (Millis and Cottell, 1998: 111). See 'How to do' box 1.9.

Guided interaction may also be provided using distance or flexible learning strategies where the 'scaffolding' is supplied in written or electronic form by an expert lecturer.

How to do 1.9: **Reciprocal teaching**

Rationale/objectives

- to help students commit a large body of information to memory (e.g. technical concepts and terminology);
- to promote deep learning by the emphasis on integrating knowledge, active learning, student–student interactions and immediate feedback;
- to increase motivation to learn.

Participant characteristics

None specified.

How does it work?

1. Students study information (a chapter from a book; a paper, etc.) independently.
2. All students are given instruction in the use of teaching techniques beforehand and act as experts to encourage their partner interact with the text. Emphasis is given to four activities: summarizing (self-review), questioning, clarifying and predicting.
3. Paired coaching takes place in class time. Pairs of students alternate in taking the role of expert, guided by instructions ('scaffolding') supplied by the teacher (the absent expert).

Outcomes

Millis and Cottell claim that the technique fulfils its aims and objectives, but provide no evidence to support their claims.

Applications

May be applied to any discipline or level of study.

Derived from Millis and Cottell (1998)

Other useful reference

Rosenshine and Meister (1991).

Scripted Co-operative Dyads (SCD) (Reading and exchange of oral summaries)

The Scripted Co-operative Dyads (SCD) model was devised, researched and refined by Dansereau and co-workers at the Texas Christian University in Fort Worth, Texas. In this system, pairs of students exchange multiple oral summaries of brief sections of textual material. In a paper reporting an early example of SCD peer tutoring, Spurlin, Dansereau, Larson and Brooks (1984) examined dyadic co-operative learning and analysed the effects of role and activity level of the learner on learning. Participants were students of general psychology randomly assigned to same-sex pairs. They participated in three one-and-a-half hour sessions, in which one member of the dyad acted as recaller/oral summarizer and the other as an active or passive listener/ facilitator. Active listeners corrected their partners and elaborated on their summaries. Facilitators shared strategies they had found useful in their own reading and studying. The roles were reversed in some treatment conditions, and students studying on their own served as a no-treatment control. The researchers found that persons alternating recaller and listener roles evaluated the experience more positively than others, and concluded that the alternating condition conferred the greatest benefit on the largest numbers.

> Even though the recallers had the best performance, the alternators also had good performance, and they evaluated the situation more positively. In the long run, the alternating technique may benefit more of the students than the fixed-recaller technique, which allows only half of the students to summarize.
>
> (Spurlin *et al.*, 1984: 461)

The key stages in the method are shown in 'How to do' box 1.10.

O'Donnell, Dansereau, Hall and Rocklin (1987) reported research into the Dansereau team's model of dyadic co-operative learning and subsequent transfer to individual learning. The O'Donnell *et al.* study related investigations of the conditions under which co-operative learning results in positive performance outcomes. In particular, the researchers wished to assess the impact of the frequency of elaboration on performance. Ninety students from an Introductory Psychology class took part, receiving credit for their participation. The study involved the use of the *MURDER text processing strategy*. Students were instructed to:

set the	Mood for learning,
and then read for	Understanding,
	Recall the information read,
	Detect errors and omissions,
	Elaborate on the information to facilitate organization,
and, finally,	Review all information from the text.

Students alternated between the roles of recaller and listener.

Students trained in SCD strategy were found to outperform individuals and dyads not trained in the technique in a transfer test (McDonald, Larson, Dansereau and Spurlin, 1985). Fixed recallers outperformed fixed-role listeners, while the performance of those who alternated roles was mid-way between the two (Larson and Dansereau, 1986).

Dansereau (1987a) later described a variation on the basic SCD strategy in which both students read the text, and follow the co-operative learning instructions. In the variant, the *co-operative teaching* version, students read different material and take turns teaching one another. Both 'scripts' are designed to promote cognitive activities which are important in academic learning. In a later publication, O'Donnell and Dansereau (1992) reviewed research which has attempted to identify variables which influence outcomes of co-operative learning in SCD, and those which may influence the kinds of interactions which take place during learning in the dyads.

Dianna Newbern and Donald Dansereau report more recent developments of this technique in Chapter 10.

How to do 1.10: Scripted Co-operative Dyads (SCD)

Rationale/objectives

- to help pairs of students understand new material and relate it to previous knowledge, using oral summarizing, metacognitive activities (comprehension, error correcting, evaluation) and elaborative activities (use of imagery or analogy);
- to practise and improve co-operative interaction;
- to encourage transfer of metacognitive skills to individual learning.

Participant characteristics

College (undergraduate) students: subject disciplines of participants are not recorded in many cases, though some work has been done involving students of psychology.

How does it work?

1 The procedure is explained to the participants.
2 Pairs of students are assigned roles of Recaller (or Presenter) and Listener.
3 Two pages of text are studied by both, silently, using normal methods.
4 The Recaller summarizes the passage out loud without referring to notes or to the text, but using diagrams or mental maps wherever possible. The Listener has access to text and notes.
5 The Listener makes corrections (in a metacognition role) and additions (in an elaboration role).
6 Discussion takes place between the two, and further correction and amplification take place, resulting in an agreed summary (with diagram if possible).
7 The two reverse roles and repeat stages 3–6 until the whole set reading is completed.

Outcomes

Students trained in SCD strategy outperformed individuals and dyads not trained in the technique in a transfer test (McDonald *et al.*, 1985). Fixed recallers outperformed fixed role listeners, while the performance of those who alternated roles was mid-way between the two (Larson and Dansereau, 1986).

Applications

The SCD strategy may be used in any situation where reading, understanding and remembering new material is required. While it has been used predominantly in higher education, it may equally well be used at other levels of education (further education and schools).

Derived from McDonald *et al.* (1985)

Other useful references

Larson and Dansereau (1986); Dansereau (1987a); Dansereau (1988); Sherman (1991).

Another variant of SCD, the *Read and Explain Pairs* technique, is described by Millis and Cottell (1998). In this variant, both partners start by studying a paragraph of assigned text. One partner then summarizes the contents of the paragraph. Both partners work together to identify the question being asked in the paragraph and agree on a summary that answers the question. They relate what they have learned to previous learning before moving on to the next paragraph. The procedure is repeated and roles may be reversed.

The use of these techniques is governed by what they can help teachers and students achieve. A summary of this information is presented in Table 1.3.

TECHNIQUES TO AID WRITING DEVELOPMENT

The final group of techniques for same-level peer tutoring with equal-status participants aim to improve some aspect of the writing process. These techniques are:

- Collaborative writing, peer criticism and peer review;
- Paired annotations;
- Peer editing;
- Peer response groups.

Collaborative writing, peer criticism and peer review

The development of writing is a major concern to many teachers, not least of all to those of creative writing. However, all academic endeavour involves writing: laboratory reports, business plans, subject specific essays, reports of statistical testing, to name but a few examples. Millis and Cottell (1998: 120) have argued that 'writing and thinking cannot be separated'.

Table 1.3 Which technique should I use? Rationales for using some same-level peer-tutoring techniques

Technique	Aim/desired outcome
Dyadic Essay Confrontations	To introduce conceptual conflict, arousal and motivation 'through integrating the writing process into the psychology curriculum' (Sherman, 1991: 3)
The learning cell	To improve learning by active involvement; to provide social support; to aid acculturation
Pair-problem-solving	To improve problem-solving skills
Reciprocal Peer Tutoring (RPT)	To help preparation for tests and exams
Reciprocal teaching	To encourage co-operative skills such as generating questions, summarizing, clarifying and predicting
Scripted Co-operative Dyads (SCD)	To help students read and understand new material

Bruffee (1978), an early proponent of peer criticism, claimed that his 'Brooklyn Plan' differed from many programmes being undertaken at the time, in that it mobilized peer influence to affect the intellectual growth of students. Under the Brooklyn Plan, 'students learn and practise judgement collaboratively, through a progressive set of analytical and evaluative tasks applied to each other's academic writing, in a context which fosters self-esteem' (Bruffee, 1978: 450).

All participants wrote papers and did critiques. The series of graded steps which constitute the technique are shown in 'How to do' box 1.11.

Dunn (1996) introduced collaboration and peer review in the context of an experimental project in a statistics course. Dunn's students selected partners to whom they were to have a contractual obligation, in that all work was to be shared equally and both partners were to receive the same grade. The written product which was to be achieved by collaborative writing was a laboratory report written in the American Psychological Association (APA) style. Details of Dunn's procedure, which was found to promote 'student appreciation of the creation, presentation and reception of ideas' (Dunn, 1996: 39), are to be found in 'How to do' box 1.12.

It should be noted that, while 'collaborative writing' is already a feature of many courses in post-secondary education, as students undertake more and more group projects, too often, these efforts are not true collaborations, and consist of patched-together individual efforts submitted immediately prior to hand-in date. Dunn's methodology might be applied to great benefit in a variety of such situations to ensure true collaboration and peer review.

Essid (1996) described a collaborative writing study which used the Daedalus Interchange Software in a writing centre for tutor training in order to develop strategies for problematic tutorials. Synchronous or real time computer conferences provided a method for encouraging student discussion and collaborative writing. Evaluations indicated that tutors favoured the new method, in that the synchronous conferences improved group discussion and their tutoring ability.

McGroarty and Zhu (1997) attempted to estimate the importance of preparing students for the task of peer revision. Their study is described in Chapters 6 and 7.

Paired annotations

This technique is designed to help students read for meaning and relate what they have read to other bodies of knowledge. Students, working individually, identify the key point of a paragraph and then reflect on this, noting their reactions and any connections they can make. They then are assigned to pairs to compare the key points identified and their reactions to them. The reasons for their choices are made explicit. Finally, each pair is required to prepare a composite summary of the whole article or chapter together with agreed annotations. This technique is elaborated in 'How to do' box 1.13.

How to do 1.11: Peer criticism: the Brooklyn Plan

Rationale/objectives

● to promote intellectual growth of undergraduates through peer influence

Participant characteristics

Students attending a Writing Center at Brooklyn College.

How does it work?

1 Students write 2 short papers on topics of their choosing.
2 Papers are read aloud to the whole class in order to familiarize everyone with the interests of peers.
3 Students attach a 'peer critique sheet' to one of their papers and exchange them.
4 *Critique 1: examination of the parts of an idea and the relationships between them.* Before the next class, each student writes a critique of the papers received, in which the main point of the paper (its thesis) is identified. In addition, reviewers say what each paragraph 'does' in terms of helping advance the line of argument.
5 *Critique 2: evaluative feedback and application of lessons derived from critique 1.* The second papers are now also exchanged and reviewed, using criteria derived from critique 1. Reviewers are also required to identify the strengths of the paper and to suggest in what ways it might be improved. Comments are limited to structural issues.
6 All materials are submitted to the teacher for comment and grading of papers and critiques.
7 *Critique 3: a critique of content.* About half way through the course peer critiques begin to focus on the content of written assignments. Reviewers are required to discuss content, stating where they agree or disagree with the author, and judging whether authors have made the best possible argument to support the position they take.
8 Papers are returned to authors who evaluate the criticism received, using an 'Author's page' and may modify their papers in response to suggestions.
9 *Critique 4: a critique of the critique.* Instructions for critique 3 are followed (description, evaluation and discussion of content). In addition, a second critique is carried out, in which another peer examines both the paper and the critique, and mediates between the two wherever necessary.

Outcomes

'It reduced the effect of one of the most serious and debilitating limitations of peer influence: the conservative tendency, potentially detrimental to academic development' (Bruffee, 1993: 90).

Applications

Applications are potentially very wide: wherever students are required to complete a written assignment. However, the time commitment necessary to replicate Bruffee's version may militate against use outside writing workshops. My modification of the plan also works well and is capable of fitting into a specialist subject programme (Falchikov, 1996).

Derived from Bruffee (1993)

Other useful references

Bruffee (1978); Falchikov (1996); McGroarty and Zhu (1997).

How to do 1.12: **Collaborative writing and peer review**

Rationale/objectives
- to enable students to teach and learn from each other;
- to develop writing skills.

Participant characteristics

Participants were psychology majors studying a course in Statistics and Research Methods of Psychological Inquiry at Moravian College in Pennsylvania, USA.

How does it work?

1 Students select partners and are told of their contractual obligation to them. Procedures are explained. Students informed about the process journal each must keep to 'reflect on the quality of the effort' of collaboration (Dunn, 1996: 39).
2 Students select a research topic and experimental design.
3 Students identify key variables, search and read relevant literature and refine the research idea.
4 Students undertake outlining, drafting and revision of a 'prospectus' (the Introduction, Method and References sections of an APA manuscript).
5 The instructor provides detailed comments on the prospectus, along with a grade.
6 Data are collected and appropriate statistical analyses conducted by students.
7 Students begin writing the final project paper based on collaborative writing, editing and revising of original prospectus, plus addition of Results and Discussion sections.
8 A draft of the final paper is taken to a peer review workshop where students are coached on how to offer constructive feedback.
9 Each pair of students shares a copy with at least one other pair. Students are instructed to make substantive evaluations of the papers they read, to note grammatical errors and deviations from APA style.
10 Pairs of students make final revisions and editorial changes to their report. (The instructor also makes herself available to discuss and comment on relatively complete drafts.)
11 Papers are submitted for grading.

Outcomes

Student reactions generally highly favourable. Ninety-six per cent indicated they had learned more as a result of collaborating. Some interesting between-group differences are reported which suggest that traditional-age students rated the exercise as more beneficial than older students.

More proof reading was carried out and more errors were corrected than in previous single-author work.

Papers contained greater discussion of the psychological import of work than those in previous years.

Applications

Dunn's methodology might be applied to great benefit in a variety of situations to ensure collaboration and peer review.

Derived from Dunn (1996)

Other useful reference

Falchikov (1996).

How to do 1.13: **Paired annotations**

Rationale/objectives

- to enable students to identify the key points in a text;
- to encourage students to make links between new and existing bodies of knowledge;
- to develop literature review research skills;
- to develop skills in preparing an annotated bibliography;
- to promote co-operative learning through individual accountability and positive interdependence;
- to improve metacognitive skills.

Participant characteristics

Any student in higher education in any discipline.

How does it work?

1   Individuals read an assigned article or chapter *out of class*. In addition, they prepare a reflective commentary on the key points of each paragraph. A prepared annotation sheet may be used for this purpose (See Table 1.4.)

2   *In class*, pairs of students compare key points and read each other's commentaries. (Students who come to class unprepared use class time to complete the individual exercise.)

3   Reasons for all choices must be discussed and made explicit.

4   Working together, pairs then prepare a composite annotation, summarizing the whole article or chapter.

5   It is recommended that this activity be repeated several times during the semester. This enables students to reflect on their thinking skills (metacognition) and compare their thinking with that of others.

Outcomes

Millis and Cottell assume that the objectives of the technique will be achieved.

Applications

Applications are potentially very wide indeed. This technique may be used in any discipline where literature reviewing and bibliographic research skills are required.

Derived from Millis and Cottell (1998)

A sheet designed to aid paired annotations is shown in Table 1.4. Millis and Cottell (1998: 119) suggest a less detailed alternative version.

Millis and Cottell (1998: 119) recommend that this technique be used on a regular basis, and that students be paired with different partners on each occasion, arguing that 'the more paired annotations they complete, the more skilled students become at identifying important points in an article'.

Team anthologies is an extended variation on paired annotation. In this, two pairs combine into a 'quad' group to prepare an annotated bibliography for a discipline-specific topic for research purposes.

Table 1.4 Paired annotation sheet

Key points identified by individuals	Individual responses and links
Paragraph 1	
Paragraph 2	
Paragraph 3	
Paragraph 4	
Paragraph 5	
Paragraph 6	
etc.	

Paired (composite) annotated summary

Peer editing

Millis and Cottell (1998) described a system of peer editing, in which students collaborate early in the writing process. Before starting writing or researching, pairs of students take turns to describe ideas for a paper they each plan to write. The listener takes notes, asks questions and produces an outline of the partner's planned composition. The roles are reversed and the procedure repeated. Next, students research their own paper, but keep in mind their partner's composition, noting any useful material or ideas for them as well. After the research stage, pairs work together to compose the opening paragraphs for each composition. The papers are then written individually. However, pairs reconvene to edit drafts of each other's papers and to comment on final drafts before submission. Millis and Cottell (1998: 120) argue that 'using writing to promote critical thinking helps students examine, evaluate, verify, analyse, weigh alternatives, and consider consequences as ideas develop'. See 'How to do' box 1.14.

Peer response groups

In peer response groups, all students write a draft of an essay and meet together to discuss questions and problems identified by each author. The philosophical basis

---

How to do 1.14: Peer editing

Rationale/objectives

Co-operative goal: for all members to check that each member's composition 'is perfect according to the criteria set by the teacher' (Johnson, Johnson and Smith, 1991: 71).

Participant characteristics

Students in higher education who have written coursework assignments.

How does it work?

1 Students work in pairs (or small groups). One describes ideas for the paper they intend to write.
2 The listener asks for clarification where necessary and produces an outline of the other student's paper.
3 Both undertake research, keeping in mind material that may be useful to their partner.
4 Student pairs work together on the opening paragraphs of their papers.
5 Students work on their own to write their paper.
6 Partners come together for editing (commentary on structure of sentences, paragraphs, whole thesis and proof-reading – grammar, spelling and punctuation).
7 Revisions made independently.
8 Students get together for a final reading before submission.
9 A record of tasks undertaken by each individually and together is made and signed by each.

Outcomes

Not stated, other than that the co-operative goal is met.

Applications

Very wide indeed.

Derived from Johnson *et al.* (1991)

Other useful reference

Millis and Cottell (1998).

---

for Bell's (1991) study of peer response groups in writing classes is Knowles' theory of adult learning. Bell described the setting up of writing groups in the ESL[2] classroom in the Language Institute at Mount Royal College, Calgary. Students were put into groups of three, on the basis of 'nationalities, personalities and friendships' (Bell, 1991: 67). Each time the group met, a 'timer' was selected whose responsibility was to ensure that every essay received equal attention. The peer-response procedure involves ten stages which are shown in 'How to do' box 1.15.

The system was evaluated by means of an anonymous, open-ended questionnaire. All participants recommended using peer response groups again.

Suggestions for answers to the question 'Which technique should I use?' for the four techniques designed to improve writing are shown in Table 1.5 in the form of desired outcomes for each.

How to do 1.15: **Peer response groups**

Rationale/objectives

- to encourage self-direction;
- to encourage critical thinking;
- to teach composition.

Participant characteristics

Participants were upper intermediate/advanced students in a college setting. Originally used in ESL writing classes.

How does it work?

1. The instructor assigns students to groups.
2. All students write an essay *out of class*.
3. Each time the group meets, a student is designated as 'timer'. It is the responsibility of the timer to ensure that all essays receive equal amounts of time and attention.
4. The writer asks for assistance with one element of the essay.
5. The writer reads aloud from her/his essay. Other group members listen. A single copy of the essay is available to them.
6. At least 60 seconds of silence follow the reading to allow thought and reflection.
7. Group members answer the writer's question, in turn.
8. Group members respond more freely, identifying something they like and something they think needs improving.
9. The writer chooses something to work on with the help of the group. Group members must do more than critique: they must help create.
10. The procedure is repeated until all essays have been responded to.

Outcomes

The system has been evaluated by means of an anonymous, open-ended questionnaire. Participants identified working in groups as one of the best things about the writing course. All recommended using peer response groups again.

Applications

May have applications in any writing situation.

Derived from Bell (1991)

Summary

We have looked at a number of same-level peer tutoring techniques involving equal-status participants which have different aims and objectives and which involve dyadic learning in a variety of contexts. Techniques have also differed in their complexity, varying from simple common-sense implementations of student co-operation to more structured examples. Same-level equal-status peer tutoring techniques are designed to aid students in a variety of ways from ice-breaking to problem solving. We can find ways to help students learn and understand materials presented to them in lectures, to help in preparation for tests and exams, to help them read and understand new materials and to encourage co-operative skills. Students may also work together to help presentation or performance skills.

Table 1.5 Which technique should I use? Rationales for using some techniques to improve writing

Technique	Aim/desired outcome
Collaborative writing, peer criticism and peer review	To promote intellectual growth of undergraduates through peer influence To enable students to teach and learn from each other To develop writing skills
Paired annotations	To enable students to identify the key points in a text To encourage students to make links between new and existing bodies of knowledge To develop literature review research skills To develop skills in preparing an annotated bibliography To promote co-operative learning through individual accountability and positive interdependence To improve metacognitive skills
Peer editing	To encourage co-operation and ensure that criteria for good writing are being met
Peer response groups	To encourage self-direction To encourage critical thinking To teach composition

We shall now investigate an example of tutoring where unequal status is introduced into same-level dyads by the teacher or co-ordinator.

SAME-LEVEL PEER TUTORING INVOLVING ONE INSTITUTION: UNEQUAL STATUS INTRODUCED BY THE CO-ORDINATOR

Unequal-status peer tutoring typically involves participants from two institutions who do not share the same status in terms of experience or level of skill, as we shall see in the next section. However, status differences may be identified, amplified or introduced into same-level student groups. We shall look at an example where this happens: teaching assistants and 'teacher-of-the-day'.

Teaching assistants and 'teacher-of-the-day'

In 1972, Grasha published a paper in which he attempted to relate teaching goals to student response styles and classroom methods. In this paper, he described a variety of methods designed to overcome problems associated with undesirable student reactions to traditional classes, such as avoidance (absenteeism), over-competitive or dependent responses. One such classroom method is a form of peer teaching, the 'teacher-of-the-day' scheme, in which students take turns at running a session. In this system, status differences are introduced by the instructor. For example, Grasha's student teachers were instructed to choose how to run a session: to give lectures, lead discussions, perform demonstrations, run experiments or show movies to the whole class or to a smaller group. 'How to do' box 1.16 provides implementation instructions for this scheme.

Grasha's evaluation of the scheme indicated that students had enjoyed the experience. There was also some evidence of a move to a more participant-response style.

How to do 1.16: 'Teacher-of-the-day'

Rationale/objectives

NB These objectives are associated with a number of classroom initiatives, including 'Teacher-of-the-day'.

- to overcome problems associated with dependent or overly competitive student response styles;
- to address 'flight from the classroom' (absenteeism) problems (Grasha, 1972);
- to help the instructor obtain her/his teaching goal;
- to help students develop learning skills.

Participant characteristics

Undergraduates, some of whom were studying introductory psychology or the history and systems of psychology.

How does it work?

'Student teachers-of-the-day give lectures, lead discussions, perform demonstrations, run experiments, or show movies' (Grasha, 1972: 145–146).

Teachers-of-the-day may work with the entire group or simultaneously with smaller groups of between 5 and 7 students.

Teachers-of-the-day are responsible for a broad issue or part of a text.

They are discouraged from reading outlines of the text to the group, and encouraged to:

- become authorities on a topic;
- identify issues;
- organize issues;
- learn by helping others learn.

(No further information supplied.)

Outcomes

NB Evaluation applied to all four classroom activities described by Grasha (1972).

Students were enthusiastic about the scheme, enjoying the opportunity to have increased responsibility in the classroom. Seventy per cent felt more involved in their own learning, and eighty per cent preferred the new initiatives to traditionally delivered courses. Grasha reported some evidence that the initiatives had moved students towards a 'Participant' response style.

Applications

May be used widely throughout the curriculum, particularly at higher levels (less experienced entrants to further or higher education may find responsibility for a whole session too stressful). More preparation and help with structuring sessions is recommended.

Derived from Grasha (1972)

Similarly, Goldschmid and Goldschmid (1976) described an example of peer tutoring where students from a class group were selected to teach their peers and were, thus, given a similar status advantage over the rest of their classmates as exists between students and lecturers. These student 'teaching assistants' were required to lead discussion groups or seminars or to conduct tutorials in exactly the same way as the teacher. However, Goldschmid and Goldschmid (1976: 29) concluded that

> despite its many advantages – including low cost – peer teaching is not a panacea for all instructional problems. In fact, it is best used together with other teaching and learning methods. It may be particularly relevant when one seeks to maximise the student's responsibility for his own learning and active participation in the learning process, and to enhance the development of skills for cooperation and social interaction.

Ney (1991) also reported a similar scheme, in which students again took turns to participate in class as lecturers teaching modern English grammar. In addition, Ney's programme required student participation in assessment. Student teachers were found to benefit from their experiences. Such schemes provide opportunities primarily to individuals, though it is to be hoped that the classes for which they had responsibility were of some benefit also to other students.

Dart and Clarke (1991) described various strategies designed to increase the responsibility of individuals for their own learning, including one strategy they rated as very successful. This was peer teaching which occurred as 'teaching episodes' in learning groups of two or three self-selected students. The teaching episode was preceded by a 'seminar statement' which identified what is to be taught, the objectives of the session and the criteria for assessment and standards of performance, to enable evaluation of the episode.

Let us now move on to examine some cross-level peer tutoring schemes in which students belong to the same institution, and in which unequal status in learning dyads and groups is built on existing differences between individuals or groups.

CROSS-LEVEL PEER TUTORING INVOLVING ONE INSTITUTION: UNEQUAL STATUS BUILT ON EXISTING DIFFERENCES

Cross-level peer tutoring may take place within an institution. In such cases, there are likely to be inequalities between participants based on existing differences such as level of achievement, degree of preparedness for study or level of study. *Supplemental Instruction (SI)* is probably the best known (and used) of such cross-level schemes, but we shall examine several other examples as well:

- mentoring;
- proctoring or the Personalized System of Instruction (PSI);
- *parrainage*.

Although some of these varieties appear to be very similar, there are certain defining differences between them. SI, for example, may be distinguished by its focus on support for 'at risk' courses. Proctors usually design and administer tests to the students they are supporting, while this does not seem to be the case in many reports of mentoring. Kerka (1998) argued that mentoring has characteristics in common with socially constructed learning theories such as experiential and situated learning. 'According to constructivist theory, learning is most effective when situated in a context in which new knowledge and skills will be used and individuals construct meaning for themselves but within the context of interaction with others' (Kerka, 1998: 2). (See Chapter 3 for a further discussion of these issues.)

This statement, however, may equally well be applied to other forms of paired and co-operative learning. *Parrainage* appears to have a wider remit than other forms of peer tutoring in that *parrains* act as counsellors and tutors to help new students adapt to their new educational environment (Goldschmid and Goldschmid, 1976).

Table 1.6 provides definitions, aims and outcomes for the four varieties to help readers choose which of these they might wish to use in their own teaching.

However, it may be that, at the end of the day, differences between the four varieties are less important than their aims and objectives which appear to be rather similar.

Supplemental Instruction (SI)

Supplemental Instruction (SI) was developed in the 1970s at the University of Missouri in Kansas City by Deanna Martin, who remains there as Director of the Center for Academic Development and International Director of the SI Program. Martin and Arendale (1992) regard the SI model as one anchored within a developmental perspective, applying concepts derived from Piaget's constructivist model of cognitive development (Piaget, 1971). They asserted that many students in tertiary educational institutions have not yet developed abstract reasoning that will allow them to learn new ideas simply by listening to lectures and reading text. Thus, they argued that, in order to be successful, learners must be actively involved in constructing knowledge themselves. Until learners have attained the ability to reason formally or abstractly, many tasks required of them in higher education may be experienced as 'overwhelming obstacles' (Martin and Arendale, 1992: 43). Constructivism is at the heart of much student-centred education.

SI works by training volunteer second-year students to act as 'leaders' to help first-year students. Leaders are facilitators whose task is to help students integrate course content with studying and learning strategies. Training of leaders includes basic input on group dynamics and verbal and non-verbal communication, as well as sessions on how to deal with sensitive issues or difficult people. Leaders are also instructed on ways of structuring an SI session. First-year students are helped to learn and understand what they have been taught in lectures in a once weekly SI session. They are not given any new material on these occasions. Student leaders typically meet with an SI co-ordinator for one hour each week for feedback and

Table 1.6 Which technique should I use?
Rationales for using some cross-level peer-tutoring techniques within an institution

Technique	Definition	Aim/desired outcome
Supplemental Instruction (SI)	A system whereby 2nd year students act as 'leaders' to help 1st year students in 'at risk' courses	To support students and help reduce drop-out and failure To encourage co-operative learning To help students master course content
Mentoring	The relationship between a less experienced person and a more experienced partner who guides and supports the less experienced in a variety of contexts (e.g. higher education; pre-tertiary education; business)	To provide guidance, advice, feedback and support to the less experienced mentee To improve overall academic performance To encourage mentee personal growth
Proctoring or Keller's Personalized System of Instruction (PSI)	A system whereby an experienced undergraduate helps a beginner, often under the guidance of an academic	To help a beginner undergraduate to achieve mastery in a particular area To help beginners become part of the academic culture To help proctors develop leadership, team building and communication skills
Parrainage	Students counselling students (Goldschmid and Goldschmid, 1976)	To provide counselling support to freshmen To help freshmen adapt to the new educational environment To improve freshmen's practical problem-solving and study skills

reflections on their session. The role of SI co-ordinator may be filled by a full-time member of staff who takes responsibility for SI schemes in a number of departments (such as a member of an Educational Development Unit or equivalent), or by someone within a department on a part-time basis, who has correspondingly fewer responsibilities in other areas of the job.

SI is typically used in the context of content heavy-courses with a demanding workload. Proponents stress that, although SI can provide help with academic problems, it is not a remedial strategy. 'Supplemental instruction targets high risk courses, such as medicine, electrical engineering and maths, rather than high risk students' (Wallace and Rye, 1994: 7–8). Richardson (1994: 15) identified this aspect of SI as 'an escape from the culture of blaming', in which students and staff 'endlessly toss the responsibility for teaching and learning into each other's court'.

Information about SI is contained in 'How to do' box 1.17.

How to do 1.17: **Supplemental Instruction (SI)**

Rationale/objectives

Wallace (1996) identified the following purposes of SI:

- to facilitate student involvement;
- to encourage empowerment of learners to become autonomous;
- to target high-risk courses rather than high-risk students, and reduce drop-out and failure rates;
- to embed study skills in course material;
- to provide discreet support and a safe place for students to admit difficulties;
- to encourage co-operative learning.

Participant characteristics

SI typically involves students from 'high-risk' courses such as engineering, medicine, dentistry, pharmacy, law, computing. It has also been used in other courses such as biological sciences and the social sciences (e.g. Isley, 1994).

How does it work?

1. Having obtained support (and resources) at an institutional level, put in place a structure to support SI.
2. Appoint and train an SI Supervisor.
3. Identify and target high-risk ('hard') courses.
4. Liaise with departmental and/or faculty staff.
5. Liaise with students (Davies and Johnston (1994) advocate consultation with Students' Union representatives, Student Rights Officer and student course representatives).
6. Recruit student SI Leaders from year 2 students (consultations between SI Supervisor and lecturers delivering courses targeted). SI Leaders should be selected for 'content competence' and interest in innovation (Wallace, 1996).
7. Train SI Leaders (in pro-active learning, study strategies, interpersonal and group management skills, etc.). Training sessions are typically of 2 days' duration.
8. Timetable rooms and times for SI sessions.
9. SI sessions take place.
10. Evaluate scheme.

Outcomes

'Studies of supplementation programmes in the United States and Britain have shown that it improves students' grades, reduces drop-out rates, and provides a forum for learning essential study strategies and developing skills in comprehension, analysis, critical thinking and problem solving' (Wallace and Rye, 1994). In addition, SI Leaders improve leadership skills. Co-operation is fostered between staff and students and within the student body.

Applications

SI was designed for use in high-risk courses, but is gradually being used more widely.

Derived from Wallace (1996)

Useful references

The SI home page provides a wealth of information and copies of many papers and book chapters dealing with SI.

http://www.umkc.edu/centers/cad/si/sidocs/siartdex.html

Mentoring

Mentoring, according to a guide prepared by the Committee on Science, Engineering and Public Policy (1999), is an ancient practice, dating back to Ancient Greece. The guide also informs us that the original Mentor, described by Homer as a wise and trusted counsellor, was left in charge of Odysseus' household during his travels. The goddess Athena, in the guise of Mentor, became teacher and guardian of Odysseus' son during his father's absence. Today, the role of experienced mentor may be filled by a variety of people:

- female executives who assist other women to break the 'glass ceiling';
- senior citizens who share their expertise with elementary students;
- business managers who guide and support new employees;
- university alumni who provide guidance to students seeking business careers;
- more experienced teachers who assist their newer, less-experienced colleagues.

(The Directory of Mentor Arts and Mentorship, 1999)

Dennis (1993) claimed that mentoring programmes generally serve three broad purposes:

1 Educational or academic mentoring helps mentees improve overall academic performance.
2 Career mentoring helps mentees develop skills needed to enter or continue a career path.
3 Personal development mentoring supports mentees during times of personal or social stress and provides guidance for decision making.

(Dennis, 1993)

In the context of higher education, mentoring 'involves a one-to-one supportive relationship between the student and another person of greater ability, achievement or experience' (Topping, 1996b: 30).

A good mentor seeks to help the student mentee optimize educational achievement and development, to encourage personal growth. A mentor serves as a 'guide or signpost' (Topping, 1996b: 30) and advises the student on the hidden curriculum. This is a way of introducing the student into the culture of the department. The mentor also assists the student's socialization into a disciplinary culture.

There is a plethora of web-based information about mentoring. For example, an experimental study of mentoring designed to improve college attendance is reported by Dennis (1993). In this, we learn that an experimental group received mentoring, while control group students did not. Attendance by experimental subjects exceeded that of their control group peers. As with other forms of peer tutoring, it is recommended that mentors receive training before embarking on mentoring activities, and that they be supported throughout by teachers. However, in spite of the importance of organization and tutor training to the success of mentoring, there is relatively little web-based information about its organization and implementation.

Witherby (1997) outlined the Peer Assisted Study Sessions (PASS) initiative which operates in the department of Geography and Planning, University of New England, Armidale, New South Wales. Although this system is described as a form of peer mentoring, it has features that suggest that it may have more in common with SI. For example, PASS 'facilitators' do not work in a one-to-one relationship with individual less-experienced students, typically having responsibility for ten to twelve students. The system was introduced to address issues of high failure rates in a Transport Planning module – another feature of SI. Facilitators are chosen from third-year students who have achieved reasonable grades. They are paid 'a modest hourly sum' to work with a 'novice' during the half day initial training and at weekly meetings throughout the semester. Study group sessions are typically held during normal teaching times and are 'driven largely by the emerging needs of the students themselves' (Witherby, 1997: 30). Operation of the PASS system resulted in increased mentee satisfaction, lowered failure rates (to almost zero), mentee ability to apply skills and competencies to other courses and increased mentor academic performance and confidence.

A similar PASS system was also implemented in the first year of a teacher education course in the context of a basic foundation science module at Queensland University of Technology (Watters and Ginns, 1997). Yet another Australian PASS scheme operates across the first year of the economics and finance curriculum within the faculty of economics at the University of New South Wales in Sydney (Watson, 1999).

A less structured example of a type of mentoring scheme was described by Topping *et al.* (1997): the Student Supported Learning (SSL) scheme piloted at the University of Central Lancashire, UK. Students who had successfully completed a year of study were given the opportunity to gain course credits for supporting other students who were currently on the course. Student 'supporters' were trained and then required to negotiate a personal learning contract with their departmental SSL tutor or co-ordinator containing personal objectives. Key competencies were provided based on National Vocational Qualifications (NVQ) criteria.

Given the similarities between many examples of mentoring and SI, no separate table for mentoring is included here.

Further information about *mentoring* may be obtained from:

The Directory of Mentor Arts and Mentorship http://www.peer.ca/mentor.html
Peer Resources http://www.peer.ca/peer.html and
http://www.peer.ca/helping.html#definitions
Other mentor sites on the internet http://www.peer.ca/mentor.html#Mentorsites
National Academy of Sciences, National Academy of Engineering and Institute of Medicine (1997), *Adviser, teacher, role model, friend: on being a mentor to students in science and engineering*, Washington, DC: National Academy Press
http://www.nap.edu/readingroom/books/mentor

Proctoring or Keller's Personalized System of Instruction (PSI)

Several writers (e.g. Goldschmid and Goldschmid, 1976) have described the Proctor Model or Keller's Personalized System of Instruction (PSI). In this, some students act as 'proctors' and work individually with other students on the same course to help them gain mastery of the material. Proctors administer tests and provide constructive feedback to students.

Wyatt and Medway (1984) reported a study in which sophomores acted as proctors to freshmen studying introductory psychology. Proctors were responsible for reviewing course material, monitoring student progress and administering and grading tests. The course was delivered by means of self-paced material. Proctors received credit for their participation in the scheme. Pre- and post-questionnaires were completed by all participants, analysis of which shed some light on issues relating to the roles of participants. It was found that student learners rated proctor characteristics as more important than their own in determining exam outcomes. This was particularly marked in the case of successful students.

Metcalfe (1992) described a similar scheme at Nottingham Polytechnic (now Nottingham Trent University) in which final-year students proctored groups of eight first-year engineering applications students engaged on a 'design and make' project. In this context, proctoring was seen as primarily of benefit to proctors.

Further details of how to organize a proctoring scheme are provided in 'How to do' box 1.18.

Parrainage

Goldschmid and Goldschmid (1976) described a scheme of *parrainage* which operated at the Swiss Federal Institute of Technology. Senior students (third- or fourth-year students of engineering) acted as *parrains* (literally translated as 'godfather or sponsor' by Harrap's Concise French and English Dictionary (1978)) to small groups of students entering higher education, known as *filleuls* ('godchildren'). *Parrains* act as counsellors and tutors to help freshmen adapt to the new educational environment. *Parrainage* has a wider remit than peer tutoring which is limited to the context of coursework. Initial encounters between *parrains* and *filleuls* assist the freshmen in solving concrete, material problems such as library use or housing. Discussions about the curriculum take place at later meetings. *Parrains* also help *filleuls* with note-taking techniques, other study methods and lab work. Some discussion about vocational goals may also take place. The Swiss scheme was rated a success by both *parrains* and *filleuls*. The performance of *filleuls* in terms of Grade Point Average (GPA) exceeded that of similar cohorts over the previous two-year period and failure rates were reduced. Most *filleuls* expressed the desire to act as *parrains* themselves in their third or fourth year of study.

We shall now go on to look at two other varieties of cross-level peer tutoring:

- Cognitive apprenticeships
- Learning with a virtual companion

How to do 1.18: Proctoring

Rationale/objectives

- 'to give students practical experience in professional engineering by providing them with the opportunity of running a team on an engineering project;
- to enable students to act as "section leaders" in an industrial sense;
- to develop the skills of communication, planning and organization in managing a team;
- to develop leadership and team building skills' (Metcalfe, 1992: 44)

Participant characteristics

Final-year students of engineering acted as proctors. Groups of first-year students of engineering applications were the student learners.

How does it work?

NB Relatively little detail is supplied by Metcalfe, particularly concerning preparation of student learners.

1 Final-year students are lectured on what is required of a proctor and on how to maximize the benefits of the experience.
2 Assessment procedures are explained fully.
3 Proctors take responsibility for managing a group of 8 students carrying out a 'design and make' project (12 hours of contact time scheduled).
4 Proctors submit a report describing the project, technical problems encountered, roles within the group and contribution of group members, personal problems encountered and how dealt with.
5 The report is assessed by a lecturer.

Outcomes

Proctors found the experience useful, believing that they, too, would have benefited from being proctored. They expressed concern about their group.

Most proctored students rated their proctors as friendly and helpful. They expressed a wish for more time being proctored, and hoped to be able to act as proctors when they reached final year.

Applications

The Nottingham scheme developed to involve second-year engineering design students, second-year computing, HND engineering and furniture design students. There is no reason why the scheme should not be applied more widely.

Derived from Metcalfe (1992)

The latter of these categories, learning with a virtual companion, leads us to the issue of how to support co-operation with technology. Issues associated with this question will be explored further in Chapter 9.

Cognitive apprenticeships

Brown, Collins and Duguid (1989) argued that concepts may be developed through a style of learning called 'cognitive apprenticeship', the name having been suggested by Collins *et al.* (1989). Cognitive apprenticeships emphasize two issues in teaching and learning:

1　teaching the processes that experts use to handle complex tasks;
2　learning-through-guided-experience and its focus on cognitive and metacognitive skills and processes.

Cognitive apprenticeships provide the novice with an insight into the variety of cognitive activities that are used in solving a complex task, and also encourage self-monitoring and reflection on the differences between expert and novice. Cognitive apprenticeships are particularly suited to collaborative learning situations. Brown *et al.* (1989: 40) proposed that '[if] ... learning is a process of enculturation that is supported in part through social interaction and the circulation of narrative, groups of practitioners are particularly important, for it is only within groups that social interaction and conversation take place'.

Starr (1991) described a number of teaching strategies based on co-operative learning, involving cognitive apprenticeships between students. Students who were 'better prepared' in learning or thinking activities (the more advanced group) were paired with less-well-prepared (or less-advanced) peers. Matching of more advanced with less advanced students took place in groups of five to seven people, in triads, where one advanced student worked with two less advanced students, and in pairs. The aim of the exercise was to improve metacognitive skills such as problem definition, selecting and ordering problem-solving components, allocating resources to the problem, and monitoring solutions to problems. Starr's scheme is described in 'How to do' box 1.19.

Trombulak's (1995) experiment in teaching and learning, combining elements of inquiry-based learning and near-peer teaching, also has some characteristics of the cognitive apprenticeship. Students from two courses took part: those studying an upper-level course in science education acting as 'instructors', and those enrolled on an introductory-level environmental science course as 'research students'. Instructors met their small groups of research students in the third week of the semester, working with them approximately eight hours per week thereafter. Research students were required to develop a research question, search the literature, choose an appropriate research methodology, collect and analyse data and communicate their results orally to the rest of the group and in writing. Instructors were expected to assist students in the execution of this project. Instructors and students evaluated each other. Both rated the experience as positive overall, and Trombulak concluded that the model has the potential to expose students to science methodology, to promote science as a career and to train future science teachers.

A study by Dong (1997) also has some characteristics of the method of cognitive apprenticeships. Dong's theoretical starting point was Lave and Wenger's (1990) situated learning theory which states that 'learning does not occur within the individual learner, but occurs in the collaboration between the master and the apprentice as well as other participants in the community' (Dong, 1997: 26).

However, Brown *et al.* (1989) argued that all work in this area is, to a greater or lesser degree, built on theory and research deriving from Vygotsky (1962). Both of

How to do 1.19: Cognitive apprenticeships

Rationale/objectives

- to improve students' learning and thinking skills;
- to provide additional support for less-well-prepared students in co-operative groups.

Participant characteristics

Psychology undergraduates studying general laboratory psychology, physiological psychology and cognitive processes. Levels not specified.

How does it work?

Students from the cognitive processes course (CP students) are required to serve as coaches for volunteer students from a general psychology course (GP students). GP students receive extra credit for participating.

1 Sections of Sternberg's (1986) book, *Intelligence Applied,* are discussed in CP class.
2 Sample metacognitive exercises are reviewed in class, and some coaching carried out by instructor and peers.
3 Each CP student meets 2 GP students for $2 \times \frac{1}{2}$ hour per week to work on metacognitive exercises.

Outcomes

Improved student attitudes towards the content area were observed. Students perceived their cognitive skills to have improved. Both CP and GP students showed some gains in content mastery. Students showed increased awareness of metacognitive processes, along with improved approaches to in-class problem solving.

Applications

Any context where improved problem solving or improved understanding of metacognitive processes is desired might use this methodology. Sources other than Sternberg's book might also be used.

Derived from Starr (1991)

Other useful references

Sternberg (1986); Collins *et al.* (1989); Trombulak (1995); Dong (1997).

these theoretical positions will be discussed in Chapter 3. Dong's study was situated within the context of ESL teacher education. Students wrote weekly entries in a dialogue journal containing 'focused topics' derived from readings and discussions which were part of the course. They were also encouraged to explore concerns and to reflect on their successes and struggles. These journals were passed around members of the peer group who read and responded to entries. The lecturer then added her own responses.

Learning with a virtual companion

It is possible for the role of peer or co-learner to be taken by a machine, or more accurately by an element within a computer program. An early and simple example of such a simulation may be found in the programmed instruction responses of Skinner's early teaching machines (Skinner, 1961) or in the reinforcing responses of Computer Assisted Learning (CAL) systems. Frasson and Aimeur (1996) described a situation where human learning was influenced by the responses of one of three 'virtual companions'. They compared three learning strategies:

1 directive learning (one-on-one) which involved a learner and a simulated intelligent tutor;
2 peer learning which involved a learner and a simulated co-learner (the companion condition);
3 learning by disturbing (the troublemaker condition).

In the third condition, the simulated troublemaker was 'a special companion with a higher competence than the learner but with unpredictable behaviour' (Frasson and Aimeur, 1996: 373–74). The troublemaker sometimes gave the wrong answer or suggestion to 'attempt to provoke the learner's motivation' and to 'force the learner to react and propose the right solution'. Frasson and Aimeur's study involved pairs of learners (students and some staff from the computing science department at the University of Montreal) who were randomly allocated to the three conditions. Self-confidence measures were taken before the experiment took place. Participants' knowledge was tested pre- and post-experiment in order to measure progress. The companion condition appeared to benefit low-confidence subjects, while the troublemaker condition was found to be 'dangerous' (Frasson and Aimeur, 1996: 380) for them. The one-on-one condition was efficient for all participants, but more so for those with low confidence.

The literature contains more and more examples of the use of technology to support collaborative learning (e.g. Tang, 1991; Chou and Sun, 1996). We shall return to this topic in Chapter 9.

Our final group of peer tutoring strategies involves cross-level peer tutoring which involves two institutions. One of these is typically an institution of higher education which provides the tutors and the second a school whose students become tutees.

CROSS-LEVEL PEER TUTORING INVOLVING TWO INSTITUTIONS

The Pimlico Connection

My first encounter with cross-level peer tutoring involving undergraduates was in Sinclair Goodlad's (1979) Community Service Volunteers (CSV) publication, 'Learning by Teaching'. Although much of the book focused on peer tutoring at primary and secondary levels, with examples often taken from schemes operating in American grade schools, one of the first peer tutoring schemes involving undergraduates to operate in the UK was also described. This was the 'Pimlico Connection'. Students from Imperial College undertook tutoring in three London schools: Pimlico School, Stockwell Manor School and Holland Park School. This study was designed to discover whether tutoring involving undergraduate tutors would be more effective than ordinary classroom teaching in increasing pupils' interest in science. It was also designed to provide final-year students of electrical engineering with practice in the simple communication of scientific ideas, and to stimulate them to reflect on the meaning and purpose of their discipline. 'One cannot teach a subject for long without pausing to reflect on the purpose of doing so', argued Goodlad (1979: 93). In addition, Goodlad pointed out the learning benefits of preparing to teach. 'One also becomes aware of the way in which a discipline holds together by trying to organise one's thoughts in preparation for teaching' (Goodlad, 1979: 93).

Starting in 1975, a small group of students visited a school each week for a period of fifteen weeks to help with the teaching of combined science to third-year classes. In addition, student tutors were required to conduct an evaluation of tutoring as part of their project. This arrangement was repeated in the second and third years of the scheme, with undergraduates undertaking more complex forms of tutoring.

A key objective of the 'Pimlico Connection' was to change pupils' attitudes and improve their school experiences in science. Tutor evaluations suggested that this objective was being met, in that pupils seemed to have improved attitudes to both school and to their science teachers. Moreover, pupils appeared to have valued the help they received from their tutors, and felt they had increased the amount of work they had done. They welcomed greater use of tutors in their classes. Advantages to the undergraduate tutors were also recorded. Tutors reported to have benefited in several ways, in terms of academic development and improvement of their transferable or generic skills. They claimed that their own subject knowledge had been reinforced and they found the practice in presentation of scientific ideas of benefit. Tutors also enjoyed getting to know people from different backgrounds and gaining insight into how their subject was perceived by others. They also reported feeling pleasure at doing something useful with what they had learned. Overall, the tutors gained considerable satisfaction from tutoring.

In the 1979 book, Goodlad not only gave a clear account of the benefits to be expected from various types of tutoring based on reports from the literature, but also included instructions for setting up a scheme. He has contributed seven golden rules for tutoring and mentoring schemes to the present volume which are to be found in Chapter 5.

Many more schemes have now been set up, including one at my own university, Napier. Many of these, the Napier one included, owe a great debt to the Imperial College model. Schemes today continue to emphasize the development of generic skills and the value of volunteering. We shall look at the Napier scheme below, as it is one of the first student-tutoring schemes in the UK to award credit to students for participation.

Tutoring for credit: the Napier student tutoring in schools scheme

Student tutoring was introduced at Napier University in 1993. A pilot scheme was set up to enable students to 'do something extra in their spare time which would provide opportunities to develop skills which would enhance their CV' (Highton and

Goss, 1997). Students spent about half a day each week in a primary or secondary school within the Edinburgh area or in nearby areas of East or West Lothian. The scheme underwent yearly evaluation and development, and is now offered to any Napier University student as a formal academic module which can become a recognized element of a student's degree programme. In order to gain credit, students are required to engage in peer tutoring in their allocated school on at least ten occasions. Prior to starting tutoring, student tutors undergo two in-university sessions on learning and reflecting in addition to a training session. During placements, volunteer tutors are supervised at all times by a qualified teacher. Mid-semester in-university progress check sessions take place. In addition to carrying out their tutoring, student tutors are required to keep a personal learning log in which lesson plans are recorded. The log also requires that a range of exercises and tasks designed to aid reflection are completed by tutors. Students also research and write an essay or report on a general aspect of primary or secondary education (such as the role of IT in schools or special-needs education), or on some aspect of their own experiences as tutors (such as how student tutors can be most effective in the classroom, on the accreditation of student volunteering, or why all students should be student tutors).

'How to do' box 1.20 provides instructions for implementing a student tutoring scheme.

Recent cohorts of student tutors, when asked to identify what they regarded as 'selling points' of the scheme, listed (in descending order of frequency):

- fun;
- opportunity to help others;
- opportunity to gain a sense of achievement from doing something useful;
- improving communication skills;
- gaining an insight into teaching;
- enhanced CV;
- improved confidence;
- improved academic knowledge;
- a challenge;
- social contact.

(Highton and Goss, 1997)

Melissa Highton reflects on her role in this scheme in Chapter 10.

We shall now move on to look at peer tutoring in the group setting. However, before we investigate some examples of peer tutoring in small groups, it might be helpful to elaborate some of the principles of co-operative learning and review some of the benefits claimed for it.

CO-OPERATIVE LEARNING

Cooperative learning is one of the success stories of educational reform. It has solid teacher support and a favorable research base.

(Adams and Hamm, 1996: 4)

How to do 1.20: **Napier student tutoring scheme: tutoring for credit**

Rationale/objectives

The module for which students may receive credit has the following objectives.
To enable and encourage students:

- to reflect on their experiences as tutor;
- to analyse the role of student tutor in the light of their experiences;
- to evaluate their own performance as tutor;
- to evaluate the oral presentations of peers;
- to develop an understanding of the wider context in which student tutoring schemes exist;
- to describe benefits of student tutoring to other students, teachers and pupils;
- to develop personal transferable skills.

Participant characteristics

Undergraduates from a variety of courses and levels.

How does it work?

1 Elective module is advertised throughout the university and students volunteer to act as tutors.
2 Students are allocated a place in a local school in response to a request from a teacher.
3 Students attend introductory sessions in university (organization, theoretical aspects of learning and reflecting) (weeks 1 and 2).
4 Students attend training session (week 3).
5 Students begin tutoring (week 4).
6 Mid-module progress check meeting takes place (week 7).
7 Presentation skills workshop (week 10).
8 Oral presentations and peer assessment.
9 Submission of essay (week 14).
10 Submission of personal learning log (week 14).

Outcomes

Initial findings 'revealed significant perceived benefits for students in terms of confidence and transferable skills gains' (Highton and Goss, 1997: 1). Many students reported satisfaction and a sense of achievement at being able to help others and 'do something useful'. Students rated the experience as fun.

Applications

Potential applications are very extensive throughout an institute of further or higher education.

Derived from Highton and Goss (1997)

Other useful reference
Goodlad (ed.) (1998).

Slavin (1985) claimed that the earliest research from which co-operative learning developed goes back to the early 1900s and that all co-operative learning methods are based on social-psychological research and theory, adapted to meet the practical requirements of classrooms. Some theoretical roots of co-operative learning and peer tutoring are explored in Chapter 3.

Characteristics of co-operative learning

Co-operative learning works best when the following conditions are present:

- . Positive interdependence ('Promotively interdependent goals').

Positive interdependence may be said to be present when individuals realise that they can achieve their own personal learning goals only when everyone in the group reaches theirs.

- Face-to-face interaction.
- Individual accountability and personal responsibility for reaching group goals.

Individual accountability has been achieved when all individuals take on the responsibility for doing a fair share of work.

- Frequent practice with small-group interpersonal skills.
- Regular group processing and reflection.

(Adams and Hamm, 1996)

Johnson and Johnson (1985) examined the internal dynamics of co-operative learning groups and isolated some potential mediating or moderating variables. They concluded that the type of task does not appear to matter a great deal, but that several identifiable processes promoted higher achievement. These included:

- the promotion of high-quality reasoning strategies;
- the constructive management of conflict;
- increased time on task;
- more elaborative information processing;
- greater peer regulation and encouragement of efforts to achieve;
- more active mutual involvement in learning;
- beneficial interaction between students of different achievement levels;
- feelings of support and psychological acceptance;
- more positive attitudes towards subject areas;
- greater perceptions of fairness of grading.

Benefits of co-operative learning

Research suggests a number of benefits to participants in co-operative learning schemes. Co-operative learning can:

- motivate students;
- increase academic performance and retention;
- help with the creative generation of new ideas;
- increase respect for diversity;

- promote literacy and language skills;
- help develop skills required in the community and the world of work;
- improve teacher effectiveness.

(Adams and Hamm, 1996)

Co-operation and competition

Contrasts between competition and co-operation were explored over 60 years ago by May and Doob (1937) who investigated social and psychological conditions under which individuals compete or co-operate. They examined the issue of co-operation or competition in a variety of contexts, including that of learning, concluding that competition and co-operation can both be promoted or disrupted by education, and point to sources of conflict between the two modes of interacting in educational settings.

They also explored the roots of conflict between co-operation and competition, identifying the influence of underlying cultural values in promoting competition.

> The system of education in any culture or sub-culture will be organized in a way calculated to perpetuate features of the culture that are most highly valued by those who control education, and to modify elements which those in control think should be changed.
>
> (May and Doob, 1937: 81)

May and Doob (1937: 82) noted a 'curious paradox' which still exists today: that the ideals of co-operation may be emphasized by society, but the basic structure of the education system is competitive.

Next we shall look at some examples of peer tutoring in small groups.

PEER TUTORING IN SMALL GROUPS

While the majority of uses of peer tutoring in higher education appear to take place within dyads, there are some examples of peer tutoring in small learning groups. For example, Fraser *et al.* (1977) varied the size of peer-monitoring learning partnership groups, assigning student participants 0, 1, 2 or 3 learning partners. Fraser *et al.*'s work on peer monitoring in dyads has been described above (see 'How to do' box 1.2). When they compared mean points totals for all group size conditions, they found that students in dyads, triads or quad groupings all outperformed individuals. However, the researchers found no performance differences between groups of different sizes, and they concluded that 'any partnership size up to four members would be equally effective in increasing academic performance' (Fraser *et al.*, 1977: 106). The only difference between groups they reported was that students in quad partnerships studied together less than dyads. Difficulties in arranging meeting times appeared to be sufficiently problematic to reduce the amount of co-operative working time. We shall return to consider composition of groups in Chapter 8 (see Felder and Brent's contribution).

In spite of the difficulties outlined above, a large number of varieties of peer tutoring are designed for use in small groups, rather than dyads. We shall limit our discussions to those that have been used in further or higher education, or to those which might be adapted for such use. Thus, although the technique of Teams-Games-Tournaments (TGT) features prominently in many accounts of small-group learning, and certainly involves some peer tutoring, we shall not include it here, as I have found no example of its use in a post-compulsory educational setting. Slavin's Student Teams and Academic Divisions (STAD) (Slavin, 1980), similarly, is largely restricted to use in pre-tertiary settings, although one series of experiments to test its effectiveness in an undergraduate setting has been located (Gnagey and Potter, 1996). However, as the technique involves team games and tournaments, it seems unlikely that they will be favoured by many students in tertiary education. Moreover, the techniques of TGT and STAD involve teachers in considerable organization, in terms of setting up achievement divisions, weekly tests and tournaments, and it is unlikely that this addition to the workload would be welcomed by lecturers, either. A key aim of TGT and STAD is to familiarize students with teacher-supplied material. As we have seen, this aim may be achieved by other peer tutoring techniques such as Supplemental Instruction (SI), proctoring or Reciprocal Peer Tutoring (RPT).

Group techniques that involve some peer tutoring and are encountered in further or higher education include:

- Guided Reciprocal Peer Questioning (RPQ).
- The Jigsaw Classroom.
- Structured academic controversy.
- Syndicate method.
- Team learning.

We shall look at each in turn.

Guided Reciprocal Peer Questioning (RPQ)

Guided reciprocal peer questioning (RPQ), devised and evaluated by King (1991, 1993), is a strategy for enhancing peer interaction and learning in terms of improving comprehension of material encountered in lectures or other oral presentations. Students are provided with a set of generic questions which act as a guide for generating their own specific questions. These questions are then answered by peers, often in small groups of three or four students (though I have found that discussion in dyads is entirely appropriate). The more frequently students practise this activity, the better the quality of the questions they ask. Group discussions involving the whole class may follow. The RPQ scheme is one of a variety of learning activities designed to promote active learning which are also capable of incorporation into lectures. King (1993) found that her students in the RPQ and self-questioning conditions benefited from using questioning strategies, in that they performed significantly better on post-test comprehension than students in the other (control) 'review' condition. Implementation instructions are to be found in 'How to do' box 1.21. Generic questions for use during such an activity, suggested by King (1991, 1993), include:

- What is the main idea of .....?
- What if .....?
- How does ..... affect .....?
- What is the meaning of .....?
- Why is ..... important?
- What is a new example of ......?
- Explain why/ how ......
- How does this relate to what I've learned before?
- What conclusions can I draw about .....?
- What is the difference between ..... and .....?
- How are ..... and ..... similar?
- How would I use ..... to .....?
- What are the strengths and weaknesses of .....?
- What is the solution to the problem of .....?
- Compare ..... and ..... with regard to ......
- What do you think causes .....? Why?
- What evidence do you have to support your answer?

Guided Reciprocal Peer Questioning can be used to beneficial effect in virtually any discipline. King reported that she and her colleagues have used it in areas as diverse as anthropology, biology, business accounting, history, mathematics, psychology, research methods and teacher education (Millis and Cottell, 1998).

The Jigsaw Classroom

Aronson *et al.*'s 'Jigsaw route to learning and liking' (1975) is a technique based on the principle of the jigsaw puzzle. Each learner has a piece of information which must be put together with those of other learners in order for all to see the whole picture. The technique fosters positive interdependence, since all must work together to teach one another. Although many examples of Aronson's Jigsaw method have involved school age students rather than those in higher education, the strategy may be applied equally well for undergraduate use. Several examples of application in the context of higher education have been encountered (e.g. Carroll, 1986; Nattiv *et al.*, 1991; Sherman, 1991; King, 1993; Wedman *et al.*, 1996; Winter, 1997).

In the Jigsaw method, textual material to be learned is divided up into segments and presented to groups of students working in 'base groups'. Individuals within each base group are allocated a particular segment, and all students working on the same segment of text leave their base groups to learn the

How to do 1.21: Guided Reciprocal Peer Questioning (RPQ)

Rationale/objectives

NB These objectives apply also to self-questioning strategies.

- to help students comprehend and remember the content of lectures, training sessions, etc.;
- to facilitate encoding and retrieval of information.

Participant characteristics

Pre-service teachers studying a teaching methods course. Predominantly female, mean age 25.5 years. Graduates and upper-level undergraduates (ratio 3:1 graduates to undergraduates).

How does it work?

NB Stages 1, 7 and 10 contain information relating to King's evaluation of the strategy.

1   Students assigned randomly to groups of 3 or 4 (and other conditions – self-question and 'review', to enable *evaluation* of RPQ).
2   Students receive training in writing higher-order questions. In addition, the benefits of metacognitive strategies of monitoring one's own comprehension during learning are stressed.
3   Students provided with a set of generic question stems.
4   Students then learn how to generate metacognitive questions such as, 'What do I still not understand about this topic?'
5   Examples of questions shared with whole class, and instructor and peer feedback provided.
6   Students receive the first of a series of oral presentations (on aspects of the theory and practice of teaching).
7   *Evaluation*: pre-test of students' abilities to comprehend and remember material from the presentation.
8   A 10–12 min. 'processing session' takes place. Groups of students use the RPQ strategy and conduct unstructured discussion on the topic being studied.
9   Further oral presentations made, followed by further RPQ activity.
10 *Evaluation*: after the last presentation of the series, a written post-test administered to assess comprehension and retention as before.

Outcomes

King's students in the RPQ and self-questioning conditions were found to benefit from using questioning strategies, in that they performed significantly better on post-test comprehension than students in the other (control) 'review' condition.

Applications

Other applications are very wide indeed. King (1993: 31) stated that 'it can be used by students in any area of the curriculum to help them actively process material presented in lectures or other classroom presentations'. RPQ may also be used by students working in dyads and to help them process material presented in textual form.

Derived from King (1991)

Other useful references

King (1993); Millis and Cottell (1998).

material together in 'study groups' (or 'expert groups'). Students become familiar with the material within the study group, and then return to their base groups as experts. There they teach their peers and learn from them about other aspects of the material. All students are tested on everything at the end, thus ensuring individual accountability. (See Aronson, Blaney, Stephan, Sikes and Snapp, 1978.)

Winter (1997) described the use of a Jigsaw learning approach taken by part-time Bachelor of Education students in a psychology module at the University of Hong Kong. Students were placed into groups and each individual allocated a chapter of the course text to study and then teach to other group members. As is usual in Jigsaw implementations, all students studying a particular chapter were encouraged to study together to familiarize themselves with the content. However, Winter reported that not all students availed themselves of this opportunity. Evaluative data indicated that Jigsaw students displayed high attendance and academic engagement and performed well in the final examination. Students appeared to enjoy working in this way.

Slavin (1990: 104) developed the Jigsaw technique into 'a more practical and easily adapted form', *Jigsaw II*. As in the original technique, Jigsaw II may be used when the material to be studied is in written narrative form, and instructional materials may be a chapter from a textbook, a story or something similar. Jigsaw II differs from the original in that all students read all the material to be studied, rather than a section from it. In Jigsaw II, each group member is supplied with a different 'expert sheet' which requires the reader to focus on the material in a particular way or in order to answer a question. As with the original Jigsaw, expert groups form to discuss their topic or issue before returning to their base groups where they take turns teaching their peers about their topic. Slavin's version also requires that team scores be calculated which may include an individual improvement score in addition to test scores. Slavin discussed advantages and disadvantages of both versions. In the original, each group member has unique information, and may, thus, be highly valued by other members in the base group. The original Jigsaw requires that each chunk of material be self-contained which has obliged some teachers to prepare special materials for Jigsaw use. With Jigsaw II, however, all read the whole which 'may make unified concepts easier to understand' (Slavin, 1990: 108). Jigsaw II does not entail preparation of special materials. Implementation steps for both the Jigsaw classroom and Jigsaw II are shown in 'How to do' box 1.22.

Johnson *et al.* (1991) suggested additional variations on a Jigsaw theme which make use of dyadic learning. Instead of expert group meetings, students meet together in 'preparation pairs' to learn how to become an expert on their section or task, and to plan how to teach the material to the others. Following this activity, students form 'practice pairs' with other class members with the same task or topic. Dyads share ideas about the best way to teach, reviewing each other's plans. They select the best from each individual plan and draw up a shared teaching plan. Johnson *et al.* (1991) also recommend that, on

How to do 1.22: **The Jigsaw Classroom and Jigsaw II**

Rationale/objectives

Aronson's original aim was to aid integration of children from different ethnic backgrounds and to improve self-esteem and liking for school of minority-group children (Aronson *et al.*, 1975).

More recent aims are:

● to improve pre-service teacher preparation through co-operative learning;
● to improve students' academic and social learning (Wedman *et al.*, 1996).

Participant characteristics

Original participants in Jigsaw schemes were at a pre-tertiary level. Varieties of Jigsaw have also been used in tertiary education with pre-service teachers and psychology undergraduates.

How does it work?

1   Text material divided into discrete chunks of information, one for each member of a 4–6 person group (original Jigsaw) OR textual material selected for the whole class (Jigsaw II).
2   'Base (or home) groups' are formed.
3   Base group members are allocated one chunk of study material, so that all chunks are studied within a base group (original Jigsaw) OR they receive 'expert sheets' each with a different question or focus for reading (Jigsaw II).
4   Learners regroup, forming 'expert (or study) groups', joining members from each base group studying their chunk (original Jigsaw) or addressing their question/focus (Jigsaw II). The task of expert group members is to become experts in their information (or question/focus).
5   Experts then return to home groups and are responsible for making sure that other members learn their chunk (original Jigsaw) OR understand the focus/question (Jigsaw II).
6   All students are tested on all material.

Outcomes

The Jigsaw technique was rated as 'an excellent motivational device' (Carroll, 1986: 210). Students using it were perceived to be having more fun than in previous traditionally taught courses. In addition, the scheme led to improved student course evaluations and to an increase in the percentage of students completing the course on time (Carroll, 1986). Wedman *et al.* (1996) reported that Jigsaw team participants seemed to have developed a higher level of understanding of strategy use than the traditionally taught controls.

Applications

Predominantly used in pre-tertiary settings, though some applications in higher education. 'Jigsaw is one of the most flexible of the cooperative learning methods' (Slavin, 1989–90: 108). The basic model may be adapted to suit a variety of purposes. Slavin (1990) identified areas in which concepts rather than skills are learning goals as particularly suitable for Jigsaw use (e.g. social studies; literature; some science).

Derived from Aronson *et al.* (1975)

Other useful references

Sharan (1980); Carroll (1986); Bossert (1988); Johnson *et al.* (1991); Nattiv *et al.* (1991); Sherman (1991); King (1993); Wedman *et al.* (1996); Winter (1997).

completion of the exercise, all participants identify actions they had found helpful and suggest strategies and actions to improve learning next time.

A variant of the Jigsaw technique has been used in an experimental laboratory course on the psychology of learning and memory. Carroll (1986: 210) reported that the technique was rated as 'an excellent motivational device', and that students using it were perceived to be having more fun than in previous traditionally taught courses. Moreover, the scheme led to improved course evaluations by students and to an increase in the percentage of students completing the course on time. Another application of the Jigsaw technique involved elementary pre-service teachers at a large mid-western university studying a course on 'diagnostic and corrective reading practices for the classroom' (Wedman *et al.*, 1996). In this evaluative study, half of the group took part in a Jigsaw exercise while the other half were taught traditionally, acting as controls. Heterogeneous Jigsaw teams were constructed so as to include students with high, medium and low Grade Point Averages (GPAs). Results of the evaluation found no differences in multiple-choice achievement between the two groups. However, the researchers reported that Jigsaw team participants seemed to have developed a higher level of understanding of strategy use than the controls. The authors concluded that the study 'provides impetus for further use of expert-jigsaw teams in education courses' (Wedman *et al.*, 1996: 121).

Structured academic controversy

This technique was devised and described by Johnson *et al.*, (1991). Its aim is to develop critical thinking skills by compelling students to examine issues for which there is no agreed interpretation. A number of steps are involved. First of all, a discussion topic with two well-documented positions is chosen, and materials to support each side supplied to students along with further references. In addition, a structure for conducting an argument around the topic and a list of discussion rules are also provided. Students work in dyads to prepare one side of the argument, and in groups of four with another pair on the opposing side of the argument to conduct the 'controversy'. Skills emphasized are:

- advocating an intellectual position;
- evaluating and criticizing the position advocated by others;
- synthesizing;
- consensual decision making.

More information is supplied in 'How to do' box 1.23

Structured academic controversy is another example of a true co-operative learning technique, in that the key features of positive interdependence and individual accountability feature prominently in it. Positive interdependence is assured by the requirement that each group submit one joint report and make one

How to do 1.23: **Structured academic controversy (SAC)**

Rationale/objectives
- to use disagreement and conflict to aid learning;
- to increase motivation and involvement of students.

Participant characteristics
College-level students. Recommended particularly for those 'facing a difficult class' (Johnson *et al.*, 1991: 9) or freshmen.

How does it work?

1 Students given a co-operative assignment, e.g. discussing a designated topic and writing a group report.
2 'Students are randomly assigned to groups of four, ensuring that both male and female and high-, medium- and low-achieving students are all in the same group' (Johnson *et al.*, 1991: 75).
3 Group divided into two pairs: one assigned the 'pro' position, the other the 'con' on an issue being studied.
4 Each pair prepares its position using a pack of information that supports the position.
5 When preparation is well under way, pairs are encouraged to compare notes with other pairs representing the same position (Jigsaw element).
6 Original groups of four reconvene and each pair presents its position to the other. Members of opposing pairs encouraged to listen carefully and take notes.
7 The group then discusses the issue, criticizing ideas not people, differentiating the two positions, and assessing the evidence and logic supporting each.
8 Pairs reverse perspectives and argue the opposing position.
9 Students drop their advocacy position and clarify their understanding of each other's information and rationale.
10 Students begin work on their group report.
11 Group reports evaluated on basis of quality of writing and evaluation of opinion and evidence.
12 Students take an individual test (and if all group members achieve a set standard, all receive bonus points).
13 Finally, all group members make 10 min. presentations to rest of class summarizing their reports. Oral presentation is also evaluated.

Outcomes
'Numerous academic and social benefits are derived from participating in structured controversies' (Johnson *et al.*, 1991: 76).

Applications
Very wide indeed: wherever there are multiple perspectives on issues. Particularly useful in social science subjects.

Derived from Johnson *et al.* (1991)

Other useful reference
Sherman (1991).

joint presentation. Interdependence is also encouraged by the awarding of bonus points to students if all group members score well on a class test covering the issues studied. Individual accountability is structured into the technique, in that each member must participate in oral discussions and presentations, and each must take an individual test on the material. In addition, this technique incorporates some Jigsaw elements (see 'How to do' box 1.23, 'How does it work?' point 5).

The following positive outcomes of well-structured, well-monitored conflict have been identified by the Co-operative Learning Center at the University of Minnesota:

- greater quantity and quality of achievement, complex reasoning, and creative problem solving;
- higher-quality decision making;
- healthier cognitive, social and psychological development by being better able to deal with more stress and cope with unforeseen adversities;
- increased motivation and energy to take action;
- higher quality relationships with friends, co-workers and family members;
- a greater sense of caring, commitment, joint identity and cohesiveness with an emphasis on increased liking, respect and trust;
- heightened awareness that a problem exists that needs to be solved;
- increased incentive to change.

(Millis and Cottell, 1998)

A group activity which is not strictly structured academic controversy, but which involved discussion of controversial topics by means of e-mail, was reported by Wizer and Beck (1996). The online discussions they describe might easily be adapted to meet the more formal requirements of a structured academic controversy.

Syndicate method

In a syndicate-based course, 'syndicates' of between four and eight students work co-operatively on a series of assignments, often in the absence of a teacher. Collier (1983) identified three distinctive features of syndicates:

- The small group work is central to academic study.
- Assignments draw on both personal experience and academic sources.
- Student syndicates are interspersed in a series of tutor-led plenary session with the whole class.

This method resembles peer criticism in some ways, in that it entails students criticizing each other's work. Collier (1983) reported case studies of implementations of syndicate methods in a variety of higher educational settings: French literature, medicine, physical education, regional studies, engineering. He also provided some 'guidelines for an aspiring practitioner' which included advice stressing the need for making clear decisions before embarking on a venture, about the design and assessment of assignments, membership and organization of syndicates, tutor training and evaluation. Although teachers using the method reported a high degree of student participation, involvement and motivation, very few accounts of implementations contained rigorous evaluations. Abercrombie (1983: 101) observed that 'perhaps the most worrying and contentious theme is that of the evaluation of the method'.

A paper by Morris and Hudson (1995) also contained a brief section on the syndicate method. According to the authors, it has 'proved exceptionally successful with both Asian and Australian students' (Morris and Hudson, 1995: 71). Unfortunately, no detail or direct reference to empirical work is provided.

Finally, we shall look briefly at a form of team learning.

Team learning

Metheny and Metheny (1997) reported the introduction of team learning into three courses: management science; operations management; mathematics education. It is not entirely clear whether the team learning they describe is a variety of co-operative learning or whether it is simply a form of group work which lacks some key features of co-operation. The authors assigned students to groups of between three and seven members in order to achieve a mix based on subject skills, interpersonal and communication skills. In addition, 'traditional' students were combined with 'older ones' who had some work experience. The authors do not provide any detail of the skills measurement techniques which this method of allocation of students to groups requires. However, some information about the types of projects, classroom activities and testing procedures for the three course groups is included in their paper. Students are required to solve textbook problems, explain problems to the rest of the class and engage in group and class discussions. Mathematics education students were also required to evaluate computer software and engage in hands-on activities in laboratories. Methods of evaluating team learning were described.

Teachers may choose from this group according to the aims and objectives they wish to achieve. (See Table 1.7.)

SUMMARY

Table 1.8 is a summary classification scheme for peer-tutoring techniques which rates each method reviewed in this chapter on seven dimensions: rationale for implementation; nature of learning; subject discipline; type of peer tutoring; method of pair selection or grouping; basis for evaluation and reward; practical requirements. The scheme is based on similar classifications devised by Bohlmeyer and Burke (1987) and Kagan (1985). The classification in Table 1.8 derives from studies reviewed and, as such, represents the position at the time of writing. As future implementations of peer tutoring may extend both the variety and range of schemes, practitioners may wish to add to the table.

Table 1.7 Which technique should I use?
Rationales for using some group peer-tutoring techniques

Technique	Aim/desired outcome
Guided Reciprocal Peer Questioning (RPQ)	To help students comprehend and remember the content of lectures, training sessions, etc. To facilitate encoding and retrieval of information
Structured Academic Controversy (SAC)	To use disagreement and conflict to aid learning To increase motivation and involvement of students
The Jigsaw Classroom	To aid integration of children from different ethnic backgrounds and to improve self-esteem and liking for school of minority-group children To improve pre-service teacher preparation through co-operative learning To improve students' academic and social learning
Syndicate method	To help cope with differing needs and expectations of international students
Team learning	To strengthen 'students' comfort with and skills in teamwork' (Metheny and Metheny, 1997: 32)

In the next chapter, we look at some of the benefits that result from participation in peer tutoring.

Notes

1 In the past, such arrangements may have been labelled 'same-age' peer tutoring. However, given the increasingly heterogeneous composition of cohorts in higher education, this term is being replaced by the term 'same-level'.
2 English as a Second Language.

Table 1.8 A classification scheme for peer-tutoring techniques

Key: (Techniques are identified by the same numbers as used in 'How to do' in the text.)

1.1 = Peer coaching	1.13 = Paired annotations
1.2 = Peer monitoring	1.14 = Peer editing
1.3 = Three-step interview	1.15 = Peer response groups
1.4 = Flashcard tutoring	1.16 = 'Teacher-of-the-day'
1.5 = Dyadic Essay Confrontations (DEC)	1.17 = Supplemental Instruction (SI)
1.6 = Learning cell	1.18 = Proctoring
1.7 = Pair problem solving	1.19 = Cognitive apprenticeships
1.8 = Reciprocal Peer Tutoring (RPT)	1.20 = Tutoring for credit
1.9 = Reciprocal teaching	1.21 = Reciprocal Peer Questioning (RPQ)
1.10 = Scripted Co-operative Dyads (SCD)	1.22 = The Jigsaw classroom and Jigsaw II
1.11 = Peer criticism: the Brooklyn Plan	1.23 = Structured academic controversy (SAC)
1.12 = Collaborative writing and peer review	

Peer-tutoring techniques

Dimensions	1.1	1.2	1.3	1.4	1.5	1.6	1.7	1.8	1.9	1.10	1.11	1.12	1.13	1.14	1.15	1.16	1.17	1.18	1.19	1.20	1.21	1.22	1.23
1 Rationale for implementation			x	x	x	x	x		x			x	x	x	x	x	x	x	x		x	x	x
Improving student learning			x	x									x	x	x	x	x	x		x	x	x	x

Table 1.8 Continued

Improving skills (incl writing)	x	x		x	x		x			x		x
Improving academic perform-ance	x				x	x	x	x		x	x	x
Supporting students	x		x		x			x		x		
Supporting high risk courses												x
Addressing problems						x	x					
Facilitating student involvement		x		x	x	x		x		x	x	
Providing practical experience							x		x		x	
Social factors/attitudinal outcomes	x	x	x	x	x			x			x	x
2 Nature of learning												
Revising lecture materials	x		x		x			x		x		
Understanding new information	x	x	?	x	x	x	x	x		x	x	x
Questions and answers	?	x	x	x		x				x		
Problem solving	?		x								x	
Improving metacognitive skills				x	x			x			x	x

Table 1.8 Continued

Dimensions	1.1	1.2	1.3	1.4	1.5	1.6	1.7	1.8	1.9	1.10	1.11	1.12	1.13	1.14	1.15	1.16	1.17	1.18	1.19	1.20	1.21	1.22	1.23
Encouraging co-operative learning	x	x	x					x		x	x	x	x	x			x				x	x	x
Peer criticism	x	x		x					x	x		x		x	x		x						x
3 Subject discipline																							
Arts & Humanities/Writing	x																						
Pre-service teachers/education			x								x				x						x		
Paramedical & Health-related																	x						
Maths & Computing							x										x						
Medicine & Dentistry																	x						
Science & Engineering																	x	x					
Social Science		x		x		x		x		x		x				x			x			x	
Mixed/Wider application	x	x	x	x	x	x	x	x	x	x	x	x	x	x	x	x	x	x	x	x	x	x	x
4 Type of peer tutoring																							
Cross-level, different institution																				x			

Table 1.8 Continued

Same-level, same institution	x	x	x	x	x	x	x	x	x	x	x	x	x	x	x	x	x	x

5 Method of selection

Randomly assigned by lecturer				x	x	x			x						x		x		x
Matched by ability/ attainment/gender	x														x			x	x
Selected for interpersonal skills													x				x		
Student self-selection/ volunteers								x						x	x				
All participate	x	x	x	x	x	x	x	x	x	x	x	x					x	x	x

6 Assessment & evaluation

Individual marks – product		x			x	x	x	x	x						x		x	x	x
Individual marks – process																	x		
Group/pair mark/bonus – product		x						x										x	x
Immediate			?		x		x	x										x	x

Table 1.8 Continued

Dimensions	1.1	1.2	1.3	1.4	1.5	1.6	1.7	1.8	1.9	1.10	1.11	1.12	1.13	1.14	1.15	1.16	1.17	1.18	1.19	1.20	1.21	1.22	1.23
Long-term (e.g. end of course)		x				x	x	x				x				x	x	x	x	x			
Evaluation of PT technique by staff	x	x		x			x			x	x				x	x	x	x	x	x	x	x	x
Evaluation of technique by students	x		x				x	x							x	x	x				x		
7 Practical requirements																							
Some lecture/tutorial time required	x	x	x	x	x	x	x	x	x	x	x	x	x	x	x	x	x	x	x	x	x	x	x
Private/directed study time used		x											x	x		x	x	x	x				
Lecturer preparation – significant	x	x					x		x	x	x			x	x	x	x	x	x	x	x	x	x
Lecturer preparation – minimal	x		x	x	x	x		x					x	x	x								

2 Beneficial effects

Why teachers use peer tutoring

It seems reasonable to assume that teachers use peer tutoring because they perceive it to be beneficial to either themselves or their students. Some of the variety of benefits associated with peer tutoring have already been indicated in Chapter 1. In this chapter, we shall explore these beneficial outcomes further. Given that the effects reported to result from participation in peer tutoring exercises are often directly linked to the aims of the teachers or researchers conducting the studies, we shall start our investigation by finding out why peer tutoring was introduced into higher education. We then look at the beneficial effects of the practice. These effects are summarized towards the end of the chapter, in Table 2.1. The table is organized so that readers may consult it in order to identify which peer tutoring technique has reported success in achieving outcomes they might wish for their own students.

WHAT ARE THE AIMS OF INTRODUCING PEER TUTORING INTO TERTIARY EDUCATION?

I recently conducted a survey of studies of peer tutoring in higher education in order to identify the reasons given by the authors for introducing the practice into programmes. These reasons were very varied and appeared to have changed over the years. An early account, in the 1960s, of why syndicate working was introduced into a teaching programme set the tone for the next decade (Collier, 1969). Collier wished to *solve a problem* he had identified, namely, the lack of involvement of his students in their learning. Subsequent researchers have also used peer tutoring to help solve a variety of problems. We shall now inspect the reasons given in each decade from the 1970s to the 1990s.

The decade of the 1970s

Research into peer tutoring in the 1970s featured studies that had been conducted for a variety of reasons, and that had a variety of aims. However, the majority of these were pragmatic.

For example, Grasha (1972: 145) introduced the 'teacher-of-the-day' system to address *absenteeism* or 'flight from the classroom', and to help overcome problems associated with *dependent or overly competitive student learning styles*. Bruffee's (1978: 449) Brooklyn Plan was designed, in part, 'to serve needs created by the current "*writing crisis*"'. Goldschmid and Goldschmid (1976) identified *the need to improve learning without increasing financial cost* to universities and *prevention of student unrest* as reasons for setting up learning cells. Many investigators identified more than one aim. As well as hoping to solve some problem within the educational setting, some practitioners also believed that peer tutoring could contribute to *improved student learning* (e.g. Grasha, 1972; Bruffee, 1978; Goldschmid and Goldschmid, 1976). Other investigators hoped for *improved performance* as a result of learning by peer tutoring (e.g. Fraser *et al.* 1977).

The decade of the 1980s

Some studies in the 1980s resembled those of the previous decade in that attempts at *problem solution* continued to be mentioned as a reason for introducing a peer-tutoring technique. Similarly, other researchers continued to investigate the effects of peer-tutoring techniques in the context of *improved student learning*. In addition to these two rationales, in the 1980s, a new reason began to appear. Many studies aimed *to investigate the processes* of peer tutoring themselves.

Annis (1983a and b), for example, wished to investigate the process of peer tutoring by manipulating variables relating to the means by which students prepared for the task of tutoring. For example, some students prepared to teach but were not required to do any tutoring when the time came, while others both prepared for the task and then engaged in tutoring. Annis then compared the performance of students who had been involved in peer learning with that of a control group. She also attempted to investigate *why* achievement gains appear to result from peer tutoring.

During the 1980s, the experimental method began to be used to help investigate and improve understanding of the processes involved in peer tutoring. Sometimes, peer-tutoring schemes were designed to evaluate predictions derived from a theoretical perspective. For example, Bierman and Furman (1981) attempted the evaluation of a role-theory analysis of the attitudinal effects of peer tutoring on tutors and tutees.

It was during this decade that Dansereau and his team (e.g. Dansereau, McDonald, Collins, Garland, Holley, Diekhoff and Evans, 1979; Dansereau, 1988) conducted many of their important investigations into the mechanisms of Scripted Co-operative Dyadic leaning, to which we shall also return later in the book.

The decade of the 1990s

Condravy (1995: 43) noted that 'as tutoring programmes have pervaded higher education, researchers and reflective practitioners have carefully examined the elements of the tutoring process to discover how and why the process works'. In other words, investigations of *how and why peer tutoring is effective* continued into the 1990s. This decade also saw an increase in the number of studies published and in the variety of researchers' aims. *Improvement of learning* was still mentioned very frequently as an aim, and schemes were implemented in order to:

- encourage critical thinking (e.g. Bell, 1991);
- improve metacognitive skills (e.g. Millis and Cottell, 1998);
- encourage students to reflect on their experiences, to analyse their roles as tutor and evaluate their own performance (e.g. Highton and Goss, 1997);
- aid learning by incorporating disagreement and conflict into peer tutoring schemes (e.g. Johnson *et al.*, 1991; Sherman, 1991);
- empower students and increase learner autonomy (e.g. Wallace, 1996).

Skills development was identified frequently as the aim of introducing schemes. Peer-tutoring schemes were introduced to:

- improve students' communication skills (e.g. Metcalfe, 1992);
- improve their literature reviewing skills (e.g. Millis and Cottell, 1998);
- improve composition skills (e.g. Bell, 1991).

Practitioners continued to acknowledge the benefits of peer tutoring in terms of *academic achievement* and *improved social outcomes* and to cite the *potential benefits* as reasons for introducing peer tutoring into courses or modules (e.g. Nattiv *et al.*, 1991; Wedman *et al.*, 1996). A few *pragmatic reasons* are still to be found. For example, Bard (1996) introduced peer learning in an attempt *to alleviate students' perceptions of isolation* and Congos and Schoeps (1997) aimed *to improve retention*.

Summary

The reasons given for introducing peer tutoring schemes during the latter half of the twentieth century seem to signal a growing awareness among the community of practitioners about the beneficial effects of the practice. We shall now look more closely at some of these effects.

THE BENEFICIAL EFFECTS OF PEER TUTORING IN HIGHER EDUCATION

In order to investigate effects of peer tutoring in higher education, we shall survey studies in the context of the four main categories that formed the basis of the taxonomy of varieties of peer tutoring in the previous chapter. These were:

- same-level peer tutoring within an institution with equal-status participants within a dyad;

- same-level peer tutoring involving one institution where unequal status is introduced by the investigator;
- cross-level peer tutoring involving one institution where unequal status is built on existing differences;
- cross-level peer tutoring involving two institutions.

As we learned in Chapter 1, the first two categories relate to peer tutoring within a cohort in which all participants are at the same or very similar levels, and the remaining two categories are relevant to peer tutoring in which tutors and tutees are at differing levels of expertise or experience. We shall also look at the effects of peer tutoring in small groups. Finally, we look briefly at the differential effects of tutoring on tutor and tutee.

CATEGORIES OF EFFECT

Even as the aims of introducing peer tutoring into higher education were very varied, so the effects of peer tutoring are equally so. My survey of studies of peer tutoring in higher education identified the following main outcome categories:

- Academic outcomes: performance in different academic settings.
- Metacognitive outcomes: learning how to learn, transfer of learning.
- Study skills outcomes.
- Non-academic outcomes: motivation, attendance, retention and attrition.

We shall look at each category of effect in the context of the four main types of peer tutoring indicated above. In some cases, effects of peer tutoring fall into more than one category, as we shall see below.

SAME-LEVEL PEER TUTORING WITHIN AN INSTITUTION WITH EQUAL-STATUS PARTICIPANTS WITHIN A DYAD

Academic and performance outcomes

A review of the same-level equal-status techniques described in Chapter 1 indicated that many effects related to the development of cognitive skills or to academic performance.

Development of cognitive skills and approaches to learning

Peer tutoring may be designed to develop a variety of cognitive skills. For example, as we saw in Chapter 1, Millis and Cottell (1998) deemed the technique of flashcard tutoring particularly suitable for developing relatively low-level cognitive skills such as *learning definitions*, *memorizing concepts* or *vocabulary building*. *Mastery of material* was also reported as an outcome of use of this technique. Similarly, Millis and Cottell (1998) claimed that reciprocal teaching enables students to commit information to memory and promote deep learning, but unfortunately provided no evidence to support their claims. However, Al-Hilawani, Marchant and Poteet (1993) described a study which compared reciprocal peer teaching by undergraduate students of education with learning by means of the traditional lecture. Data obtained from multiple-choice tests the investigators administered indicated no relationship between instructional method and achievement. However, 70 per cent of students reported that they preferred the reciprocal method of teaching.

Bell's (1991) peer response system, designed to encourage self-direction and critical thinking as well as to teach the principles of composition, however, was evaluated by means of an anonymous, open-ended questionnaire. Participants identified working in groups as one of the best things about the course. All recommended using peer response groups again. However, it is not clear whether the aims of the technique relating to the development of critical thinking were achieved.

Thus, on the present evidence, while it seems clear that peer tutoring has a role in the development of low-level cognitive skills, and is liked by participants, we might do well to exercise caution regarding some claims that it encourages the development of higher-order skills.

Improved performance

Results of an early investigation by Goldschmid and Goldschmid (1976) found that use of the peer-tutoring technique of the learning cell led to significantly better performance than the traditional system of learning in a large psychology class. The technique also attracted good student ratings in terms of morale and experiences. Another early study of peer tutoring in tertiary education, peer monitoring (Fraser *et al.*, 1977), led to superior performance compared with individual working, in that no student involved in the scheme received a lower grade than would have been the case if they had worked individually, and some students' scores were increased. Similarly, Koch (1992) described an experiment using pair-problem-solving which found improved performance in the experimental group in a post-test, although all students were equivalent pre-test. Reciprocal Peer Tutoring (RPT) has resulted in higher examination scores and lower levels of subjective distress than control conditions (Fantuzzo, Dimeff and Fox, 1989a). In addition, RPT received higher satisfaction ratings from participants than a more traditional type of learning engaged in by those in control conditions. However, some studies of RPT report only limited success. For example, Griffin and Griffin (1998) investigated the effects of RPT on academic achievement, academic self-efficacy and test anxiety in sophomore undergraduate education students. While they had noted that a typical effect size for improved academic achievement in elementary school students was 0.99, the effect size calculated for one of their own tertiary level studies was 0.13. Thus, these results suggest that students in higher education may benefit to a much lesser extent than school students. Similarly, Griffin and Griffin (1998) found no consistent clear-cut positive effects in terms of either academic self-efficacy or test anxiety.

Metacognitive outcomes, learning how to learn and transfer of learning

As we saw in Chapter 1, the Scripted Co-operative Dyads technique is designed to help pairs of students understand new material and relate it to previous knowledge, using oral summarizing, metacognitive activities (comprehension, error correcting, evaluation) and elaborative activities (use of imagery or analogy). Students trained in this strategy have been found to outperform individuals and dyads not trained in the technique as evidenced in a transfer test (e.g. McDonald *et al.*, 1985). Thus, the researchers' aim to encourage transfer of metacognitive skills to individual learning seems to have been met. Moreover, further research found that fixed recallers outperformed fixed-role listeners, while the performance of those who alternated roles was midway between the two (Larson and Dansereau, 1986). In other words, students who engage actively in their learning seem to do better than those who are more passive. We shall return to this important body of work in Chapter 10.

Study skills

Reading and note taking

The co-operative note-taking pairs technique (Millis and Cottell, 1998) is designed, as its name suggests, to improve student note taking. Although I have anecdotal evidence to suggest that the technique is appreciated by students, I know of no formal measures of its benefits. Similarly, Millis and Cottell (1998) identified the technique of paired annotations as capable of helping students read for meaning, claiming that the more paired annotations students undertake, the more skilled they become at identifying the main points in an article. Once again, while this claim has some face validity, I have not been able to find any hard evidence to support it.

Techniques to aid writing development

Johnson *et al.* (1991) claimed that their peer editing technique enables all members to check that each peer's composition meets all the criteria set by the teacher and asserted that this co-operative goal is met. My own work on peer review also suggested that students find the technique helpful (Falchikov, 1996). Similarly, Dunn (1996) found that student reactions to collaboration and peer review were generally highly favourable. Moreover, Dunn also found collaborative writing to be better than previous single-author work. For example, it was noted that more proof reading was carried out and more errors were corrected in the collaborative product. A very large majority of Dunn's participants indicated they had learned more as a result of collaborating. Dunn also reported some interesting between-group differences which suggested that traditional-age students rate the exercise as more beneficial than older students.

Non-academic outcomes: affect and motivation

The relatively simple exercises in peer tutoring or paired learning outlined in Chapter 1 (co-operative note-taking pairs; peer coaching; peer monitoring; think-pair-share and think-pair-square; the three-step interview; flashcard tutoring) can have non-academic benefits. For example, Fraser *et al.* (1977) described an example of peer monitoring which appeared to give rise to *improved attitudes towards the subject* and *increased student motivation*. The researchers considered whether differences in responses pre- and post-implementation of the scheme could be attributed to the Hawthorne effect (Roethlisberger and Dickson, 1939) on the experimental group, and designed another study to investigate this possibility. In the follow-up study, students were assigned to learn with 0, 1, 2 or 3 learning partners. Results replicated those from the initial study, and, additionally, indicated that all partnerships were equally effective.

Other simple peer-tutoring techniques appear to have other non-academic benefits. As we saw in Chapter 1, students in a peer coaching scheme perceived it to *increase participant confidence* (Levene and Frank, 1993). Additionally, both participants and organizers claimed that the scheme *strengthened collegial relationships*. Similarly, the think-pair-share technique, too, seems to help build up student confidence and encourage students to *participate in discussion*.

More complex peer tutoring techniques have also been found to have non-academic beneficial effects. For example, Koch's (1992) study which featured students engaged in pair-problem-solving showed a significant *drop in partici-pants' maths anxiety* post-study and an *increase in positive attitudes to themselves* as learners of mathematics. Control students not participating in pair-problem-solving showed no significant differences pre- to post-test. In terms of perform-ance, experimental students' scores were highly significantly higher than those of control students at the end of the study. Moreover, *completion rates* were 50 per cent for control students and 64 per cent for the experimental group.

Summary

It seems that while some peer-tutoring techniques are very successful at helping students improve their academic performance, others are particularly beneficial in terms of skills development. The most researched skill appears to be that of writing, and techniques designed to improve writing have been rated as successful by both practitioners and participants. Reading and note-taking skills may also be improved by paired learning. However, there is less hard evidence to support claims of peer tutoring aiding the development of higher-order cognitive skills. This does not, of course, mean that peer tutoring does *not* help such development. Lack of evidence of cognitive development may simply reflect the difficulty of measuring it. Work by the Dansereau team has found that experience of paired learning can transfer to subsequent individual learning.

We shall now move on to examine the effects of same-level peer tutoring involving one institution where unequal status is introduced by the investigator.

SAME-LEVEL PEER TUTORING INVOLVING ONE INSTITUTION WHERE UNEQUAL STATUS IS INTRODUCED BY THE INVESTIGATOR

Academic and non-academic outcomes: affect and motivation

An example of this category of peer tutoring is Grasha's (1972) scheme of teaching assistants and 'teacher-of-the-day' which was designed to help them develop learning skills and help overcome problems associated with dependent or overly-competitive student response styles. Grasha found participants enjoyed the opportunity to have increased responsibility in the classroom and were enthusiastic about the scheme. Nearly three-quarters felt more involved in their own learning, and over three-quarters preferred the new initiatives to traditionally delivered courses. Grasha reported some evidence which indicated that the initiatives had *moved students towards a 'participant' response style*. Although the initiative also aimed to address problems of absenteeism, no data are reported to enable us to see whether this aim was achieved.

Frasson and Aimeur's (1996) study of learning with a virtual companion indicated some benefits in the area of *knowledge acquisition*. However, these benefits were not universal, and different outcomes were associated with different experimental conditions and different sub-populations. As we learned in Chapter 1, the researchers found that learning with the help of the simulated intelligent tutor benefited all participants, particularly those with low-confidence. Learning with a virtual companion also seemed to benefit low-confidence subjects particularly. However, learning with the virtual troublemaker was deemed to have adverse outcomes for the low-confidence group.

Summary

Although there are few examples of same-level unequal-status peer tutoring initiatives, some benefits to participants are reported in the two examples described. However, both studies involve a very novel situation for traditionally taught students, and the effects may, thus, be as much due to this novelty as to the techniques themselves. As with so many initiatives, follow-up studies are needed.

We shall now examine the benefits reported to result from cross-level peer tutoring involving one institution where unequal status is built on existing differences.

CROSS-LEVEL PEER TUTORING INVOLVING ONE INSTITUTION WHERE UNEQUAL STATUS IS BUILT ON EXISTING DIFFERENCES

Multiple benefits

Some peer-tutoring techniques within this category have multiple benefits. As we saw in Chapter 1, Wallace and Rye (1994) reported that studies of Supplemental Instruction (SI) programmes in the United States and Britain have shown *improved grades* and *reduced drop-out rates* among tutees. SI has also been found to provide a forum for *learning essential study strategies* and *developing skills* in comprehension, analysis, critical thinking and problem solving. In addition, SI leaders have been found to *improve leadership skills*, and *co-operation is fostered* between staff and students and within the student body (Wallace and Rye, 1994).

Mentoring, too, appears to have benefits in several categories. For example, Witherby (1997) reported that his Peer Assisted Study Scheme (PASS) resulted in *increased mentee satisfaction* and a *reduction in failure rates* to almost zero. Additionally, the ability of mentees to *apply skills and competencies* to other courses appeared to be improved and mentor *academic performance and confidence* was also increased. Other peer-assisted study schemes, too, appear to confer similar benefits to students.

Watson (1999) described another type of PASS scheme, the Peer Assistance Support Scheme which is modelled on Supplemental Instruction, but, unlike SI, was offered to all first-year students who wished to participate as mentees. Watson's evaluations of the scheme have found benefits in both affective and skills development areas, and in improved participant performance. In qualitative self-report data, student mentees reported an *improved understanding of concepts* and of the *wording of problems* as a result of participating. The latter effect was noted particularly by participants whose first language was not English. All students appeared to enjoy the friendly atmosphere and helpfulness of leaders. Leaders (predominantly second-year students) also noted deepened understanding of the lower level material as a result of their mentoring activities, which they believed helped their understanding of second level subjects. In other words, a *learning to learn effect* was identified. Leaders also reported *improvement to their communication, presentation and teamwork skills*. Quantitative data relating the number of attendances at the voluntary PASS sessions with examination scores suggested that the scheme had performance benefits, too. Attendance was categorized into levels which varied from zero to 'more than six attendances' and the performance of high and low attenders was compared. The pattern was found to be the same for all modules which offered a PASS scheme (quantitative methods; microeconomics; finance): those who had attended at least six sessions had *significantly better performance* than non-attenders. The percentage of students who performed at the highest level in each subject area was at least doubled by attendance at PASS sessions. Of course, as attendance was voluntary, we cannot be sure that the groups of attenders and non-attenders were matched. However, the philosophy of the scheme is that it is for everyone, not simply for those who are in difficulty.[1]

Parrainage, too, seems to have benefits in both performance and non-academic spheres. In Chapter 1, we learned that *parrains* aim to provide help to *filleuls* in a variety of contexts: with practical problem solving, learning skills development, discussion about vocational goals and help with mastery of content. The Swiss scheme reported by Goldschmid and Goldschmid (1976) was rated a success by both *parrains* and *filleuls*. *Filleuls* showed *improved academic performance* in terms of grades compared with that of similar cohorts over the previous two-year period. In addition, *failure rates were reduced*.

Multiple benefits are also reported for cognitive apprenticeships. Starr (1991) noted improvements in the area of academic achievement (participants showed some *gains in content mastery*), in the area of *skills development* (students perceived their cognitive skills and approaches to problem solving to have improved), in the *affective area* (student attitudes towards content were improved) and in terms of *metacognition* (students showed increased awareness of metacognitive processes).

Study skills

Improving writing

Bruffee (1978) described the effects of the Brooklyn Plan, a scheme which, he claimed, provided the conditions identified by Newcomb (Newcomb and Wilson, 1966) as essential for promoting intellectual growth of undergraduates through peer-group influence. As we saw in Chapter 1, peer tutors were trained in a section of the English Department's Intermediate Composition course to provide help for students with their writing in a drop-in writing centre. The written work of tutors was found to improve 'dramatically'.

Non-academic outcomes: affect and motivation

Proctoring seems to be particularly beneficial in the non-academic area. For example, Metcalfe (1992) reported that proctors expressed *concern for their group* and stated a belief that they themselves would have benefited from being proctored. Most proctored students rated their proctors as friendly and helpful. They expressed a wish for more time being proctored, and hoped to be able to act as proctors themselves when they reached final year.

Summary

Different-level unequal-status techniques such as SI, proctoring and mentoring appear to confer many benefits to participants. There is also some evidence to suggest that techniques designed to improve writing appear to do just that.

We now move on to look at our fourth category, cross-level peer tutoring involving two institutions.

CROSS-LEVEL PEER TUTORING INVOLVING TWO INSTITUTIONS

Multiple benefits: generic skills development, reinforced knowledge and personal satisfaction

Tutor evaluations of the 'Pimlico Connection', in which undergraduates tutored school-age students, suggested that a key objective of the scheme, to change pupils' attitudes and improve their school experiences in science, was being met (Goodlad, 1998, 1979). However, we shall focus primarily on benefits to the undergraduate tutors. Tutors felt themselves to have benefited in several ways: in terms of *reinforcement of subject knowledge*, in *improvement of communication and presentation skills* and in terms of *improved understanding of people* of different ages and from different backgrounds. They also reported considerable *satisfaction* from doing something useful with what they had learned. Evaluation of the Napier student tutoring in schools scheme also found that student tutors perceived themselves to have benefited in terms of *increased confidence* and *development of transferable skills* (Highton and Goss, 1997). These students also registered satisfaction and a *sense of achievement* at being able to help others and to do something useful with their skills. Many students rated the experience of tutoring in schools as *fun*.

Thus, students may benefit in a variety of ways from participating in a tutoring in schools programme. Benefits to tutors are increased in cases where they gain credit for tutoring. We shall now consider some benefits of small-group peer-tutoring techniques.

PEER TUTORING IN SMALL GROUPS

Multiple benefits

In a very early example of syndicate learning, Collier (1969) reported the results of a self-report survey of students. Syndicate participants believed they had gained more satisfaction, experienced greater stimulus to thinking, developed more personal interest in the subject and found increased meaningfulness in an academic course than would have been the case when learning in a more traditional way. Collier also reported a subjective impression that students working in a syndicate wrote more cogently than those in traditional courses. As we saw in Chapter 1, Collier (1983) reported a number of case studies of syndicate methods in use. Although teachers using the method reported a high degree of student participation, involvement and motivation, very few accounts contained rigorous evaluations.

Structured Academic Controversy (Johnson *et al.*, 1991) aims to use disagreement and conflict to aid learning and intellectual development and to increase motivation and involvement of students. Numerous academic and social benefits appear to derive from participating in structured controversies. For example, the following positive outcomes of well-structured, well-monitored conflict have been identified by the Co-operative Learning Center at the University of Minnesota:

- greater quantity and quality of achievement, complex reasoning, and creative problem solving;
- higher-quality decision making;
- healthier cognitive, social and psychological development by being better able to deal with more stress and cope with unforeseen adversities;
- increased motivation and energy to take action;
- higher-quality relationships with friends, co-workers and family members;
- a greater sense of caring, commitment, joint identity and cohesiveness with an emphasis on increased liking, respect and trust;
- heightened awareness that a problem exists that needs to be solved;
- increased incentive to change.

(Millis and Cottell, 1998)

Academic outcomes and performance

Guided Reciprocal Peer Questioning (King, 1991) was designed to help students comprehend and remember the content of lectures and to facilitate encoding and retrieval of information. Participants were found to benefit from using questioning strategies, in that they performed significantly better on post-test comprehension than students in a control condition.

Study skills

Although, as we shall see below, the Jigsaw technique's main area of benefit is in improved affect and motivation, Wedman *et al.* (1996) also reported that Jigsaw team participants seemed to have developed a higher level of understanding of strategy use than the traditionally taught controls.

Non-academic outcomes: affect and motivation

The Jigsaw technique (Aronson *et al.*, 1975) has been rated as an *excellent motivational device*. Students using it are reported to give the impression of having more *fun* than in previous traditionally taught courses. In addition, Aronson's team found that participants came to see the course in a more favourable light and *evaluated it more positively*. An additional benefit of the Jigsaw technique reported in another account was that an increased percentage of students *completed the course* on time (Carroll, 1986).

Thus, peer tutoring in small groups can also confer benefits in academic and non-academic spheres.

Summary

Table 2.1 summarizes the reported effects in the four categories of dyadic learning and small-group settings. Desired outcomes are listed along with some peer-tutoring techniques that have reported success in achieving them.

Table 2.1 Benefits likely to result from different peer-tutoring techniques
N.B. Please note that when a technique appears in brackets there is little or no hard evidence to link it with the desired effect.

Desired outcome	Technique reporting such an effect
	EQUAL-STATUS SAME-LEVEL PEER TUTORING
Academic Improved memorization/learning of definitions/vocabulary building	Flashcard tutoring
Improved ability to commit information to memory and promotion of deep learning	(Reciprocal teaching)
Promotion of self-direction and critical thinking	(Peer response system)
Improved performance	The learning cell
	Peer monitoring
	Pair-problem-solving
	Reciprocal peer tutoring
Metacognitive Improved metacognitive skills (comprehension; error correcting; evaluation)	Scripted Co-operative Dyads
Improved elaborative activities (use of imagery and analogy)	Scripted Co-operative Dyads
Transfer of learning	Scripted Co-operative Dyads
Skills development Improved note taking	Co-operative note taking pairs
Reading for meaning	(Paired annotations)
Writing development	Peer editing
	Peer review
	Collaborative writing
Non-academic Improved attitudes to subject	Peer monitoring
Increased motivation	Think-pair-share

Table 2.1 Continued

Increase participation	Think-pair-share
Increased confidence	Peer coaching
Strengthen collegial relationships	Peer coaching
Decreased anxiety about mathematics	Pair-problem-solving
Improved attitudes to selves as learners of maths	Pair-problem-solving
	UNEQUAL-STATUS SAME-LEVEL PEER TUTORING
Academic and non-academic Development of a participant response style	Teacher-of-the-day
Improved affect	Teacher-of-the-day
Improved motivation	Teacher-of-the-day
Decreased absenteeism	(Teacher-of-the-day)
Improved knowledge acquisition	Learning with a virtual companion
	CROSS-LEVEL PEER TUTORING WITHIN AN INSTITUTION
Academic Improved grades (recipients)	Supplemental Instruction
Improved academic performance (recipients)	Mentoring/ Peer Assisted Study Scheme
	Peer Assistance Support System
	Parrainage
Improved understanding of concepts (recipients)	Peer Assistance Support System
Improved understanding of wording of problems	Peer Assistance Support System
Deepened understanding of lower-level material (leaders)	Peer Assistance Support System
Mastery of content	*Parrainage*
	Cognitive apprenticeships
Metacognitive Transfer of learning (application of skills to other courses)	Mentoring/ Peer Assisted Study Scheme
Transfer of understanding to higher level material	Peer Assistance Support System
Improved awareness of metacognitive processes	Cognitive apprenticeships
Skills Improved leadership skills (SI leaders)	Supplemental Instruction
Improved communication skills (leaders)	Peer Assistance Support System

Table 2.1 Continued

Improved presentation skills (leaders)	Peer Assistance Support System
Improved teamwork skills (leaders)	Peer Assistance Support System
Help with practical problem solving	*Parrainage*
	Cognitive apprenticeships
Learning/academic skills development	*Parrainage*
	Cognitive apprenticeships
Vocational goal identification	*Parrainage*
Improved writing	Brooklyn plan
Non-academic Reduced drop-out (recipients)	Supplemental Instruction
Decreased failure rates (recipients)	Mentoring/Peer Assisted Study Scheme
	Parrainage
Increased confidence	Mentoring/Peer Assisted Study Scheme
Increased student satisfaction (recipients)	Mentoring/ Peer Assisted Study Scheme
Increased student enjoyment (recipients)	Peer Assistance Support System
	Proctoring
Improved attitudes to subject	Cognitive apprenticeships
	CROSS-LEVEL PEER TUTORING IN 2 INSTITUTIONS
Academic Reinforcement of subject knowledge (tutor)	Tutoring in schools
Skills Improved communication skills (tutor)	Tutoring in schools
Improved presentation skills (tutor)	Tutoring in schools
Non-academic Improved understanding of people of different ages and from different backgrounds (tutor)	Tutoring in schools
Increased satisfaction (tutor)	Tutoring in schools
Increased confidence (tutor)	Tutoring in schools
	PEER TUTORING IN SMALL GROUPS
Academic Improved learning	Structured Academic Controversy
Increased academic development	Structured Academic Controversy
Improved comprehension	Guided Reciprocal Peer Questioning

Table 2.1 Continued

Improved memory for lecture content	Guided Reciprocal Peer Questioning
Improved performance	Guided Reciprocal Peer Questioning
Facilitate encoding and retrieval of material	Guided Reciprocal Peer Questioning
Metacognitive Development of understanding of higher levels of strategy use	Jigsaw
Non academic Improved motivation	Jigsaw
Increased satisfaction	Jigsaw
Improved course evaluation	Jigsaw
Increased completion rates on time	Jigsaw

Readers may, thus, select outcomes they wish for their own students and identify appropriate peer-tutoring techniques to help them achieve their aims.

DIFFERENTIAL TUTOR–TUTEE EFFECTS

We shall now move on to investigate effects of peer tutoring which may be different for tutors and tutees. I surveyed peer-tutoring schemes from the 1960s to the end of the 1990s with the aim of locating any differential tutor-tutee effects.

Very early studies, all of which were same-level (e.g. Collier, 1969), tended to involve the participation of all class members in group learning, and, thus, no tutor-tutee differences in outcomes are reported. Similarly, schemes in the 1970s also described methodologies in which all learners participated as group members (e.g. Bruffee, 1978) or as equal partners in a dyad (e.g. Fraser *et al.*, 1977). Goldschmid and Goldschmid's (1976) review of peer tutoring studies concluded with an observation that the dyadic structure permits an easy 'teacher'–'student' role change which prevents passivity of any participant. Once again, no tutor-tutee differences were apparent.

However, reports of *tutor advantages* seem to dominate the 1980s. Work by Dansereau and team contributed about half of all studies conducted during this time. In general, as we saw above, they found that partners with an active tutoring role outperformed those in passive roles and recommended alternating roles as a means of maximizing benefits to all participants (e.g. Larson and Dansereau, 1986). Other tutor advantages are found in the work of Bargh and Schul (1980) and Annis (1983a and b). My own initial exploration of peer tutoring in higher education was also characterized by greater tutor than tutee gains (Falchikov, 1990).

Great variety in terms of tutor-tutee outcomes are reported in the explosion of peer-tutoring studies in the 1990s. In about a third of all papers located, all students within a class participated and had equal status within a dyad or small group (e.g. Bell, 1991; Scott, 1995; Bard, 1996). A smaller number of studies involved role reversal within dyads (e.g. Al-Hilawani *et al.*, 1993; King, 1993; Griffin and Griffin, 1998), and, thus, once again, there were no tutor-tutee differences in outcomes. This decade witnessed the emergence of *cross-level peer-tutoring* activities such as mentoring (e.g. Starr, 1991; Dennis, 1993) and Supplemental Instruction (SI) (e.g. Price and Rust, 1995). In these studies, *tutee benefits* were often seen as being of greater importance than those of tutors. Reports certainly tended to focus on benefits for tutees. However, towards the end of the decade, some studies began to report that both *tutors and tutees can benefit, though in different ways* (e.g. Carroll, 1996; Watters and Ginns, 1997; Rubin and Herbert, 1998). Finally, a very small number of studies reported *tutor advantages* and omitted mention of tutee outcomes (e.g. Metcalfe, 1992; Congos and Schoeps, 1997). However, although there may be an absence of information about benefits to one class of participant, we cannot conclude that there are none.

Summary

Several differences in the patterns of benefits to tutors and tutees have been noted over the past 40 years. Peer tutoring schemes today are structured so as to provide benefits to all participants, and the key to maximizing benefits in dyadic working seems to be for participants to alternate between roles of tutee and tutor. When fixed-role and alternating-role performance is compared, it is generally the alternation of roles that has most benefits, and in cases where fixed roles are successful in terms of participant benefits, it is the active partner who benefits at the expense of the more passive one.

In the next chapter, we shall look at a number of theoretical frameworks that underlie peer tutoring.

Note

1 Watson continues the evaluation and should be contacted in the School of Economics at The University of New South Wales about future developments which, I gather, are likely to include an analysis along gender lines.

3 Theoretical frameworks for peer tutoring

In this chapter, we shall look at a variety of theoretical frameworks which underlie peer tutoring. These may be classified as:

- early cognitive theories;
- theories from social psychology;
- theories relating to personal and professional development.

We shall also consider why a theoretical basis is regarded as important for any educational practice or innovation.

INTRODUCTION

Too many educational initiatives appear to be devoid of theoretical underpinnings, seeming to be driven by expediency, economics or political agendas. Cross (1981: 109) argued that theory is 'one of the most under-utilized vehicles for understanding various aspects of adult education'. While Cross was advocating the usefulness of theory in the context of adult learning, her conclusion applies equally well to any field of education. Others have argued that absence of theory has 'a pervasively debilitating influence' (Mezirow, in Cross, 1981: 135). Some educational practice is not only devoid of a theoretical basis, but also lacks rigorous testing by research. Even when research is conducted, it may be perceived as inadequate. For example, a large body of educational research has attracted criticism from UK government inspectors (Tooley, 1998).

Seemingly well-established educational beliefs and practices may be lacking in some key respects. For example, although generic or transferable skills development has become an established feature within much current higher education in the UK, this topic still gives rise to lively debate among educators. The Confederation of British Industry requires that graduates should possess generic transferable skills for a flexible labour market (CBI, 1997/8). However, it has been argued that universities will never be able to define and assess a set of key skills acceptable to industry, and that, in any case, an emphasis on key skills threatens the intellectual development of students (Baty, 1997). The *Times Higher Education Supplement* featured an article which provided further evidence of the gulf between what was termed 'the culture of universities and the practical problem-solving world of work' (Levin, 1998). Both staff and students are reported to have expressed concern about the atheoretical status of generic skills and competence-based modules (Saunders and Kingdon, 1998). While these debates are taking place in the UK, colleagues in other parts of the world assure me that they are engaged in similar discussions centred on the conflict between external requirements and perceived educational standards.

Similarly, the concept of lifelong learning has taken the educational spotlight in the UK with the publication of government reports on continuing education and lifelong learning (e.g. DfEE, 1997). It is envisaged that lifelong learning will include a variety of forms of learning, all characterized by flexibility. These forms include distance and open learning in the context of home, the community or work. However, initial research conducted as part of the Economic and Social Research Council's (ESRC) Learning Society project found that much of the government's policy on life-long learning is based on 'fallacy' (Baty, 1998). Researchers at the University of Wales, Cardiff, discovered that a person's lifetime participation in education is largely determined at birth, and that intervention to promote learning in later life is often fruitless.

Even educational objectives such as the development of students as autonomous learners, which can be said to have a philosophical and theoretical base (e.g. Maslow, 1954; Perry, 1970), may be undermined by other factors. Wall (1997) argued that 'what most university teachers might once have thought of as a high educational ideal has been highjacked by those whose main concern is to balance the books'. Wall also maintained that the achievement of a significant degree of autonomy is a lifetime project which cannot be achieved by reducing contact hours and increasing the length of reading lists. Students, too, may be suspicious of much independent learning now that they are required to pay for the privilege of receiving it.

Before starting our investigation of the theories themselves, we shall begin by considering a question:

What are the benefits of situating peer-tutoring schemes within a sound theoretical and research framework?

Why is a theoretical base important? I would argue that it provides a framework within which to gain understanding of events and enables us to make predictions and evaluate our initiatives. Studies that are well designed, and structured so as to enable us to test hypotheses and answer questions, can provide invaluable information about both the outcomes of innovations and about their processes. There are a number of useful, well-grounded and researched theories that may help inform much current educational debate and illuminate many aspects of peer-assisted learning. We shall examine some of these below.

THEORETICAL FRAMEWORKS OF PEER TUTORING

We shall begin our overview of theoretical influences on peer tutoring with the seminal work of *Jean Piaget* and *Lev Vygotsky*.

COGNITIVE DEVELOPMENTAL THEORY: THE WORK OF PIAGET

The explicit or implicit aim of much higher education is the development of students' cognitive abilities, and active, co-operative peer learning is no exception to this principle. Much of what we believe about cognitive development derives from the work of the Swiss biologist Jean Piaget, who saw a progression of cognitive developmental stages as being inevitable, each building on the one which preceded it, and each being a prerequisite for the next. He also believed that the rate of progression from one stage to another varied from person to person, and that progression through the stages involved multiple determinants: *maturation*, *experience* and *social environmental factors*. It was Piaget who stressed the value of *cognitive conflict*. He argued that, when individuals encounter new information which does not fit into their current mental organization of knowledge and thought (their existing mental schema), a contradiction occurs which causes '*disequilibrium*'. This enables learners to '*accommodate*' the new information and modify their current understanding of aspects of the world, thus achieving a new '*equilibrium*'. In this way, learners construct their own knowledge.

Although evaluations of Piaget's theory have suggested that some modification may be necessary (e.g. Donaldson, 1978), many educators, myself included, find its basic tenets extremely useful.

Towards the end of his career, Piaget (1971, written in 1969) looked at developments in pedagogy, noting that a very large proportion of innovators were not professional educators. He argued that education was not respected as a discipline and had low prestige. This argument has parallels today, for example, in terms of the status of pedagogical research compared with subject-specific research in universities. However, Piaget's recommendations to aid progress in experimental pedagogy in the 1960s might suggest some ways forward for educational researchers today.

> If experimental pedagogy wishes to understand what it is doing and to complete its observations with causal interpretations or 'explanations', it is obvious that it will have to employ a precise psychology, not merely that of common sense.
>
> (Piaget, 1971: 23–24)

Piaget argued that classic educational theorists were hampered by their lack of a psychology or psycho-sociology of childhood, and believed that his theory relating to the active nature of knowledge would benefit the educator. Intelligence, according to Piaget, derives from *action*, even when the action takes the form of thought. He questioned whether knowledge is simply a copy of reality, or 'an assimilation of reality into a structure of transformations' (Piaget, 1971: 28). He supported the transformations alternative with his developmental theory of cognitive growth. However, he regretted that the 'knowledge-copy' concept was slow to be replaced. 'The ideas behind the knowledge-copy concept have not been abandoned by everyone, far from it, and they continue to provide the inspiration for many educational methods' (Piaget, 1971: 28). Unfortunately, this may still be true today.

Piaget believed that *co-operation between peers* is likely to encourage real exchange of thought and discussion, and that such co-operation among children has an importance as great as that of adult action. In other words, he deemed co-operation among peers essential for the development of a critical attitude of mind, objectivity and discursive reflection.

Piaget's cognitive theory has influenced generations of educators. McCormick and Pressley (1997) suggested some ways in which to encourage conceptual change in students which derive from Piaget's theory.

- Diagnose students' current developmental stages so that developmentally appropriate assignments and instruction can be given.
- Design instruction so that students are active participants in their own learning. Construct learning environments conducive to exploration by students.
- Make students aware of conflicts between their approaches to problems and the features of the problems. Probing questions should be asked. Present counterexamples, and point out inconsistencies that may lead to disequilibration.
- Reduce adult power as much as possible. Foster collaboration with peers who have mutual interests.
- Encourage children to think in their own ways. Analyse students' errors to gain a better understanding of their thought processes.

(McCormick and Pressley, 1997: 160–61)

Piaget's influence is clearly evident in the context of peer tutoring, and his name is mentioned frequently in current accounts of peer tutoring initiatives. For example, Forman and Cazden (1985) asserted that most past research into peer collaboration has been based upon Piaget's ideas. They themselves designed experiments to examine the effects of collaboration, making use of Piagetian and Vygotskian perspectives and concluded that a Piagetian perspective can be particularly useful in understanding situations where cognitive conflict is present.

Rings and Sheets (1991) identified 'student development theory' as an appropriate research-based theoretical model in which to ground tutor training programmes. A key element of this theory is Piaget's *dynamic active learning* which challenges students to become more self-directed. In addition, the authors identified another important element of Piaget's theory, namely, its developmental nature, and stressed the importance of taking into account the different levels of development, differing skills and abilities and different rates of progression of student learners.

Koch (1992), too, emphasized the importance of Piaget's constructivism in the context of learning mathematics. Koch's model of instruction which involved pair-problem-solving and small co-operative groups for the learning of mathematics was based on a constructionist view. Similarly, early chapters of Hertz-Lazarowitz and Miller's (1992) book on co-operative group working emphasize the social construc-tionist theories of Piaget and Vygotsky (1978). Mann (1994) also made use of Piagetian theory (Inhelder and Piaget, 1958) in her study of peer tutoring journals. She argued that the role-taking aspect of acting as tutor 'can also facilitate the transformation of adolescent thinking away from the egocentric perspective of childhood toward a more decentred perspective that recognizes multiple points of view and that is more reflective' (Mann, 1994: 164).

VYGOTSKY'S ZONE OF PROXIMAL DEVELOPMENT

As we have seen, Forman and Cazden (1985) argued that a Piagetian perspective on the role of social factors is useful in attempting to understand situations that are characterized by cognitive conflict. However, they also argued that 'if one wants to understand the cognitive consequences of other social contexts, Vygotsky's ideas may be more helpful' (Forman and Cazden, 1985: 343).

Vygotsky also proposed a general theory of cognitive development. Although much of his original work was done in the context of language learning in children (Vygotsky, 1962), later applications have been broader (e.g. Wertsch, 1985). Principles of Vygotsky's theory are that, at any given age, full cognitive develop-ment requires social interaction. Vygotsky argued that the range of skill that can be developed with adult guidance or peer collaboration exceeds that which can be attained alone. Central to his theory is the idea of the '*zone of proximal development*', defined as

> the distance between the actual development as determined by individual problem solving and the level of potential development as determined through problem solving under adult guidance or in collaboration with more capable peers.

> (Vygotsky, 1978: 86)

While Vygotsky's theory is used at all educational levels, and has helped many researchers to both frame questions and interpret the results of a variety of empirical studies, it is particularly relevant to peer tutoring. For example, Palincsar and Brown (1984) described a series of studies of reciprocal teaching involving teachers and 7th grade students with poor comprehension, in which an adult model guided the student to interact with a text in increasingly sophisticated ways. Significant gains in children's comprehension test scores were noted. Palincsar and Brown's method is grounded in Vygotsky's theory as it stresses the importance of the social context and the presence of '*expert scaffolding*' (Palincsar and Brown, 1984: 117). Forman and Cazden (1985) also used the framework of Vygotsky's zone of proximal development to help explain the results of research which compared performance of singletons and dyads. Similarly, Brown *et al.* (1989) acknowledged the debt owed by proponents of situated cognition and cognitive apprenticeships to activity theorists such as Vygotsky. More recently, Doolittle (1995) discussed the relationship between Vygotsky's zone of proximal development and co-operative learning, and elucidated some 'Vygotskian suggestions of the use of co-operative learning'. Examples of these are:

> Create classroom exercises that require social interaction with peers, parents, teachers or professionals....
>
> Provide opportunities for verbal interactions....
>
> Construct activities that are designed to stimulate both behavioural change and cognitive/metacognitive change.
>
> (Doolittle, 1995: 20, 21, 23)

Similarly, Watters and Ginns' (1997) Peer Assisted Study System (PASS) was based on Vygotsky's 'constructivist-inspired strategies such as collaborative learning, conceptual change through discourse and the development of autonomy' (Watters and Ginns, 1997: 6). Topping (1997: 110) also identified a 'neo-Piagetian interpretation of individual development through the cognitive conflict and challenge' inherent in many forms of peer-assisted learning (PAL), but claimed that PAL may be better understood through the social interactionist or constructivist view of cognitive development which is traceable back to Vygotsky.

SOCIAL-PSYCHOLOGICAL THEORETICAL BASES OF PEER TUTORING

In addition to general theoretical and philosophical roots, and to the influence of Piaget and Vygotsky, several specific theories from social psychology might also be seen as relevant to peer tutoring. Indeed, Slavin (1985) claimed that all co-operative learning methods are based on social-psychological research and theory, adapted to meet the practical requirements of classrooms. We shall now take a brief look at some of these theories, starting with role theory.

After the brief description of each framework, problems that are highlighted by the theory will be listed, and practical suggestions for dealing with peer tutoring problems considered.

Role theory

To some extent, people's behaviour may be understood by looking at the roles they occupy. However, Goffman (1956) pointed out that the term 'role' involves more than the conduct of particular behaviours. In addition to a set of behaviours, a role may also involve attitudes, obligations and privileges expected of an individual who occupies a status. Subsequently, Tajfel and Fraser (1978) argued that people become what they are obliged to be.

As adults, we occupy many roles. We may be both parents *and* daughters or sons. We may also have professional roles. We fill the roles of consumers and members of a community. Some individuals are criminals. More and more adults are also taking on the role of student. Some of these roles may conflict with others, and occupying too many roles may give rise to *'role overload'*. Failure to fulfil *role expectations* may give rise to discomfort and embarrassment. 'When one is "not himself" in the presence of others who expect him to be just that ... embarrassment ensues' (Gross and Stone, 1964: 356).

Let us start by looking at role expectations in the context of teaching and peer tutoring.

The role of teacher

Allen and Feldman (1973) suggested that the role of the teacher represents competence, prestige and authority, and Medway (1991) argued that enacting the role of teacher will convey these attributes. Owen (1983) provided some evidence to support these predictions. He described student perceptions of the faculty tutor as an authority figure even in situations where teachers were attempting to achieve a more equal status with students, and argued that, however liberal the intentions, 'no tutor can avoid being perceived as a frame of reference, a legitimator of knowledge', and one who sets 'the parameters of acceptability' (Owen, 1983: 94).

The roles of peer tutor and tutee

More recently, Gillam, Callaway and Wikoff (1994) investigated the role of the peer tutor and the authority it carries. These researchers concluded that tutor–tutee relationships were influenced by traditional preconceptions about the tutor's role and authority. Clearly, fulfilment of the tutor's role is crucially dependent on the presence of a tutee. The mere presence of a peer constitutes an audience which influences the tutor. Moreover, Gillam *et al.* (1994) noted that tutees expected the tutor to take charge, and 'this expectation shaped each encounter in one way or another' (Gillam *et al.*, 1994: 193). Thus, tutees are both influenced by their role and influential within it. Tutee behaviour influences the tutor, in that passive tutee behaviour can act to confirm the tutor's role, while tutee action can help the tutor and the interaction. For example, the tutor will benefit if the peer asks questions (Forman and Cazden, 1985).

Although a study reported by Bierman and Furman (1981) involved fourth-grade children rather than undergraduates, the results of their analysis of the effects of the experimental manipulation of the rationale for selection as tutor or tutee may be of relevance to this discussion. Bierman and Furman's study made *predictions from role theory*, according to which, 'enactment of a role produces changes in behaviour, attitudes and self-perceptions consistent with role expectations' (Bierman and Furman, 1981: 33). In other words, assignment to the role of tutor can lead to perceived similarity with the teacher, and student tutors may grow to perceive competence and prestige in their role. Tutees, on the other hand, may begin to perceive themselves as relatively deficient in these qualities. Children involved in the study were given one of four rationales for selection as tutor or tutee:

Condition 1: a competence rationale ('teacher-like').
Condition 2: a physical characteristic rationale ('had a clear voice').
Condition 3: a chance rationale.
Condition 4: no rationale.

The researchers reasoned that it might be expected that Condition 1 would give rise to greater tutor–tutee differences than other conditions, followed by Condition 2, with Condition 4 giving rise to fewest tutor–tutee effects.

Results of Bierman and Furman's analysis of performance and attitudinal data indicated significant effects for role and condition. Tutor–tutee differences indicated that, overall, tutors scored well above tutees in all conditions on attitude measures, and this difference was statistically significant in Condition 1, and nearly so in Condition 2. Investigation of differences due to condition indicated that attitudes of tutors and tutees were significantly more positive in the no-rationale Condition 4, compared with other conditions. The authors concluded that children seemed to perceive the roles of tutors and tutees as representative of particular characteristics, and, 'in the course of enacting these roles, begin to apply these characteristics to themselves, thus influencing their self-perceptions' (Bierman and Furman, 1981: 37).

Thus, however egalitarian the dyadic relationship at the onset of the exercise, peer tutors and their tutees can come to see tutors as having teacher-like characteristics. One might predict that, under such circumstances, tutor self-esteem might improve. In addition, the individual occupying the role of tutee may come to share perceptions of their erstwhile peer as having developed increased competence and authority, which might, in turn, give rise to role conflict in the tutee.

Summary

Thus, the roles of both tutor and tutee may carry problems with them. However, it has been argued that the role of tutor is more problematic than the role of tutee, and very much more has been written on the tutor role than that of tutee. Garrett (1982: 94), for example, identified the need to maintain a 'delicate balance between the "tutor" element and the "peer" element in the development of peer tutors' perceptions of their role' as a potential problem for tutors. Similarly, Hawkins acknowledged the difficulties of the dual role of the tutor as instructor and friend, arguing that 'this subtle, sometimes precarious juggling of a dual role is a pedagogical stance unique to peer tutors' (Hawkins, 1982: 30). Gillam *et al.*

(1994), exploring the roles of tutor and tutee in the context of a writing laboratory, also found that peer tutors found the double role as fellow-student and 'more capable peer' problematic (Gillam *et al.*, 1994: 165). It is not difficult to see why this might happen. As tutor, a student may identify with the system which placed her in the position of tutor and invested her with what Gillam *et al.* described as 'a certain institutional authority' (Gillam *et al.*, 1994: 165), while as fellow-student, she/he may feel conflicting social allegiances.

Problems highlighted by role theory and advice for avoiding or minimizing these in the context of peer tutoring are summarized below.

Problems highlighted by role theory

- Identification with a particular role may act to enhance the tutor's experience and detract from that of the tutee.
- Peer tutors may experience dissonance between their new role as tutor and their pre-existing role as equal.
- Tutees may experience dissonance between their new role as tutee and their pre-existing role as equal.

Advice

- If same-level tutoring is to be implemented, choose a variety in which tutors and tutees change roles. Avoid fixed roles.
- Include work on how to boost the self-esteem of tutees in tutor training for cross-level tutoring situations.
- Use tutor training sessions to stress collaboration in tutor–tutee interactions.
- Design tutoring tasks that require co-operation and work sharing rather than reinforcing the traditional authority structure.

We have seen that the roles of teacher and tutor carry with them a degree of authority. We shall now look more closely at issues of authority in relation to peer tutoring.

Issues of authority in relation to peer tutoring

Around 40 years ago, Homans (1961) considered the effects of authority on those without it. He differentiated between authority that is earned and that which is acquired by appointment, and attributed different effects to the two types. As we have seen, authority of peer tutors may be earned (as in cases where more advanced students are selected on merit to tutor less advanced students) or acquired by appointment (where same-status dyads are formed for the purpose of peer learning and the role of tutor allocated randomly). Homans defined authority as 'differences between members in the amount of influence they exert', and 'specialized authority' (Homans, 1961: 286) as influence in a narrow field of activity, which is generally the case in peer tutoring.

Social psychologists have noted an inverse relationship between authority and liking. Homans explored this relationship, illustrating it by work conducted by Bales

(1950) and Lippitt (1947). Homans (1961) argued that, as the leader's authority gets established, it becomes more and more incongruent with the social equality which existed earlier. Followers may have ambivalent feelings towards leaders, and in some cases they may not like leaders very much, or may envy them and the position they occupy. This effect may be explained in terms of the control exerted by a leader over a follower which incurs 'costs' to the follower. Similarly, Homans argued, the leader may feel an obligation to respond critically to the ways in which followers have carried out instructions. Lippitt's classic research (in Newcomb and Hartley, 1952) found that choices of working with another group member and spending social time with them tended to be more highly correlated at the beginning of a project than at the end.

Simon and Feather's (1973) study of causal attribution for success and failure in university examinations illuminated another aspect of authority imbalance in tutor–tutee relations. In many examples of peer tutoring, such as when tutors are supplied with tutoring materials by the lecturer, the tutor has access to information and knowledge which is not available to the tutee. In other instances, tutors have been selected because of their superior knowledge and skills compared to tutees. An analysis of variance conducted by Simon and Feather (1973) found that the amount of preparation or knowledge contributed most to students' confidence ratings. This finding may help explain other problems associated with tutee status.

Problems highlighted by issues of authority together with advice for minimizing these are summarized below.

Problems highlighted by issues of authority

- Tutors may exert too much control and influence within the relationship.
- Tutors may be disliked.
- Tutees may envy the tutor.
- Tutees may lose confidence as a result of an imbalance of knowledge within the tutoring relationship.

Advice

- Reciprocal tutoring relationships are likely to restore social equality and ameliorate tutee hostility.
- Make every attempt to structure tasks so as to share the preparation and knowledge and re-establish social equality between partners.

Strain deriving from role-associated behaviour is described as either 'role ambiguity' or 'role conflict'.

Role ambiguity and role conflict

The terms 'role ambiguity' and 'role conflict' are described and analysed by Kahn, Wolfe, Quinn and Snoek (1981). *Role ambiguity* relates to the availability of role-related information to the person occupying a particular role. 'All too often people are unclear about the scope of their responsibilities; they simply do not know what they are "supposed" to do' (Kahn *et al.*, 1981: 24). A person occupying any role, particularly a new one, needs to know what kinds of behaviour will be rewarded or punished. It is also desirable that the nature of the rewards and punishments be known, along with their likelihood of occurrence. Finally, a person needs to assess what is likely to be personally satisfying in relation to existing values, needs and aspirations. Lack of information can be stressful to the person occupying a role, and it has been observed that individuals are more likely to suffer role conflict in cases where the role is not well defined. Information may be missing because it does not exist or because it is not available to the person who needs it. In some cases, information may be communicated inadequately. Healy (1991) argued that, in the context of tutoring in a writing centre,

> Inadequate information may be the result of various factors, including inexperience, lack of familiarity with particular content areas, insufficient communication from supervisors or tutees, or simply the inherent nature of the job – a job that demands a degree of flexibility which renders specific and detailed job descriptions problematic.
>
> (Healy, 1991: 43)

Role conflict may be caused in a variety of ways, but all types appear to derive from the differing expectations that may be placed on a person occupying a role by those in what Kahn *et al.* (1981) call the 'role set'. For example, in the context of peer tutoring, the teacher or peer-tutoring organizer may impose certain restrictions on the behaviour of the student tutor, such as requiring her/him to engage tutees actively in their education, while tutees may wish for a more passive role in the process.

Kahn *et al.* (1981) identified 5 types of role conflict:

1   *Inter-role conflict*
    In inter-role conflict, expectations attached to an individual in one role clash with those of the same person in another role, as we have noted above. For example, a peer tutor's role which requires her to become a leader within the relationship may conflict with her perception of herself as a friend and equal of the tutee.

2   *Person–role conflict*
    In person-role conflict, role requirements violate the particular values or needs of an individual. For example, an independent, autonomous individual may experience the role of tutee dependent on her/his tutor as violating her/his preferred mode of being.

3   *Role overload*
    In role overload, the role involves more expectations than can be realistically fulfilled by one person. An example of this may be where a peer tutor perceives her/his role as having too many facets (such as Brannon's (1982) peer tutor roles of facilitator, supporter, leader and resistor to which we shall return in Chapter 6).

4   *Intra-sender conflict*
    In intra-sender conflict, one member of the dyad has mutually incompatible

expectations. For example, tutees may say that they want critical helpful feedback, while also signalling that they really wish to hear that things are fine as they are. Similarly, tutors experience conflict between the need to provide critical feedback and encouragement to the tutee.

5   *Inter-sender conflict*
    In inter-sender conflict, the two members of the dyad have differing expectations. An example of this type of conflict, as we saw above, might be when the tutor sees her role as being one of facilitator of learning while the tutee wants correct answers to problems.

Kahn *et al.* (1981) claimed that role conflict may be particularly marked in cases where innovations are being implemented. Intra-role conflict within a person involved in an innovation may stem from a tension between enthusiasm for and commitment to the creative, non-routine aspects of the innovation and lack of interest in the routine aspects. Interpersonal conflicts can arise between the innovator and those keen to preserve the old ways: 'a kind of continuing battle of new guard versus old' (Kahn *et al.*, 1981: 127).

Role conflict in tutees

Tutees have been found to behave in negative ways as a means of coping with role conflict. Roberts (1994) described a number of difficult tutoring situations, all of which involved *disruptive tutee behaviours*. Many of these behaviours resembled those Kahn *et al.* (1981) had attributed to role conflict and individual attempts to cope with it, and it may be useful to conceptualize these dysfunctional behaviours as manifestations of role conflict in the tutee. For example, Roberts included blocking, resisting, evasion and passivity in her list of difficult situations facing a peer tutor. She described seven styles of disruptive tutee behaviour in total:

1   Blocking
2   Confusion (a variation of blocking)
3   Miracle seeking
4   Over-enthusiasm (a variation of miracle seeking)
5   Resisting
6   Passivity (a variation of resisting)
7   Evasion

Blocking behaviour on the part of tutees was characterized by low frustration tolerance, immobilization or hopelessness and freezing up or blocking. Remarks such as 'It's beyond me' or 'I'll never get it' can be associated with such behaviour. The type of disruptive behaviour labelled '*confusion*' is characterized by bafflement, disorientation or disorganization and helpless feelings. Roberts noted that remarks such as 'I just don't know what to do', 'I studied for the test and got a "D"', 'I'm not sure where we're going' characterized this behaviour category. *Miracle-seeking behaviour* is characterized by global interest or concern. Those displaying this type of behaviour often express enthusiasm about being with the tutor, but take a fairly passive part in the tutoring process. They have high and often inappropriate expectations. Roberts also found that their behaviour may be characterized by evasion or inability to concentrate on tasks. *Over-enthusiasm* is characterized by high expectations or demands on oneself, talk of limited time, long-range goals versus immediate tasks, global interest and enthusiasm. It is often associated with older students. *Resisting behaviour* is characterized by variations of sullenness, hostility, passivity or boredom, lack of interest in the class, the work or the tutor, or a defensive posture towards the class, the work or the tutor. Easily-triggered anger may also characterize this type of behaviour. *Passivity* is characterized by non-involvement, inattention, low affect or boredom. Those displaying this type of behaviour initiate little discussion and ask few questions. *Evasive behaviours* are characterized by manipulation, verbal ability or glibness. Global or non-specific praise of the tutor's skill or the course content may also occur.

While Roberts (1994) was writing for those primarily involved with peer tutoring in the context of the community college, many of us may recognize some of our own students in her descriptions of disruptive behaviours.

Below is a summary of problems highlighted by issues of role ambiguity and role conflict, together with advice on how to minimize these.

Problems highlighted by issues of role ambiguity and role conflict

- People may be unclear about their responsibilities.
- Lack of information can be stressful.
- Different individuals may have differing or incompatible expectations of a person.
- A role may involve too many expectations.
- Tutors may withdraw from their role, appeal to authority figures or become over-friendly with tutee.
- Tutors may work excessively hard.
- Tutors may use inappropriate approaches; they may use an over-directive approach or may become over-friendly.
- Tutees may engage in disruptive behaviour in an attempt to cope with role conflict.

Advice

- Define the role clearly.
- Be explicit about the extent of a person's responsibilities.
- Be explicit about rewards and punishments and about the types of behaviour that can earn them.
- Have open discussion between all parties involved about their expectations.
- Carry out training to familiarize tutors with different approaches to tutoring and their benefits.
- Carry out training in appropriate conflict-reduction techniques.

These issues will be explored further in Chapter 4 in which theoretical frameworks are used to analyse problems encountered in a case study of dyadic peer tutoring, and Chapter 6 in which advice is provided to help students become peer tutors.

Issues of status

Groups may be structured in a variety of ways. Group members may occupy particular roles, as we have seen, and different individuals may have different statuses within the group. Status can derive from two main sources: task proficiency and socio-emotional skills competence. Perceived importance, prestige and liking are also related to the status of individuals. These factors influence the group dynamic as 'relative statuses of group members influence the amount and quality of communication they initiate or receive from others' (Dörnyei and Malderez, 1997: 72). High-status individuals have been found to be more likely to criticize others than their lower-status peers, but are often evaluated more positively than those with lower status. The perceived statuses of individuals within a group or dyad can have other consequences. Early work by Adams (1953) on the effects of status on social and emotional behaviour made use of the concept '*status congruence*', or '*status consistency*'. Status congruence or consistency is a measure of the extent to which an individual's ranks on a number of relevant status dimensions are perceived to be comparable. Adams concluded that there appears to be a tendency for social relationships and personal emotional states to improve as group status congruence increases. However, the relationship between status congruence and performance has been found to be complex. Adams found that, initially, performance improved as status congruence increased, but then deteriorated as status congruence continued to increase. Thus, a degree of *incongruence* may act as a motivator which drives improved performance. Goffman (1956) also investigated status consistency in a very large sample of citizens of the United States. He found that those with a high degree of status consistency sought less change than those with a low degree of consistency. Once again, inconsistency seemed to act as a motivator for change.

Some consequences of status incongruence

'Status congruence' and 'status incongruence' also involve notions of fairness, and while the former is desirable and unproblematic, the latter incurs costs. Homans (1961: 248) claimed that a relationship is fair and just when, 'if the investments of the two are equal, their rewards and their costs are equal too'. Fair exchange is regarded as an important principle of social behaviour. Jackson (1962) argued that all forms of status inconsistency are psychologically disturbing and identified two consequences of such conflict: frustration and uncertainty.

Frustration, Jackson (1962) argued, stems directly from the conflicting expectations experienced by an individual who holds high rank on one status dimension and low status on another. The expectations of other people regarding this individual will be partly contradictory, and it is, therefore, impossible for the individual to meet all of them. In addition, the aspirations of the individual with status inconsistency may be raised by the high-status component and then blocked by the low-status one. *Social uncertainty* may then develop, which can reduce the stability of the self-image.

An example of status inconsistency in the context of peer tutoring is the mature student who has high status in the domestic sphere, perhaps as head of a household or parent, and perceived low status as tutee within a tutoring dyad. For example, a student who is chair of the local Parent Teacher Association (PTA) or chair of a Student Association (SA) committee may find the role of tutee particularly at odds with her or his position in the other status hierarchy. In fact, such students may also find the role of student problematic. To some extent, people's status rankings control their expectations of others, their expectations of themselves and others' expectations of them. Where there is inconsistency, as in the examples above, expectations may be in conflict. Status congruence and incongruence has relevance in both cross-level and same-level fixed-role peer tutoring.

Problems highlighted by issues of status within a dyad and advice on ways of minimizing these are summarized below.

Problems highlighted by relative status within a dyad

- Status inequalities are detrimental to dyadic or group learning.
- Social behaviour can be undermined by perceived unfairness.
- Status inconsistency can give rise to ill-effects such as frustration and uncertainty.
- The relationship between degree of status congruence and behaviour is not straightforward: some status incongruence may be motivating, but too much may cause a deterioration in performance.
- Social uncertainty can lead to a reduction in the stability of the self-image.

Advice

- The adoption of a student-centred andragogic approach can act to minimize status inconsistency where students have high status in non-educational spheres of their lives.
- Avoid situations which can give rise to status inequalities (e.g. fixed-role same-level peer tutoring) (see also above).
- Make instructions very clear to minimize uncertainty.
- Ensure that, wherever possible, knowledge is shared equally.
- Where not possible to attain equality, try for balance and respect for diversity. If an individual is not strong in one area, then she/he may be in another.
- A little status inconsistency may be motivating.

Equity theory and helping behaviour

Equity theory (e.g. Walster, Berscheid and Walster, 1973; Homans, 1976; Nadler and Fisher, 1986) maintains that partners are most satisfied with a relationship when both experience a similar ratio of benefits to effort expended.

When both parties perceive that the ratios of their rewards to contributions are equal, the distribution of rewards is said to be fair, just or equitable. Homans (1976) pointed out that comparisons of rewards and contributions are based on outward and visible measures. For example, students may see the role of tutor as having desirable high status, or, conversely, may see the amount of preparation needed to conduct a tutorial as undesirable. They may perceive that tutees do not need to prepare for tutorials, and so on. In other words, they focus on present rewards and costs rather than the longer-term benefits of these activities.

The basic equity equation has been described as:

$$\frac{\text{Your benefits}}{\text{Your contributions}} = \frac{\text{Your partner's benefits}}{\text{Your partner's contributions}}$$

(Brehm and Kassin, 1996: 205)

If one partner experiences greater benefits than the other, but also expends more effort, then the relationship between the two may still be seen as equitable. However, some researchers (e.g. Cate, Lloyd and Long, 1988) have argued that many people may find that the calculation of this equation is complex and time consuming, and resort to the simpler comparison of observable *rewards*.

The effects of helping behaviour

Kurt Lewin (1935, 1948) believed that we all need continuous help from each other, and that the interdependence this generates is 'the greatest challenge to maturity of individual and group functioning' (Lippitt, 1947: 92). While peer-assisted learning methods are designed to foster helping behaviour, in an attempt to enhance student achievements, certain types of helping behaviour have been found to be not helpful (Bossert, 1988). The acts of giving and receiving help appear to be problematic. Equity theory predicts that recipients will find non-reciprocal helping psychologically disturbing, as dependence is contrary to the norm of self-reliance. Very early work by Walster *et al.* (1973) applied equity theory to a study of helping and harm-doing relationships. Before helping begins, benefactor and recipient enjoy an equitable relationship, but after help is given, their association becomes inequitable, being unprofitable for the benefactor and profitable for the recipient. Equity theory predicts that *both* giver and receiver should experience some discomfort at this point, and attempt to alleviate it by restoring 'actual equity or psychological equity' (Walster *et al.*, 1973: 166) to their relationship. This may be achieved by either altering the overall balance of inputs to outputs or by cognitive distortion of elements (Fisher, Nadler and Whitcher-Alagna, 1982). For example, in the context of peer tutoring, tutees in receipt of help may increase the amount of tutorial preparation they do in an attempt to achieve actual equity, or tutors may persuade themselves that they, too, are deriving benefit from the helping behaviour to achieve psychological equity.

In most same-status dyadic peer-tutoring relationships, the participants share a long-term goal to do well in terms of improved grades or increased understanding of the course of which peer tutoring is a part. Thus, one might expect their relationship to be a co-operative one. However, there may be occasions when sight of the shared long-term goal is lost and immediate, day-to-day experiences and perceptions come to the fore. In addition, participants may become competitive in relation to longer-term goals, and further negative elements enter the relationship.

Another, perhaps simpler, way of trying to understand some of the problems associated with helping behaviour is to separate the effects of giving and receiving help. Receipt of help does not always result in improved performance. The type of help given can also affect outcomes. Webb (1985) reported results of studies which distinguished between giving and receiving help, and others which looked at the type of helping behaviour. She concluded that while giving explanations is beneficial to achievement, giving 'terminal responses', such as correct answers or pointing out errors, is not. Similarly, receiving explanations also tended to be beneficial to achievement, but receiving information without explanation or receiving no help when it was needed were found to be detrimental to achievement.

Webb (1992) also reviewed studies which investigated the relationship between learning outcomes and help received, and found that matches between the amount of help received and achievement produced only 20 per cent positive significant correlations. Giving help (in terms of explanations or non-elaborate information) was found to carry important benefits for the giver as well as the receiver. While it may be possible to argue that, in the studies to which Webb refers, the receipt of help did not produce improved learning outcomes because some of the conditions identified as necessary for learning were not being met, it may be equally possible that recipients were in some way threatened by help.

The conditions necessary for help to be effective were identified by Webb (1992). She saw effective help as being:

- timely;
- relevant;
- of sufficient elaboration;
- capable of being understood by the recipient;
- applied by the recipient to the problem in hand.

Helping as the ratio of rewards to costs

Perceptions of participants concerning the outcomes of their interactions are also important, and tutors and tutees may calculate different reward/cost ratios. Thibaut and Kelley (1959: 117) argued that, in a dyadic relationship with unequal power, the person who has greater power can enjoy the best 'reward-cost positions'. For example, in non-reciprocal peer tutoring, opportunities for decision making, access to information and power due to superior knowledge reside with the tutor rather than the tutee. Moreover, the tutor is given the responsibility to help the tutee learn, which confers enhanced status. In other words, the tutor has more to offer (or threaten to withdraw) and power to induce behaviours he or she desires. The individual with high power is advantaged by the ability to set the pace, to call for changes and so on, and can keep the values with which the relationship was entered. The low-power partner often takes care to avoid offending or annoying the high-power partner.

The threat to self-esteem approach

Homans (1961) argued that asking for help from another might suggest inferiority of status and reduce self-esteem. Homans also reasoned that, if the two individuals involved are of equal status, then the request for help will be incongruent with this equality, and the experience may be seen as demeaning to the one making the request. 'Thrusting help upon a man who thinks he is your peer is an act of hostility to him, and your generosity is apt to earn you resentment and not gratitude' (Homans, 1961: 252). If these statements remain true today, and there is no reason to suppose this not to be the case, they may also have a bearing on difficulties within the tutee role.

Fisher *et al.* (1982) also described a *threat to self-esteem approach* which incorporates factors such as *situational conditions* (e.g. similarity of attitudes between recipient and donor, or degrees of friendship) and *recipient characteristics*. The self-esteem model predicts that recipients who are threatened by aid will experience negative affect, and may engage in *defensive attempts to restore positive feelings* and the self-esteem status quo. Such behaviours may include derogating the donor and the aid, or recipients engaging in self-help to avoid further aid or seeking little subsequent external help.

The disruptive behaviour on the part of tutees described above may also result from perceived threats to self-esteem.

Reactions to help

Reactions to help can be quite negative, as we have seen. This is not always the case, however. Fisher *et al.* (1982) claimed that, although recipients of help may experience negative consequences such as feelings of failure or inferiority and dependency, they may frequently view aid as a positive, supportive act that reflects donor care and concern. In an attempt to better understand the giving and receiving of help, Nadler and Fisher (1986) reviewed past research and theory relating to the characteristics of the help, characteristics of the helper and those of the recipient. We shall look at each of these in turn.

Nadler and Fisher's (1986) review of research and theory relating to the helping relationship

Characteristics of the help

Nadler and Fisher found that greater amounts of help are more often accepted than smaller amounts. Moreover, greater amounts of help lead to stronger perceptions that the helper is motivated by concern for the recipient. In addition, the giver's attractiveness is enhanced.

Characteristics of the helper

Help from friends was found to produce 'more positive attributions of donor intent' (Nadler and Fisher, 1986: 86) than is the case when help comes from strangers. Moreover, help from friends gave rise to less tension and greater willingness to accept the help on the part of the recipient than was the case when help came from a stranger.

Characteristics of the recipient

Research suggested that:

- individuals with high self-esteem are more likely to be threatened by help than those with low self-esteem;
- those with high authoritarianism, high achievement motivation and 'externals' (those who have an external locus of control) are more negative in relation to help-seeking than others low in these characteristics, and are, consequently, relatively unlikely to seek it;
- men are far less disposed to seek help than women.

Other factors affecting reactions to help

1   Intentionality has been found to be important in that, 'when the inequity is intentionally produced, participants .... will experience more distress and will have stronger desires to restore equity to the relationship than if the inequity occurs inadvertently' (Walster *et al.*, 1973: 167). This may be more of a problem for matched peer tutoring dyads than for those paired randomly.
2   The ability of the beneficiary to repay has also been identified as a potent determinant of how helping affects the benefactor–recipient relationship. If the participants know the recipient can and will reciprocate, the inequity is viewed as temporary, 'and .... produces little distress and little need to justify the inequity' (Walster *et al.*, 1973: 168). This approximates to the situation in reciprocal peer tutoring where roles are reversed.
3   Clark, Gotay and Mills (1974) conducted laboratory experiments using college students to investigate under what conditions help may be accepted or rejected. Their results supported Walster's claim and also suggested that it may be useful to consider *how similar to themselves* people unwilling to accept help perceive the helper to be.

   If they perceive the helper as similar to themselves, then one should try to make it possible for them to do something of value for the helper. If the helper is per-ceived as dissimilar, one should try to minimize the possibility of repaying the aid.
                                                                    (Clark *et al.*, 1974: 229)

This again indicates that same-level peer tutoring relationships should be reciprocal. However, it also suggests that different-level peer tutoring relationships should not be.

Studies by Rosen, Powell and Schubot (1977) provided some support for these claims. *Reactions to aid* are complex phenomena and the receipt of help may be either a self-threatening or self-supportive experience for the recipient.

Problems highlighted by equity theory and helping behaviour, together with advice on how to minimize these, are summarized below.

Problems highlighted by equity theory and helping behaviour

- Small amounts of help may be less acceptable to the recipient than larger ones.
- Help from strangers may be more difficult to accept than that from friends.
- Some individual personal characteristics make the receipt of help difficult.
- Dependency is contrary to the norm of self-reliance.
- Some people, having accepted help, are more able to benefit from it than others.
- Help may be given at the wrong time.
- Help offered may be irrelevant to the recipient's needs.
- Help may be inadequate to the recipient's needs.
- Help may not be understood by the recipient.

Advice

- Peer-tutoring schemes should take place over a relatively extended period. Benefits of 'one-off' help are likely to be minimal.
- Self selection of partners may enhance students' willingness to accept help.
- Help should be given in a form that the recipient can understand, yet be sufficiently elaborated so as to be useful.
- Reciprocal helping is advisable (see also above).
- Take care to time the giving of help to coincide with the recipient's needs.
- Help should be relevant and useful to the recipient.
- Unless extensive psychometric measurement is to take place we cannot address problems of particular individuals. In any case, within an individual, some characteristics associated with adverse reactions to help may be balanced by others which are not. For example, students who are rated as 'externals' and are, thus, likely to have negative views in relation to help-seeking may also have low self-esteem which acts to reduce the threat posed by help.

Reactance theory

Reactance theory (Fisher *et al.*, 1982) suggests that receipt of help can pose restrictions upon the recipient's freedom of future action. For example, the recipient may experience the obligation to repay the donor, or feel the need to act upon the help in a particular way. When aid threatens the freedom to perform present or future actions, Fisher *et al.* (1982) argued that it will arouse '*reactance*', a negative psychological state which, 'presumably leads to attempts by the recipient to re-establish his or her freedom' (Nadler and Fisher, 1986: 88). Modifications in perceptions and judgements may again occur, and unfavourable evaluations of the helper or of the help may be explained in these terms.

Problems highlighted by reactance theory, together with advice on how to minimize these, are summarized below.

Problems highlighted by reactance theory

- Recipient's future actions are restricted.
- Negative psychological states may result.
- Modifications in perceptions and judgements may lead to unfavourable evaluations of the helper.

Advice

- Aim for reciprocal helping relationships in cases of same-level tutoring (see above).

Attribution theory

Attribution theory (e.g. Heider, 1958; Simon and Feather, 1973; Wyatt and Medway, 1984; Nadler and Fisher, 1986) is a generic term for theories that attempt to clarify how we analyse our behaviour and incidents in the world. *Attributions* are the inferences we make in our attempts to explain and understand people and events. Early work by Heider (1958) grouped explanations into two main categories: those relating to the personal and those relating to the situation. Once again, these findings may be generalized to the context of peer tutoring where tutees in particular may perceive themselves to be receiving help, and may examine their beliefs about why they appear to need it. They will make attributions in an attempt to explain the situation to themselves. Recipients are concerned to gain answers to questions relating to the intentions of the donor or the reasons for help being deemed necessary (Fisher *et al.*, 1982). These answers can affect both their reactions to help or to their seeking help in future. For example, Nadler (Nadler and Porat, 1978) found that if needing help is believed to reflect personal inadequacy, then help is less likely to be sought than when this is not the case. This finding has clear implications for tutee behaviour within a tutoring dyad.

Attributions have been classified as being external or internal. Kelley's (1967) theory of attribution specifies conditions under which the recipient internalizes or externalizes the need for aid. Internal-dispositional factors (e.g. one's inadequacy) are contrasted with external-situational factors (e.g. the difficulty of the task). The former attribution is associated with unfavourable self-perceptions on the part of the recipient, an unwillingness to expose inadequacy and a tendency to avoid seeking help.

Problems highlighted by attribution theory, together with advice on how to minimize these, are summarized below.

Problems highlighted by attribution theory

- Participants may make inaccurate attributions about the intentions of the giver of help.
- Participants may make inaccurate attributions about the difficulty of the task.
- Participants may experience personal inadequacy as a result of needing help and choose not to seek it.
- Individuals may make internal-dispositional attributions in cases where an external-situational attribution may be more appropriate and vice-versa.

Advice

- Be very explicit about all reasons for requiring students to give or receive help.
- Set tasks that are at an appropriate level of difficulty for participants.
- Provide full and clear task instructions.
- Organize help giving and receiving within a reciprocal tutoring relationship.

Summary

Peer tutoring and other dyadic interactions are complex phenomena involving many variables which may act in isolation or interact with each other. Nadler and Fisher (1986) observed that predictions deriving from equity, reactance and attribution theories are lacking in some respects, and because each theoretical orientation has a different focus, each will look at a different aspect of the phenomenon. What seems to be required is research which integrates predictions from several theories. In addition, research studies have typically concentrated on prediction of outcomes from variables acting in isolation rather than in interaction in context. Future research would do well to focus on the wider picture.

We are now in a position to make some suggestions about minimizing peer tutoring problems and maximizing its benefits. Table 3.1 summarizes problems and advice deriving from the theoretical perspectives which underlie peer tutoring.

Using social-psychological theory to help minimize problems and maximize benefits

Table 3.1 shows that most perspectives endorse *the importance of training* for tutoring. Collaborative dyadic roles require training to stress collaboration. Tutors require training on how to boost tutee confidence and on how to facilitate and support tutees. They need to be made aware of different approaches to tutoring and to appreciate which of these are beneficial for learning. Training which includes exercises in how to deal with problem behaviours in tutees will stand tutors in very good stead. Similarly, tutors need to be made aware of conflict-reduction techniques and given some training in how to use them.

Another frequently mentioned piece of advice concerns the *desirability of a reciprocal role structure* in tutoring. The strategy of tutor–tutee role change is

Table 3.1 Summary: social-psychological theoretical perspectives, problems and solutions

Theoretical perspective	Problems predicted	Solutions suggested
Role theory: the tutor role	Identification with a role may enhance tutor's experience and detract from tutee's; tutors may experience conflict between 'peer' and 'tutor' aspects of role	Training to help tutor boost tutee's confidence; avoid fixed roles; training to stress collaboration; tasks structured to require co-operation; use reciprocal peer tutoring
Issues of authority	Tutors may exert too much control and influence; tutees may dislike and envy tutor or lose confidence due to growing imbalance of knowledge in partnership	Reciprocal tutoring; tasks structured to ensure preparation and knowledge are shared
Ambiguity and role conflict	Tutors may withdraw from their role, appeal to authority figures or become over friendly with tutee. Tutors may work excessively hard	Training in appropriate conflict-reduction techniques; clear definition of roles
Disruptive tutee behaviour	Tutees may engage in: blocking; confusion; miracle seeking; over enthusiasm; resisting; passivity; evasion	Training exercises to deal with disruptions
Status incongruence	Status inequalities detrimental to learning (although a *little* incongruence *may* be motivating); perceived unfairness undermines social behaviour; frustration and uncertainty may result; social uncertainty may de-stabilize self-image	Adopt student-centred andragogic approach; avoid fixed-role tutoring; minimize uncertainty; ensure that when possible, knowledge is shared equally; respect diversity and aim for balance
Equity theory, rewards and costs, threat to self-esteem and helping behaviour	Small amounts of help not acceptable; help from strangers can be difficult to accept; recipients vary in extent to which they can benefit; timing of help may be wrong; help may be inadequate to needs; help may not be understood	Avoid 'one-off' peer tutoring schemes; choose partners carefully – self-selection may help; ensure help is useful and relevant to needs of recipient, is at an appropriate level, in appropriate form and given at appropriate time; reciprocal helping advisable
Reactance theory	Recipient's future actions restricted; negative psychological states may result; perceptions and judgements modified leading to unfavourable evaluations of helper	Aim for reciprocal helping relationships
Attribution theory	Inaccurate attributions about intentions of help giver; inaccurate attributions about difficulty of task; experiences of personal inadequacy; inappropriate internal-dispositional and external-situational attributions	Be explicit about reasons for requiring students to give/receive help; set tasks at appropriate level of difficulty; provide full and clear instructions; organize reciprocal help giving and receiving

particularly useful in the context of same-level higher education situations where ability ranges are less marked than in the pre-tertiary sector. Given that, in same-level schemes, the roles of tutor and tutee may each lead to negative reactions which threaten the learning potential of peer tutoring for both partners, systematically changing roles within the dyad seems a wise strategy. Most tutors and tutees within different-level dyads do not appear to experience the negative reactions that characterize same-level pairings. The strategy of role reversals emerges from our analysis of various theoretic perspectives and is recommended by many teachers and researchers.

Third, the importance of *organization* and *structure* is also stressed. Schemes need to be very well organized and tasks well structured. Organization and structure should support social equality. *Clarity* is also stressed. Roles should be defined clearly and instructions unambiguous.

We shall look further at these practical issues in Chapters 5 and 6.

THEORETICAL BASES OF PEER TUTORING FOR PERSONAL AND PROFESSIONAL DEVELOPMENT

Saunders and Kingdon (1998) identified further theoretical frameworks relating to personal and professional development in the context of peer tutoring. These included:

- experiential learning;
- Perry's deep, surface and strategic learning;
- dualistic and relativistic reasoning;
- self-actualization theory;
- personal construct theory.

These theories have a different relationship to peer tutoring than those from cognitive and social psychology discussed above. While classic psychological theories can aid our understanding of the processes and problems of peer tutoring, and can help with hypothesis testing and study design, the theories identified by Saunders and Kingdon have more to say about what peer tutoring can *achieve*. For example, intellectual development or self-actualization may be facilitated by the act of tutoring, but knowledge of Perry's conceptualizations of intellectual development or Rogers' work on self-actualization (Rogers, 1969) does not increase our understanding of peer tutoring to any great extent. However, we shall look at each of these in turn, and then go on to consider two further frameworks which may have relevance to peer tutoring: situated learning and andragogy.

Experiential learning

An early formulation of what is meant by '*experiential learning*' is to be found in a paper delivered in 1969 by Carl Rogers to a Harvard conference. He differentiated experiential learning from cognitive learning and argued that 'the only learning which significantly influences behavior is self-discovered, self-appointed learning' (Rogers, 1969: 153). Moreover, he stressed that learning must be experienced for oneself, as it cannot be directly communicated to another person. He advocated doing away with teaching, examinations and grading of all kinds. To Rogers, experiential learning is equivalent to personal change and growth, and learning is facilitated when:

1   the student participates completely in the learning process and has control over its nature and direction;
2   it is primarily based upon direct confrontation with practical, social, personal or research problems; and
3   self-evaluation is the principal method of assessing progress or success.

Rogers also emphasized the importance of learning to learn and an openness to change (TIP, 1999).

The personal involvement and active learning that peer tutoring entails can constitute experiential learning. In many cases of peer tutoring, the conditions that facilitate learning suggested by Rogers are present. However, for some students, peer tutoring is a course requirement rather than self-appointed learning and, thus, cannot be regarded as experiential learning. Barbara McCombs explores a related issue in her contribution to Chapter 10.

Deep, surface and strategic learning

The concepts of deep and surface learning and the more recent addition, strategic learning, derive from the work of Ference Marton in Sweden and Noel Entwistle in the UK (Marton and Säljö, 1997; Entwistle, 1997). A *deep approach* to studying is characterized by the desire to 'transform', to understand and engage with material and ideas and to relate new material to existing cognitive structures. Students become actively engaged with course content. A *surface approach* may be described as a 'reproducing' orientation, and is characterized by studying without reflecting on either purpose or strategy. A student using this approach, has the intention to cope with course requirements and will attempt to do this by memorizing material. A *strategic approach*, or 'organizing' approach, is character-ized by the desire to maximize grades. Students taking this approach tend to be cue-conscious and cue-seeking, scrutinizing previous exam papers for clues and questioning the lecturer. Such students are particularly sensitive to assessment requirements and criteria. They generally put consistent effort into studying. (See Entwistle, 1997: 19.)

Marton's research identified qualitatively different approaches used by students in order to understand a text. This research also led to the development of *phenomenography*, a methodology which allows the exploration of students' conceptualizations of phenomena. The identification of three approaches to studying also led to the development of the Approaches to Studying Inventory

(ASI), an instrument containing statements relating to the three distinctive approaches as well as, in some versions, to some other factors (e.g. lack of direction and academic self-confidence) (Entwistle and Tait, 1990; Tait and Entwistle, 1996).

Work on student approaches to studying is often linked to, or contrasted with, the work of Pask (1975) who identified two different groups of learners differentiated on the basis of their learning strategies: *serialists* who progress in a sequential fashion and *holists* who look for higher-order relations. Pask's work comes together in the *conversation theory of learning*. Principles of this theory are that students must learn the relationships among concepts in order to learn subject matter, that explicit explanation or manipulation of the subject matter facilitates understanding and that individuals differ in their preferred manner of learning relationships. The critical method of learning, according to conversation theory, is 'teachback' in which one person teaches another what they have learned (TIP, 1999). Here the parallels with peer tutoring are obvious. Later in the book (Chapter 7), a mature student, Lana Freeman, describes the importance of conversation and teachback to her learning and intellectual development.

Perry's dualistic and relativistic reasoning

In 1970, Perry published the results of an interview study undertaken to document the experiences of undergraduates during four years in a liberal arts college. This study has become a much-quoted classic which described nine 'positions' through which students might progress from an understanding of the world in absolute terms of right and wrong answers to personal commitment and affirmation of identity. Perry (1970: 9–10) noted that not all students get to the higher levels. The nine positions are:

Position 1: 'The student sees the world in polar terms of we-right-good vs. other-wrong-bad.' An Authority exists whose role is to teach Right Answers.

Position 2: The student perceives diversity of opinion and uncertainty, but attributes these to poorly qualified 'Authorities' or interprets them as exercises set so that 'we can learn to find The Answers for ourselves'.

Position 3: Diversity and uncertainty are accepted as legitimate but *temporary* states. Authority has yet to find The Answers.

Position 4: (a) The student perceives legitimate uncertainty and diversity of opinion to be extensive and interprets these as evidence that everyone has a right to her or his own opinion.
(b) The student perceives qualitative contextual relativistic reasoning and interprets it as a special case of 'what They want'.

Position 5: The student perceives all knowledge and values including those of the Authority, as contextual and relativistic, and subordinates dualistic right–wrong functions to 'the status of a special case, in context'.

Position 6: The student sees the need for some form of personal commitment distinct from 'unquestioned or unconsidered commitment to a simple belief in certainty'. The student sees the need to orient one's self in a relativistic world.

Position 7: An initial commitment is made in some area.

Position 8: The implications of commitment are experienced and subjective issues of responsibility are explored.

Position 9: 'The student experiences the affirmation of identity among multiple responsibilities and realizes Commitment as an ongoing, unfolding activity through which he expresses his life style.'

Perry's developmental stages were used in a study of peer-tutoring journals which attempted to gain insight into how tutors conceptualize and respond to the activity of tutoring, and to chart the progress of development of tutors, using qualitative data from their journals (Mann, 1994). Cognitive development was measured pre- and post-test using Moore's (1987) Learning Environment Preference Instrument which is based on Perry's work. Mann found that all experimental tutors outperformed controls on all outcome measures, though not to the same extent. Thus, it has been demonstrated that the experience of tutoring may help intellec- tual development. What is not clear, however, is whether stage of development of participants influences their experience of peer tutoring.

Self-actualization theory

Maslow (1954) proposed that human motives took the form of a pyramid, with basic biological and physiological motives such as hunger, thirst or sex forming the base. Building from this base were motives of safety, security, order and stability, followed by 'belongingness' and love, esteem, self-respect and success. At the top of the pyramid was *self-actualization*. Maslow claimed that motives were organized into an hierarchy, such that those at each level must be achieved before the next level can be addressed. The self-actualizing person is 'spontaneous, creative, and has a sense of humour' (Houston, Bee, Hatfield and Rimm, 1979: 297). However, according to Maslow, self-actualization is not reached by many people. Existential and humanistic branches of psychology maintain that people have an inborn drive towards psychological growth which has been called the '*actualizing tendency*' (Houston *et al.*, 1979: 565). This drive motivates us to express needs in ways that are constructive and healthy. Great emphasis is placed on personal choice and personal responsibility. It is not difficult to see that measures deriving from self-actualizing theory might be used to evaluate the effects of paired learning and peer tutoring.

Personal construct theory

Personal construct theory takes into account the effects of experience and change on development, and may thus be a useful framework in which to interpret personal or professional growth. The theory, originally formulated by Kelly (1955), is formally stated as a fundamental postulate which is that we all have our own view of the world and our own expectations about what will happen, and that 'our behaviour is our continual experiment with life' (Bannister and Fransella, 1980: 17). Saunders and Kingdon (1998) included personal construct theory as of relevance to peer tutoring, given the experiential nature of paired learning.

Situated learning

This theory is associated with Jean Lave (Lave, 1999; Lave and Wenger, 1990) who believes that normal learning is a function of the activity, context and culture in which it occurs. In other words, learning is situated. This belief contrasts with many classroom learning activities which involve abstract and apparently context-free knowledge. Two main principles of situated learning are that knowledge needs to be presented in an authentic context and that learning requires social interaction and collaboration. Learners move from the periphery of a learning community to take on the role of expert as they become more active and engaged within the culture. Other researchers have contributed to the theory of situated learning. For example, Brown *et al.* (1989) discussed the role of cognitive apprenticeship in the social construction of knowledge. 'Cognitive apprenticeship supports learning in a domain by enabling students to acquire, develop and use cognitive tools in authentic domain activity. Learning, both outside and inside school, advances through collaborative social interaction and the social construction of knowledge' (Lave, 1999: 1).

It has been claimed that situated learning has Vygotsky's social learning as an antecedent, though there are also some parallels with Piagetian theory. The centrality of interaction within this theory makes it particularly relevant to peer tutoring and, as we saw in Chapter 1, the concept of cognitive apprenticeship has been developed as a peer-tutoring technique.

Andragogy

As more and more mature students enter higher education, we should take a brief look at Knowles' *theory of adult learning* or *andragogy* (Knowles, 1984), and at Cross's work on adult learners (Cross, 1999, 1981, 1976). Knowles' theory of andragogy was developed specifically for adult learning. Andragogy theory assumes that adults need to know why they need to learn something, that they need to learn experientially, that they approach learning as problem solving and that they learn best when the topic is of immediate value. Knowles also emphasized that adults are self-directed and expect to take responsibility for decisions. It can be argued that these assumptions might be applied beneficially to learning more generally. Indeed, Brown (2000) has maintained that andragogy is actually good pedagogy in disguise.

Differences between pedagogy and andragogy are shown in Table 3.2.

Table 3.2 Differences between pedagogy and andragogy

Pedagogy	Andragogy
Authority-oriented, competitive, formal	Mutuality stressed, respectful, collaborative, informal
Planning carried out by teacher	Incorporates mechanisms for mutual planning
Needs diagnosed by teacher	Mutual diagnosis of needs
Objectives formulated by teacher	Mutual negotiation of objectives
Activities based on transmission model of education	Activities based on experiential learning model
Assessment by teacher	Self, peer and collaborative assessment
Evaluation by teacher	Evaluation by teachers and learners

Cross (1981) argued that pedagogy is characterized by dependency, by personal experience of learners being of little worth and by the postponement of the application of learning. In contrast, andragogy aims for increasing self-directedness, and is characterized by the learners themselves being recognized as a rich resource for learning. Andragogy also usually involves the immediate application of learning. While children's biological development continues throughout the school years, adults are seen to have completed the process. However, Cross argued that 'it is possible for a 50-year-old adult to remain at a "childish" level of ego development, while a 30-year-old may attain the highest possible level of ego maturity' (1981: 238). Cognitive development, too, may not bear a simple relation to age. Although Piaget proposed an age-related model of cognitive development, suggesting that adolescents enter the final, formal operations stage (and gain the ability to deal with abstract information and theoretical propositions) between the ages of about 12 and 15 years, research has found that this is not true for some adolescents and even for some adults (e.g. Neimark, 1975). Similarly, Perry reported that about a quarter of undergraduates had not attained the final stage of intellectual and ethical development by the end of their final year of study (Perry, 1970).

Cross (1981) attempted to integrate andragogy and experiential learning theories with aspects of human life-span development. Her Characteristics of Adults as Learners (CAL) model consists of personal developmental characteristics such as age-related changes, and situational characteristics such as part-time versus full-time learning, and voluntary versus compulsory learning. The CAL model is intended to provide guidelines for adult education programmes. However, there is no known research to support it (Cross, 1999).

SUMMARY

We started this chapter with a question, 'What are the benefits of situating peer-tutoring schemes within a sound theoretical and research framework?' It is worth repeating that I believe there are many good reasons for doing this. Theory enables us to identify interesting and important questions. It enables us to make predictions, frame and test hypotheses. In other words, it helps us to conduct high-quality research with good experimental design and, thus, enables us to evaluate educational initiatives. Lack of a theoretical basis to an educational initiative can lead to the problems and arguments which characterize much current educational debate.

In developing my own approaches to peer learning, Piaget's theory has been particularly influential, but as a social scientist, I believe that all events may be viewed from multiple perspectives and I value the benefits brought about by the disagreement and conflict which can result. As I began to develop peer teaching initiatives, I found role theory and help-seeking models particularly useful in providing an insight into why things didn't always work out as I had planned and hoped.

In the next chapter, we shall see how theory can inform practice, by re-examining a case study of peer tutoring using new questions derived from theory.

4   How theory can inform practice

In previous chapters, I argued that teachers use peer tutoring because of the benefits it brings to participants, and because of its theoretical basis which enables practitioners and researchers to frame and test questions. In this chapter, I shall use one of my case studies to illustrate how we may gain a deeper understanding of what happens during tutoring, and learn how theory can help us understand why some things went wrong. In this way, we can use theory to help us inform our future practice.

A CASE STUDY OF PEER TUTORING

Some time ago, Carol Fitz-Gibbon and I designed and implemented an experimental pilot study of same-level peer tutoring, in order to explore the operation of the technique in higher education (Falchikov and Fitz-Gibbon, 1989). Our evaluation identified a number of problems. I recently revisited this study, using social-psychological frameworks as the basis for framing questions and seeking answers not explored in the original analysis. I shall start by summarizing the original study and report results of our primary analyses, before going on to the secondary theoretically based analysis.

Up to the time of the original study, the bulk of work on peer tutoring in the UK had been conducted in pre-tertiary settings, where the technique had proved very successful. While we had no reason to doubt that peer tutoring would also be beneficial in higher education, there were some worrying indications from the school experiments about same-level implementations. For example, we noted the growing evidence that same-level peer tutoring involving children is less effective than the cross-age variant, and Posen's young offender study (1983) had found that, while tutors were happy with their role, tutees expressed many reservations about the scheme, as well as some hostility to tutors. However, we reasoned that university or college students might be expected to be more mature than school pupils and, given the voluntary nature of higher education, that undergraduates would be better motivated than either young offenders or school-age participants. We embarked on our investigation of how same-level tutoring might operate in higher education.

Participants

Our participants were first-year students studying psychology as part of a four-year degree in what was then called, 'Catering and Accommodation Studies' at Napier College (now University), Edinburgh. They had all entered college straight from school. Females were in a marginal majority.

Phase 1

Method

As preparation for the first phase of the experiment, students were given background information about the benefits and operation of peer tutoring. They were then randomly allocated to one of three groups: tutors, tutees or independent study students. Pairing of tutors and tutees was also made on a random basis. Tutors prepared for the first task of tutoring by watching a video of a lecture on alcohol and alcoholism delivered by an experienced lecturer, and by making notes to help them teach the material to their tutees. The video was available for further study in an open-learning facility. Tutors and tutees then attended one-to-one tutorials which they arranged at mutually convenient times. All students were encouraged to spend additional time studying the topic. On completion of the first tutoring exercise, all participants completed an evaluative questionnaire. Three weeks after the exercise was completed, participants took a short test during class time, comprised of multiple-choice items requiring simple recognition and short essay questions which required exercise of higher-level cognitive skills. They were tested on the material again in the end-of-term examination.

Performance measures

Approximately 84 per cent of participants were present for the class test, but there were interesting tutor-tutee-independent study student differences in rates of attendance. Attendance was 100 per cent for the tutor group, 84.6 per cent for the independent study group, but only 62 per cent for the tutees. While the poor attendance of tutees made interpretation of test performances difficult, it may tell us, in a very direct way, something about the motivation and attitudes within this group. However, both the immediate post-performance test results and performance in the end-of-term examination showed no statistically significant differences between groups.

For more details and information about the performance of the independent study control group see Falchikov and Fitz-Gibbon (1989).

Qualitative evaluation

Responses to the question, 'What did you like *best* about this scheme?' were different for tutor and tutee groups. While tutors identified features relating to the benefits they felt they had experienced in terms of development of personal and study skills, tutees chose the flexibility of the scheme as best feature. Similarly, the groups differed in response to the parallel question, 'What did you like *least* about this scheme?' Tutors mentioned time as the least desirable feature, while tutees frequently identified lack of confidence in their partner. A few tutees also referred to lack of motivation. However, overall, the scheme was well received by participants who perceived it to have conferred many benefits to them.

Problems identified after phase 1

1   Tutee attendance was poorer than that of tutors.
2   Many tutees appeared to lack confidence in their tutors.

Phase 2

Method

The second phase of the experiment took place six months after the first, and followed much the same pattern, except that phase one independent study students were also given the opportunity to tutor or become a tutee. Student tutor and tutee pairs from the first phase worked together again on the second experiment. A further experimental manipulation was included relating to mode of preparation for tutoring, but, as there did not appear to be any patterns in the subsequent performance and evaluations of the two tutor groups, we looked at both groups together in analyses.

Performance measures

The results of this phase of the experiment relating to immediate test and retention scores indicated that, overall, tutors seemed to have slightly higher scores than their tutees. However, when entrance qualifications were taken into account, I concluded that 'total post-test scores for tutor groups seem entirely consistent with their differing ability levels', but 'performance of tutees ... cannot be accounted for simply in terms of ability' (Falchikov, 1990: 136). It seemed that some tutees with low entrance qualifications were performing at roughly the same level as high-ability tutors. No differences in scores on the retention test were found on this occasion.

Qualitative evaluation

Best and least liked features of the scheme were again identified, and resembled those recorded after the first phase, in some respects. Tutors again rated the development of personal and study skills as best feature, while tutees once more chose flexibility of the system, with benefits of having one-to-one sessions coming a close second. However, after the second experience of tutoring, some students failed to identify any best-liked feature. While least-liked features for tutors again focused on the time-consuming nature of the exercise, several also mentioned their own lack of motivation. Lack of motivation featured again in the second evaluation by tutees. Peer tutoring was described by one tutee as a scheme which 'propagates laziness'. However, for tutees, time was most frequently rated as least liked feature. In addition, there were several undifferentiated negative ratings in the repeat evaluation.

Thus, there appeared to be an increase in the number and type of problems identified in the evaluation conducted after the repeated experience of tutoring or being tutored.

Problems identified in the phase 2 evaluation

1   Overall evaluation of the scheme was *less positive* than after phase 1.
2   Some participants were *unable to identify any 'best-liked' feature.*
3   *Lack of motivation* was mentioned by both tutors and tutees.
4   Many tutees perceived that *time* had been a problem.

Further research of the literature soon found that the problems experienced by our peer-tutoring students were not uncommon to those working in dyads.

We shall now look at the reanalysis of pilot study data carried out in order to investigate the problems the study identified and test further questions derived from some of the theories outlined in Chapter 3.

Revisiting the data: framing questions and testing predictions from some social-psychological theories

The tutor role

If, as Bruffee (1993) claims, the peer-tutoring relationship is compromised by a task which reinforces the authority structure of traditional education, we might predict that tutors who see their task in terms of an interaction between teacher and learner may begin to see themselves as enacting the role of teacher. This role, as we have seen, conveys competence, prestige and authority (Medway, 1991). Tutors may, thus, change their conceptions of themselves and may experience an increase in self-esteem as a result. I, therefore, felt it would be illuminating to seek answers to the following questions:

1   Do tutors take on characteristics of teachers? Do their perceptions of themselves change?
2   Does tutor confidence increase over the period of the scheme?
3   At the end of the scheme, are tutors seen as more confident or authoritative by tutees?

Role theory leads us to predict that the answers to all these questions would be 'Yes'.

Role conflict and coping mechanisms

We may also ask whether tutors are able to maintain the 'delicate balance between the "tutor" element and the "peer" element' of their tutor role (Garrett, 1982: 94). It is possible that, if the *peer* aspect of the peer tutor role remains important, and the delicate balance is achieved, then ratings of friendliness by both tutee and tutor will be relatively unchanged. However, we might predict that both tutors and tutees will experience some degree of *role conflict*. Tutees, seeing authority and prestige in a formerly equal-status peer, and *decreased social equality* within the dyad, might respond by engaging in *negative coping behaviours*, or might experience a *decrease in friendly feelings* towards their partner. Inspection of enjoyment ratings might provide some clues. If tutors do not appear to enjoy their task as much at the end of the exercise as at the beginning, we might hypothesize that either the balance has not been achieved or that they are having to expend increasing amounts of effort to attempt to maintain it.

As we shall see later (Chapter 6), Hall (1972) suggested that redefinition of roles may act as a way of coping with role conflict. Are we able to ascertain whether these mechanisms have been used by our participants? To what extent do they redefine their roles? We may gain a little insight into these issues by looking for changes in ratings of self-confidence, particularly in tutors.

We learned in Chapter 3 that tutees can behave in negative ways as a means of coping with role conflict. As we saw, Roberts (1994) described a number of difficult tutoring situations, all of which involved some form of disruptive tutee behaviour. She identified seven styles of behaviour in total:

- blocking;
- confusion;
- evasion;
- miracle seeking;
- over-enthusiasm;
- passivity;
- resisting.

It is possible that there may be some evidence of negative coping behaviour by the tutees in the evaluative data from the pilot study. Evidence of some of the seven styles of disruptive tutee behaviour may be present in ratings of best- and least-liked features of the scheme. As we learned in Chapter 3, Roberts (1994) claimed that over-enthusiasm is often characterized by talk of *limited time*. Do we have any evidence of such behaviours in our study?

In the absence of personal and sociometric data for the participants, we might ask the following questions following on from those on p. 117;

4   Do levels of tutor enjoyment remain stable over the period of the exercise?
5   Do levels of tutee enjoyment remain stable or change towards the end of the exercise?
6   Are there any indications of tutee resistance, passivity, withdrawal, rejection, boredom or hostility in participant evaluations?

7   Is there any evidence of over-enthusiasm, miracle seeking or other evasive measures on the part of tutees? Does time feature prominently in evaluations?
8   Do we have any indications of tutee hopelessness, helplessness, disorganization or disorientation?

Role theory would predict that answers to questions 4 and 5 would be 'No', and to questions 6, 7 and 8 would be 'Yes'.

Authority and liking

Is there any evidence of an inverse relationship between authority and liking such as that found by Homans (1961) and Lippitt (1947)? It seems reasonable to assume that tutees, placed in a position where the authority of a former peer is enhanced, may begin to like their partner less. Tutors, experiencing the increase in authority, are less likely to react in this way towards their tutees.

Thus, we might ask further questions:

9   Do tutees start to perceive tutors as less friendly as the scheme progresses?
10   Do tutor ratings of tutee friendliness remain relatively stable?

We might predict that the answers to both questions will be 'Yes'.

Equity theory: rewards and costs

As we saw in Chapter 3, Walster *et al.* (1973) argued that if a relationship becomes inequitable, both participants are likely to experience some discomfort. Tutees may experience an increase in levels of perceived status incongruence and undergo a lessening of 'social ease' in interaction with tutors (Homans, 1961). Inequality may also be experienced in terms of perceived rewards and costs. Qualitative evaluative data reported in Falchikov and Fitz-Gibbon (1989) have already suggested some perceived rewards and costs (e.g. tutors benefit from access to information; tutees benefit from a flexible system of learning; tutors pay time costs; tutees lack confidence in their tutors). These data may also provide us with some insights into the perceived reward–cost ratios of our tutor and tutees. As Homans (1976) has argued, comparisons are likely to be based on observable factors such as the sort of rewards and costs identified above, rather than on subjective estimates of longer-term personal benefit. Enjoyment ratings may also tell us something about perceived equality in the tutoring relationship. Again, we might expect an inequitable relationship to be enjoyed less than an equitable one. Specific questions might be:

11   What evidence do we have of tutors and tutees experiencing costs and rewards associated with peer tutoring?
12   What is the ratio of rewards to costs for each? Do benefactors (tutors) experience an increase in *rewards* as the experiment progresses? Do recipients (tutees) experience an increase in *costs*?

Once again, we might look at answers relating to enjoyment ratings (see questions 4 and 5 above) for further evidence. Do they fall as the exercise progresses? Given that these questions are of a 'look and see' type, no predictions will be made.

Reactance theory and reactions to help

As we have learned, reactance theory (Nadler and Fisher, 1986) predicts that those who receive help are likely to give an unfavourable evaluation to either the helper or the help received. It has also been argued that giving help as well as receiving it may have adverse effects. The tutoring relationship involves one person helping another. In the case study under consideration, the amount of help was relatively small, as the study was of short duration. However, Nadler and Fisher (1986) found that small amounts of help were often less acceptable than larger ones, so we may find evidence of adverse reactions to helping in the present study. These are likely to vary according to the degree of friendship present within dyads at the start of the tutoring study, but, unfortunately, we do not have access to such sociometric information. Similarly, although self-esteem is a variable which has been found to affect reactions to help (Homans, 1961; Nadler and Fisher, 1986), once again, we do not have a direct measure of this in the present case. However, although we cannot explore this relationship directly, we are able to look for differences in self-confidence in tutors and tutees. We wish to obtain an insight into some of these issues and wish to obtain answers to the following question:

13   Is there evidence for tutee reaction against helping behaviour?

Once again, no specific prediction will be made.

Do multiple theoretical perspectives lead to conflicting predictions?

It may be claimed that a multiplicity of ways of looking at any phenomenon will lead to conflicting predictions. This does not seem to be the case here. It is common for the same question or prediction to be derived from several theoretical standpoints. For example, tutor or tutee ratings of friendliness of their partner may tell us not only about reactions to a new role, but also about the inverse relationship between authority and liking or about the approach to tutoring taken by the tutor. Similarly, enjoyment ratings may indicate the presence of role conflict or relate to predictions from equity theory or tell us something about reactions to helping behaviour.

We shall now return to the data from the pilot study of peer tutoring in higher education, bearing in mind the questions posed above.

RE-ANALYSIS OF DATA

Tutee ratings

Paired t-tests were carried out comparing tutee ratings of enjoyment and self-confidence after phases 1 and 2. Enjoyment ratings were found to *decrease* significantly, from an average of 2.86 after phase one to 1.23 on completion of the second phase ($p = 0.005$).

Tutee self-confidence was also reduced from 3.71 to 2.86, but this was not found to be a significant reduction.

Changes to tutees' perceptions of organizational and teaching skills of tutors

Tutees rated tutors on the following dimensions:

- clarity;
- knowledge;
- organization;
- preparedness;
- quality of explanation.

These ratings provide information relating to the tutor role. All ratings of skills listed were found to *increase* from first to second phase. In other words, tutors were seen as being clearer, better at explaining, more knowledgeable, better organized and better prepared after phase 2 than they were after phase 1. Changes in ratings were found to be significant for the category 'clear' (an increase from 3.40 to 4.00, $p = 0.04$) and 'organized' (an increase from 3.27 to 3.71, $p = 0.04$).

Changes to tutees' perceptions of personal qualities of tutors

These ratings also tell us about the tutor role. Tutee ratings of all categories within this group *increased* after the second experience of being tutored. In other words, tutors were perceived as more confident, enthusiastic, relaxed and motivated on the second occasion compared with the first. Most marked change was in the perception of the confidence of the tutor which changed from 3.33 after the first exercise to 4.00 on completion of the second ($p = 0.03$). Tutors were also perceived to be more relaxed, with ratings increasing from 3.33 on the first occasion of tutoring to 4.14 on the second ($p = 0.05$).

Changes to tutees' perceptions of interpersonal skills of tutors

Tutees rated tutors on the following dimensions:

- approachable;
- friendly;

- helpful;
- reassuring;
- supportive.

These ratings provide information relating to authority and liking. There was no overall pattern to changes within this category, with small increases in ratings being associated with the categories 'reassuring' and 'supportive', and decreases in the three other categories. The only change which reached significance was that of the tutor's perceived decrease in friendliness, with ratings decreasing from 4.60 to 3.71 (p = 0.03).

Tutor ratings

Changes to tutors' ratings relating to their role

On re-examination of tutor ratings of best- and least-liked features of peer tutoring, there are also interesting indications of tutors identifying with the role of teacher after their first attempt at tutoring. Some examples of best features which might suggest this were:

> I got the chance to try to teach, which gave me confidence.

> It gave me more responsibility.

> (It gave me) an understanding of the organization necessary for teaching.

> It gave me a chance to do a lecture from another point of view.

However, there were also some indications of lack of confidence after the first session:

> I wasn't sure if I had taken all the important points down.

After the repeated experience, tutors indicated less enthusiasm for the exercise, largely on the grounds of the time they had spent on it. At least one tutor saw the time spent on the exercise as a *cost* to tutors. There was no sign of identification with the teacher role or enjoyment derived from it on this occasion.

Tutor ratings of enjoyment and self-confidence

Once again, we may learn about the tutor role by inspecting these ratings. Paired t-tests were carried out, and tutor enjoyment ratings were also found to *decrease* significantly, from an average of 3.67 after phase one to 2.58 on completion of the second phase (p = 0.04).

Tutor self-confidence was reduced from 4.25 to 3.83, but as with the equivalent tutee ratings, this was not found to be a significant reduction. It should be noted, however, that tutor levels of confidence were higher than those of tutees on both occasions, and that tutor levels on the second occasion are higher than tutee first-time levels.

Changes to perceived skills of tutees

Tutors rated tutees on the following dimensions:

- confidence;
- enthusiasm;
- motivation;
- relaxation;
- willingness to learn.

These ratings may tell us about the tutors' perceptions of disaffection among tutees or disruptive tutee behaviour. All categories in the task-related group attracted *lower* ratings on the completion of the repeat study. In other words, tutees were perceived as having less enthusiasm, motivation, willingness to learn or to ask questions compared with the first occasion. However, paired t-tests showed that these differences were significant in only two of the cases: tutee motivation and willingness to learn. Perceived tutee motivation fell from 4.00 to 2.92 ($p = 0.03$) and tutee willingness to learn from 4.50 to 3.93 ($p = 0.03$).

Perceived tutee confidence and tutee relaxation both *fell* after the second experience of tutoring, though the fall in tutee relaxation was the only significant change. Tutee relaxation was reduced from an average of 4.08 on the first occasion to 3.00 on the second ($p = 0.04$).

ANSWERS TO QUESTIONS

We now return to the questions listed earlier in the chapter and attempt to use the results of the new analysis to frame some answers. To what extent do theoretical perspectives help us to interpret the data from our simple experiment in same-level peer tutoring? We shall group together questions which illuminate similar theoretical perspectives.

Roles and role theory

Question 1: Do tutors take on characteristics of teachers? Do *their* perceptions of themselves change?

Question 2: Does tutor confidence increase over the period of the scheme?

Question 3: At the end of the scheme, are tutors seen as more confident or authoritative by tutees?

As we have noted already, tutor ratings of best- and least-liked features of peer tutoring suggest that some tutors do see themselves as occupying the role of teacher. On conclusion of the first phase of the exercise, tutors identified the responsibility of teaching and the insights into teaching they had experienced as beneficial. However, there were few such comments in the evaluation of the second phase, which might suggest that a fleeting visit to the role might be satisfying, but a longer sojourn in it is not. Tutor confidence ratings throughout the exercise were significantly higher than those of tutees. Tutee perceptions of tutors' confidence and relaxation increased significantly from the first to the second phase. Similarly, organizational and teaching skills of tutors were rated as improving over the duration of the exercise. Tutors were perceived by tutees to be better organized and to give clearer deliveries and explanations in the second evaluation. The only significant decrease in tutee ratings of tutor interpersonal skills was in the area of friendliness.

The re-analysis of data suggests that tutors had started to take on some teacher-like characteristics and had experienced some increase in their confidence. Both tutor and tutee ratings support this conclusion. Thus, it appears that our predictions from role theory are supported.

However, tutors may have experienced a greater degree of role conflict during the second phase of the exercise as fewer mentions of the benefits of the teacher role were evident in phase two evaluations.

Role conflict and coping mechanisms

Question 4: Do levels of tutor enjoyment remain stable over the period of the exercise?

Question 5: Do levels of tutee enjoyment remain stable or change towards the end of the exercise?

Question 6: Are there any indications of tutee resistance, passivity, withdrawal, rejection, boredom or hostility in participant evaluations?

Question 7: Is there any evidence of over-enthusiasm, miracle seeking or other evasive measures on the part of tutees? Does time feature prominently in evaluations?

Question 8: Do we have any indications of hopelessness, helplessness, disorganization or disorientation?

The re-analysis of data confirmed that both tutor and tutee enjoyment ratings decreased significantly between the completion of phases 1 and 2 of the exercise.

It also appeared that tutors perceived tutee motivation and willingness to learn to have dropped during the second phase of the study. One tutor commented that

> it (the second phase of the scheme) did not seem to achieve anything, and no-one really seemed to want to be involved.

Several tutees reported lack of effort on their part.

> I didn't put as much work into it as I should have.

It seems very clear that tutee resistance and passivity was a feature of the second phase of the exercise.

As we have learned, Roberts (1994) described miracle-seeking behaviour as characterized by a focus on time as well as by a global interest or concern, evasion or inability to concentrate on tasks. In our data, time was rated as least-liked feature by tutors on both occasions and by tutees on the second occasion. There were also some indications of global evaluations of the scheme. The second-phase evaluation included several contributions, particularly from tutees, which referred to the whole scheme, rather than to particular liked or disliked aspects. One tutee disliked 'the whole aspect of it', while another liked it 'not a lot'. As we saw above, there were frequent blanks left in the second evaluation sheet, and several terse answers to questions. It is easier to condemn the whole than to spend time and thought identifying what was particularly disliked and why this was the case. There are, thus, some indications of Roberts' (1994) disruptive tutee behaviour in our data.

Our data do not supply us with sufficient detail for us to answer questions relating to hopelessness, helplessness, disorganization or disorientation with any degree of confidence. However, the marked drop in tutee confidence noted after the second phase of the exercise might be interpreted within this framework. In addition, tutors rated tutees as less relaxed during the second tutoring phase.

As Hall (1972) argued, redefinition of roles may be interpreted as a mechanism for reducing role conflict. In the re-analysis of data, we see that tutors appear to retreat from a teacher-like role in the second phase of the experiment which might constitute an example of such role redefinition.

Returning to our predictions from role theory, we find that answers to questions 4 and 5 are 'No', which supports our prediction. There is also some support for predictions concerning tutee behaviour. We predicted that there would be some evidence of disruptive behaviour which was found to be the case.

A change in perceptions of friendliness might also tell us something about the effects of role conflict. An analysis of friendliness data is included in the next section.

Authority and liking

> Question 9: Do tutees start to perceive tutors as less friendly as the scheme progresses?

Question 10: Do tutor ratings of tutee friendliness remain relatively stable?

Small decreases in tutee ratings of tutor helpfulness, approachability and friendliness were evident in the data. The drop in perceived friendliness reached statistical significance. However, tutors tended to rate tutee friendliness as slightly, though not significantly, greater than after phase 1. It is possible to interpret the tutee ratings as evidence of the development of greater social inequality and an increase in the kind of ambivalent feelings described by Homans (1961). Once again, both our predictions are supported by the data.

Equity theory: rewards and costs

Question 11: What evidence do we have of tutors and tutees experiencing costs and rewards associated with peer tutoring?

Question 12: What is the ratio of rewards to costs for each? Do benefactors (tutors) experience an increase in *rewards* as the experiment progresses? Do recipients (tutees) experience an increase in *costs*?

There is a hint that some students are aware of rewards and costs associated with the experience of peer tutoring. There is also slight evidence of the calculation of comparative costs by at least one tutor after the second phase of the study, who concluded that 'It was very time-consuming for the tutors. We spent more time working on it than anyone else.' Such a perception (if shared more widely) might go some way towards explaining the reduction in tutor enjoyment, and the negative ratings of some aspects of tutee behaviour within the dyad. We do not have enough information to enable us to answer question 12, though the sort of negative tutee reactions that we have already encountered might support the perception of an increase in costs to them as the exercise progresses.

Reactance theory and reactions to help

Question 13: Is there evidence for tutee reaction against helping behaviour?

There appears to be some evidence to support the answer 'Yes' to this question. We have already seen that tutees rate both tutors and the scheme less favourably after the repeated experience of being tutored. This might be seen to support Homans' (1961) argument that the thrusting of help upon a peer may result in resentment rather than gratitude. Similarly, it provides support for Fisher *et al.*'s (1982) assertion that aid threatens freedom and gives rise to the negative psychological state of reactance which can result in unfavourable evaluations of the helper or the help received.

We can now begin to frame an explanation for some of the problems identified in the pilot study. Tutors appear to experience some degree of role conflict as the scheme progresses and tutees indicate some awareness of the growing inequality between them and their erstwhile peers, the tutors, and perceive them to become less friendly as a result. Some tutees seem to resort to dysfunctional coping mechanisms such as hostility or miracle seeking which are likely to detract from their enjoyment of the experience. Few miracle seekers are rewarded with their miracle.

Thus, the re-analysis of data carried out in this chapter has illustrated the importance of theoretical frameworks to peer tutoring. Predictions from theory succeeded in explaining many of the problems encountered in the pilot study. In the next chapter, we look at ways of helping teachers plan and promote peer tutoring.

5 Planning and promoting peer tutoring

In this chapter, we shall consider ways of helping teachers to plan and promote peer tutoring. As nothing will change in the absence of people who are prepared to innovate, we begin by discussing ways in which we may allay the fears of colleagues, by exploring some answers to frequently asked questions. Next, Sinclair Goodlad supplies advice on the importance of organization and programme structure. Although Sinclair's own work is mainly concerned with cross-level peer tutoring, his advice may usefully be applied to the setting up of any tutoring venture. The chapter also contains a staff-development activity designed to introduce lecturers to current research in peer tutoring, and to its academic and other benefits. A set of overhead projector (OHP) slides suitable for both staff development purposes and for introducing co-operative or paired learning to students is included for the use of practitioners. The chapter ends with a brief consideration of planning to avoid problems.

PERSUADING COLLEAGUES: RESISTANCE TO CHANGE

In Chapter 6, we shall look at ways of persuading students and preparing them for peer tutoring. However, resistance to innovation may not be restricted to the student body. Our colleagues, also, may prefer to cling to well-tried familiar old ways. As Millis and Cottell (1998) argued, it is not difficult to understand why changes come slowly, given that it is far easier, and requires less effort, to maintain the status quo. Institutional support will clearly help any attempts at innovation, but many of us know that this may not be enough to ensure implementation. More important is the 'selling' of the project to colleagues and students by a respected peer.

Over twenty years ago, Cornwall (1979) observed that some teachers feel that teaching is, by definition, the prerogative of the teacher. This belief seems to continue to be true today, as some teachers still express professional concerns that their 'real' jobs may be taken by unqualified substitutes. These fears may be fuelled by institutional strategies for dealing with financial crises. Anxieties about non-replacement of recently vacated full-time posts, reductions in numbers of part-time lecturers and tutors, or replacement of full-time teachers with temporary part-time staff, and fears of possible redundancies, naturally may make some teachers sceptical of, and threatened by, the idea that students should take on the role of tutor. Such resistance is difficult to address in the absence of good relationships between management and teaching unions, or, indeed, if the fears are well founded.

In order to become actively committed to peer tutoring (or any other innovation), teachers may need to redefine their roles. This often presents problems, as it involves 'a subtle power shift' 'away from the authority figure of the instructor to the students themselves' (Millis and Cottell, 1998: 41).

Whitman (1988) identified public relations as another key issue which must be considered in advance of implementation. As peer tutoring needs to be 'sold' to lecturers, students and administrators, all groups should be included in public relations activities. All are likely to be influenced in a positive way by hearing verbal accounts of successful schemes, and by having access to dossiers of evaluative reports. In proposing the introduction of any scheme, explicit statements of aims and objectives, rules and regulations regarding peer tutoring will reduce misunderstandings. Whitman's (1988) review of studies of resistance to change in the context of peer teaching suggested that opposition may be reduced if the role of peer tutor is defined very clearly. Clear definition benefits both lecturers and students alike. Similarly, teachers must be helped to appreciate that, as Svinicki (1991) argued, 'the weight of the world of learning does not rest on our shoulders alone; that responsibility is shared with students. They are the ones who must do the learning' (Svinicki, 1991: 29).

Fears and uncertainties about the functioning of peer tutoring schemes should be voiced and addressed, and clear answers provided to questions concerning the financial and time costs of the initiative proposed. It may be beneficial to provide information about the origins of peer tutoring, and it is essential to elaborate its benefits and advantages. In addition, potential risks and problem areas should be made explicit. Whitman (1988) also recommended that staff need to be helped to see how peer tutoring relates to the institution's goals and objectives. Of course, as Whitman (1988: 36) concluded, 'the best public relations is the good news spread by a successful programme'.

Let us now look at some responses to frequently asked questions.

ALLAYING FEARS: RESPONSES TO FREQUENTLY ASKED QUESTIONS

Colleagues may have many concerns relating to implementation of peer tutoring or co-operative learning schemes. As Whitman (1988: 34) argued, 'the key to overcoming resistance is to deal with the causes, not its symptoms'. We shall now address some more common anxieties about peer tutoring by providing answers to frequently asked questions. Some of the questions and statements are developed from Millis and Cottell (1998).We shall start by examining a concern about peer tutoring which derives from what many regard as its historical roots: the monitor system.

1. Isn't peer tutoring really the old monitor system in new clothing?

The historical legacy of expediency and social control associated with the monitor system may give rise to attitudinal problems, as some teachers may see modern peer tutoring as simply 'reverting back to the old monitor system', and reject the modern form. The modern practice of students teaching students is readily associated with the monitor system of Joseph Lancaster and Andrew Bell. We shall look a little more closely at the old system to examine the basis of current fears. A method of boy-instructors was devised in Madras by Andrew Bell, who was reported as saying, 'Give me twenty-four pupils at night, and I will deliver you twenty-four teachers in the morning' (quoted by Vaile, 1881: 266). Indeed, Bell found the system so successful that he promptly dismissed his teachers and became very wealthy as a result. On returning to England, he wrote a pamphlet describing his method which, according to Vaile (1881), caught the attention of Joseph Lancaster, a benevolent and enthusiastic Quaker, who set up a similar scheme in the UK. Lancaster's scheme also was an overnight success.

The context in which the monitorial system emerged in Britain may also contribute to modern fears about peer tutoring. Concern that the 'contagion of the French Revolution' should not spread to England encouraged a major effort 'to promote the diffusion of knowledge among people of the lower classes' and 'to transplant intelligence and reverence' (Vaile, 1881: 265). Educational agencies such as Sabbath Schools and Mechanics' Institutes were set up. There was an increase in the production of cheap publications designed to 'dispel adult ignorance' and instruct juveniles. Among these educational endeavours was the monitorial or Lancastrian system of instruction which met the need for mass instruction, was economical and perceived to be effective. However, 'It was a scheme without any foundation in philosophy, and not deserving to be called a method' (Vaile, 1881: 265). Nonetheless, the monitor system attracted the enthusiasm and praise of scholars and statesmen.

It is easy to see how even a passing knowledge of these events might prejudice colleagues against peer tutoring, or indeed against any form of student involvement in teaching. Vaile's account of the monitor system contains many seeds of current anxieties about peer tutoring:

- it is an economic expediency;
- it threatens jobs;
- it threatens standards and quality;
- it lacks any philosophical or theoretical foundation;
- it is a social control measure;
- students do not have teaching skills or enough knowledge to teach others.

Peer tutoring today, however, is very different from these early manifestations.

As we saw in Chapter 2, peer tutoring gives rise to many academic and non-academic benefits. Modern peer tutoring can encourage a rich type of learning. For example, studies of reciprocal teaching found that it encouraged high-level cognitive activities (Palincsar and Brown, 1984). King's Reciprocal Peer Questioning (1991, 1993), similarly, requires students to engage with the material at a deep level. Schemes such as those implemented by Dansereau and colleagues (e.g. O'Donnell and Dansereau, 1992) aim to assess the effectiveness of metacognitive and elaborative activities. Such outcomes bear little resemblance to the rote learning which characterized the monitor system.

Additionally, peer tutoring facilitates the development of desirable generic skills such as interpersonal and communication skills (Metheny and Metheny, 1997) and the ability to apply skills and competencies to other courses and increased confidence (Witherby, 1997).

2. Won't peer tutoring lower standards?

Research suggests that this does not seem to be the case. For example, Fantuzzo *et al.* (1989a) found higher examination scores and lower levels of subjective distress after participation in reciprocal peer tutoring. Further examples may be found in Chapter 2. In any case, lecturers remain involved in student learning and can monitor progress associated with a peer-tutoring scheme.

3. Why use peer tutoring when lectures are more efficient than students teaching and learning from each other? You run the risk of not being able to cover the course content

In order to address this issue, we need to differentiate between teaching and learning. For a teacher to simply tick off all the topics listed in the syllabus does not guarantee that any learning has taken place. I have been known on occasion to throw the question, 'How much do you remember of the content of your degree course?' into discussions about the importance of 'covering the syllabus'. The answer, after some thought and a little embarrassment, is often, 'Not much' or 'Nothing'. It is frequently acknowledged that skills such as the ability to evaluate, criticize, synthesize and continue to learn after graduation are more lasting and important than content which, in any case, requires constant updating.

An alternative answer to this question, suggested by Millis and Cottell (1998), is that syllabus coverage does not require lecturing. It may equally be achieved through out-of-class learning.

4. If students teach each other, won't the lecturer lose control?

Many would argue that 'keeping control' over students is undesirable, and much current educational debate emphasizes the benefits of transferring power from teacher to learner. Millis and Cottell (1998) argued that control of teachers over students may, in any case, be illusory. Those who stand at the front and lecture might do well to investigate the range of activities that are taking place in the lecture hall which fall totally outside the control of the lecturer. Even seemingly attentive students may be daydreaming.

Lecturers who feel most comfortable with a silent audience may fear loss of control when students communicate with each other in class. Noise levels will, necessarily, rise as dyads and small groups communicate with each other. However, the lecturer can always attract the attention of the class by an agreed signal. Millis and Cottell (1998: 62) suggest that instructors and students agree on the 'quiet signal' at the beginning of the course or module. They proposed that instructors explain the need for such a signal to the class, offer several options and invite suggestions from students. They rate the most frequently chosen signal as the instructor's raised hand, though more exotic options such as a collection of tinkling glass bells and flickering or dimming of lights have also been used.

5. The problem with peer tutoring is that you don't know what goes on in dyadic learning

A quick response to this statement is that you don't know what goes on in most people's heads, most of the time. Students, however they work, are usually required to provide some evidence of scholarly and creative activity in the form of reports, essays, solutions to problems, designs and so on. They are quite aware of these requirements, and will spend some time addressing task issues. We should also remember that group (or pair) 'maintenance' issues are important in any kind of co-operative learning. Time spent resolving interpersonal conflict, for example, is not time wasted. The participants will have learned or practised an important skill. If students who have worked in dyads can work amicably and fulfil course requirements, maybe it doesn't matter that the processes are hidden to us.

6. Don't students want to learn from an expert rather than from peers who are as inexperienced as themselves?

This statement describes a very frequently encountered reservation about peer tutoring. Both sceptical colleagues and reluctant students need to be reassured that the system can, and will, 'work'. I have found that producing 'hard evidence' is useful in these contexts. Knowledge of the benefits and working of whichever variety of peer tutoring you are planning should be shared with colleagues and presented to students before attempting to organize them into learning pairs or groups. Data derived from work in your own institution may be more persuasive than evidence from studies carried out elsewhere, given that there will always be at least one sceptical colleague who will argue that 'Oh, yes, I think X is a good idea, but it wouldn't work here/things are different here/our students are different'.

Where appropriate, it is important to point out that you are not planning that all learning will take place in pairs or groups. Students will continue to experience a wide range of learning situations.

7. I don't know how peer tutoring works. I wasn't taught that way

I hope that we all do things each day that were not explicitly taught in our own formal education. Colleagues who claim ignorance about any new technique might be provided with the opportunity to attend a staff-development event in order to expand their repertoire and allay their fears.

8. Don't student tutors simply give the answers to tutees?

It should be stressed that the student tutor's job is not to provide tutees with ready-made answers, but rather to support them in their quest for their own solutions.

9. Isn't peer tutoring just a way of saving the lecturer's time?

Any colleague who is labouring under this misapprehension should be directed to Sinclair Goodlad's contribution below. Successful peer tutoring requires preparation, very careful planning and organization and on-going monitoring on the part of the teacher. Start-up time is high, as with any innovation. However, colleagues can be reassured that all the effort is worth it. Once a scheme is up and running, some lecturer time *may* be saved, but this is not the aim and purpose of peer tutoring.

10. I don't know how to assess students who have been learning in this way

There are a number of issues in this area that deserve consideration. For example, whether we like it or not, grades or marks are primary extrinsic motivators in higher education. As Millis and Cottell (1998: 190) observed, '[no] teacher who has heard the dreaded words, "Will this be on the exam?" can doubt their power'. While acknowledging the veracity of this observation, we hope that our students will get more from their educational experience of peer tutoring than this. We wish for them to experience personal and educational rewards as well as a good grade.

There is a growing acceptance that responsible assessment promotes learning. Similarly, there is growing consensus that assessment and grading policies should be visible and clearly understood by teachers and students. These views apply to assessment in co-operative situations as well as in more traditional ones. Teachers espousing peer tutoring and co-operative learning must be explicit about their grading policies and explain these to students. In assessing peer learning, as in more traditional situations, assessments should be carefully linked to course or module objectives. As Millis and Cottell (1998) argued, in a co-operative classroom, grading practices should also encourage and reinforce co-operative practices. Colleagues might wish to read more about this issue in Chapter 10, where Cohen *et al.* reflect on the problems of assessing peer learning.

11. How can you grade a group effort?

Some colleagues may be particularly concerned about group grading. It can be unfair to award the same mark to students for group work, and Millis and Cottell (1998) claimed that group grades foster resistance to co-operative learning. They also raised the question of the legality of group grading, citing an example of a lawsuit brought by an 'A' student in the USA whose grades were perceived to have been depressed by less talented team mates. The issue of how to differentiate between group members has received considerable attention in recent years, and many papers have been written suggesting ways round the problem (e.g. Goldfinch and Raeside, 1990; Oldfield and Macalpine, 1995; Ritter, 1997). Some studies attempt to measure student participation. However, unless 'participation' is defined in terms of contribution of a number of useful behaviours which have been identified before the group work commenced, awarding marks for mere presence may be problematic. None the less, students frequently argue that they deserve extra marks because of their presence or amount of effort. Millis and Cottell (1998: 193) suggest a witty response to such students. 'If students raise participation points as an issue for each assignment completed, instructors can simply mention that Professor Graybeard down the hall does not assign participation points based on his students' attentiveness during his lecture.'

12. I don't know how to evaluate peer tutoring

Most academics will be keen to know if peer tutoring has improved learning outcomes. There are a number of mechanisms for evaluation available. When there's a rich source of theory on which to base study design and evaluation, it is regrettable that so many studies reported do not appear to have benefited from a knowledge of it. Colleagues should be directed to Chapter 7, where a number of evaluation mechanisms are described and other issues relating to evaluation discussed.

13. What do I say to students who say they're paying to be taught, not to do it themselves?

Svinicki (1991) conceded that both teachers and students can experience the adjustment from teacher-centred to student-centred education as a difficult one, even though students may be better off in the end. How can we persuade students that this is the case when they subscribe to what Trevor Habeshaw (1999), in an electronic discussion on student power and responsibility, described as 'the Thatcherite dogma' that, as they are paying for their education, it is the job of the staff 'to teach them MORE, be MORE helpful, give them MORE feedback, do ALL the teaching, teach TO the exam, NOT demand reading outside the course etc.'. However, Habeshaw also produced a useful response to such student demands.

> Higher education does cost students and/or their parents a lot of money, but it's important for them and us to be clear what they are, in fact, paying for. What the students pay for is the opportunity to have an education. They are not, however, paying for a qualification. Qualifications can be bought off the Internet if that's what they want. How well they really qualify (first, 2:1, distinction etc.) is primarily their responsibility. Our 'job' then becomes that of creating the highest quality educational environment, and of motivating the students by initiating a range of learning experiences, so as to make it possible

for them to qualify well SO LONG AS THEY MAKE THEIR CONTRIBU-
TION TO IT ALL

(Habeshaw, 1999).

Peer-assisted learning can provide part of Habeshaw's supportive educational environment which encourages learning and development.

14. I don't have the time to make any changes to my teaching programme

I have great sympathy with this objection. It is a valid concern. Time *is* required, and time is something we seem to have less and less of. My response would echo that of Sinclair Goodlad, which would be to suggest that one might start small and keep the initiative simple. For example, relatively little material preparation time is required in order to implement some straightforward paired learning activities in timetabled tutorial slots. Scripted Co-operative Dyadic reading or King's generic questioning may be applied to ready-made readings such as a course text. Of course, you need to know about these activities before they may be used. Staff developers have a role here. Any available resources should be used: educational development units, teaching resource centres, staff development activities.

THE SEVEN GOLDEN RULES FOR TUTORING AND MENTORING SCHEMES

Sinclair Goodlad, Imperial College, UK

Despite the volume of activity, there are still many things that we do not know about tutoring and mentoring, and on which research needs to be conducted. Until we know more, we need to establish precise, and limited, objectives for schemes and to beware of over-selling the ideas lest we discredit them. Meanwhile, there are certain matters that, if not attended to, can cause schemes to fail. Seven are examined.

Although we may not yet know exactly what makes tutoring and mentoring work effectively (see Goodlad, 1995a), we have a pretty good idea of what will make a scheme fail. The observations that follow are based upon the experience of running a large student tutoring scheme (The Pimlico Connection – see Goodlad, 1979, 1985; Goodlad and Hirst, 1989), of talking to practitioners in other tutoring schemes, and of reading the research literature. I would submit that if any of the following seven matters is neglected, trouble will follow. I shall be interested to learn from readers whether or not you agree.

1. Define aims

In a tutoring scheme, who is to teach what to whom for what purpose? In a mentoring scheme, are the benefits sought primarily professional/academic or social?

If a compromise has to be made between benefits accruing to tutors and those accruing to tutees, in whose favour will the scheme operate? (See Fitz-Gibbon, 1978.)

Although the intended benefits of a scheme may seem self-evident to the planner of a tutoring or mentoring scheme, it can be very useful to have a short 'statement of intent' that can be given to prospective participants and inquirers about a scheme. If the focal objective can be stated in a single sentence, this can be useful: e.g.

- to give school pupils support in learning mathematics and science by the provision of undergraduates as tutors;
- to assist first-year undergraduates in the transition from school to university by the provision of mentoring by second-year undergraduates.

If the focus of a scheme is not completely clear, problems may result. For example, Houston and Lazenbatt (1996) report that in a scheme to support independent learning in mathematics some participants felt insecure and resented the innovation. The authors suggest that the students' discontent was more with the independent learning aspect of the course than with the ideas of peer tutoring and peer support. One innovation was colliding with another.

If a scheme is to be the subject of research (see section 7 below), it may be helpful to phrase objectives in terms of precise behavioural outcomes, e.g.

- First-year physics students who receive help in mathematics from third-year physics students will achieve X points better in test Y than students from a matched control group who do not receive tutoring but who spend an equal amount of time in normal classroom instruction.

2. Define roles

As I have indicated elsewhere (Goodlad and Hirst, 1989: 137), when tutoring schemes have failed, two major factors have been present:

- There was a lack of communication – people who should have known what was going on did not.
- There was a loss of initiative and impetus – nobody seemed to know who was responsible for what.

Most of these difficulties can be avoided if there is one single person with whom the buck stops! This in turn suggests keeping a scheme to a scale in which one organizer can be realistically in touch with what is going on. The lack of such a person can be catastrophic. For example, Saunders and Gibbon (1998) report that one scheme, the Peer Assisted Student Support (PASS) scheme at the University of Glamorgan, foundered after one year for lack of overall co-ordination by a member of staff. As a 'bottom-up' scheme initiated by students, it suffered from the inevitable transitoriness of student union executives.

As with aims, so with roles, it is important to write these down – particularly if inter-institutional contacts are involved. For example, in a scheme linking schools and a university it is necessary to write down as a minimum the tasks of: the university organizer, the school heads, the receiving teachers, the tutors – especially any who help with the administration of the scheme (as they often do).

Matching

Part of the assignment of roles involves the complex issue of pairing up tutors and tutees, and mentors and mentees. The jury is still out on this topic, but some research findings may be of interest.

Cloward (1967) found no significant effect of different-sex pairings, nor did Mevarech (1985). Cicirelli (1972) studied the effect of sibling relationships on the concept learning of young children taught by child-teachers, and found that irrespective of the sex of the younger child:

(a) sisters were more effective than brothers when teaching younger siblings;
(b) sisters were more effective in teaching younger siblings than girls in teaching younger unrelated children;
(c) boys tended to be more effective in teaching unrelated younger children than in teaching younger siblings; and
(d) boys and girls did not differ in effectiveness as teachers of unrelated younger children. Drawing on extensive experience of running tutoring schemes, Mainiero, Gillogly, Nease, Sheretz and Wilkinson (1971) recommend that an older boy should never be matched with a younger girl, but offer no research findings in support of this suggestion.

More recently, Topping and Whiteley (1993), studying the matching of tutors and tutees by sex in paired reading, found that male–male combinations did particularly well all round. Female–female combinations were good for the tutees but poor for the tutors. Mixed-sex combinations were good for the tutors but poor for the tutees. This latter was particularly true for the combination of female tutors with male tutees. They do, however, caution that the supposition that same-sex pairings are more effective than mixed-sex pairings is a gross over-simplification, and the interactions between sex combinations and outcomes for tutors and tutees are more complex than previous research has indicated.

Friendship

In a study designed to explore the influence of friendship upon the process and outcome of learning in peer tutoring, Foot and Barron (1990) found that far from reducing task demands upon eight- to nine-year-old tutors, friendship appeared to impose greater burdens on children's limited resources. This came from their need to renegotiate their new social relationship arising from the unfamiliar and unequal roles into which the tutoring had thrust them.

Ethnicity

In the PERACH project in Israel, Fresko found that the relationships between student tutors and young people were easier when pairs were matched by ethnicity (Fresko, 1996).

In the absence of unequivocal guidance from the research, a sensible strategy might be to always ask the participants! Suffice it to say that the assignment of roles, particularly face-to-face roles, is a complex area.

3. Train the tutors and mentors

Not surprisingly, it has been known for many years that untrained tutors are less effective than trained ones (see, for example, Niedermeyer, 1970; Conrad, 1975). Evidence about this continues to be produced (Fuchs, Fuchs, Bentz, Phillips and Hamlett, 1994; Shore, 1995). Barron and Foot (1991), for example, found that children who have a fuller understanding of a task and its rationale are not only better prepared for performing the task themselves, but are also better equipped to manage the demands of the task when teaching it to others. Again, Wheldall and Mettem (1985) found that 16-year-old tutors who had been trained in the 'pause, prompt and praise' technique were effective, whereas those who had not been trained made almost no use of praise at all.

The particulars of training will, of course, depend upon what the tutors or mentors are going to do; but the following items constitute the irreducible minimum of matters that need to be addressed:

- how to start a tutoring or mentoring session by establishing a friendly atmosphere;
- familiarity with the content of the tutees' syllabus;
- what to do when the tutee gives a correct answer;
- what to do when the answer is wrong;
- what to do if a session goes badly;
- how to vary the content of tutoring or mentoring sessions;
- how to end a tutoring session.

Record-keeping

Even postgraduate students acting as tutors for undergraduates are anxious not only about the possible limitations of their subject knowledge, but also how to cope with students who are too talkative or, more frequently, not talkative enough (see Goodlad, 1997a, 1997b).

A similar agenda can readily be constructed for mentoring where the process of disengagement at the end of a mentoring arrangement is even more complex than ending a tutoring relationship.

Elsewhere, I describe at length the fertility of student tutoring as a focus for academic study (Goodlad, 1998: 10–17) and argue the case for building the preparation of tutors and mentors into their formal education. Where this has been done (e.g. Saunders and Kingdon, 1998; Wood, 1998), not only have the students benefited personally and professionally, but also it has been easier to argue the case for a tutoring scheme having a claim for part of a university's tuition budget.

4. Structure the content

For the organizer of a tutoring scheme, a major decision concerns the degree of control to exercise over the content of the tuition/teaching. The two extreme conditions are (a) when tutors are given complete responsibility for choosing materials, and (b) when tutors operate with programmed texts and/or CAL (Computer Assisted Learning) in which steps for the tutee are laid down very precisely.

It has long been known that striking benefits to tutees can come from the administration by tutors of programmed materials (see, for example, Ellson, 1986; Ellson *et al.*, 1965; Ellson, Harris and Barber, 1968, 1969; Ellson and Harris, 1970; Harrison, 1969, 1971a, 1971b, 1972a, 1972b). Not only does careful structuring ensure that learners are given material in appropriate sequence, but it has also been found that tutors still find the human interaction with their tutees rewarding. Tutors' originality and creativity can be built around the content whose structure is the prime responsibility of the trained teacher. Tutors, in short, do not reinvent the wheel; rather, they use other people's wheels to travel further and faster.

For those of you running tutoring or mentoring schemes that involve placing numerous tutors or mentors, this suggestion may seem like a counsel of perfection. However, it is an important management task for an organizer to urge receiving teachers to deploy tutors on clearly defined tasks for the tutees or to provide mentors with a list of matters to raise in encounters with their mentees.

To ease the dilemma about offering too much content or too little, Bloom (1976) offers sensible advice. She urges organizers to choose materials that

- make learning more meaningful and salient to tutees – based on the skill-needs of tutees, organized as a sequence of planned tasks, providing clear models of correct responses and desired behaviours;
- involve the maximum participation and human interaction;
- incorporate appropriate reinforcement – because tutors may not offer this spontaneously;
- offer some choice to participants – so that a mixture of structure and freedom is encouraged.

Benware and Deci (1984) suggest that one of the areas that merits research is whether it is reflecting about the deep structure of academic disciplines, as much as doing the tutoring itself, that offers benefits to students – as some of the early phenomenographic work by Marton and Säljö (1976a, 1976b) might imply. Annis (1983b), however, demonstrated in one experiment that the benefits to students seemed to come from actually doing the tutoring, rather than just preparing to do it.

5. Support the tutors and mentors

Providing the necessary support to tutors and mentors is one of the most difficult aspects of running a scheme – but also one of the most rewarding. The teacher's work moves from being direct instruction to being more one of management. The teacher effectively passes to non-professionals responsibility for tactics while retaining responsibility for strategy. But the teacher cannot just train tutors or mentors and then let them loose, hoping for the best: some regular feedback is needed on how a scheme is working. Ideally, this should be achieved through regular debriefing sessions. If the tutoring or mentoring is built into students' studies, debriefing sessions are a legitimate and fruitful call on the organizer's time, and the learning from experience of the tutors or mentors can be actively encouraged.

Well-structured materials will, of course, have built-in instructions to keep the tutors on the right lines. Whether or not such materials are available, it is useful to give tutors or mentors a ready-reference list of instructions to review regularly – before and/or after sessions, maybe on the bus, possibly with sound or video recordings of sessions for checking their own performance.

Many tutoring schemes involve parties and other gatherings for tutors to generate a feeling of collegiality, and contact with others with whom to share and compare experiences.

6. Keep logistics as simple as possible.

Writing of paired reading, Rhodes (1993: 18) observes that '[this] kind of project is practical: that is, it can fit into the working patterns and routines of mainstream school without extra effort and time'. As readers who run tutoring or mentoring schemes know, that is no small thing! Logistics can make or break tutoring and mentoring schemes.

Time

In a survey of 82 peer-tutoring projects, Fitz-Gibbon (1978: 29) found that scheduling problems occurred in 52 per cent of them! Likewise, in mentoring, Marc Freedman (1995: 221) identifies time as the biggest single problem with adult mentoring schemes: mentors are often better at signing up than showing up!

There is no easy answer to this problem, either for tutoring or for mentoring. One approach, which we have consistently used in 'the Pimlico Connection' tutoring scheme, is to ask students to make only a limited commitment of time (2 hours per week for 15 weeks) – and not to sign up if they do not think they can manage this. Again, in a scheme mobilizing volunteers to act as tutors or explainers in the London Science Museum, Stephanie McIvor and I found that volunteers preferred making a defined commitment of time rather than an open-ended one (Goodlad and McIvor, 1998).

Then there is the related problem of finding time for all those involved in tutoring schemes (organizers, teachers, tutors) to meet each other. It is one of the laws of nature that organizers of schemes soon discover – Timetables never fit!

Space

Likewise, space is a problem. We are encountering it at present in Imperial College with a peer-tutoring scheme in which we are facilitating the pairing up of students who speak French or German and who want to improve their English with English students who want to improve their French or German. We have lots of huge, raked lecture theatres, but very few small rooms. And from this month, we also have a complex space-charging system so that we have to pay for the rooms that we use!

In schools, I have seen tutoring taking place in locker rooms, store-cupboards, dining rooms, corridors, and corners of libraries in which lack of privacy can be a nuisance.

For mentoring schemes, the choice of places for meetings is a non-trivial issue. Not only must the meeting places be geographically accessible, but they must also make both mentors and mentees feel comfortable – culturally as well as physically.

It is these very practical matters that lead to the suggestions:

> Start small!
>> Keep it simple!

7. Evaluate the scheme

In a book on tutoring and mentoring, it hardly seems necessary to stress the importance of evaluation; so I will be brief. There are at least three good reasons for evaluating your tutoring or mentoring scheme:

- one's perception of suitable objectives for a scheme will be sharpened if one tries to determine how those objectives will be achieved;
- everyone involved in the scheme will feel satisfaction if there is 'something to show for it all';
- self-contained evaluation reports can be very useful instruments for telling other people (including putative participants) about the idea.

But once again, we need to proceed with caution. The late Vernon Allen, one of the best-known advocates of children teaching children (Allen, 1976), warns that evaluation tests can be seen by teachers as spying – and testing sessions can be very disruptive of class time. He recommends that test materials should be made available to teachers before the scheme is instituted. Researchers should avoid springing things on people, should avoid scheduling tests at busy times of the school year, and should give teachers the results as soon as possible after the testing.

Evaluation procedures that are too complex can fail. For example, Topping, Simpson, Thompson and Hill (1997) achieved only a 30 per cent response rate from student tutors when evaluating a faculty-wide accredited cross-year student-supported learning programme. It appears that this may have been a result of reporting schedules being too complex. All were, it seems, critical of the long list of NVQ (National Vocational Qualifications) competencies, which they thought too vague and too numerous. When compiling the portfolios required of them, some student supporters were unsure about what to include or leave out and what level to aim for. Again, the message is: keep it simple!

And finally, for all their many attractions, tutoring and mentoring schemes are complex and difficult to get right first time. As Mary Kennedy has argued (Kennedy, 1990: 59), the links between research findings and established educational theory are often tenuous. Likewise, as Keith Topping has reminded us (Topping, 1998: 51), the number of variables to be controlled is daunting. Mentoring programmes, which are often more diffuse in aims and looser in organisation, can be even more difficult to study.

You would probably not be reading this book if you did not think tutoring and mentoring to be important. Indeed, their rediscovery and reinvention over the last 35 years could be as important as that of printing. Coupled with use of the Internet (see Beardon, 1998), they hold quite stunning promise for the spread of education. We have everything to gain by persevering with our experiments, but I suggest we need to keep in mind at least the simple rules explored above.

INNOVATION AND CHANGE: ESTABLISHING PEER TUTORING

No change will take place to the status quo unless there is considerable effort expended to ensure that it happens and, for any innovation to succeed, at least one person's commitment and enthusiasm is required. A peer-tutoring scheme will not get off the ground unless it has a champion. Many schemes have been introduced into institutions as a result of the presence of just one committed individual. Champions may be lone enthusiasts who may have encountered like-minded individuals at conferences or workshops and other scholarly meetings, or sometimes in less formal settings. For example, my own first encounter with Carol Fitz-Gibbon with whom I first worked on a peer-tutoring project was in a social setting, facilitated by a mutual friend. Such individuals may have gathered information about peer tutoring from a variety of sources. Their enthusiasm may stem from reading about peer tutoring in the research literature. They may have talked with colleagues from other institutions. They may have found evidence of its effectiveness in evaluative reports in the literature. Such individuals are well up the learning curve before they design and implement their own schemes. Some may have also developed an understanding of the theoretical underpinnings of peer tutoring, although I suspect that many skilled practitioners develop an intuitive feel for the methodology well before they explore its theoretical bases.

However, not all institutions have champions, and in the absence of individual enthusiastic teachers, peer tutoring may also be introduced into an institution by means of staff development activities. An example of such an activity designed to encourage teachers to set up peer-tutoring schemes is described below.

STAFF DEVELOPMENT ENCOURAGING PEER TUTORING

Lecturers need to be convinced of the benefits of an innovation before they will consider introducing it into their own teaching programmes. Any psychologist will confirm that to change attitudes and behaviour is, perhaps, one of the most difficult things for anyone to achieve. Advertisers spend millions of pounds to persuade us to buy their products, using state-of-the-art technology and endorsements from stars. Governments introduce legislation to enforce certain behaviours and prohibit others. Educators have to try other means, and our tools of persuasion may have to rely on the need of the scientist in all of us for evidence. Lecturers may be persuaded to consider changing their habits as a result of either their personal experience or of having been introduced to evaluative research literature. Sometimes motivation for change may come from the realization that the old ways of teaching no longer work for all students. Sometimes staff may become sensitive to institutional policy which advocates new methods of teaching and learning.

Staff development activities should make use of all methods and means of persuasion available. Although Millis and Cottell (1998) argued that teachers more readily acquire new ideas about teaching from their colleagues than from readings or workshops, they advocate four strategies to engage teachers:

***How to do* 5.1: Starting a peer-tutoring scheme: a staff-development activity**

Materials required: Overhead projector (OHP) slides and pens
                          Workshop handouts I to III
                          Paper and writing implements
Time allocation: Approximately 3 hours
                          Total and individual times are approximate and will
                          vary according to numbers present.

Procedure

1. An introduction to the activity, outlining some of the benefits of peer tutoring delivered by the workshop leader. (See OHPs 5.1.1–5.1.9 and Chapter 2 for more detail.)   **(20 mins)**

2. Participant activity: paired reading
(a) Each participant is supplied with a copy of a short article and instructions on how to proceed (see workshop handouts I and II), blank OHPs and pens. Participants are allocated a randomly chosen partner.

(b) Paired reading/studying activity takes place, alternating roles in the SCD methodology. All pairs should try *both* methods of paired learning.

(c) Each pair prepares 2 multiple-choice (MC) questions on an OHP slide. In addition, the pair submits 1 short-answer question based on the material, together with a model answer, also on an OHP.
(a) to (c)   **(45 mins)**

(d) Workshop leader selects 10 MC questions in total and 2 short-answer questions. Questions are displayed on the OHP.

(e) Participants complete the test in pairs. Meanwhile, the workshop leader prepares a MC questions answer sheet on OHP slide, using answers supplied by participants.   **(15 mins)**

(f) Pairs mark their own work, using the MC answer guide provided and the 2 model answers to the short-answer questions.   **(10 mins)**

(g) Designers of short-answer questions invite comparisons between their model answers and learner answers and lead discussions on matches and mismatches.   **(15 mins)**

(h) Reflection *in different pairs* on the experience of learning with a partner. (See handout III for prompt questions.)   **(20 mins)**

3. Plenary session   **(20 mins)**

The workshop pack might also include references to Chapter 2 in the present volume.

If the workshop leader has the facilities and expertise to set up an internal electronic peer tutoring/learning discussion group this should be done and participants encouraged to join it in order to share experiences and to diagnose and solve problems.

- dissemination activities through libraries and resource centres of broad-based literature (preferably discipline-specific);
- institutional support;
- workshops to introduce teachers to new methods and encourage experienced practitioners to share their teaching ideas and experiences;
- networking, within an institution and across campus and discipline lines.

Resource rooms should be stocked up with relevant literature. There is now a wealth of useful and stimulating material available on *the internet* (embedded in the dross), and teachers should be encouraged to access this. As we shall see in Chapter 8, much useful debate takes place on *electronic discussion groups* such as the USA-based AERA-J, the Australasian HERDSA and the UK-based isl (improving student learning), seda (staff and educational development association), ed-dev-resnet (educational development research network) and others. Discussion groups are a ready way of *networking*, too.

In some places, *institutional support* may be long in coming. However, there are clear indications, in the UK at least, that some change will receive institutional support. The setting up of the Institute for Learning and Teaching to oversee the accreditation of teachers in higher education has already caused some institutions to evaluate their policies on learning, teaching and assessment.

Workshops

Workshops are an effective way of helping teachers learn about new techniques and about how they might improve the learning of their students. 'How to do' box 5.1 describes a staff-development activity designed to introduce staff to the benefits of peer tutoring.

A set of overhead projector (OHP) slides suitable for both staff development purposes and for introducing co-operative or paired learning to students (see Chapter 6) constitute Tables 5.1.1 to 5.1.9. Tables 5.1.1 to 5.1.7 are located at the end of the chapter (pp. 151–53) and Tables 5.1.8 and 5.1.9 below.

Table 5.1.8 Some frequently asked questions concerning co-operative and paired learning

---

1   Isn't it wrong to teach using co-operative learning methods when we must prepare students for a competitive world?
2   Doesn't co-operative learning mean forcing some students to work with others they don't like?
3   Doesn't co-operative learning mean a 'free ride' for some and extra work for others?
4   How much learning should take place co-operatively?
5   Doesn't co-operative learning focus on the process of learning at the expense of content?

I respond to slide 5.1.8 (Some frequently asked questions concerning co-operative and paired learning) in the following ways.

1 Isn't it wrong to teach using co-operative learning methods when we must prepare students for a competitive world?

   The world is becoming less competitive in some respects, and employers require graduates to be able to co-operate in teams.
   There's a place for a variety of learning methods.

2 Doesn't co-operative learning mean forcing some students to work with others they don't like?

   No. Initially hostile and reluctant students have been found to become drawn into co-operative learning schemes and grow to percieve the benefits.
   Safety-net procedures are designed to deal with problems that students cannot resolve themselves.

3 Doesn't co-operative learning mean a 'free ride' for some and extra work for others?

   No. Co-operative learning methods are structured to ensure contributions from all members. Learning can be assessed individually or in groups by peer assessment.

4 How much learning should take place co-operatively?

   Some, but not all. Variety is important (see below).

5 Doesn't co-operative learning focus on the process of learning at the expense of content?

   This depends on the objectives of the co-operative learning scheme. Peer tutoring and paired learning are good ways of helping students learn new content.

Table 5.1.9 Benefits of paired learning in a Life-span development module

Method of study	Mean score (s.d. in brackets)
Reciprocal Peer Tutoring (RPT)	10.00 (3.41)
Reciprocal Peer Questioning (RPQ)	9.14 (2.80)
Scripted Co-operative Dyads (SCD)	8.50 (2.90)
Individual study	5.67 (1.53)
Absent from tutorial	6.25 (1.72)

The last slide, Table 5.1.9, shows the results of a paired-learning study I conducted in a life-span development class at Napier University. This is my *pièce de résistance*. 'Home-grown' results can be very persuasive!

Worksheets are located in Tables 5.2.1, 5.2.2 and 5.2.3.

Table 5.2.1 Workshop sheet I

Worksheet I Study extract

Participants should be supplied with a study extract on the topic of the effectiveness of peer tutoring.

Suitable extracts:

Topping, K. (1996a) Effective peer tutoring in further and higher education: a typology and review of the literature, *Higher Education*, 32: 321-45 (Teachers may wish to select extracts from within this paper)

or

Parts of **Chapter 2 in the present volume**. In the absence of any fixed plans on the part of participants, I would suggest choosing sections to support Dansereau's Scripted Co-operative Dyads methodology ('How to do' box 1.21 see Chapter 1, 'How to do' box 1.10, for further details) or King's Reciprocal Peer Questioning methodology (Chapter 1, 'How to do' box 1.21). However, when teachers have decided on other forms of peer tutoring, the section on beneficial effects should be chosen to match these.

Worksheet I, Table 5.2.1, contains suggestions for study extracts to be investigated during the workshop.

Worksheet II, Table 5.2.2, contains brief instructions relating to the paired reading techniques to be used. It is important to remember that teachers may differ in their approaches to learning in ways similar to students, so participants are given first-hand experience of two paired-learning activities: Dansereau's Scripted Co-operative Dyads and King's Reciprocal Peer Questioning. These activities not only allow teachers to experience each learning technique, but also familiarize them with material on the effectiveness of peer tutoring in further and higher education.

Worksheet III, Table 5.2.3, contains questions designed to help participants reflect on their experiences.

This workshop requires the leader to watch the time very carefully. It is imperative that there is ample time for discussion and reflection in both pairs and the plenary session at the end. By the end of the workshop, once participants are convinced of the possible benefits of peer tutoring, the next task is to make *practical plans* to implement some paired learning in their own teaching programmes. This process should be started before participants leave the workshop, attention being given to what it is that they hope to gain by introducing peer tutoring.

Table 5.2.2 Workshop sheet II

Worksheet II Paired reading/teaching instructions
All pairs will use both methodologies listed below. Half the pairs will use methodology A to teach paragraphs 1 and 2, the other half will use methodology B on this material. Pairs will change methodology after completing work on paragraphs 1 and 2. Full methodological details are to be found in Chapter 1.

A. Dansereau's Scripted Co-operative Dyads methodology (See Chapter 1, 'How to do' box 1.10 for further details)

Workshop organizers should make sure that How to do 1.10 is available to participants.

B. King's Reciprocal Peer Questioning methodology (See Chapter 1, 'How to do' box 1.21)

How does it work?	**(Abbreviated version suitable for learning from text)**
1	Students assigned randomly to groups/pairs.
2	Students are provided with a set of generic question stems (see below).
3	Students receive the extract on peer tutoring.
4	Pairs of students use the RPQ strategy, alternating roles of completing questions and answering them. Unstructured discussion on the extract being studied should also be conducted.

King's generic question stems
Workshop organizers should make sure that examples of King's generic question stems are available to participants (see Chapter 1 and King, 1991, 1993).

Table 5.2.3 Workshop sheet III

Worksheet III Questions to prompt reflection

1　Which of the two paired learning methods did you prefer?
　　Why?
2　Do you think these methods of paired learning are better for encouraging an increase in knowledge or improved understanding?
　　Why?
3　To what extent do you think your experience of paired learning might have been different with another partner?
　　Why?
4　In which of your classes might you use one or both of these techniques?

A follow-up workshop to help participants with their plans may be very beneficial.

PLANNING AND PROMOTING PEER TUTORING

When considering whether or not to embark on a peer-tutoring scheme, the first and most basic question to ask is, 'Who is to teach what to whom for what purpose?' (see Sinclair Goodlad's contribution above). In other words, aims and objectives need to be clarified. Potential innovators need to pose, reflect on and answer a number of questions:

- Why do I wish to introduce peer tutoring into my programme?
- What are my objectives?
- Which students do I wish to involve as participants?
- What benefits do I hope to achieve (for my students or myself)?
- How can I evaluate my scheme?
- What problems might I encounter in my attempts to get this initiative off the ground?
- Where might I seek help?

All these questions need to be addressed before the first concrete step towards implementation may be taken. Teachers need to be clear whether they are intending to remedy a deficit or add value through peer tutoring. If the aim is to add value, they must be clear in which area the peer-tutoring scheme envisaged is likely to benefit the participants. For example, will it enhance academic performance, help in the development of transferable skills or aid social interactions? Is the scheme designed to reduce student non-attendance or encourage progression? Does the current ethos of the course or department or institution support the innovation? Are they likely to encounter apathy, inertia or resistance from either colleagues or students, and how might this be dealt with?

Once these questions have been answered and aims and objectives clarified, practical planning may begin. As Topping (1996b: 37) has noted, 'a first peer tutoring project is inevitably front-end loaded with planning and preparation'. Sinclair Goodlad's seven golden rules for tutoring and mentoring schemes, elaborated above, provide practical guidance on how to go about this process.

PLANNING TO AVOID PROBLEMS

Organizers need to be aware of a number of problems in order to 'head them off' before they can disrupt the whole scheme. Safety-net procedures need to be in place to deal with problems that have the power to disrupt peer tutoring such as partner absences, partner incompatibility and absenteeism.

Safety-net procedures

(a) *Partner absence procedure*

Topping (1996b) recommends that a 'partner absence procedure' should be in place to enable tutoring to proceed. Topping's solutions include:

- Re-matching the partner-less person with another in the same situation, possibly renegotiating roles for that session.
- Appointment of a spare or stand-by tutor.
- Merging the partner-less individual into another group (again some role change may be necessary).
- If no alternative is possible, a simple system of communication between pairs should enable rescheduling the tutoring session at a different time.

The issue of absenteeism more generally will be considered in greater detail in Chapter 8 and, by Daphne Hampton and Margo Blythman, in Chapter 10.

(b) *Partner incompatibility procedure*

With the best will in the world (which is not always present), some student pairs will fail to get on well enough to enable them to give their attention and energies to the task of learning. In such cases, they need to be able to change their partners. Peer-tutoring schemes need to include arrangements to deal with these occurrences, and all students and lecturers involved need to be aware of the safety-net procedures.

Problems in operation

Evaluation procedures may identify further problems within your scheme. Qualitative feedback from both participating staff and students may shed light on these and suggest modifications for next time. A final word of advice – don't be put off by a shaky first run. Perseverance will pay dividends.

SUMMARY

Information supplied throughout this chapter is summarized in 'How-to-do' advice in Table 5.3.

We shall return to many of the points made above later in the book. For example, Chapter 7 is devoted to the important question of evaluation, and, in Chapter 8, Felder and Brent discuss further issues relating to group composition and the matching of participants. Tutor training and support for tutors are discussed in some detail in the next chapter, Chapter 6.

Table 5.3 'How-to-do' advice

What to do	What it will achieve
Ground your scheme within a theoretical framework.	This will give you the ability to make informed predictions, formulate and test hypotheses.
Define your aims and objectives.	This will help you select an appropriate variety of tutoring.
Persuade your colleagues of the wisdom of your plan. Be prepared to discuss their fears and answer questions.	This will enable you to proceed with your plan and rely on some support from your colleagues.
Keep your design simple. Start with a modest implementation.	You will minimize the complications that are inevitable whenever human beings are involved in any venture.
Identify one person with whom the buck stops. Define roles.	If communication structures and responsibilities are made clear, the chance of ultimate success for your scheme is enhanced.
Provide training in the technique to be used. Train tutors in the art of tutoring.	Trained tutors are more effective than untrained ones. Students who know what is expected of them are more likely to succeed than those who are unclear of how a scheme works or why it is beneficial to them.
Structure the materials that are to be used. Make this relevant to students' needs. Build in interaction between learning pairs.	This increases participation and makes learning active.
Support tutors and mentors for the duration of the scheme.	Regular contact and feedback benefits student tutors (who gain help with problem solving) and also teachers (who can monitor the progress of the scheme).
Test your hypotheses. Evaluate the scheme. Pay particular attention to what went wrong.	This will provide essential information: (a) suggestions for improvements to the scheme next time you carry it out, (b) insights into the processes of learning and (c) useful information with which to persuade students and colleagues to give peer tutoring a try on a future occasion.

Tables 5.1.1 to 5.1.9 Overhead projector slides for introducing peer tutoring to teachers and students (Tables 5.18 and 5.19 are on pp. 144–45).

Table 5.1.1 Introduction to co-operative and paired learning

Is co-operative learning new?
Where does it come from?

- Earliest research out of which co-operative learning was developed goes back to early 1900s.
- All co-operative learning methods are based on social-psychological research and theory, adapted to meet practical requirements of classrooms (Slavin, 1985).
- The roots of peer tutoring: the monitor system (e.g. Andrew Bell and Joseph Lancaster in late eighteenth century) or earlier?

Table 5.1.2 What is co-operative learning?

Basic elements of co-operative learning

1 Clearly perceived positive interdependence.
2 Considerable face-to-face interaction.
3 Clearly perceived individual accountability and personal responsibility to achieve goals.
4 Frequent use of the relevant interpersonal and small group skills.
5 Frequent and regular group processing of current functioning to improve the group's future effectiveness.

(Johnson, Johnson and Smith, 1991)

Table 5.1.3 What is peer tutoring?

Keith Topping's definition (1998):
People from similar social groupings who are not professional teachers helping each other to learn, and learning themselves by teaching.

Peer tutoring is characterized by specific role taking: at any point someone has the job of tutor while the other(s) are in roles as tutee(s).

Table 5.1.4 Research into co-operative learning: improved achievement

Results of a meta-analysis of 122 studies indicated that co-operative learning tends to promote *higher achievement* than competitive and individualistic learning experiences.

Processes that promote higher achievement include:

- high-quality reasoning strategies;
- constructive management of conflict;
- increased time on task;
- more elaborative information processing;
- greater peer regulation and encouragement of efforts to achieve;
- more active mutual involvement in learning;
- beneficial interaction between students of different achievement levels;
- feelings of support and psychological acceptance;
- more positive attitudes towards subject areas;
- greater perceptions of fairness of grading.

(Johnson and Johnson, 1985)

Table 5.1.5 Outcomes other than improved achievement

Co-operative learning has positive effects in a number of other areas such as:

- increased deep and strategic approaches to studying;
- increased internal academic locus of control;
- inter-group relations/inter-group acceptance;
- prosocial behaviour;
- self-esteem/self-concept;
- liking for topic or institution;
- increase in motivation;
- time-on-task;
- attendance.

Table 5.1.6 Benefits of paired learning

Evaluations of peer monitoring/peer teaching/paired learning schemes

1   An experiment in learning in order to teach another found that students who had prepared to teach had **higher scores** than a study-for-self group.

(Bargh and Schul, 1980)

2   Use of co-operative strategy (SCD) facilitated initial learning and subsequent individual learning. **Positive transfer** occurred.

(McDonald, Larson, Dansereau and Spurlin, 1985)

3   Paired and small-group learning students showed a significant **drop in math anxiety** post-study and an **increase in positive attitudes** to themselves as learners of mathematics.

(Koch, 1992)

4   **Completion rates:** traditionally taught students 50 per cent; paired and group learning students 64 per cent.

(Koch, 1992)

Table 5.1.7 Is it better to be tutor or tutee?

Annis designed a study to compare the effects on learning of five combinations of tutoring or being tutored. These were:

- Read only.
- Read to teach but not actually teach.
- Read and teach.
- Taught only.
- Read and were taught.

Results indicated significantly **greater gains** in both content-specific and the generalized cognitive area **for the tutor group** compared with tutees. Moreover, students who prepared to teach and did the teaching outperformed the group who prepared to teach but did not carry it out.

(Annis, 1983a)

6 Helping students become peer tutors

This chapter is designed to help teachers prepare their students for peer tutoring. In the same way that our colleagues may react against change, our students, too, may be reluctant to try a new way of learning. Therefore, we start the chapter by considering some methods of persuading students to give peer tutoring a try. We then look at ways of ensuring that essential training takes place, and a number of training methods and techniques for supporting students are reviewed. We then look very briefly at some guidebooks and training materials. The chapter concludes with a brief review of an evaluation of peer-tutor training.

We shall start the chapter with the question:

'How do I persuade my students to take part in peer tutoring?'

PREPARING STUDENTS FOR PEER TUTORING: THE NEED FOR A ROLE CHANGE

Before we can consider training our students to act as peer tutors, we must attempt to make them ready for learning in a way which is different from the traditional. Many students believe that their task is to assimilate what the teacher says, or what they read in a textbook or extract from the Internet. Some may see their role as passive absorbers of information. Topping (1996b) stated that

> Many students are deeply conservative and have formed ingrained habits of superficial and rote learning. They may lack any spontaneous interest in active and interactive learning, let alone in personal responsibility for their own learning outcomes. Arguably this is largely the result of years of conditioning by the educational system.
>
> (Topping, 1996b: 31)

However, as we have argued, even traditional higher education now aims to change this view and bring about some redefinition of the student's role. For example, if intellectual development, from Perry's (1970) dualist position of right and wrong answers, to relativism and personal commitment, is to occur, by whatever means, a number of changes are necessary. Learners must change their views of themselves, their views of the nature of knowledge and of what it is to learn. Student-centred learning, which aims to facilitate intellectual development, shifts the balance of power from teacher to learner, and responsibility for learning from teacher to student. However, the adjustment required of students accustomed to learning, and teachers used to teaching, in a traditional teacher-centred way, may be difficult, and both parties will need to be convinced of the benefits of such a transition.

Given that we need to persuade our students to try a different way of learning and to begin to see themselves in a different light, we may learn some useful tips on how to achieve these changes by looking to theories of attitude change or persuasion. Any good social psychology textbook will include useful advice, and any ex-student of psychology may remember that persuasion involves 'who says what to whom, for what purpose and with what result' or some variant on this.

Persuasion by communication

Brehm and Kassin (1996) differentiate between '*the central route*' and the '*peripheral route*' to persuasion by communication. The central route is 'the process in which a person learns and thinks carefully about a communication and is influenced by the strength of its arguments', while the peripheral route is 'the process in which a person does not think about a communication and is influenced instead by cues that are peripheral to the message' (Brehm and Kassin, 1996: 378). Both routes are used by politicians seeking election to office. We, the voters, are supplied with information to tempt us to pledge our support. We are also wooed by emotional appeals and catchy slogans. Although we may attempt to persuade our students (or colleagues) by methods associated with the central route, both routes probably come into play in our attempts at influence. However sound our message, it will not be appealing to our audience if it is delivered in ways which intimidate or overwhelm. Neither will it be received with enthusiasm if it is delivered by a poor speaker or by one who appears to be arguing from self-interest. Students are unequivocal in their condemnation of lecturers who are 'boring'. Thus, we need to make our enthusiasm for peer tutoring manifest, and make it clear that the technique has benefits for students.

The importance of information

Initially, students may have little or no knowledge of the benefits of peer tutoring. They do not understand how it works, or know what to expect as participants. It is absolutely necessary, but clearly not sufficient, to instruct students in the new procedures. It is reasonable that they should be made aware of the rationale behind the changes proposed, the benefits that are likely to result from participation and what is expected of both themselves and their teachers. However, some continuing support is also needed. Many new ventures flounder because the initiators think their task is over after implementing the first stage.

Introducing students to peer tutoring

Persuading students to learn in a different way from that involved in the traditional lecture model requires careful preparation. First of all, as has been argued, learners must be made aware of the characteristics of the new method and assured of its benefits. Bossert (1988) argued that introducing a new method or idea to students involves three procedures:

1 providing instructions and instructing students to work in the new way;
2 varying the reward contingencies to support the new technique;
3 constructing tasks that are interdependent.

Bossert's second and third procedures for successful introduction of a new technique relate to two of Johnson and Johnson's (1985) characteristics of co-operative learning: interdependence and co-operative reward structures. These are structural features that require the students to co-operate and reward them for so doing. Co-operative learning can be supported by *co-operative reward structures*. For example, my students involved in group project work are able to 'earn' bonus marks if all members of a group attain a pre-designated, challenging but achievable mark for the individual reflective component of the assignment. Dyads may also benefit from such arrangements. The interdependence of partners engaged in peer tutoring is obvious.

Materials for introducing paired learning to students

Some of the overhead projector slides included in Chapter 5 for staff development use might also be used for introducing paired learning to students (see Tables 5.1.1 to 5.1.8). Comment, questions and discussion should be encouraged throughout an introductory session. Once students have been introduced to the new method, they need help with preparation for their task. Chapter 1 contains tables and How-to-do boxes with descriptions for implementing a variety of peer tutoring techniques. One such table or box is the minimum information students require. Most will benefit from further information. The Napier tutoring-in-schools project log book (Highton, 1999) is a good example of such provision. It supplies students with not only all essential information about the scheme, but also a wealth of material to support their learning. Advice on setting personal goals (Table 6.1) and diary pages to stimulate reflection are included in the log. Instructions to students on how to complete the diary are shown in Table 6.2. Assessment requirements are also made very explicit.

Although Highton's scheme involves undergraduates tutoring school students, much of her structured log may be adapted for wider use.

However, Hawkins (1978) argued that manuals and handouts do not provide sufficient support, as they may be misinterpreted by students. He recommended that additional reading be provided. Highton's (1999) handbook follows this advice, providing references to further reading and guided reading notes for the course textbook, Goodlad (1998).

Table 6.1 Setting personal goals

Setting your goals

In order to get the most from your time in the school you should have a clear idea about what the benefits to you might be. Below is a list of some of the most common things students feel they want to achieve through student tutoring.

1 Read each one and decide whether it applies to you. There is space at the bottom to add in a few of your own. If it does apply to you, tick the box in the *first* column on the right-hand side of the page, *if it doesn't apply to you leave the box empty.*

	Applies to me	Priority (1,2,3, ...)
I want to improve my active-listening skills.		
I'd like to feel part of the school community.		
I want to learn more about children with special needs.		
I would like to develop better verbal communication skills.		
I need to feel more confident in new situations.		
I am interested in building a trust relationship with the pupils.		
I want to learn about 'on your feet'- based decision making.		
I want to make commitment to something and see it through.		
I want to find out how young people react to me as an adult.		
I would like to learn practical skills, e.g. IT skills.		
I would like to find out if I am suited to a career in teaching.		
I want to learn about working as part of a team.		
I would like to learn how to empathize with people.		
I would like the challenge of preparing a task to do with pupils.		
I would like to see how pupils approach the subject I am studying at University.		
I want to give something back to the education system.		
I would like to share my enthusiasm for my subject with other people.		
I want to get to know people from different social backgrounds.		
I want the chance to see how others handle difficult situations.		
If you have other personal goals, please add them in here.		

2 Now go back and read the statements you have ticked, including any you have added. As you are reading ask yourself 'How important is it that I achieve this?'

Fill in the *second* column by putting in a number that corresponds to how badly you want to achieve that goal. Start by marking '1' by the most important and working through the statements you have ticked.

3 List the three goals you have identified as your top priorities

i.

ii.

iii.

4 How do you hope to achieve these goals?

(Highton, 1999)

Table 6.2 Instructions for completing diary sheets

Completing your diary sheets

This log is a record of the work you did, but it is also a record of your reflective process. When you are writing your log you should think about using phrases which show that you have really thought about what happened. Some phrases you might use are:

I realized....   I decided....   I made a connection between....   the consequence of this was ....

considering alternative outcomes....   intended effects....   unintended effects ....   I planned....

I struggled....   making a difference....   looking back, I could have....   next time I will....

I regret ....   I wish ....   I learned from this that ....   It occurred to me that .... I managed ....

I considered ....   I felt ....   I experimented....

and words like: *evaluating, purpose, outcomes, aims, response, goals, meaning, reactions, benefits, challenge, motivation, evidence.*

Work done today: Should be a brief account of the important features of the lesson(s). There should not be lengthy descriptions of everything which took place but should focus particularly on what you did, what contribution *you* made to the lesson and how *you* worked with the pupils.

Successful outcomes: Might refer to work done by a particular pupil, groups of pupils or the whole class; or could be progress in the interaction between you and the pupils; or an improved working relationship with the teacher. A number of student tutors in the past have noted that 'success' may be something relatively simple like a previously quiet pupil being encouraged to talk more openly or a less confident pupil completing a piece of work that they felt would be beyond them.

Areas to improve/difficulties encountered: Problems and difficulties come in all shapes and sizes; the significance of recording them is so that you can try to overcome them, perhaps in subsequent sessions in the school. If you do not feel you are encountering any particular problems, use this space to concentrate on areas in which you feel you could improve.

Action on difficulties: You should analyse the situation and explain why a difficulty may have arisen and how it can be overcome. There should be some justification for the course of action you intend to take and evidence in later log sheets that the action has been carried out.

Forward planning: Should provide an indication of what you intend to do in subsequent lessons to improve your contribution to the class, generally after discussion with the teacher. For example, this could be a reminder of materials to take to the next week's lesson or ideas for new approaches to try with pupils, possibly with some explanation as to the reasoning behind your planning. You should also indicate on subsequent log sheets what happened when you implemented this plan. Remember to keep referring back to your log sheets from weeks before.

Personal qualities: Over the tutoring period you should try to provide examples which indicate that you were able to use your initiative to make the most of a situation and have demonstrated such skills as adaptability, creativity, decision making, negotiation, prioritizing, responsibility and teamwork. You should refer back to the skills section at the beginning of the log. Simply listing the skills will not be enough, you must give examples of how you used the skills and whether you found this enjoyable or challenging.

Examples:

'*creativity: I used an analogy of water in a hosepipe to explain the concept of electrical resistance. It was quite a challenge to think of a way to explain it that the kids would understand.*'

'*evaluation: we gave the pupils a questionnaire we had devised to see what they thought of student tutors. I struggled to find a way to word the questions so that there was no ambiguity. The responses we got back were very positive.*'

'*responsibility: I assisted on a school excursion to the Royal Mile. I had six children to look after in the midst of all the traffic and the crowds. This was a very daunting responsibility and I was worried that I might do something wrong but everything went well and the teacher said afterwards that I handled everything okay.*'

Your log entries do not have to fit exactly in the space provided. You should insert pages to give yourself more space as required.

(Highton, 1999)

TUTOR TRAINING

Training is one of the key ways in which students may be helped to become good peer tutors. Tutoring can be seen to derive from the task of the classroom teacher or lecturer, and may be mistaken for a form of teaching. However, it is important to remember that tutoring differs from teaching, in that tutors are typically less well-qualified and less experienced than teachers. This difference is particularly marked in the context of peer tutoring, and participants need to undergo some training before they may be able to act effectively.

Ellson (1976) stressed the importance of taking into consideration three groups of factors, each of which have implications for the nature of tutoring. These are:

- structural factors (the abilities of students);
- affective factors (including emotional, attitudinal and motivational factors);
- learning or environmental factors.

Sherwood (1982) argued that tutors need training in all three areas and that training in both task and process domains must be seen as equally important.

Tutor training can emphasize either or both of the two elements of the tutor's role (i.e. tutor and peer), and Garrett (1982), quoting Bruffee, raises a potential problem in this context:

> to have a strong effect on tutees, tutors have to be fairly well-trained ... yet if they're too well-trained ... tutees don't perceive them as peers but as little teachers, and the collaborative effect of peers working together is lost.
>
> (Garrett, 1982: 94)

Garrett argued that training programmes that emphasize the need for expertise can lead to tutor-role dominance (tutors as mini-teachers), whereas those which emphasize the 'responsive' element in peer tutoring more readily lead to peer-role dominance. The responsive element in peer tutoring is that which requires tutors to respond to psychological and social needs of tutees (often at the expense of task-based issues). It is, however, possible to strike a balance between the two elements and Garrett devised a training protocol designed to help tutors achieve this balance. We shall return to this below.

There is widespread agreement that tutor training is a necessary component of a successful peer-tutoring scheme. There is also agreement about what constitutes an appropriate balance of approaches to tutoring. However, there is little consensus in answers to questions such as, 'Do student tutors require more training in the content of their tutoring session or in the techniques of delivering it?'

What should be the balance between the technical, educational, social, structural and affective aspects of the delivery? Although training in all aspects is necessary, the balance will vary from situation to situation. Competent cross-level tutors, chosen for their mastery of content, may require greater emphasis on delivery aspects than those lacking in subject-content knowledge, who may require a more balanced training. The better we know our students and the clearer our aims and objectives, the easier it will be for us to answer these questions. The following questions for reflection and discussion may be put to trainee tutors during training as well as to teachers in staff-development activities.

Questions for reflection

In which area do student tutors need most help: content or delivery?
What is an appropriate balance between the different aspects of the delivery?

WAYS OF ENSURING THAT TRAINING HAPPENS

However good one's training programme, it is of no value unless potential student tutors attend training sessions and participate in them.

Payment

One way in which students may be encouraged to spend their time training to be a tutor is to pay them for it (e.g. Arfken, 1982; Randels, Carse and Lease, 1992). This solution is not common outside the United States, and Topping (1996a) observed that, in the UK, accreditation is seen as a more acceptable form of extrinsic reward than payment of tutors.

Accreditation: credit-bearing training courses

In the UK, at the University of Newcastle, the University of Northumbria at Newcastle and at my own university, Napier, for example, students may gain credit for training for and participating in student tutoring-in-schools schemes (see Chapter 1, and contributions by Melissa Highton and Jim Wood to Chapter 10). At present, tutors, but not tutees, have the opportunity to gain credit for peer tutoring, and Topping (1996b) reasoned that, in same-level schemes, as both tutors *and* tutees stand to gain from the practice, maybe both should be eligible for the award of credit. Accreditation is also used in the USA (e.g. Bruffee, 1980; Wyatt and Medway, 1984; O'Donnell, Dansereau, Rocklin, Hythecker, Lambiotte, Larson and Young, 1985). In a review of 26 Writing Fellow programs, Soven (1993) reported that most schools in the USA required tutors to enrol in a credit-bearing course that combined theory and practice.

Are there disadvantages to rewarding students for peer tutoring?

Reward for tutoring, whatever its form, raises issues about the relative values of *intrinsic and extrinsic rewards*. It can be argued that increasing the extrinsic motivation of tutors by means of providing them with a reward, in the form of either money or academic credit, may detract from the intrinsic satisfaction they derive from the experience. For example, Fresko (1988) reported results of a questionnaire survey of Israeli college students acting as tutors who were about to receive a tuition rebate for tutoring disadvantaged elementary-school children as part of the PERACH project. Tutors were presented with a list of five possible motives for tutoring, two representing intrinsic, and three extrinsic, motivation. Results of the analysis of attitudinal data indicated that tutors who listed at least one intrinsic motive felt more positive about their tutoring experiences, and reported greater tutee improvement than other tutors. Extrinsically motivated tutors, on the other hand, were more critical of their tutoring experiences and expressed less satisfaction than the intrinsic group. Fresko advocated giving serious thought to the question of tutor motivation.

TRAINING METHODS AND TECHNIQUES AVAILABLE

It should be noted that much that has been written about tutor training to date derives from the training of tutors for work in a writing centre, often in the United States (e.g. Hawkins, 1982). However, there are plentiful suggestions in the literature that have more general applicability. We shall now look at some strategies and techniques.

There are three key *stages of training*:

- the preparatory phase;
- the period during which tutoring is taking place;
- the post-tutoring phase.

The great majority of training takes place in the context of a *workshop*. These workshops vary in terms of length, timing and content. Supervision arrangements also vary from weekly to 'periodic' meetings. Although workshops tend to be concentrated at the beginning of a peer-tutoring scheme, they may also take place during tutoring and after tutoring has finished. Training sessions may often seem to be time consuming and lengthy. However, the more time you can spare for tutor training, the greater the likelihood of successful peer tutoring.

Initial preparation for tutoring

There are a number of techniques that may be used to help prepare students for tutoring before they commence formal training. We shall look at two activities which help students begin to think about how they might act as tutors. These are self-rating of tutoring skills and tutoring style assessment.

Tutoring skills assessment

Hawkins (1982) identified two key tutoring skills: listening and explaining. He developed a checklist of tutoring skills to enable students to rate themselves on these two skills before tutoring. This checklist is published in Harris (1982). Trainee tutors are invited to assess their own levels of usage of skills on a three-point scale ('Infrequently', 'Sometimes', 'Most of the time').

Examples of statements relating to *listening skills* are:

> I avoid interrupting, even for purposes of clarification, until a student has completed his/her message.

> To check my understanding of what the student has said, I briefly paraphrase the tutee's idea(s) in my own words.

(Harris, 1982: 286)

Listening skills are defined widely to encompass questioning skills. Techniques to stimulate thinking, and reveal tutee strengths and weaknesses, include the use of relatively few questions that are 'brief but specific'. Techniques also include waiting a while between asking a question and saying something to break a silence, and balancing open and closed questions.

Examples of statements relating to *explaining skills* are:

> In addition to giving my own examples, I also ask students to provide examples after they have understood my explanation.

> I am cautious about giving prescriptive advice based on my own experiences because I am aware that my students' background may be considerably different from mine.

(Harris, 1982: 287)

Some statements draw attention to individual differences, while others refer to potential personal bias of the tutor.

> I delay my correction of a 'wrong answer' so that I can first question my own preconceptions ...

(Harris, 1982: 288)

As the desired response is usually clear from the structure of the checklist, in that the 'Infrequently' response is never an appropriate one for a sensitive skilful tutor, the checklist seems particularly useful for individual, personal use.

Tutoring style assessment

Another useful self-assessment instrument for use by potential peer tutors is Hawkins' (1982) tutoring style typology. It may be helpful to students who are planning to train as peer tutors to heighten their awareness of their individual tutoring style. Hawkins' tutoring typology was designed to encourage students to do this. Ten styles are included in his typology:

- Expert.
- Guide.
- Scholar.
- Mentor.
- Academic adjunct.
- Medic.
- Counsellor.
- Psychologist.
- Referee.
- Advocate.

Each label carries a short description. For example, 'Guide' is defined as:

> I am a good listener and I ask many questions. I want my students to learn how to think for themselves, but I also need to know what they're thinking if I'm to help them.
>
> (Harris, 1982: 289)

'Medic' is described as:

> I don't want to see anyone fail, and I do everything in my power, short of doing the person's work, to get someone through a course. All of my tutees deserve as much of my energy, knowledge, and time as I can give them.
>
> (Harris, 1982: 290)

'Advocate' carries the following description:

> I am on the student's side, and if I have to disagree with the instructor I will. Sometimes the problem is in the course, not the student.
>
> (Harris, 1982: 290)

During preparations for tutoring, trainees are reminded that 'there is no right or wrong in teaching, but rather a variety of methods and approaches which can be adapted to each learning situation' (Harris, 1982: 289). A number of stages are involved:

1   Tutors are advised to think of a particular student tutee and rate themselves using the typology.
2   They are then asked to repeat this focusing on a different student in a different situation.
3   They then compare their scores on the two occasions and note changes in their style.

Hawkins' typology might also be used as the starting point for discussion of the variety of ways of tutoring. It may also be used to attempt to relate particular tutor or tutee profiles to the effectiveness of tutoring outcomes, though I have not yet found an example of this type of use in the literature. Tutors might be asked to complete the typology after particularly successful or unsuccessful tutoring sessions, then compare the two sets of ratings and attempt to identify any patterns. Such an activity might be useful in a post-tutoring debriefing and reflection session.

Tutor roles and approaches to tutoring

Other researchers and practitioners have also categorized tutoring behaviour. Brannon (1982) identified approaches to tutoring which closely resemble Garrett's (1982) categories. Brannon's three approaches are:

1   the sociable approach;
2   the directive approach;
3   the balanced approach.

In the *sociable approach*, the tutor regards camaraderie or friendship between tutor and tutee as desirable. However, although the tutor must not be hostile towards the tutee, an over-friendly approach may become a problem for learning within the relationship. The *directive approach*, too, can hinder learning as the tutor who adopts it may do too much for tutees and not allow them to discover things for themselves, while in a *balanced approach*, tutors are both sociable and task-centred. They are caring and supportive, yet allow students to discover their own errors. The balanced approach integrates qualities of effective communication, and Brannon, like Garrett, rates it as the most effective style.

However, Brannon also pointed out that other approaches may be valid in certain circumstances, such as where building self-confidence in the tutee is a desired outcome of the relationship or when the pair are working to very tight deadlines.

Brannon also identified four basic tutor roles:

1   facilitator;
2   supporter;
3   leader;
4   resister.

The role of *facilitator* is seen as an appropriate one which is helpful to the tutee as tutors focus on the work in hand. The role of *supporter* of tutee learning, too, is beneficial to tutees. The roles of *leader* and *resister*, however, are usually dysfunctional as they can involve tutors pressurizing the tutee. Brannon's classification of tutor roles has much in common with Hawkins' typology and a comparison of the two might stimulate useful discussion during tutor training.

WORKSHOPS TO SUPPORT STUDENTS BEFORE AND DURING TUTORING

Pre-tutoring training

Pre-tutoring training features in many peer-tutoring schemes (e.g. Hawkins, 1978; Glassman, 1982; Arfken, 1982; Groccia and Miller, 1996). In Arkfen's study, in the pre-tutoring sessions stress was placed on:

- the need for punctuality and reliability;
- methods for establishing a working relationship with tutees (listening and responding with probing questions);
- ways to handle problems in tutee co-operation.

In addition, advice was given on administration and assessment. In later training sessions, tutors brought specific questions for discussion.

We shall now look at some examples of workshop activities.

Workshop activities

Student tutors may be supported during tutoring in a variety of ways, and regular workshop meetings are common. Once again, much of what we know about these activities comes from Writing Lab settings. Activities which take place at meetings for tutors, which take place during tutoring, are very similar to those used in pre-tutoring situations. Commonly occurring activities include role play and simulations and writing and critiquing. Because of this overlap, I shall focus the discussion on activities irrespective of whether they take place in pre-tutoring or during-tutoring settings.

Role play and simulations

Sherwood (1982) suggested several techniques to help tutors learn to encourage tutee learning, all of which might be practised by means of role playing. For example, tutors may be taught that they should verify whether or not learning has taken place by asking a clarification question and by reviewing the concept if necessary. Other techniques are elaboration and closure. The tutor should always ask the tutee to elaborate on an ambiguous answer. Closing questions to check tutee's understanding are also recommended. Use of the tutee's name is recommended.

> e.g. Now would you summarize what I've just said, X?
>
> Do you understand how to ... , Y?

Several training regimes make use of the role-play technique (e.g. Garrett, 1982; Randels *et al.*, 1992).

Garrett (1982) advocated the use of role tutor- or peer-role playing and peer-criticism activities in tutor training to help tutors avoid adopting teaching styles which lead to either extreme tutor- or peer-role dominance. Garrett's mock-tutoring session using role play to help tutors achieve balance between 'directed-ness' and 'responsiveness' is summarized in Table 6.3.

Students in the role of tutee are required to analyse the performance of the peer playing the tutor in terms of both 'Directedness' (tutor-role dominance) and 'Responsiveness' (peer-role dominance). Features associated with 'Directedness' are diagnosing problems, developing tutoring strategies and focusing the tutoring sessions with well-timed, well-phrased questions. 'Responsiveness', on the other hand, involves developing flexibility in tutoring techniques to meet the tutee's needs, responding to the tutee's cues and becoming sensitive to the attitudes of the tutee.

Mann has argued that such a role-taking experience can 'facilitate the transformation of adolescent thinking away from the egocentric perspective of childhood toward a more decentred perspective that recognises multiple points of view and that is more reflective' (Mann, 1994: 164).

Modelling experienced-tutor behaviour

Some training schemes provide opportunities for trainees to model experienced-tutor behaviour. An example of this was reported by Glassman (1982). After initial preparation, new tutors were paired with experienced tutors for team tutoring. At first, the new tutor observed the experienced tutor during tutorials and, only later, began to participate. All tutors were required to attend student workshop sessions.

Another popular workshop activity involves writing and critiquing.

Writing and critiquing

Very many students who act as tutors in writing laboratories use critiquing as both a training and learning activity. A study by McGroarty and Zhu (1997) reported the effects of training for peer revision in college freshman English composition classes. Peer revision, as we saw in Chapter 1, is a learning technique in which students work in pairs or small groups to provide feedback on each other's writing. McGroarty and Zhu attempted to estimate the importance of preparing students for this task. Volunteers participated in training conferences at which they practised the skills necessary to carry out effective peer revision activities working in groups. Analysis of trained student discourse during peer revision was compared with that of untrained groups, and the trained groups were found to have engaged in 'more extended and livelier interactions than those in the control group' (McGroarty and Zhu, 1997: 25). However, peer revision did not significantly improve grades awarded for writing.

Table 6.3 A training protocol

A training protocol: a practice tutoring session using role play to help tutors achieve a balance between directive and responsive styles

1 Features associated with directive and responsive styles are discussed

- *Features associated with Directedness:*

    Diagnosing (writing) problems.

    Developing tutoring strategies.

    Focusing the tutoring sessions with well-timed, well-phrased questions.

- *Features associated with Responsiveness:*

    Responding to tutee's oral and written cues.

    Developing flexibility in tutoring techniques to meet tutee's needs.

    Becoming sensitive to tutee's attitudes (to task and tutoring) (Garrett, 1982).

2 Role play

Student trainee tutors work in triads, one playing the role of tutor, one the tutee and the third an observer-commentator. They focus on a particular problem concerning either the task or attitude of tutee. The session lasts about 30 minutes. Participants then switch roles and repeat the exercise twice, after which all will have experienced all roles.

(Total time = 90 mins.)

3 Peer criticism follows: analysis sheets are completed from the perspectives of the different roles

First, **the tutee is asked to analyse the tutor** in terms of

- diagnosis of problems;
- clarity of purpose;
- whether she/he involved the tutee in activities;
- whether she/he used the tutee's (writing) strengths to identify and explain weaknesses;
- whether she/he was sensitive to cues revealing attitudes and ideas;
- whether she/he encouraged the tutee to take notes of main points;
- whether the session had an organized conclusion.

4 Tutors then respond in writing to tutee analyses

5 Observer commentators comment on both and add their own analysis of the session

6 Oral exchange of views within the triad takes place, followed by

7 Class discussion

Critical reflection

Critical reflection is regarded as being of major importance in tutor training by authors of a collection of six essays on tutoring writing (Okawa, Fox, Chang, Windsor, Bella Chavez and Hayes, 1991). In this collection, Okawa sees posing questions as a key 'tool' for critical reflection. Questions may concern many aspects of peer tutoring: questions about writing issues, tutoring methods, learning theories and so on.

Tutoring logs

Many students are now required to complete learning logs in a variety of educational contexts, including peer tutoring. For example, Highton (1999) supplies her student tutors with prompts to stimulate individual reflection throughout their tutoring log, as we saw above.

In same-level peer tutoring, tutees as well as tutors benefit from keeping a learning log to aid reflection and record meetings. An example of a simple format suitable for use by both tutors and tutees is included in Table 6.4.

Tutor–tutee pairs should work together to complete the last section, the agreed action plan. Tutors and tutees who have established a comfortable and trusting relationship might also wish to compare notes on other sections. However, it is recommended that, initially, sections other than the last be completed individually.

Reviewing key books and materials

Some training schemes require participants to review key texts or other materials (e.g. Glassman, 1982). At Glassman's weekly tutors' meetings, after completing their reviews, participants wrote a brief paper which was then critiqued in small groups.

Letters and informal records

Soldner (1992, in De Stephano, Miller, Clegg, Vanderhoof and Soldner, 1992) supported her tutors by sending them weekly letters which included information on the following:

- what transpired in the class attended by tutees;
- the week's assignment;
- how to evaluate the assignment;
- plans for the weeks ahead.

Tutors kept these letters in chronological order along with their anecdotal notes which were submitted to the instructor every two to three weeks. The writing of anecdotal notes was aided by an *'anecdotal record sheet'*, supplied by the lecturer, one of which had to be completed after each tutoring session. These sheets

Table 6.4 Evaluation form for tutors and tutees

PEER TUTORING PROGRESS REPORT: TUTOR/TUTEE

Date ....

Aims and objectives of the session

1 ....

2 ....

3 ....

4 ....

Description of activities used during the session (tutors only)

....

....

....

....

Evaluation of the session   (What worked? What didn't? Why?
                                 Were aims/objectives met?)

....

....

....

....

....

Problems needing attention

(a) Concerning the work

1 ....

2 ....

(b) Concerning the interaction between us

1 ....

2 ....

What can I (the tutor/tutee) do?

....

....

What can the tutee/tutor do?

....

....

Plan of action agreed by tutor and tutee

....

....

....

....

....

contained space for recording the date, details of the assignment of the week and tutors' comments on tutees' performance, motivation, interests or needs. Tutors were also encouraged to record their plans for future individual instruction. At the bottom of each form was space for comments from the instructor. All records were open to students as well as to staff. In addition, Soldner further supported her tutors by means of a monthly group meeting at which information about what had and had not worked was exchanged, advice given and concerns aired.

MANAGING CONFLICT

There is wide agreement that conflict can and should be managed (e.g. Healy, 1991). A number of strategies have been suggested to help in this endeavour.

Coping strategies

Hall (1972) identified *three types of coping strategy* from a survey of role conflict in college-educated married women. These strategies may suggest some ways of helping tutors deal with conflict in the context of peer tutoring. Hall's three types of strategy encompassed sixteen individual strategies:

Type I coping

This type of coping was achieved through structural role redefinition (a person is permitted to change the external reality of the role demands) and involved six strategies.

a   Eliminating role activities, but not entire roles.
b   Role support from outside the role set.
c   Role support from inside the role set.
d   Problem solving with role senders.
e   Role integration.
f   Changing the societal definition of one's role.

Type II coping

This type was achieved through personal role redefinition (the person changes her/ his perceptions of the conflict) and contained seven strategies.

a   Establishing priorities.
b   Partitioning and separating roles.
c   Overlooking role demands.
d   Changing attitudes towards roles.
e   Eliminating roles.
f   Rotating attention among roles.
g   Developing self and own interests.

Type III coping

This type was achieved through reactive role behaviour (an intensification of attempts to cope with the conflict) and involves three coping strategies.

a   Planning, scheduling and organizing (but making no change in the way time is managed).
b   No conscious strategy.
c   Working harder.

Hall's pilot study suggested that satisfaction is positively related to Type I strategies. However, this correlation failed to reach significance in the main study, and Hall concluded that success in *any* kind of coping may be more strongly related to satisfaction than the particular strategy employed.

Hall's (1972) categories may be applied to tutor training to help tutors and tutees cope with role conflict in at least two ways:

1   Extracts from Hall's paper might be used as a study and discussion document in training sessions either before or during tutoring.
2   Secondly, tutor and tutee learning logs might be structured to focus on aspects of role conflict and include prompts to action and reflection about possible ways of coping with it.

Examples of Types I and II coping should be included. Two of these coping types are not suitable for inclusion in either a training session or a reflective log, however (Type I (f): *Changing the societal definition of one's role* and Type II (e): *Eliminating roles*). Students should be advised to avoid Type III coping strategies wherever possible as these are likely to be very energy-intensive and, ultimately, to give rise to intensified levels of stress and strain. It is probably better for very busy people to work smarter rather than harder.

Some examples of training activities and learning log prompts to reflection using Hall's coping strategies are shown in Tables 6.5.1 and 6.5.2.

Confrontation

Sometimes *confrontation* is necessary in order to deal with conflict and Adams and Hamm (1996) described some ways of *helping students develop confrontation skills* for use in such cases. They made nine suggestions:

1   Describe behaviour. Do not evaluate, label, accuse or insult.
2   Define the conflict as a mutual problem. The conflict is not a win–lose situation. Aim for a win–win situation.
3   Use 'I' statements.
4   Communicate what you feel as well as what you think.
5   Be critical of ideas not people. Affirm the competence of the other.
6   Give everyone a chance to be heard.

Table 6.5.1. Examples of tutor-training activities and learning-log prompts using Hall's Type I coping strategies

---

Strategies involving action

Type I (a) coping: *Eliminating role activities, but not entire roles*

> Prompt to reflection: 'If tutees are pushing you to do more for them than was agreed, what should you do?'

Type I (b) coping: *Role support from outside the role set*

> Prompt to action/reflection: 'Discuss any problems you have with the role of tutor with someone from within the university (e.g. peer tutoring co-ordinator). What does she/he suggest?'

Type I (c) coping: *Role support from inside the role set*

> Prompt to action/reflection: 'Discuss your role as tutor with other tutors. What do they suggest?'

Type I (d) coping: *Problem solving with role senders* and Type I (e): *Role integration*

> Prompt to action: 'At your next meeting with your tutee, set aside some time to discuss your two roles. Before starting the discussion, both of you should write down what you think being a tutor involves in terms of responsibilities or behaviour. Now both repeat this exercise for the role of tutee. Compare your lists and spend some time discussing areas of disagreement. Try to agree on two job descriptions before ending the meeting.'

> This activity may also be used as the basis of a role-playing exercise.

> A successful outcome will lead to the redesigned roles necessary for Hall's role-integration strategy.

---

7   Follow the guidelines for rational argument.
8   Make sure there is enough time for discussion.
9   Take the other person's perspective.

(Adams and Hamm, 1996: 26)

Student tutors should be encouraged to implement these suggestions in their dealings with tutees. Other behaviours with the potential to aid conflict resolution are *negotiation* and *active listening*. All these behaviours might be practised during role play activities. Alternatively, trigger video clips illustrating 'real-life' examples of situations where there is conflict or confrontation might be used to stimulate discussion.

Coping with disruptive tutee behaviour

As we saw in Chapters 3 and 4, tutees, too, may suffer from role conflict. Roberts (1994) described seven disruptive styles. We shall now consider each one in turn,

Table 6.5.2 Examples of tutor-training activities and learning-log prompts using Hall's Type II coping strategies

---

Strategies involving changes in personal perceptions and attitudes

Type II (a) coping: *Establishing priorities*

> Prompt to reflection: Include a time management exercise in the tutor log.
>
> 'Write down all the tasks and responsibilities you have as tutor. Now try to prioritize them and rank them in order of importance.'

Type II (b) coping: *Partitioning and separating roles* and Type II (f) coping: *Rotating attention among roles*

> Prompt to reflection: 'What are the *defining characteristics* of the different roles you occupy (e.g. tutor; peer group member; friend; flat mate; spouse; parent; others)? Make a list for each role.
>
> Think about how the emphasis on different roles might change during a day on which you are involved in peer tutoring. Complete the chart below, writing in the predominant role for each period.'

Time period	Breakfast time	Mid morning	Late morning	Lunch time	Early afternoon	Late afternoon	Early evening	Late evening
Predominant role								

Type II (c) coping: *Overlooking role demands*

> Prompt to reflection: 'Are there any aspects of your role as tutor or tutee that you have been neglecting? What have been the consequences of this? What might be the consequences?'

Type II (d) coping: *Changing attitudes toward roles*

> Prompt to action/reflection: 'Repeat the exercise listed under type II (b) (above) after a period of time has passed. Compare your responses on the two occasions, looking for examples of change. What might have caused you to change? Is the change for the better, on the whole?'

Type II (g) coping: *Developing self and own interests*

> Prompt to reflection: 'Which aspect of your role gives you most satisfaction? How might you develop this aspect?'

adapting Roberts' advice to the context of student–student interactions. It may be necessary for teachers to intervene to support student tutors.

- Coping with blocking

The best approach here is to determine what the student *does* know and use this as the starting point to new learning. Roberts also recommended that simple steps be used and that success be reinforced consistently. Teachers may assist here by structuring the tutoring materials supplied to student tutors appropriately. Tutor training might provide tutors with some practice in identifying student problems and levels of knowledge and understanding and in reinforcing tutee learning.

- Coping with confusion (a variation of blocking)

Roberts emphasized the need for structure and order as a remedy for this behaviour. As in the context of blocking behaviour, confusion may be reduced by the use of well-structured tutoring materials and well-ordered tutoring sessions.

- Coping with miracle seeking

In order to combat student lack of specificity, a feature of miracle seeking, Roberts urged that the teacher should continually focus on the specific task in hand, involving the student with questions and problems. The student tutor, too, might be trained to behave in this way in the face of tutee miracle seeking. The teacher can also help by stressing the importance of active participation in the learning process.

- Coping with over-enthusiasm (a variation of miracle seeking)

Roberts recommends similar measures to those used to combat miracle seeking as a means of dealing with over-enthusiasm.

- Coping with resisting

Student resistance may be reduced by teachers presenting a well-planned introduction to the peer-learning activity. Roberts recommends the use of the first and second sessions to build up a relationship between tutor and tutee, and to establish the credibility of the technique. This may be done by a short presentation outlining the benefits of the scheme. Student resistance later in the scheme should be addressed by providing students with opportunities to 'ventilate'. This job is probably more appropriately undertaken by the teacher. In the context of peer tutoring, a well-designed safety net will provide such opportunities.

- Coping with passivity (a variation of resisting)

Passivity may be more a feature of the teacher–student relationship than of the student–student one. However, Roberts' advice to teachers might also help peer tutors. Use as many 'mobilizing techniques' (Roberts, 1994: 26) as possible: questions, problems, mini-tasks and reinforce all activities and successes. Tutor training should include activities to help tutors in this respect.

- Coping with evasion

Roberts suggests that the evading students be asked in a non-threatening way why they are attending the class and what they hope to gain from attendance. She suggests a question for the evading student: 'My biggest concern is your success in this class; how, specifically, can I help you with that?' This type of dysfunctional behaviour is very difficult for an experienced teacher to handle, let alone an inexperienced peer tutor, and the student tutor should refer such a problem to the scheme's organizer for action, or the tutee should be encouraged to self-refer. However, it is perhaps more likely that this type of behaviour would translate into absenteeism in the context of higher education. In either case, once again, safety-net procedures should be made known to both tutors and tutees.

AFTER THE TUTORING: STIMULATING REFLECTION

Goodlad and Hughes (1992) described an interesting way of stimulating reflection in their undergraduate tutors. Once the tutoring had been completed, students were required to write an analytic report on some aspect of their tutoring. To start them on this process, they were asked to think about the tutoring they had completed and to say the first word or phrase that sprang to mind. Goodlad and Hughes call this the 'Gestalt Fix'. 'Typically the words the students utter are: "noise"; "enthusiasm"; "chaos"; "satisfaction"; "bad discipline"; "friendly"; "mixed ability"; "teachers under siege"; "frustration"; and so forth. Our response to such suggestions is: "Fine, you have the beginnings of an essay!"' (Goodlad and Hughes, 1992: 48).

The authors argued that this strategy of enabling tutors to identify their concerns, and teachers to react to them, gives students the opportunity for 'academic engagement' with their experiences.

A more usual strategy for aiding reflection on completion of tutoring is to return to the *learning outcomes* identified at the start of the exercise and ask students to evaluate the extent to which each has been achieved.

HANDBOOKS, GUIDEBOOKS AND OTHER TRAINING MATERIALS

Glassman (1982) prepared a series of self-study materials which were then developed into a handbook as a *distance learning strategy* for training of writing tutors where there were no funds with which to pay them. This document included information about the philosophy of the programme, tutoring objectives, notes on professionalism and commitment, policies and procedures, methods and materials, notes on study skills and information about tutoring handicapped students and those whose first language was not English. Tutors were supplied with the handbook and self-paced individual activities to brush up their grammar, acquaint them with materials available and give them practice in commenting on sample essays.

There are several other peer-tutoring handbooks and guides available, though most have a focus other than peer tutoring in higher education. Harris (1982), for example, is a collection of essays written by writing laboratory directors from a variety of High Schools, Colleges and Universities in the USA, including Glassman (above). Other authors whose contributions are useful more generally are Arfken (1982), Garrett (1982) and Sherwood (1982). The focus of this collection is the supporting of tutoring for writing improvement.

Slaughter, Blaukopf and Toohy's (1991) guidebook, on the other hand, is designed to help tutoring for reading improvement. Topping's (1988) *Peer tutoring handbook* has a more general focus, but is targeted at peer tutoring in pre-tertiary settings. However, a more recent paper (Topping, 1996b) contains advice relating to peer tutoring in further and higher education.

EFFECTIVENESS OF TUTOR-TRAINING PROGRAMMES: EVALUATION STUDIES

As we shall see in the next chapter, evaluation may contain qualitative or quantitative elements. It may be formal or informal, using questionnaires designed for the purpose, pre-existing checklists or questionnaires, reflective learning logs or self-evaluation measures. In the context of peer tutoring, it can involve students, teachers and co-ordinators. Some study designs involve a comparison of pre- and post-measures, while others compare outcomes for an experimental group with those of a matched control. Other studies use several measures and compare results of these. Quantitative evaluations involve statistical analysis of data. As Soven (1993) has pointed out, the purpose of evaluation is to provide immediate feedback to student tutors, teachers and co-ordinators, to boost tutor confidence and provide evidence to administrators of the success of programmes.

Not all training schemes are evaluated, and some evaluations may not be reported in the literature. Sometimes, evaluation of training forms a part of evaluation of the scheme as a whole, while at other times it is for personal use. For example, training evaluation may be included as a small part of tutor reflective learning logs. Those schemes which report evaluation of training procedures seem to conclude that training is beneficial to students (e.g. Mann, 1994; Sobral, 1997, 1998).

SUMMARY

Table 6.6 shows a five-session plan for preparing students for peer tutoring. It is appreciated that this involves a considerable investment of time, but, as with many things, the quality of the outcome is likely to reflect the extent of the investment.

If you do not have sufficient time to complete all sessions, a condensed programme may be constituted from session 1 (plus a brief inclusion of questions from session 2), session 3 or 4 and session 5. If you have longer time at your disposal, you might want to consider designing a self-standing training module similar to that described by Sobral (1997, 1998).

In the next chapter we shall look more closely at evaluation.

Table 6.6 A plan for pre-tutoring training

PRE-TUTORING TRAINING

Session 1. Introductory meeting: lecture on background, theory, aims and objectives

- Write brief notes on the lecture, listing the aims and objectives very clearly (2 sides A4 max.).
- What was the most important/surprising/useful thing you learned at this meeting?
- What questions about peer tutoring would you now like to be answered? List at least 3.

Session 2. Follow up Q and A meeting

- Trainee tutors should bring lists of the 3 most pressing questions they wish to discuss to this meeting.
- Group question-and-answer sessions take place, based on the questions identified.
- Make a record of these discussions in your log.

Session 3. Trigger video discussions: problems in tutoring

- Write a brief report of this activity, identifying which situations portrayed you feel more confident about and which you would like more help with.

Session 4. Role-play sessions based on problems requiring further exploration

- All students will take an active part in this session which will conclude with a debriefing exercise, during which the following questions will be considered:
  1 What did it feel like to be 'your' character?
  2 (How) did this help you understand the problem?
  3 (How) did this help you understand the other person?
  4 If you found yourself in the same situation, would you do anything differently? If so, what would this be?
- Write a brief reflective report (1 side A4) on the role-play session.
- Read through the materials required in your first tutoring session and think about how you are going to tackle it.

Session 5. Evaluation of training and preparation for tutoring

- Students should complete a simple evaluation of the training they have received. This might take the form of completing simple sentence stems:
  1 What did you find most/least helpful about the training you have undergone?
  2 What would you like to see included in future training?
- Students then work on preparing action plans.

  Work with a partner on the preparation of your first tutoring session plan. Compare your plans with those of other tutors. Modify your plan if you feel this would be beneficial.
- Include your plan in your log.

---

7 Evaluation of peer-tutoring schemes

WHY IS EVALUATION IMPORTANT?

Most academics will be keen to know if peer tutoring has achieved what it set out to achieve. In other words, they wish to know the results of study evaluations. Positive evaluative data may prove very useful in a number of ways. Beneficial outcomes may prove invaluable in persuading colleagues and students to try peer tutoring, as we have seen in previous chapters. They may also be useful in helping you secure funding for your scheme. As Soven indicates, 'When budget time rolls around again, no argument may be more compelling than data gathered during the evaluation process' (Soven, 1993: 66). Evaluations may indicate problems as well as successes, and it is extremely useful to learn what is *not* working in your scheme. Modifications may be implemented to ensure more positive outcomes in future.

Thus, we might expect that all schemes will be evaluated as a matter of course. Unfortunately, this is not the case. Moreover, Whitman (1988: 59) noted that, even where evaluations are carried out, they are 'fairly primitive' and plagued by problems such as lack of a control group and 'fluid changes in programs'. He also rated much 'evidence' in support of schemes as anecdotal and impressionistic. It can be all too easy to accept your experimental results at face value – particularly when they confirm your hypotheses. However, a dash of scepticism can help improve both evaluative procedures and confidence in one's results.

Given that we are interested in many aspects of the students' experiences, evaluations should reflect this. However, many teachers do not have the time to conduct very lengthy and time-consuming evaluations and we shall bear the following question in mind and return to it at the end of the chapter.

> Can peer tutoring schemes be evaluated without significantly adding to the lecturer's workload?

EVALUATION METHODOLOGIES

A simple first step towards building confidence in results is to *replicate your study*. Replications are not reported in the literature with any frequency, probably due to publication policies which favour 'original' work. However, a few such studies are reported (e.g. Fraser *et al.*, 1977).

There are many methodologies available for use in the evaluation of peer-tutoring schemes, several of which are also used for assessment purposes. Some are relatively quick and easy, others more lengthy and complex. The two main types are qualitative and quantitative, but methodologies may be conceptualized as representing a continuum.

Qualitative evaluation

Qualitative research has been described as having a multi-method focus and as 'involving an interpretive, naturalistic approach to its subject matter' (Denzin and Lincoln, 1994: 2). Qualitative evaluation, therefore, attempts to understand and judge a phenomenon in its natural setting and in terms of the meanings partici-pants bring to it. Qualitative evaluation often relies on self-reports, introspection and reflection. Other qualitative methods can involve observations or interviews. Although necessarily subjective, these methods should not be thought of as chaotic or valueless. Reflective self-reports used to evaluate peer learning and tutoring may be linked to course or module outcomes, and many qualitative methods are quite formal and highly structured. A formal, structured report can constitute a graded assessment exercise. Qualitative methods can to be informal, however, relying on unstructured or semi-structured self-reports from participants. If such reports contain rich reflective statements about the processes of learning as well as about perceptions of outcomes, they, too, can play a useful role in the evaluative process.

Qualitative evaluations or subjective measures can take a number of forms:

- formal or informal feedback from student participants;
- peer evaluations;
- formal or informal feedback from colleagues;
- observation of peer tutoring by a third party;
- surveys and questionnaires.

As we all know, some colleagues may not be persuaded by the outcomes of qualitative evaluations. If we are to encourage them to introduce our favoured peer-learning methods into their teaching programmes, and persuade our institutional administra-tions to provide some financial support, we may need some less subjective 'hard evidence'. The second type of technique, quantitative evaluation, can provide this.

Quantitative evaluation

Quantitative evaluation typically involves the use of numbers, such as percentage marks or grades, which represent a measure of how people perform in particular learning situations, or how much difference a technique makes to attainment. Quantitative evaluation options often follow 'the research method' and involve more objective measurements of outcomes than those recorded in qualitative evaluations. Careful experimental design, the use of control groups and attention to the effects of other factors within the learning environment characterize quantitative methodologies. Such methodologies also typically employ statistical methods to test for differences or similarities in study outcomes. Quantitative techniques are particularly useful in providing 'hard evidence' of the effectiveness of a particular type of peer learning, as we have argued, and many teachers take comfort from, and are persuaded by, quantitative data. However, it can be claimed that many quantitative methods on their own tell us little about the experience of peer tutoring, or about the reasons why things do or do not work.

Quantitative evaluations can vary from simple measures such as test scores to methodologies involving more complex experimental designs and sophisticated statistical techniques.

Qualitative and quantitative techniques have both strengths and weaknesses, and the use of a combination of measures may go some way towards ameliorating problems associated with either method when used on its own. Moreover, peer tutoring can affect many aspects of learning and development, and requires the use of a variety of techniques in order to explore benefits and problems to the fullest extent.

WHICH METHODOLOGIES DO RESEARCHERS USE?

Willson (1988) conducted a survey of methodologies and techniques used in educational research generally which indicated that the quantitative *ANOVA-regression paradigm* currently dominates. However, this does not appear to be the case in the context of peer-tutoring studies where more qualitative methodologies seem to predominate. For example, Soven's (1993) review of 26 curriculum-based peer-tutoring programmes across the USA included an examination of evaluation procedures used in each. Soven found that all programmes included an evaluation component, usually consisting of a *survey* of the views of tutees, tutors and faculty sponsors. The purpose of evaluation was to provide immediate feedback to tutors, to boost tutor confidence and provide evidence to administrators of the success of programmes.

VARIETIES OF METHODS

Given the popularity of qualitative methodologies in peer-tutoring evaluation, we shall start by looking at these, and then move on to consider more quantitative options. The section ends with a discussion of the experimental method.

1 Informal feedback from students or colleagues

Informal feedback is usually delivered verbally. It can be quite anecdotal and gathered unsystematically. Metheny and Metheny (1997) reported an appraisal of their scheme of team learning which involved such informal feedback from participating students. In addition to this anecdotal evidence, they also cited the unexpected support they received from their Dean as indicative of the scheme's success. They concluded their account of evaluation with the comment that 'our courses have developed a good reputation and other students look forward to them' (Metheny and Metheny, 1997: 34).

2 Participant evaluations

Some studies report evaluations that are carried out by the participants themselves (e.g. Slaughter *et al.*, 1991; Scott, 1995; Singh-Gupta and Troutt-Ervin, 1996). The stated purposes of such evaluations are to aid participant reflection, personal development and future planning. For example, Slaughter *et al.*'s (1991) guidebook of tips for tutoring recommended that student tutors should evaluate each session they conducted. In the guidebook, they include a short peer-tutoring progress report form designed to elicit information on problems needing attention and encourage tutors to judge the success of the activities undertaken. Similarly, Singh-Gupta and Troutt-Ervin (1996) used peer evaluation as part of their schemes of collaborative writing and peer review at post-secondary level in Southern Illinois University. The evaluation procedure they described was aided by teacher-supplied criteria and checklists, and was felt to help students develop critical thinking and interpersonal communication skills, and to estimate their own contribution to the process.

3 Reflective logs

As we saw in Chapter 1, some student tutoring in schools projects enables students to gain credit for tutoring, though not all those participating choose to do this (e.g. Highton and Goss, 1997). Those wishing to earn credit are required to keep a reflective log which is submitted as part of the formal course work requirements. The log is also used to help evaluation of the module. Teachers award marks to the log based on the extent to which it shows reflective self-awareness and indicates whether course objectives have been met. In addition, students also complete an evaluation form, shown in Table 7.1. Similar logs feature in many peer-tutoring schemes.

4 Reflective coursework essays

Below is reproduced, with permission of the author, an extract from a reflective essay written by one of my students as a coursework requirement as part of a 'Psychology of higher education' module. She was about to sit her final exams and graduate. In her second year, she was a member of a class who, on first being introduced to the technique, dramatically rejected paired learning. It was, therefore, particularly gratifying to me to read that conversations and teach-back techniques seem, eventually, to have played an important part in her learning.

Table 7.1 A sample module evaluation form

Module Evaluation

General

What was the **best** feature of this module?

Why?

What was the **worst** feature of this module?

Why? How might this be improved?

Class time

The time spent in class for this module was designed to support you in completing the module and making the most of student tutoring. How useful did you find these sessions?

	Very useful			Not very useful	
Introduction and matching in weeks 1 & 2	1	2	3	4	did not attend
Evening training session with other tutors	1	2	3	4	did not attend
Halfway progress check with course leader	1	2	3	4	did not attend
Presentation skills discussion	1	2	3	4	did not attend

Contact with course leader

While you were working in the school how important do you feel it is to have regular contact with the course leader?

	Very important			Not very important
	1	2	3	4

Why?

How does the Student Tutoring module compare to other modules you have taken at this level?

More work   The same amount of work   Less work   (please circle)

Any comments?

Future developments

In the future do you think course materials for this module should be available

on paper   on disk   on the Internet?

(Highton, 1999)

Extract from the 'Memoirs of a mature student' by Lana Freeman

This is the last coursework essay I shall ever write, as I intend to graduate in July with an Ordinary degree, and so it is particularly fitting that it should be a reflection on my learning experience. I entered this educational establishment late in life (as students go) – aged 50 – not as a near-empty vessel hoping to be filled up, but more like a knickerbocker glory, short of the cream and chocolate chips; a pizza, requiring that final something to add richness to all the other ingredients, to bring together a variety of existing flavours in a complete and satisfying way, which would leave me with a memorable taste in my mouth – a reminder of a totally self-indulgent experience.

Lana then went on to reflect on how a number of learning theories had helped her understand her own learning: social learning theory and conditioning, rote learning and subsumption theory. She described her learning style preferences, her fear of failure and hopes for success. She continued:

Today, as I lurch – frazzled, exhausted and disillusioned – towards the finishing post, I am inclined to wonder if the journey was really necessary. In the course of my travels in this world of Academia – a learning maze with blurred directional signs, sometimes written in strange languages and often seeming to move or change just as you approach them – I have been forced up many blind alleys, often with strange travelling companions I would not have voluntarily chosen to accompany me. I have tripped over many carefully concealed obstacles, been attacked in the head by all manner of 'monsters' and have often nearly drowned in seemingly endless seas of coursework. The only thing that saved me was talking to myself. I would stop for a while, gather different pieces of information together to try to make sense of it all, relate it to something else I knew about and then feed or 'teach' it back to myself to see if I could really understand it. This way I could apply what I now knew, in dealing with a new or different situation. Occasionally, I would meet a like-minded fellow traveller and we would compare our understandings and help each other fill in the gaps or see things from a different perspective. Together we could forge ahead with more confidence and a deeper understanding.

This is the basis of *Conversation theory* (Pask, 1976). This theory describes how a student works his or her way to full understanding of a topic by questioning or trying out ideas on either another person – student or teacher – or on an alter ego; that part of the student's own mind which interacts with and monitors the learning process. Pask argues that full understanding occurs when the student can explain the topic by reconstructing it and applying the principles learned to a new situation. He calls this the 'teach-back' technique.

Lana passed her exams and obtained her degree, and her reflective essay provided me with feedback about the longer-term effects of paired learning.

5 Questionnaires and surveys

Questionnaires may be structured instruments, requiring categorical responses or the rating of statements, or open-ended self-reports. They can, thus, provide both quantitative numerical data and qualitative responses. Surveys commonly make use of questionnaires. Sometimes, this methodology enables a quick and easy evaluation, particularly where 'off the shelf' questionnaires are used. On other occasions, such as when a questionnaire is designed from scratch, or when open-ended statements are used, more time and effort are required. However, the time investment is likely to pay dividends in terms of increased understanding of processes and answers to difficult and important questions. Questionnaires have the advantage of being applicable to any situation. They can take on a number of different forms, as we have seen.

Common response formats

- Categorical
  Some questionnaires make use of *Yes/No answers*. Such responses are quantitative;
  e.g. 'Did the independent learning sessions make you feel that you had the chance to learn more by talking?' (Houston and Lazenbatt, 1996).
- Rating scales
  Surveys often require participants to *rate statements*. The respondent is presented with a series of statements relating to the experience of tutoring or being tutored, and asked to select one of a number of degrees of agreement, using a scale which generally ranges from 'strongly agree' to 'strongly disagree'. Such data are readily converted into numbers. For example, Scott's (1995) evaluative survey required students to rate statements such as, 'The more feedback I can get the better. I'll decide whether to take the advice or not', on a five-point scale. The five-point scale seems the most commonly occurring, though, sometimes, seven points are used (e.g. Rosen, Powell and Schubot, 1977).
- Open-response formats
  Sometimes, surveys or questionnaires include *open-ended statements or questions*. Respondents are asked to respond in any way they choose. Self-report questionnaires consist of a number of open-ended questions relevant to the topic under investigation. Hammond (2000) argues that the use of these questionnaires owes much to the assumption that the best way to find out about an individual is to ask them direct questions. Thus, data collected in this way are qualitative.

For example, Scott (1995) included the following:

e.g. The thing I enjoy most/like least about group writing is ...

The greatest value of group writing as a learning experience is ...
The biggest problem with group writing is ...

Similarly, Houston and Lazenbatt's (1996) Peer Tutoring Evaluation Question-naire contains open-ended questions which require students to think about and justify their responses (e.g. Did you find it easy to work collaboratively in a group? Why or why not?). It also seeks student views on a variety of issues such as group composition and group skills.

Uses of questionnaires

Questionnaires can focus on any area of student experience, and can provide feedback to teachers. In a study of paired learning in dental education, Qualtrough (1996) sought information from participants on many aspects of the technique: their understanding of *why the scheme had been introduced*, and their perceptions of the *advantages* to themselves, to teaching staff, dental nurses and patients. Information about the extent to which students had *enjoyed* the scheme was also solicited. Other questionnaires have sought feedback from students on process issues such as the *usefulness of training, the nature of supportees, supporting activities, difficulties encountered, assessment* and *evaluation* (Topping *et al.*, 1997: 50). Scott (1995) reported the results of a survey designed to determine *students' attitudes* to peer assistance and group writing which focused on the participants' views on the *usefulness of the feedback* they received and their *confidence* about the validity of suggestions made.

Measures of *self-concept, self-esteem, stress* and other factors may also be made in order to explore the effects of peer tutoring (e.g. Goldberg, 1978; Goldberg and Williams, 1988). These instruments are generally structured, involving numerical ratings by respondents.

Questionnaires may be administered *pre- and post-*tutoring or used to compare tutoring groups with those taught more traditionally.

Choosing a questionnaire

Care must be taken when choosing a questionnaire to select a well-designed instrument. Even more care is necessary if you decide to design your own. It is advisable to take careful note of the problems of questionnaire design and analysis elaborated below. The information you gather is only as good as the questions asked, and leading or ambiguous questions can make interpretation of results very difficult. You should, similarly, avoid any value judgements, hidden assumptions or very sensitive issues. You should also consider who should complete the questionnaire. Is the same format appropriate eliciting the views of both tutors or tutees?

In their very useful book, Millis and Cottell (1998) include a variety of question-naires and evaluation forms suitable for use in the context of peer-tutoring schemes.

e.g.

Dyadic Essay Confrontation Evaluation form
Feedback form for interdependent self-directed learning
Co-operative learning peer evaluation form

Questionnaires described by Houston and Lazenbatt (1996) may also be used in a variety of contexts. Two particularly useful instruments are:

Attitudes to Peer Tutoring Questionnaire
Peer Tutoring Evaluation Questionnaire

Full versions of both questionnaires are contained in Houston and Lazenbatt's paper.

Several other researchers make use of questionnaires in their investigations of peer tutoring (e.g. Rosen *et al.*, 1977; Wyatt and Medway, 1984; Carroll, 1986; Fresko, 1988; Bell, 1991; Mann, 1994; Witherby, 1997). Thus, there is a great deal of material available for either direct use or modification to suit any particular purpose.

Problems of questionnaire design, analysis and administration

Although the use of questionnaires or surveys is a popular way of acquiring information relatively quickly and painlessly, too few people appreciate the difficulties associated with the practice. Students are particularly prone to this when carrying out project work, I find. Problems and issues include:

Development and reliability of the instrument

Questionnaires need to be well prepared and reliable. Preparation can be a lengthy procedure, as instruments which are not tested can contain ambiguous statements or include statements which do not differentiate between members of the target population. In order to be deemed reliable, questionnaires may be subjected to one of three kinds of reliability testing. The first of these tests *parallel form reliability*. Two versions of the instrument are prepared, and scores on each compared. The second form, *test-retest reliability*, requires that the same question-naire be administered on two occasions. For it to be rated as reliable, the questionnaire should produce very similar results on each occasion. There are problems in deciding how far apart these two testing sessions should be. If they are too close in time, respondents may remember their first responses at the second testing. However, if too much time elapses between testing and re-testing, other factors may have influenced their ratings. Indeed, when questionnaires are used pre- and post-tutoring, we are hoping for such intermediate influence. The third type of reliability concerns *internal consistency* and is sometimes known as *split-half reliability*. This has been rated as the most practical method for estimating reliability (Hammond, 2000). This method is based on the principle that each part of the test should be consistent with other parts. Reliability may be calculated by correlating scores on even-numbered items with those on odd items.

Relatively few tests of reliability are reported for questionnaires used in peer-tutoring evaluations. However, Houston and Lazenbatt (1996) described the development of their Peer Tutoring Evaluation Questionnaire in some detail. They also reported results of a principal components analysis and the Chronbach's α calculation carried out to test the internal consistency of their instrument. Few questionnaires receive such thorough attention. However, as we shall see below, in spite of their thoroughness, there remains a hint of *bias* in Houston and Lazenbatt's instrument.

Bias in the design

Houston and Lazenbatt (1996) use only three rating categories in their questionnaire: 'Excellent', 'Good' and 'Fair', rather than using a wider range to include 'Very poor', for example. Similarly, Bell (1991) described a very simple and easy-to-administer open-ended questionnaire which invited students to identify two things they had liked about peer response groups. Bell did not, however, appear to balance this by asking students to identify things they had disliked about the scheme, thus introducing bias into the evaluation. In addition, it is often wise to ask the question, 'Who requires the information and for what purpose?' Sometimes, the motivation for collecting information can give rise to bias. For example, it is possible to bias the design of a questionnaire so as to encourage positive or negative responses, according to your purpose. For example, it is harder to disagree with a leading question such as, 'Do you agree that peer tutoring promotes better learning than traditional teaching?' than with one worded more neutrally. Thus, an unscrupulous teacher or researcher might choose to include leading questions in order to maximize the chances of gaining support for a favoured technique. You may have noticed that politicians sometimes make use of such strategies in designing questions for referenda.

Do the items included give you the information you want? e.g. Do they relate to objectives of the scheme?

An important problem with evaluation and questionnaire design is that scheme objectives are not always tested. For example, although the promotion of 'a deeper understanding of the subject' (Topping *et al.*, 1997: 45) was listed as an objective of their student-supported learning scheme, there were no items to test whether this had been achieved in the evaluation questionnaire. Similarly, 'the promotion of intellectual and personal development' was another objective, but no measure of this was made either before or after completion of the scheme. However, some attempt at measurement of effects was included, in terms of perceptions of cognitive and transferable skills and attitudes.

For whom is the questionnaire designed?

It seems to be not uncommon for questionnaires to be completed by one member of a learning partnership only, particularly in cross-level tutoring (e.g. Qualtrough, 1996; Topping *et al.*, 1997). This seems regrettable, as one side of the tutoring equation is ignored.

Administration

Administration of questionnaires to large numbers of students may be problematic, not least of all in terms of preparation and duplication of the instruments. Computer-based versions can often reduce such problems and assist with simple analysis.

Bias in responses

Questionnaires may be criticized because of the possibilities they provide for respondents to complete them inaccurately, by 'faking good' or supplying deliberately misleading information. Respondents usually do not wish to present themselves in a negative light, and may choose responses to try to avoid that possibility. Also, if, in spite of your best efforts, questions of a sensitive nature appear in your questionnaire, some respondents may be upset or offended by them, and withhold their response.

Return rate

Topping *et al.* (1997) point to another difficulty associated with the use of questionnaires as evaluation instruments, namely the return rate. They reported that only 30 per cent of supporters returned completed questionnaires, and wisely concluded that this return rate was 'far too low for the data to be considered representative' (Topping *et al.*, 1997: 51).

Problems of analysis and interpretation

Analysis of open-ended format data can be time consuming, as responses are often very varied. It is not possible to carry out easy numerical analysis in the way that closed-format response formats allow. However, on close inspection of the qualitative data, patterns are usually discernible and categories of response may be identified. It is advisable to test the categories you identify by asking a colleague to use them to rate a set of responses. You then compare the colleague's ratings with your own. In this way, you can calculate yet another form of reliability, the *inter-rater reliability*. Hammond (2000) argues that the degree of agreement expressed as a percentage gives a rough estimate of reliability, but recommends the calculation of an index of agreement for greater reliability. Clearly, a high level of agreement is desirable. Further caution is required in *interpreting* open-format data due to the possibility of response bias on the part of the experimenter, as well as response bias of participants.

6 Checklists

Checklists generally consist of a number of clearly defined categories or descriptions of behaviour. They are typically used by observers to note the presence or absence of the categories or behaviours, but may also be used by individuals to help analyse their own behaviour. Totalling all occurrences gives a measure of frequency of the behaviour. The duration of each occurrence may also be noted where this is of interest to the investigator. Topping (1996b) recommends the use of standardized checklists to help monitoring of peer tutoring.

Hawkins' (1982) checklist of tutoring behaviours and his tutoring style typology are examples of this type of measurement in the context of peer tutoring (see Chapter 6). Another example of a checklist used to help evaluation is to be found in Arfken (1982). These instruments may be used before tutoring commences, during tutoring and at the end to help evaluate skills development or personal growth.

7 Monitoring quality indicators

Some varieties of peer tutoring aim to improve retention, reduce absenteeism or ameliorate similar problems. Indicators of its effectiveness in these spheres should also be monitored. Quality indicators include:

1   a reduction in dropout rate for a course;
2   a reduction in absenteeism;
3   an increase in completion of assignments;
4   a reduction in re-submissions and retakes;
5   an improvement in overall grades for completed assignments.

Your institution may hold some of these data centrally and others may be calculated within a department or unit.

8 Use of pre- and post-attainment tests

Although this quantitative practice may share some characteristics with the traditional examination (see below), it may be used to compare attainment before and after tutoring. In addition, attainment tests may be used to compare performance of peer-tutoring participants with that of a non-participant control group. Several peer-tutoring studies use this methodology (e.g. Mann, 1994; Sobral, 1997, 1998).

9. A traditional examination

Another example of a quantitative method of evaluation is the traditional examination. However, Topping (1996b: 46) describes this as a 'crude outcome measure' in the context of peer tutoring, given the complexity of this method of learning.

We shall conclude the review of evaluative techniques by looking at a quantitative method which involves careful study design as well as statistical analysis of data. Some might argue that we have left the best until last! Others would disagree vehemently. Whatever your view, we shall now investigate the experimental method.

THE EXPERIMENTAL METHOD

Experiments involve a comparison between two groups who are equivalent, or matched in key respects. Matching is achieved by randomization, a procedure which gives every subject an equal chance of being assigned to either group. One group experiences an experimental manipulation of some sort, while the other does not. All other aspects of the situation are held constant as far as is possible. For example, one group of students may participate in peer tutoring (the 'experimental' group) while a matched group are taught in a more traditional way (the 'control' group). Elmes, Kantowitz and Roediger (1992: 105) describe experiments as 'tests to arrive at a causal explanation'. Thus, experiments into peer tutoring are likely to be investigating the *processes* involved in the technique or the *reasons why it works* as well as its *effects*.

Congos and Schoeps (1997) described an experimental evaluation procedure designed to assess the effectiveness of a peer-tutoring intervention programme. They elaborated an *eight-stage model* which may be applied to the evaluation of a very wide range of educational initiatives:

1   Identify the relevant variables
    Both dependent and independent variables should be identified. *Dependent* variables are factors which may be influenced by the initiative. In other words, they are the outcomes of an initiative. In educational settings, these may include class of degree, final course grades, test grades or, if retention and attrition are being targeted, progression or graduation rates. *Independent* variables are factors which may influence the outcomes of dependent variables and may be manipulated by the experimenter. Independent variables include such things as participation in a new method of learning or previous achievement scores.

2   Operationalize variables
    Many variables such as marks in class tests or class of degree, as well as gender and age, may be sampled directly. Others may present more of a problem. For example, where attendance at your initiative is voluntary, you may wish to define the criterion which determines who is regarded as an attender or participant, so that you may compare subsequent performance of attendees and non-attendees. This is referred to as operationalizing the variable. You may choose a cut-off point such as a number of attendances, representing more than 50 per cent or 75 per cent attendance, for example. Sophisticated analyses can incorporate degrees of attendance. Graduation rate may also present problems. For example, Congos and Schoeps (1997) ask whether graduation rates are calculated taking into account graduation in the

minimum number of years possible or whether graduation in a slightly longer time frame may be allowed. All variables must be defined clearly.

3   Collect relevant information for each participant.

4   Gather data and maintain records of dependent variables as the initiative progresses.

5   Enter data into a computer package ready for analysis
    e.g. SPSS (Statistical Package for the Social Sciences).
    Enlist the help of a colleague who has both computer and statistical skills to help with this if necessary.

6   Analyse the data using an appropriate data analysis software package. Some re-coding and combining of variables may be necessary. Your helpful statistically literate colleague's services should again be sought if necessary. Congos and Schoeps (1997) suggest the use of chi-square tests, t-tests and analysis of variance or covariance.

7   Display the results graphically and include a verbal summary of the key points.

8   Interpret and draw conclusions from the data.

There are any number of problems associated with interpreting results, often associated with issues of *reliability* and *validity*. 'An experiment that can be replicated is a reliable one, as is a test whose results are consistent' (Elmes *et al.*, 1992: 245). Data are deemed to be valid if 'several results converge on an understanding of a concept' (Elmes *et al.*, 1992: 227). However, we hope for results that unambiguously support or refute our predictions or hypotheses.

Congos and Schoeps' (1997) eight-stage procedure will provide you with not only the 'hard evidence' with which to persuade your colleagues, but also the makings of an action research publication.

If you are interested to see an example of this type of evaluation in use, I would recommend reading Price and Rust (1995) who report the evaluation of the effectiveness of Supplemental Instruction in an introductory course in business at Oxford Brookes University.

Key steps in quantitative evaluation are shown in Table 7.2.

MULTIPLE MEASURES

As we have seen, there are a wide variety of qualitative and quantitative methodologies in use in the evaluation of peer-tutoring studies. However, given the broad remit of most peer-tutoring schemes, it may be wise not to rely on one single evaluative measure. While experiments are the only means of investigating causal questions, they are frequently criticized because they lack *ecological validity*. In other words, they do not tell us anything worth knowing about life outside a laboratory. Davis and Rose (2000) argue that the weaknesses of non-experimental techniques may be complemented by the strengths of the experimental method and vice versa.

We shall now look at examples of studies which make use of more than one measure.

Table 7.2 Key steps in quantitative evaluation

Key steps in evaluation
1   Clarify your aims and objectives.
2   State your experimental question or hypothesis.
3   Identify relevant variables. What, other than the peer tutoring, might influence outcomes? Which variables are dependent? Which independent?
4   Operationalize variables.
5   Select an appropriate evaluation instrument.
6   Identify a control group where possible.
7   Carry out any pre-measurements before onset of the scheme.
8   Collect relevant information as the scheme progresses.
9   Carry out any post-measures at the end of the scheme.
10 Distribute evaluation instruments (e.g. questionnaires) for completion or collect qualitative measures (e.g. reflective learning logs).
11 Compare pre- and post-measures for experimental and control groups.
12 Enter data into a computer package for further analysis where appropriate.
13 Compare results from different evaluation measures where possible.
14 Reflect on and interpret your results and draw conclusions from data.
15 Consider writing up your study for internal or external dissemination (e.g. publication in a refereed journal or, in the UK, preparation of portfolio for membership of the Institute for Learning and Teaching (ILT)).

A stage model of the evaluation process

Arfken (1982: 121) argued that evaluation of the programme of tutoring at her university should be 'ongoing and a total process' and should involve both tutor and tutee. Moreover, evaluation should include personal, social and academic matters. She described the evaluation process as having four stages:

1   *Observation*
    This approach is taken by the administrator, instructor or teacher who takes time to observe tutoring in progress or a videotaped record of it.

2   *Administrator–tutee conferences*
    At these conferences, the administrator receives feedback from tutees, and together they evaluate recent writing in the tutee's folder. A checklist is used to help evaluation (but Arfken does not include a copy of this in her

account). Administrators check the personal rapport developing between tutor and tutee. Tutors and tutees are asked the same questions on this topic.

3   *Tutor–administrator co-operative evaluation seminars*
Tutors are questioned on the rapport between themselves and tutees. They are then required to complete a self-appraisal form which elicits information relating to aspects of the job, personal development, communication and job satisfaction.

4   *Tutor performance review*
Administrators are asked to rate the performance of each tutor as 'weak', 'good' or 'excellent' on a number of dimensions (rapport with tutee; ability to explain ideas; skill in critiquing composition; development in tutoring skills) on an evaluation form. In addition, administrators identify obstacles to achieving progress in any area and suggest methods for helping the tutor to develop further. Finally, areas in which tutors have made most and least progress are identified.

In this way, a large amount of information is amassed, from a number of sources, using a variety of techniques. Arfken's evaluation also compared some of the responses from different sources.

Evaluation comparing qualitative and quantitative results

Similarly, Dunn (1996) compared results of two qualitative methods. In addition to completing a *process journal*, participants were asked to take part in a *survey* in which they commented on the following:

- division of labour in the pair;
- their liking for collaboration vs preference for working alone;
- the amount of learning achieved;
- the extent to which they found collaboration helpful.

Dunn compared the two measures and noted that the survey responses were consistent with what students had written in their journals.

Qualitative and quantitative evaluations by teachers and students

Bard (1996) used a variety of measures in the evaluation of co-operative learning, although student performance was rated as the most important measure. Post-performance measures of participants were compared with those from previous classes who had learned in a more traditional way. However, Bard's report includes suitable caveats regarding this procedure. Student co-operative learning evaluations took the form of periodic short, individual, anonymous assessments of activities. Participants were supplied with the following criteria, and asked to rate themselves on a scale from poor to excellent:

1   Were the participants listening to each other?
2   Did most people participate or did just a few dominate?
3   Did we maintain a focus?
4   Did our discussion 'scratch beneath the surface' or 'open up the topic'?
5   Did I learn something new?
6   Did I challenge my own thinking or 'work hard' at it?

Interactive television monitoring enabled the instructor to keep an eye (literally) on students' interpretation of questions, their progress on task, areas needing clarification, group member interaction and students who dominate. Thus, there is some overlap between the content and focus of instructor monitoring and student evaluations which allows the two perspectives on the same experiences to be compared. Comparisons are the key to the next methodology: triangulation.

Triangulation in evaluation

Triangulation is defined as 'any situation involving three parties or points of view' (Collins English Dictionary, 1991). Thus, triangulation in evaluation requires that three points of view be sampled using different methods of measurement and results compared. In this way, where different methods produce the same results, conclusions about outcomes may be strengthened. However, it should also be noted that, when results from different techniques differ, 'the differences may be the result of the methods used to obtain the data rather than the result of misinterpreting data' (Lyons, 2000: 280), and caution should be exercised before rejecting the usefulness of findings.

We have already encountered McGroarty and Zhu's (1997) study of training for peer revision in college freshman English composition classes in previous chapters. The authors wished to estimate the importance of preparing students for peer revision. In order to achieve this, their study made use of a triangulation procedure involving multiple methods of evaluation. Results derived from qualitative analysis of how far student *discussions*, instructor *interviews* and researcher *observations* corroborated each other. The authors concluded:

> The combination of measures, data sources, and methods not only allowed triangulation of the finding that training for peer revision improved students' ability to critique peer writing and their attitudes toward peer revision but also illuminated other aspects of peer revision processes.
>
> (McGroarty and Zhu, 1997: 2)

Further details of their study may be found in Chapters 1 and 6.

HOW TO CHOOSE AN APPROPRIATE METHODOLOGY

Schallert, Alexander and Goetz (1988) use the analogy of a photographic lens to help illuminate choice of methodology. We may be interested to investigate a global phenomenon or wish to explore a very small aspect of learning in some detail – both valuable ventures in the advancement of knowledge. We may choose to zoom in and enjoy a detailed close-up view of a small part of the scene, or we may prefer to make use of the wide-angle lens for a glimpse of the bigger picture. Experimentalists may prefer the former, closely focused, often quantitative option, while those preferring more naturalistic or qualitative methods will opt for the latter. Advocates of naturalistic methods stress the richness of the data they collect and the sensitivity of the methodology to unexpected outcomes and its ability to depart from the expected, while critics of these methods point to the impossibility of formally comparing competing treatment outcomes by their use. Advocates of a more formal experimental method, on the other hand, stress its ability to compare competing treatments, and critics 'have charged that current methods are prescriptive and preordinate, that they focus the enquiry process on things that are already known and miss the anticipated' (Willson, 1988: 263).

Willson also argued that 'each discipline is informed by the methodology it employs'. In other words, we are able to learn only what our methodology (or our discipline) allows us to learn. However, the purposes of our research will determine the methodology we employ to some extent, so we do have some choice in the matter. If we are interested in improved academic performance and design our study to achieve this end, we cannot evaluate it by means of an attitude questionnaire. Conversely, attitudinal and affective changes cannot be measured by course grades (though the two may be linked of course).

As answers to all kinds of questions are needed, some synthesis of evaluative technique seems desirable. However, Topping warns against 'death by questionnaire avalanche' (Topping, 1996b: 47). None the less, he advocates that evaluation should not stop at the formal end of a project, in order to see whether benefits are long-lasting or whether students spontaneously continue to tutor each other after the project has finished.

Table 7.3 provides information and advice on how to select an evaluative technique. Selections and combinations other than those suggested may also be possible.

Conclusion

Returning to the question posed at the beginning of the chapter, 'Can peer tutoring schemes be evaluated without significantly adding to a lecturer's workload?', I would argue that the answer is, 'Maybe'. We *can* say that schemes that are well designed and implemented, which use appropriate evaluation methods and instruments, will be more easily evaluated than those implemented haphazardly or than those with muddled objectives where many issues remain unclear and results, therefore, ambiguous. If your experimental question or hypothesis is simple and your chosen measuring instrument straightforward, the evaluation may be quickly achieved. If, for example, you are marking a reflective log for assessment purposes, then the additional information you extract for evaluation may add little to your workload. Many universities and colleges now

Table 7.3 Selecting an evaluative technique

What does your scheme hope to achieve?	Suggestions for suitable evaluative techniques
Attitudinal and non-academic outcomes	
To improve attendance	Monitor quality indicator, i.e. compare *attendance* with a control group or previous cohort who did not use the technique
To increase retention	Monitor quality indicator, i.e. compare *retention data* for peer-tutoring cohort with those of a traditionally taught control group or cohort from a previous year
To increase completion of assignments	Monitor quality indicator, i.e. note completion rates and compare with traditionally taught control group or previous cohort
To reduce re-submission and re-sit rates	Monitor quality indicator, i.e. compare *re-submission and re-sit rates* for peer-tutoring group and traditionally taught control group or previous cohort
To reduce feelings of isolation	Direct measures: • Teacher observation • Informal feedback from students Indirect measures: • Inspect attendance; completion; re-submission; re-sit and retention rates (see above)
To improve student attitudes to themselves or the subject	• Pre- and post-measurement and comparison of attitudes using an appropriate attitude questionnaire • Participant evaluations • Informal feedback
To increase self-esteem of participants; to improve self-concept	Pre- and post-comparisons of self-esteem/self-concept using an appropriate standardized questionnaire
To reduce student stress	Pre- and post-comparisons of stress levels measured by means of a standard instrument
Academic outcomes	
To improve learning	Pre- and post-comparisons of scores on a learning style or approaches to studying inventory
To encourage critical thinking	Reflective logs; reflective essays Pre- and post-comparisons of performance on high-level cognitive task

Table 7.3 Continued

To improve metacognitive skills	Reflective logs; reflective essays
To promote an effective learning style or approach to studying	Pre- and post-comparisons of scores on a learning style or approaches to studying inventory
To improve performance	Examinations; tests Observation
To improve skills, e.g. communication; writing; reading; composition; literature reviewing	Pre- and post-comparisons of performance Participant evaluations

Developmental outcomes

To encourage reflection	Reflective logs; reflective essays
To aid personal/intellectual development	• Reflective logs; reflective essays • Checklists
To encourage autonomy	• Learning logs; reflective essays • Checklists

Process outcomes

To explore the processes of tutoring	Formulate and test hypotheses derived from theory or research using the experimental method
To answer a causal question	Formulate and test hypotheses derived from theory or research using the experimental method

Module evaluation

To evaluate the effectiveness of a peer-tutoring module or module/course of which peer tutoring is a major part	Mixed instrument (e.g. Table 7.1 which contains open-ended questions and questionnaires)

require module or course evaluation to be carried out routinely as a means of ensuring quality and maintaining standards. In such cases, there is no addition to the workload. However, where evaluation involves more than one methodology, where there is qualitative data from very large numbers of participants, or where advanced statistical tests are required, more time will be needed. However, as with so many aspects of peer tutoring, the potential benefits in terms of increased understanding make the extra effort well worthwhile.

In the next chapter, we consider some problems associated with peer tutoring.

8 Problems associated with peer tutoring

Peer tutoring does not always work out as we would wish. Problems that arise may be seen as inherent within the tutoring relationship (endogenous), as in the case study in Chapter 4, or external to it (exogenous). Sometimes problems can relate to a number of factors, and very often the factors are inter-connected. We may be able to learn a great deal and increase our understanding of peer tutoring by looking for examples of schemes which have reported qualified or limited success. However, the asymmetry in educational publishing which favours 'successful' experiments makes this endeavour difficult. Nonetheless, researchers reporting successful schemes often refer to difficulties they have experienced, and staff developers recount some resistance on the part of colleagues to give peer tutoring a try.

As we have seen, the first barrier to the introduction of peer tutoring in undergraduate programmes may be the lecturers themselves. Similarly, students may be reluctant to participate. In Chapter 4, we saw that a variety of features associated with the roles taken by students within the tutoring dyad can also give rise to problems. In this chapter, we shall consider some frequently asked questions relating to other problems associated with peer tutoring:

> Why do people make such a fuss about organization?
> How can I improve my students' motivation?
> Why do some students miss peer-tutoring sessions? What can be done about it?
> Why do some students dislike working in groups?

FREQUENTLY ASKED QUESTIONS 1: PROBLEMS OF ORGANIZATION AND PREPARATION

Why do people make such a fuss about organization?

Preparation and organization are crucial to the success of any educational innovation, and this is nowhere truer than in the case of peer tutoring. In Chapter 5, Sinclair Goodlad identified seven golden rules for organizing peer-tutoring and mentoring schemes: define your aims, define roles, train tutors and mentors, structure the content, support tutors and mentors, keep logistics as simple as possible and evaluate the scheme. However, where peer tutoring takes place in small groups, or involves same-level participants, other problems may also arise. For example, Goldschmid and Goldschmid (1976) identified the selection of student partners as a potential problem in peer tutoring, particularly when staff choices, made on the basis of grades or other performance criteria, result in the creation of an 'equal peer' and 'unequal peer'. I, too, have encountered problems of this nature, and anyone who has used group project work as part of their programme will be likely to be able to testify to the problems inherent in this practice. We shall now focus on the important organizational decision regarding the composition of groups. Richard Felder and Rebecca Brent discuss some issues relating to this topic below.

We shall now move on to the issue of motivation, without which any educational venture may be compromised. We may be better able to persuade our students to try peer learning if we improve our understanding of what motivates them.

FREQUENTLY ASKED QUESTIONS 2: MOTIVATING STUDENTS

How can I improve my students' motivation?

An obvious but relatively little-used method of learning more about the motivation of our students is to ask them about their reasons for learning. Patricia Cross, whose work we encountered in Chapter 3, reported the results of several surveys of adult learners, and found that, while most respondents gave a number of reasons for their participating in learning or for wishing to do so in the future, the key reason was in order to be able to put it to immediate use (Cross, 1981). Most adults gave practical, pragmatic reasons for learning and most were clearly goal-oriented. However, some surveys also showed that some people gave socially desirable reasons for learning such as an eagerness to pursue knowledge for its own sake or to become better citizens and happier people though the pursuit of education. Cross found that her adult interviewees spoke of *barriers to learning* which may also provide us with useful insights about learning and motivation.

Barriers to learning

Cross's research on perceived barriers to adult learning indicates that obstacles may be categorized into three groups:

- situational;
- institutional;
- dispositional.

ISSUES RELATING TO GROUP COMPOSITION

Richard M. Felder and Rebecca Brent (North Carolina State University, Raleigh, and East Carolina University, Greenville, USA)

Research and design projects, laboratory experiments, and homework problem sets can all be effectively completed by teams of students. The teams may function as formal co-operative learning (CL) groups, remaining together until the completion of an assignment and then disbanding, or as co-operative base groups, remaining together for an entire course or even longer (Johnson *et al.*, 1991). The periodic reforming of formal co-operative learning groups exposes the students to a larger variety of learning styles and problem-solving approaches than they would see in base groups; the base groups tend to provide more assistance and encouragement to their members. A third category, informal co-operative learning groups, refers to teams that come together and disperse within a single class period, as in the exercises listed previously.

Following are several *suggestions for setting up CL groups and structuring assignments*:

- Give assignments to teams of three or four students. When students work in pairs, one of them tends to dominate and there is usually no good mechanism for resolving disputes, and in teams of five or more it becomes difficult to keep everyone involved in the process. Collect one assignment per group.
- Try to form groups that are heterogeneous in ability level. The drawbacks of a group with only weak students are obvious, but having only strong students in a group is equally undesirable. First, the strong groups have an unfair advantage over other groups in the class. Second, the team members tend to divide up the homework and communicate only cursorily with one another, omitting the dynamic interactions that lead to most of the proven benefits of co-operative learning. In mixed-ability groups, on the other hand, the weaker students gain from seeing how better students study and approach problems, and the stronger students gain a deeper understanding of the subject by teaching it to others, a phenomenon familiar to every teacher.
- Avoid groups in which women and minority students are outnumbered. Studies have shown that women's ideas and contributions are often devalued or discounted in mixed-gender teams, and the women end by taking passive roles in group interactions, to their detriment (Felder, Felder, Mauney, Hamrin and Dietz, 1994; Heller and Hollabaugh, 1992). Groups containing all men, two women and one or two men, or all women are acceptable, but one woman and two or three men should be avoided. The same rule applies to minority students.
- If at all possible, select the teams yourself. In one study, 155 students surveyed claimed in a 2/1 ratio that their worst group-work experiences were with self-formed groups and their best were with instructor-formed groups (Feichtner and Davis, 1985). Other studies in the CL literature generally support this finding.

On the first day of class, we have the students fill out a questionnaire indicating their sex, ethnicity, and either overall GPA or grades in selected prerequisite courses. (Students who do not wish to provide this information are free to withhold it, but few do.) We use the collected questionnaires to form the groups, following the guidelines given above. We have also occasionally let students self-select into groups, stipulating that no group may have more than one student who earned A's in specified courses and strongly recommending that women and minority students avoid groups in which they are outnumbered. While not perfect, this system at least assures that the very best students in the class do not cluster together, leaving the weaker ones to fend for themselves.

A problem may arise if assignments require long periods of time out of class and many students live off campus and/or have outside jobs. Instructor-formed groups may then find it almost impossible to agree on a suitable meeting time and place. We have shuffled groups to allow commuters to work together to the extent that they can, recognizing that they will lose some of the benefits of CL by not having as much face-to-face interaction as the other students in the class.

Assign team roles that rotate with each assignment. Johnson et al. (1991) suggest

1   The co-ordinator (organizes assignment into sub-tasks, allocates responsibilities, keeps group on task).
2   The checker (monitors both the solutions and every team member's comprehension of them).
3   The recorder (checks for consensus, writes the final group solution).

In addition, Heller and Hollabaugh (1992) suggest:

4   The sceptic (plays devil's advocate, suggests alternative possibilities, keeps group from leaping to premature conclusions).

Only the names of the students who actually participated should appear on the final product, with their team roles for that assignment identified.

Promote positive interdependence: all team members should feel that they have unique roles to play within the group and that the task can only be completed successfully if all members do their parts. Strategies to achieve this objective include the following:

1   Require a single group product.
2   Assign rotating group roles.
3   Give each member different critical resources, as in Jigsaw;
4   Select one member of each group to explain (in an oral report or a written test) both the team's results and the methods used to achieve them, and give every team member the grade earned by that individual. Avoid selecting the strongest students in the groups.
5   Give bonuses on tests to groups for which the lowest team grade or the average team grade exceeds a specified minimum.

The last two strategies provide powerful incentives for the stronger team members to make sure that the weaker ones understand the assignment solution and the material to be covered on the test.

Promote individual accountability: the most common way to achieve this goal is to give primarily individual tests; another is the technique mentioned above of selecting an individual team member to present or explain the team's results.

Some authors suggest having each team member rate everyone's effort as a percentage of the total team effort on an assignment, and using the results to identify non-contributors, and possibly to adjust individual assignment grades; others recommend against this procedure on the grounds that it moves the team away from co-operation and back towards competition. We occasionally use it, but only in classes in which students have repeatedly expressed complaints about irresponsible team members.

Have groups regularly assess their performance: especially in early assignments, require them to discuss what worked well, what difficulties arose, and what each member could do to make things work better next time. The conclusions should be handed in with the final group report or solution set, a requirement that motivates the students to take the exercise more seriously than they otherwise might.

Offer ideas for effective group functioning: working effectively in teams is not something people are born knowing how to do, nor is it a skill routinely taught in school. Quite the contrary, in fact, as Bellamy, Evans, Linder, McNeill and Raupp (1994) observe, working together in college courses is more likely to be regarded as cheating and punished than viewed positively and encouraged. The same authors note that the traditional approach to team building in academe is to put three to five students together and to let them 'work it out' on their way to solving a problem. A better approach is to prepare the students with some instructional elements that will generate an appreciation of what teaming (as opposed to just working in groups) involves, and to foster the development of interpersonal skills that aid in team building and performance.

Some *elements of effective group functioning* are relatively self-explanatory and might be given to teams as a check list.

These elements include showing up for meetings on time, avoiding personal criticisms, making sure everyone gets a chance to offer ideas, and giving those ideas serious consideration. Other recommendations we make to homework teams working on quantitative problems are these:

1   Set up all assigned problems individually (no detailed mathematical or numerical calculations), then meet as a group to put the complete solution set together. We tell the students that if they simply parcel out the work, each of them will understand their own part but not the others, and their lack of understanding will hurt them on the individual tests. On the other hand, if they only work as a complete group, certain quick-thinking students will tend to begin every problem solution, which will put their teammates at a disadvantage on the tests.

2   Don't allow a situation to develop in which one or two students work all the solutions out and then quickly explain them to teammates who didn't really participate in obtaining them. If this happens no one is getting the full benefits of co-operative learning, and the explainees will probably crash and burn on the tests. This message may not get through to some students until after the first test.

3   Don't put someone's name on the solution set if they did not participate in generating the set, especially if it happens more than once. We don't like using test threats (as in Items 1 and 2) to goad students into following good teamwork practices, but we have never found another motivator as effective for most engineering students, especially in their first and second years.

> *Provide assistance to teams having difficulty working together*: teams with problems should be invited or required to meet with the instructor to discuss possible solutions. The instructor should facilitate the discussion and may suggest alternatives but should not impose solutions on the team.
>
> We allow teams to fire non-co-operative team members if every other option has failed, and we also allow individuals to quit if they are doing most or all of the work and team counselling has failed to yield improvements. Fired team members or members who quit must then find other teams willing to accept them. In our experience, just the knowledge that this option is available usually induces non-co-operative team members to change their ways; in chemical engineering classes containing as many as 50 teams, rarely does more than one team dissolve in the course of a semester.
>
> Don't reconstitute groups too often. A major goal of co-operative learning is to help students expand their repertoire of problem-solving approaches, and a second goal is to help them develop collaborative skills – leadership, decision making, communication, etc. These goals can only be achieved if students have enough time to develop a group dynamic, encountering and overcoming difficulties in working together. Co-operative groups should remain together for at least a month for the dynamic to have a chance of developing.

We may benefit by looking at some of these barriers, given that an increasing proportion of undergraduates are now 'mature students'. Additionally, many of us believe that helping school leavers learn in the context of higher education should more closely resemble andragogy than pedagogy.

Cross found that *situational barriers* to learning included, in descending order of mention, the costs involved (e.g. tuition, books, child care), lack of time, home responsibilities and job responsibilities. Over half of the adults interviewed mentioned the financial costs of learning. Most frequently mentioned *institutional barrier* to learning was the difficulty posed by having to attend full time. Over a third of adults mentioned this barrier. Other institutional barriers included inconvenient scheduling of courses and insufficient information about what is on offer. *Dispositional barriers* were less frequently identified than situational or institutional barriers, but, nonetheless, are worth noting, given recent moves world wide to support lifelong learning. Dispositional barriers included the fear that the individual may be too old to begin learning. Unsurprisingly, low grades in the past appear to leave individuals lacking in confidence of their ability to succeed in the future. Some people also mentioned lack of energy and stamina (Cross, 1981).

It can be argued that some progress is being made by universities and colleges to address institutional barriers to learning. Flexible and distance-learning initiatives are more common in higher education than at any time in the past, and part-time studying continues to be encouraged. Links between higher and further education institutions not only increase access to higher education, but also help dissemination of information, as does advertising by individual institutions in newspapers, on television and in cinemas. Adult learners are being wooed back into education.

While dispositional barriers may be more difficult to surmount, some attempts to boost confidence and provide up-to-date educational experience to adult learners before they embark on formal courses are not uncommon. As we shall discuss below, traditional theories of motivating students also involve consideration of self-worth, self-efficacy and the effects of previous experience. Dispositional barriers are not limited to adult returners to education. Indeed, they can apply to all learners.

Motivation

In the context of learning, motivation has been defined by McMillan and Forsyth (1991) as

> a process in which students value learning and involve themselves in class-room assignments and activities. Motivated students ... take learning seriously and try to get maximum benefits, rather than merely getting by or doing the minimum amount of work necessary.
>
> (McMillan and Forsyth, 1991: 39–40)

In higher education, it can be argued that, as students have chosen to be there, they are self-motivated. However, many would agree that the self-motivated student is a myth. In fact, Beard and Hartley (1984) maintained that some students lack any motivation at all; students who have been persuaded into higher education by parents or school or those with personal problems. If this was the case in 1984 when rates of student participation in higher education in the UK were much lower than is the case today, how much more accurate is the claim today? Students often find themselves having to study compulsory courses which do not interest them. Some courses are seen as not relevant to a student's needs and goals. In addition, Forsyth and McMillan (1991) argued that some courses may be too challenging, which can result in student discouragement, while others may be too easy and disillusioning. Moreover, even the most dedicated students do not spend all their time studying, and extra-curricular activities may prove more involving than lectures or tutorials. Additionally, as we shall discuss below, poverty requires some students to miss classes in order to undertake paid work.

Many colleagues who have introduced peer tutoring or other forms of paired learning into their classes have found that poor student motivation and sporadic absenteeism pose a problem for both students and teachers. Although, as we shall see later in the chapter, absenteeism may be caused by a variety of factors, poor motivation may be a direct cause. As McMillan and Forsyth (1991: 45) argued, 'When students believe that an upcoming situation holds little hope for obtaining scarce rewards, behaviors are adopted to avoid the feelings of negative self-worth that would accompany low achievement.' In other words, students may be motivated to absent themselves, to do very little, to procrastinate or to cheat.

Theories of motivation

McCombs and Pope (1994) claimed that current theories of motivation emphasize cognitive, social-cognitive and social-behaviourist perspectives. The major focus of *cognitive theories* is the mind and how it structures and organizes experience. McCombs and Pope argue that, when looked at from this perspective, motivation may be based on individuals' learned beliefs about their worth, abilities, competencies, goals and expectations for success or failure, and the positive or negative feelings that result. *Social-cognitive* and *social-behaviourist* theories emphasize external factors in motivation, such as the social or emotional support from others or external rewards and incentives. Thus, McCombs and Pope categorize motivation theories as either intrinsic or extrinsic. However, they also argue that more recent theories of motivation are beginning to focus on higher-level processes such as metacognition and on an understanding of the self as agent.

Some theorists claim that there are two determinants of motivation: needs and expectancies (McMillan and Forsyth, 1991). Needs initiate actions, and actions are continued if actors believe they are able to achieve goals. Let us start by examining some of the needs our students may have.

Needs of learners

McMillan and Forsyth (1991) suggested that the following needs are important to learners:

- self-actualization;
- the need to achieve;
- competence;
- self-worth;
- developmental level and goals.

We shall look at these factors briefly.

As we saw in Chapter 3, needs relevant to motivation to learn are usually thought to be situated towards the apex of Maslow's well-known hierarchy of needs (Maslow, 1954), though recent reports which suggest that students now participate in higher education primarily in order to get a well-paid job may refer to needs lower in the hierarchy.

Self-actualization relates to the striving to maximize human potential and personal growth. Self-actualization is not achieved in isolation. It involves the need for 'positive regard' from others, as well as positive self-regard. Acceptance by others indicates value and worth. McMillan and Forsyth (1991: 43) argued that 'this suggests that as professors offer approval and support for what students see as important for their self-actualization, their motivation will be enhanced'.

Maslow's level of 'esteem, self-respect and success' within his hierarchy of needs encompasses several factors relating to what McClelland, Atkinson, Clark and Lowell (1953) call 'achievement motivation'. Achievement-motivation theory is based on the premise that the *need to achieve* is an important determinant of behaviour. This has particular relevance in educational settings. During childhood, some people develop a strong desire to achieve success and enjoy challenges, while others develop the need to avoid failure, and prefer easy tasks with little or no risk of failure attached. People who aim to avoid failure often appear anxious but may try to minimize feelings of failure by over-achieving.

Self-worth is another aspect of the second-highest level of Maslow's needs hierarchy ('esteem, self-respect and success'). It is a 'fundamental need that pervades achievement situations ... for individuals to maintain a positive view of themselves' (McMillan and Forsyth, 1991: 44). Too often, self-worth is directly related to grades, particularly in competitive situations where rewards are scarce. As we have seen, adults with low self-worth based on previous poor performance experience this as a barrier to learning.

As we saw in Chapter 3, Perry (1970) described nine 'positions' representing different developmental levels through which students might progress from an understanding of the world in absolute terms of right and wrong answers to personal commitment and affirmation of identity. In terms of increasing motivation, it can be argued that students may be most motivated when they are challenged by thinking that is beyond their current level of development. For example, a dualist will be challenged and motivated by the views of a relativist. McMillan and Forsyth (1991) claimed that students are least likely to be motivated by activities or discussions that are consistent with their own developmental position.

Goals

Needs and goals are related: needs are both influenced by the goals students set themselves, and, at the same time, may exert an influence on those goals. Weinstein and Meyer (1991) have argued that, in order to be able to become effective learners and achieve their goals, students need to know a great deal about themselves as learners. They need to be aware of their preferred approach to studying or learning style, the ease or difficulty they experience in learning particular subjects or topics and their optimal study habits. Students also need to be aware of how being at university or college and studying the course on which they are enrolled fits in with their personal, occupational and social goals. As we saw in Chapter 3, student approaches to studying may differ, and a student's preferred approach may also act to create educational needs. For example, a deep approach to studying is characterized by the need for understanding which can become the student's goal. Similarly, the surface approach with its requirement for memorization can give rise to a different kind of need.

Expectancies

We shall now move on to consider the part played in the motivational process by student expectancies. McMillan and Forsyth (1991) suggested a number of key aspects:

- self-efficacy;
- previous experience;
- the success of others;
- feedback;
- attributions.

Self-efficacy has been defined, simply, as 'people's beliefs about what they can do' (Kaplan, 1998: 36), and personal judgements about one's own self-efficacy will affect what one chooses to do, whether or not these judgements are accurate. Bandura (1982) claimed that people will attempt activities and tasks they believe to be within their capabilities, and avoid those which they believe to exceed them.

We can all look to our own lives to find examples of the influence of our *previous experience* on our present actions. We can be motivated towards activities which we associate with success and against those which have brought failure in the past. Conversely, we can be motivated to make a second attempt at actions which have been unsatisfactory in the past. Many factors interact to determine what we are motivated to do. We compare ourselves with other people to enable us to refine our impressions of ourselves. This process is formalized in *social comparison theory*. McMillan and Forsyth (1991) argued that we are particularly influenced by *the success of others*. However, Brehm and Kassin (1993) claimed that people sometimes cope with personal inadequacies by focusing on others who are less able or less successful than themselves.

The concept of *feedback* is closely related to that of social comparisons. We check our own behaviour by monitoring the reactions of others around us, by impression checking. Feedback is the means by which we are supplied with reactions to our performance which enable us to reflect and bring about improvements and, thus, feedback plays a particularly important role in education. Schmuck and Schmuck (1975: 151) asserted that 'for feedback to communicate and engage the student in dialogue, it should arise out of empathy for the student, not out of the teacher's need for catharsis'.

It is also useful for us to know what other people are like, and how they feel, in order that we may interact with them successfully. We are, thus, motivated to try to understand others. We observe and analyse their behaviour in an attempt to explain it. As we saw in Chapter 3, 'the explanations we come up with are called *attributions*, and the theory that describes the process is called attribution theory' (Brehm and Kassin, 1993: 107).

External factors

So far, our consideration of student motivation has focused on internal factors relating to students themselves. Motivation may also be affected by external factors. As we have seen, McCombs and Pope (1994) described social-cognitive and social-behaviourist theories of motivation which emphasize external factors such as the social or emotional support from others or external rewards and

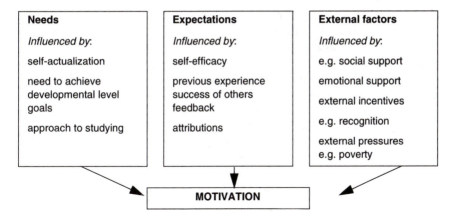

Figure 8.1 A model of student motivation

incentives. Other influential external pressures affecting student motivation in current higher education are the need to undertake paid work and the desire for a job on graduation.

Summary

It is possible to summarize factors relating to student motivation in a model of student motivation which incorporates needs, expectations and external factors. (See Figure 8.1.)

We now need to consider how we may put all this interesting and helpful information to good use.

Facilitating learning: using what we know about motivation to help us persuade and motivate students

How may a knowledge of theories of motivation help teachers to motivate their students or persuade them to participate in paired or co-operative learning? McCombs and Pope (1994) suggested three basic principles:

1 Students are motivated by learning situations that challenge and involve them and allow them personal choice and control matched to their capabilities.
2 Students' motivation is enhanced if they perceive that tasks are related to personal interests, needs and goals and are capable of being achieved.
3 Students have a natural motivation to learn which can be elicited in supportive environments.

As we have seen, motivation is a complex phenomenon, including individual personal factors which may be difficult or impossible to influence. There are, however, opportunities for intervention to promote student motivation within the educational context. Peer tutoring, peer-assisted learning and true co-operation require involvement and activity on the part of learners and, thus, meet the requirements of McCombs and Pope's first principle. These learning methods also provide learners with a greater degree of control and choice than occurs in traditional teacher-centred learning. In order to address the second principle, we need to ascertain what are our students' needs and goals in order to try to make the tasks we set relevant to these wherever possible, as we might in a variety of learning situations. Finally, well-organized peer-assisted learning should provide the supportive learning environment deemed necessary in order to elicit students' natural motivation. This fulfils the requirements of the last principle.

Barbara McCombs from the University of Denver Research Institute at Denver, Colorado, reflects on some issues relating to motivation in the context of peer learning in Chapter 10.

Next, we shall explore the problem of absenteeism.

FREQUENTLY ASKED QUESTIONS 3: ABSENTEEISM

Why do some students miss peer tutoring sessions? What can be done about it?

Absenteeism is, perhaps, the most critical of the problems that are general to higher education and particularly relevant to the working of paired or co-operative learning. Debates on electronic discussion lists about the problems of absenteeism seem to indicate two polarized positions on this topic. While some teachers advocate the use of penalties for absence, others discuss ways of motivating students to ensure that they *want* to be present. Yet others discuss the philosophical implications of regarding absence as a problem. Whatever one's views on absenteeism, it is not possible to learn from one's peers if you or they do not participate in any interaction. Thus, absenteeism must be regarded as a central problem in the context of peer tutoring and paired learning.

Let us look more closely at some of the arguments and issues raised in electronic list discussions. John Ogden made three observations about absenteeism which provide a good starting point to our investigation.

First, in increasing numbers, students are being obliged to find paid employment in order to make ends meet. While this may not conflict directly with lectures and other academic commitments, it does set up a whole new dynamic of priorities for the students to juggle with. They may take the view that lectures are not their highest priority.

Second, and perhaps related to the first point, is it not the responsibility of the lecturer in charge of the class to ensure that the learning experience to be found at our lectures is such that students do in fact give it the priority we think it should have?

Third, if students are regularly absent from lectures what is our normative means of communication with them? That is: what understanding is there, between department and student, as to the trustworthy means of communication, that which if we have used it we have discharged our obligations to the give the student due notice?

(isl,[1] 17.3.99)

We shall explore some of these issues further, starting with the question of student employment.

Student employment

There is growing evidence to support the claim that more and more full-time students are engaging in paid employment. For example, Taylor (1998) conducted a survey of paid employment undertaken by full-time undergraduates in an established Scottish university and reported that the amount of paid work increases in each year of study, with the exception of the final year. He concluded that, during term time, over one-quarter of respondents were working at weekends and 10 per cent were working during week-days. Not surprisingly, he reported that the primary reason given for working during term time was financial. Personal experience and anecdotal evidence suggest that a much higher proportion of students now do paid work while studying for a degree. McNair supplied some UK-based evidence to support this claim, pointing out that a large number of so-called full-time students now face the kinds of problems that, previously, were limited to their part-time peers. 'Such students now face the same problems which part-timers have always faced when programme changes are made, or when their employers require them to work additional hours at short notice' (ed-dev-resnet,[2] 15.3.99).

Brigitte Gemme from Quebec alerted us to possible effects of student paid employment on motivation. She pointed out that goal commitment to high grades may be lower for students who do paid work outside university or college. She argued that these students 'may be more ready than others to accept a compromise (lower grades, some money) in order to pursue at the same time a degree and a decent lifestyle' (AERA-J,[3] 15.3.99).

However, Margo Blythman from the London College of Printing argued that engaging in paid work may not be the sole explanation for absenteeism. In addition, she provided a useful suggestion about how to investigate the phenomenon.

My only other suggestion is to be up front and ask the students why they don't attend – either a telephone survey of non-attenders (and attenders) or some focus groups (but the latter is of more limited value if the non-attenders are not there!). It is important to gather the views of the attenders as well as the non-attenders since the FE evidence shows that external factors – like paid work – are likely to be as big for the attenders as for the non-attenders and therefore are not in themselves the explanation.

(ed-dev-resnet,15.3.99)

Margo Blythman and Daphne Hampton describe their scheme of study support networks designed to encourage attendance in Chapter 10.

Other factors in absenteeism

In his contribution to the discussion, Phil Race from Newcastle, UK, explored a number of factors relevant to the topic of absenteeism, suggesting reasons other than the need to undertake paid work why students might miss classes:

- the growing percentage of the population in our universities means that this population includes many students who are not as motivated as once was the case (showing my age here!!);
- students are (sensibly) strategic, and they often don't attach value to small-group work when they don't see the time spent being reflected in our assessment processes and instruments (this one we CAN do something about directly);
- students sometimes don't seem to be told clearly enough about the expected learning outcomes directly associated with small-group work, and other learning processes apart from 'core' lectures;
- in the age of info technology and photocopies, students (often wrongly) think that they can catch up on missed sessions by capturing someone else's handouts or notes, or from the web;
- we are now so pressed in most institutions that WE can't afford the time and energy to make small-group work a central plank in students' learning;
- the small groups are often not small enough any more, and students feel that one less won't be missed in the larger-group size;
- sometimes students tell me that they don't value small-group work because WE give them the impression that WE don't value it: they report that tutorials are sometimes cancelled through illness (or TQA[4] preparations!) whereas lectures seldom are. They say WE turn up unprepared for them in a way we wouldn't for lectures.
- Probably, of all these things, the one we can most tackle is the driving force of assessment. Once we get our students into our small groups, however, we still have to get them learning while they're there – it's not enough to turn up for an attendance mark and sit there mentally sleeping. Is assessed work DURING small groups one of the answers?

(seda[5]-request, 15.3.99)

This contribution captures vividly the complexity of the problem and suggests positive ways of moving towards a solution.

Attendance policies and their rationales

A majority of contributors to the electronic discussion argued for the introduction of attendance policies to combat student absenteeism. Abbe Herzig from the University of Wisconsin-Madison and Tony Green from University College Worcester described schemes in which class participation accounts for a percentage of grades. Most contributors who advocated some sort of policy for absence described schemes which were designed to be 'realistic' rather than punitive, and which had the best interests of students at heart. For example, Ray LaManna of New York University argued that if we wish to help our students for life, we should give them 'a dose of that life in higher education'. Thus, in LaManna's classes, absentees have their grades reduced. He explains the reasoning behind this strategy:

> This is not the lone cry of some conservative here ... It is, instead, the reasoned response of a quite progressive professor who is concerned with the obvious disconnect which I see between higher education and the world of work.
>
> (AERA-J, 17.3.99)

Similarly, Russ Hunter from New Brunswick, Canada, argued that one of the functions of an attendance policy is to teach students that attendance facilitates learning, that absenteeism has a personal moral dimension and that non-attendance has real consequences.

> I try to help my students see that there are arbitrary, imposed consequences, and there are real consequences. If the consequence of jaywalking is that you get a ticket, that's one thing; if it's that you get hit by a bus, that's quite another. Someone can *decide* not to give you a ticket. The consequences of non-attendance have to be (and be seen to be) real, not imposed, in order for them to facilitate learning. My view is that if attendance in my class actually facilitates learning, then non-attendance doesn't, and that's a *real* consequence. Nothing I can do about it.
>
> My students have an *extremely* hard time understanding this distinction, because everything about their educational careers has effectively obliterated it.
>
> (AERA-J, 17.3.99)

Hunter's statement might form a useful discussion starter for students or teachers investigating the phenomenon of absenteeism.

Some contributors to the electronic list debates provided information relating to implementation of attendance policies.

Implementing a policy on absenteeism

John Simons reported that the introduction of the attendance policy which operates within the School of Humanities and Arts at Edge Hill College, UK, was preceded by discussions between teachers, heads of subjects and student represent-atives. The aim of that policy is reported as being to change the culture, so that non-attendance is not seen as an option and to ensure that students feel a sense of responsibility for their course. It was not designed or introduced to force students to see attendance as an end in itself.

> Students have actually been reported as saying in module feedback that they are glad the system is in place because they find it supportive. It is also note-worthy that although the system is only operative in modules within my school there is some evidence that attendance has improved across the modular scheme. The library has also reported increased use presumably because stu-dents feel that once they are in they might as well do something with their time!
>
> We still need to run the scheme for a year before we can fully evaluate it but what we seem to have done is to change the culture for the better. It must be stressed that what we set out to do was to create responsibility not obedi-ence and so I think that part of what, at this stage, looks like success has to be down to the fact that we did consult carefully with student reps and get their support before we did anything.
>
> (isl list, 16.3.99)

It might be argued that the attendance policies discussed above represent an act by teachers to attract students into classes. However, some colleagues reasoned that this responsibility should go further.

Lecturers' responsibilities

Velda McCune from Edinburgh raised the issue of negotiation of responsibilities between students and teachers:

> I have recently been discussing this issue (absenteeism) with colleagues and the one common theme seems to be negotiation of responsibilities. Several ex-perienced staff felt this was important, and staff who did this seemed to get better attendance. The discussions typically involved asking what their stu-dents felt their responsibilities were in terms of preparation and attendance and the staff member might also discuss their own responsibilities (such as guaranteeing a supportive atmosphere). Colleagues varied in how they broached the issue, some were quite up-front, others more gentle. I doubt this would work without a culture which supports attendance, but if you could get that, then negotiation might help further.
>
> (ed-dev-resnet, 15.3.99)

Kathleen Ellis of Texas Technical University argued that the responsibility for absenteeism should be shared by teachers, students and administrators, and that some people may be placing the blame for absenteeism on the wrong shoulders.

She informed us that absence from her classes was a rare event and then went on to consider some of the possible reasons for this.

> I do not take credit for being such an excellent teacher. There were other contributing factors – the class was one of only thirty students, the students were primarily non-traditional (i.e. older and wiser). The blame for high absenteeism must be shared. If at all possible, classes of 250 students in a lecture pit should not be offered for freshmen. That responsibility would have to be placed squarely on the shoulders of the administration. Faculty, students, and administration must work together to create an environment of higher learning rather than a boot camp with drill sergeants calling out roll.
>
> (AERA-J, 17.3.99)

A number of participants in the discussion argued that students would be more likely to attend classes if the benefits of so doing were stressed.

Student responsibilities

Several discussants maintained that students should be responsible for their own learning, and for decisions to be absent from classes. Some argued against attendance policies and against those who advocate forced attendance. For example, Kathleen Ellis (a regular participant in this discussion) wrote:

> Have they (teachers) forgotten that their students are adults paying for a service? It is the option of the customer to attend or not attend. I always told my students that if they could pass with the grade that was acceptable to them without attending my classes, that was fine with me. I never took attendance and always had a full house. ... Perhaps faculty should look at their teaching methods and material rather than a punitive system directed at their customers.
>
> (AERA-J, 17.3.99)

Similarly, Russ Hunter (another regular participant) commented that

> We keep them children by making up all these rules; one of the ways we protect children and make it possible for them to make mistakes is to intervene between real consequences and artificial ones. But at some point we need to pull back. My view is that in this case that point is well before university.
>
> (AERA-J, 17.3.99)

Dewey Dykstra Jr of Boise State University agreed that the responsibility for attendance resided with students, but felt that the consequences of this view could lead to problems and potential conflict. For example, Dykstra described a scenario in which lecturers, particularly those who attempt non-traditional teaching, may be blamed for poor student attendance and performance by both the administration and students themselves.

Maybe this 'problem' is in part brought on by the non-adult manner in which we are treated by the system which we supposedly set up for 'teaching evaluations'.

I also don't mind if someone can do well without me, the problem is that many usually don't when they try and then I pay the consequences of their wrath both financially and promotionally.

(AERA-J, 17.3.99)

Attendance and the learning community

Jody Fernandez's contribution is particularly pertinent to student co-operative learning or learning by peer tutoring as it highlights the importance of the learning community in student learning. Fernandez reported having once believed that attendance was entirely at the discretion of the student.

I used to agree with you but have changed in recent years. Here's why.

There's more that occurs in the classroom than is testable. Learning occurs through discourse, just as we are doing here. Students who are able to read the book and pass the test but do not attend class are missing out on an important part of the learning community we call higher education. If they do not attend, they are basically using the course as a correspondence course, certainly a viable form SOMETIMES, but not always. Attendance is built into my syllabi, but I'm always willing to make exceptions in certain circumstances, i.e. childbirth. If a student cannot attend a Friday class due to other commitments, perhaps s/he should sign up for another section. If the course is not important enough to attend every session, what does that show about the student's level of commitment to his/her education and about the real necessity of even offering the course?

(AERA-J, 17.3.99)

Summary

Our examination of electronic list discussions has indicated that the topic of absenteeism has the power to stimulate fierce debate among academics. We have seen, too, that teachers hold very different views on the subject. We have looked at the extent and role of student employment in absenteeism, and considered other factors which may influence students' decisions to attend classes. Some attendance policies have been discussed, and some issues relating to implementation of these considered. Lecturers' responsibilities in the context of absenteeism have been explored. Finally, the importance of the peer group and of the learning community at large has been emphasized.

We shall now move on to consider some problems of learning in groups, based on a case study of positive and negative experiences of group learning.

FREQUENTLY ASKED QUESTIONS 4: PROBLEMS OF LEARNING IN GROUPS

Why do some students dislike working in groups?

The work of Feichtner and Davis (1985) makes an excellent contribution to our understanding of learning groups and provides some answers to the question. Below is a summary of the findings of their survey of positive and negative group-learning experiences.

A CASE STUDY OF GROUP LEARNING: FEICHTNER AND DAVIS' (1985) SURVEY OF POSITIVE AND NEGATIVE EXPERIENCES

The authors reported the results of a study of views of undergraduates from two major south-western US universities entitled, 'Why some groups fail: a survey of students' experiences with learning groups'. Students were asked to nominate examples of their least and most positive experiences of group working, and to identify factors which may have led to either success or failure. As Felder and Brent observed earlier in the chapter, Feichtner and Davis found their students were more likely to report positive experiences when groups were formed by the instructor than when students self-selected their group mates. In fact, if students formed their own groups they were likely to list the group working among their worst experiences. Students rated their best experiences of group learning as those where no class presentation was required and where there was no requirement for a written report. However, best experiences were also associated with the presence of a number of examinations. The researchers reported a straightforward relationship between time spent working together (in and out of class), group cohesion and positive experiences. When group work counted for more than 20 per cent of the course grade, Feichtner and Davis (1985) found that the majority of students reported a best-group experience. When group work contributed less than 20 per cent, the number of students rating their experiences in learning groups as good was reduced to one in six. The researchers also felt it important to use some peer evaluation as part of the course grade, but recommended that it be used with caution, as problems may arise if student influence on grades is too great. Contributions from peer evaluation of between 21 per cent and 40 per cent were found to be associated with the greatest number of positive group-learning experiences.

My summary of advice to teachers derived from Feichtner and Davis (1985) is to be found in Table 8.1.

A final comment from Feichtner and Davis (1985: 68), based on their analysis of student questionnaires is that students are likely to 'blame the group's problems on the attitude or lack of competence of the instructor'. Teachers do not receive credit when groups are effective, however.

Table 8.1 Minimizing problems associated with learning in a group

Problem area	Guidelines and advice
Reluctant students **(1) Rationale**	Think carefully about why you are planning to use group learning. Communicate your rationale to students.
Reluctant students **(2) Student expectations**	Help students develop realistic expectations about their role and that of the teacher.
Structuring groups	Structure groups carefully: • 4–7 member groups tend to do best. • Permanent groups are better than temporary ones. • Heterogeneous groups formed by the instructor are better than homogeneous student-selected groups.
Preparation	Be 'meticulously prepared'.
Group activities	It is important to have enough of these to ensure some development of group cohesion, but too many (and particular types, e.g. presentations and group reports) tend to be associated with poor student experiences. Fechtner and Davis (1985) suggest: • Design activities likely to be perceived as relevant to course content. • A variety of activities will help achievement of course objectives and increase group cohesion. • Give a series of group exams. • Provide the opportunity to work on group assignments in class.
The role of the teacher	Try to listen in on groups as they work together in class. This allows for the early detection of errors or group problems. It 'also seems to provide them (students) with a visual demonstration that we're still doing our job'.
Grading	Provide grade incentives. Aim for between 21% and 40% group-work contribution to course-assessment grade.

Derived from Feichtner and Davis (1985)

SUMMARY AND REFLECTIONS

This chapter has focused on a variety of problems relating to peer tutoring, paired and co-operative learning. We started by considering some issues concerning organization and preparation. Next, motivation of both colleagues and students was explored. This was followed by a brief exploration of student needs and expectancies, and consideration of some external factors which may influence student motivation. Next, through an examination of electronic list discussions, we explored the topic of absenteeism. Finally, some problems of learning in groups were examined in Feichtner and Davis' survey of positive and negative group learning.

We can conclude that some problems associated with peer tutoring are more amenable to solution than others. We have the opportunity to improve our planning and organization (though these skills come more easily to some than to others). We can obtain information from our students about their needs and expectations, and, where these are compatible with our conceptions of higher education, we can attempt to meet student needs. Solution becomes more problematic when student and lecturer needs are at odds. However, openness and negotiation may help save the day. We can organize group learning so as to maximize the chances of our students having a positive learning experience. My views on absenteeism somewhat resemble those expressed by Jody Fernandez above. I believe that students should make their own decisions about how they use their time so as to maximize their learning. I also think that we can help them do this by planning interesting courses, structuring and preparing them well and delivering them with flair. However, I also know that, even in the best of circumstances, some students will choose to absent themselves. While this may not matter too much in a small number of cases, I believe that it does matter in general. As was argued in Chapter 3, many theorists believe that learning cannot take place in isolation and that it requires the presence of others. Social interaction is thought to be a critical component of situated learning. It is not only peer tutoring, paired learning and co-operative learning that require the presence and active participation of learners. Quality learning in general cannot take place on one's own.

In the next chapter, Nils Tomes discusses some of the issues involved in the use of technology to support co-operative learning.

NOTES

1 Improving student learning discussion list (isl@mailbase.ac.uk)
2 Educational development research network discussion list
  (ed-dev-resnet@mailbase.ac.uk)
3 American Educational Research Association (LISTSERV@ASU.EDU) 'J' division is
  the post-secondary education forum.
4 Teaching Quality Assessment.
5 Staff and Educational Development Association (seda@mailbase.ac.uk)

9 Technology-supported collaborative learning

Nils Tomes

INTRODUCTION

Communication and computing technologies have a special importance for collaborative learning in overcoming some of the bounds of distance and time, making possible collaborations which might not otherwise be able to take place. Technologies can also extend the possibilities for collaboration, offering new opportunities to work in richer or more varied ways. And technologies can change the very nature of collaborative learning.

The increasing prevalence of computing and communications infrastructure offers realistic options for educational use. Within Europe and America, a high proportion of households have access to a personal computer and the second half of the 1990s saw an exponential growth in internet subscriptions. At a policy level, educational technologies are seen as a key component of the European vision of the global information society (Bangemann Report, 1995), the UK's growth of lifelong learning through superhighways for education and industrial training, and the USA's Education Plan. Within the education sector, information and communications technologies are valued for their potential to extend educational opportunity and promote economic growth.

Increasing bandwidth has delivered more power to the desktop and to the classroom. With this has come a more convincing sense of immediacy and personal presence, which has brought an interpersonal depth to communication across a distance. This growth in bandwidth also makes it possible to share more detailed and more dynamic activities with collaborators, opening new possibilities for working for distributed communities. At a broader level, the introduction of high-bandwidth networks connecting educational institutions, the superhighways, has begun to blur traditional institutional boundaries. This impacts on how we see our involvement in learning. Not only are groups of learners distributed across different locations, but so, too, are the groups of tutors who facilitate and shape their learning. More flexible approaches to learning are needed.

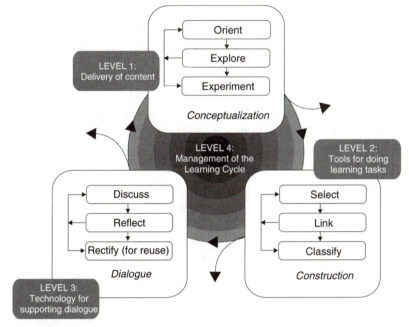

Figure 9.1 The learning cycle
(Adapted from Mayes, T., Coventry, L., Thomson, A. and Mason, R. (1994) 'Learning through telematics', report to British Telecom)

THE PEDAGOGICAL FRAMEWORK

Let us look first at the pedagogical framework for learning using communications and information technologies. A key element, here, is the underlying model of what is happening when a student is engaged in learning.

A helpful model of the learning cycle is defined by Mayes, Coventry, Thomson and Mason (1994), which assists in identifying where technology can support the key processes of learning (Figure 9.1). Learning is not seen as a sequence of activities which the lecturer specifies and the learner follows: it is far more dynamic than that.

This model draws an important concept found in the work of Laurillard (1993) which may be familiar to readers: that the teacher and learner are engaged in a dialogue. The learner's activities are shaped and redirected as an outcome of this dialogue. The three levels in this learning cycle focus upon:

1   Conceptualization, which is enabled through the online delivery of content.
2   Construction of a mental model of the topic, supported by tools for doing learning tasks.
3   Dialogue between teacher and learners, as well as learner and learner, supported by communications technologies.

These levels equate, broadly, to the development of knowledge, understanding and empowerment.

A fourth level overlies Mayes' three levels: the management of the learning cycle itself (McAndrew, Foubister and Mayes, 1996). This encompasses the scheduling of learning activities, monitoring and the assessments which are used by learners, their teachers and the institution to monitor progress towards their individual educational goals.

Technology creates new opportunities within the learning cycle by capturing the collaboration and communication between groups of learners and teachers in a form which allows that collaboration to become an educational resource for other students. The inclusion of technology can convert a *process* into a re-usable *product*: it reifies the act of collaboration or dialogue and makes it available to others. This product can also be assessed for grading purposes.

A key point which follows from this conversion of process to product is that the student must be considered as a creator of learning materials, as well as being a consumer. Within this context, the student's creations are most likely for use within their local learning community, but it is not uncommon for these products to be utilized more widely through essay-banks, structured sets of queries, such as answer-gardens, and other opportunities for vicarious learning.

At the highest level, learners need to develop a strategic overview of their discipline and acquire the tactical knowledge to further develop their understanding. This can be achieved within the learning dialogue both through peer-assisted learning and through a tutor's shaping of the learning process. Dialogue is a crucial aspect of deeper learning and the development of higher-order thinking. But it is an aspect which can be hard to develop among distributed groups of students.

> [We] feel that much of the learning which comes through dialogue is being squeezed out of the formal education system, particularly in higher education, often because of the growing emphasis on the use of educational technology to deliver content and activities. By exploiting the potential of the emerging networked communities, we can try to reintroduce this component and even expand it to those students who would not otherwise have had the opportunity at all, such as distance learners.
>
> (McKendree, Stenning, Mayes, Lee and Cox, 1998: 113)

An important aspect of the learning dialogue is the pace at which it progresses, and there are advantages and disadvantages on each side. Here, technology offers the options of collaboration in real time, with everyone working simultaneously, or of contributing asynchronously to an ongoing discussion at a time which suits the individual learner. Synchronous communications offer the most natural pacing, but there are significant technical, psychological and organizational difficulties in being able to scale up these approaches to deal with larger groups.

With distributed groups of learners, computer conferencing offers the potential to deliver collaborative learning more efficiently than face-to-face group work, and in ways which suit the demands on learners' and tutors' time. There is some evidence that this increased flexibility may be at the expense of increased effort for the teacher (European Commission, 1998).

Technology-based learning adds additional requirements to the students' repertoire of learning skills, and these needs must be recognized if technology-supported collaboration is to work effectively. Littlejohn and Stefani (1999) asked teachers which skills their students needed to learn effectively in a technological environment. Over half of the skills identified were independent of the students' learning environment, whether virtual or real (such as basic information technology skills, and an open mind about the role of new technology in learning). But to these were added the need for a concept of virtuality, the ability to work with others in a virtual environment and engage in asynchronous discussion. The same is, of course, true for the teacher or tutor. In some cases, the adjustments which teachers make to their teaching strategies when they introduce educational technologies are those which correspond to good practice in teaching, regardless of the medium. Here, technology is the Trojan horse of pedagogical change.

Another important issue concerns the design of computer tools to support co-operation. As Tang (1991: 143) argued, 'the needs of a group using tools collaboratively are different from those of an individual user'. These differences should be reflected in the design of technology.

There is a need to tackle skills and design requirements head-on, to empower people who are learning and collaborating online.

THE ORGANIZATIONAL CONTEXT

Let us turn now to look at the organizational context. Conventionally, innovation is seen as being driven by the supplier of new technologies, a model which worked well in developing an understanding of the introduction of technologies such as the radio and the television. In telematics-based learning, as with other multimedia technologies, the users play 'an active and creative role in appropriating the new functionalities into working practices and relations' (Proctor, Williams and Cashin, 1999). This is social learning, a highly distributed process which impacts upon personal, technical and organizational change. It involves both consumer and supplier, and the contexts within which they work. Users configure and use collaborative technologies to meet their own educational needs, not necessarily to reflect the needs anticipated by the designer. The evolution of the innovation is itself an inherently collaborative exercise. This means that particular care needs to be taken in monitoring and evaluating pedagogical innovation based upon telematics technologies to ensure that the multiple motives and expectations are being met. The key actors should be involved in this evaluation process.

The impact of this kind of educational innovation relies upon the distribution of technical and educational understandings among the various key actors such as learners, teachers, facilitators and trainers (Flannagan and Miles, 1999), and consequently the way in which the innovation is implemented reflects organizational structures and personal development needs.

Institutions must manage the transition from traditional teaching approaches to ones which are suited to integrating technology-based collaborative working. A review of 30 pilot distance-learning projects carried out within the 'Telematics for Flexible and Distance Learning Programme' (European Commission, 1998) concluded that positive learning outcomes were observed particularly where telematics-supported distance learning was combined with periodic face-to-face interactions in the form of seminars or residential meetings. Why should this be? Educational providers operate within an existing institutional context and learners have preconceptions as to how that context affects the ways in which they work. Both learners and their teachers bring well-developed expectations with them to the learning process, often based on previous experience and specific to their own cultural context. There can be a misalignment between the intentions of the education providers and the expectations of the teachers and students involved, which can be resolved in a straightforward manner with face-to-face discussions at a local level.

New specialist services are beginning to develop throughout the education sector, to meet the needs of technology-based communication and collaboration. Content-design, systems-design, review, procurement of resources, integration, maintenance, service-provision, and report-generation are tackled by a growing class of specialists. Teaching will soon no longer be a lonely activity which a lecturer carries out in private with 50 (or 500) students: there are many more people involved in technology-based collaboration. A multidisciplinary approach is becoming essential, bringing together subject specialists, service providers, learners, educational designers, senior managers and staff trainers. Collaboration in the design, delivery and use of technology-based learning is vital to its success. In setting out to define a collaborative learning activity, the educational designer must take specific account of the technology-based system which is to be used to enable and monitor that collaboration, and to add this additional level of design to creating their task description.

As well as offering new ways to support familiar patterns of working, technology also creates opportunities for new styles of collaborative working. For example, electronic seminars give unanticipated advantages over more traditional face-to-face tutorials, in allowing learners to develop their techniques in presenting and responding to arguments. 'A system of asynchronous conferencing gives seminarians time to reflect on and research their contributions, rather than feeling they are being put on the spot by having to make instant judgements on unfamiliar and sometimes difficult or complex material' (Duffy, Arnold and Henderson, 1995: 42).

COLLABORATION AND COMMUNICATIONS

Different kinds of collaboration are enabled by synchronous and by asynchronous communications. Each technology imposes its own limitations and offers its own rewards. Synchronous collaborations require people to be collaborating at the *same time*, and include applications-sharing, video or teleconferencing, audioconferencing and text-based 'conversations'. Asynchronous communications can be used by people working at *different times* and include bulletin boards, voicemail, e-mail, work-groups, and structured discussion lists. You will be able to add your own examples to this list.

Synchronous communications

Synchronous collaborations convey the best sense of the collaborator being present. They can also be expensive, where good-quality images are required, and work best with smaller groups. Early adopters of these technologies are found among the educators of health professionals, where small groups are the norm and visual information is crucial. Surgical techniques, for example, are taught by videoconference, making specialist professional expertise available to a wide audience while overcoming the practical limitations of putting large numbers of students into a sterile operating theatre.

Synchronous collaborations technologies do not scale up straightforwardly to deal with large numbers of collaborators, as they become more like presentation media where there is a large group at one of the networked classrooms. Despite their capacity for spontaneity, synchronous collaborations benefit from a degree of formality, with participants taking specific roles in maintaining the communication and people using more overt techniques for turn-taking, interrupting or identifying themselves. In addition, there can be different social constraints on participants, depending whether they feel part of the main group, where the collaboration is being co-ordinated, or whether they are in a distant group. Those who are remote feel less involved in the collaboration unless specific strategies are used to include them within the discussion. As an example, a speaker whose seminar was being video-conferenced to a remote audience found that, when his exposition overran, those in the main group remained to participate in the discussion, while the entire far-end audience had already left for lunch. Where there is a large group at the far end, it can help to have a local co-ordinator who is assigned to manage aspects of the group's communication.

Communications and group-work technologies inevitably place a conceptual distance between participants, due to the limitations in achieving real telepresence, that is, the sense of really being there. For audio or textual synchronous conferencing, groups can find it difficult to establish a rapport if they know little about their collaborators' identities. Often, this kind of synchronous conferencing is facilitated by arranging an early face-to-face meeting, for example at a residential school, where participants can build up a more detailed picture of their classmates. Once identities are firmly established, audio or textual conferencing can be sufficient to maintain the ongoing collaboration. 'When creating a virtual community … it is important to remember that an electronic community is composed of people, not computers, and as such it has to be built one person at a time' (Reid, 1999: 45).

Asynchronous collaboration

Asynchronous collaboration allows learners and teachers to participate at a time which suits their working needs or the time zone in which they live. The technologies involved tend to require lower bandwidth and simpler software, being more economical. They can, nonetheless, be powerful tools in collaborative work.

Within the UK, for example, there are over 150,000 teachers and learners who use Mailbase-structured discussion lists.

> A discussion list is more than e-mail; it has the potential for becoming a learning community. Essentially, it allows for reflective and considered debate. Responses can be prepared off-line and sent to either all members of the list simultaneously or to a select number or to only one. Only when the first option is taken is the message entirely open to the whole list. An untold number of exchanges take place between individuals 'behind the scenes' and these form part of the list activity but have an ambiguous relationship in relation to the concept of the list's learning community.
>
> (Burke, 1998)

Building a sense of community is the key to fruitful collaborative learning. But one impediment to this is the difficulty in growing this group knowledge through the use of asynchronous technologies. Answer-gardens provide useful opportunities here, supporting the development of a collective memory among a collaborative group or organization (e.g. Ackerman and McDonald, 1996). This class of tool allows groupings of similar questions and answers to be evolved, providing a sense of context which can aid the independent learner in diagnosing and developing their understanding of a topic.

THE BENEFITS OF COMPUTER-MEDIATED COLLABORATION

Computer-mediated collaboration benefits groups of teachers as well as their students.

> The global community, through the medium of Communications and Information Technology (C and IT), is already a reality for researchers. [...] It will bring benefits to scholars in the arts and humanities as well as researchers in science and technology.
>
> (Dearing Report, 1997: section 13.6)

Increasingly, new courses are created by collaborative teams of teachers and supported by distributed groups of tutors, as well as defining collaborative activities for learners, all of whom can benefit from the support which telematics applications can offer. Learners from all parts of the world sharing a common language and appropriate Internet technology may experience these benefits (e.g. Chou and Sun, 1996).

One specific advantage to computer-mediated collaboration is that it provides an audit trail of the collaboration process itself, which is often missing from unmediated discussions. This opens up new opportunities for assessing an individual's contribution to group work, and their competency with teamwork. The recording of a collaboration produces a new learning resource which can become part of the learning process for other groups of students, for evaluation or to provide an exemplar.

Technologies can create new educational opportunities. Video or audioconferencing can, for example, bring together distant experts or native speakers with foreign language learners, providing speech models at a time when the student needs authentic input.

As most tutors are aware, women learners can often take a back-seat in small-group interactions. This is attributed variously to cultural expectations, lack of confidence, or different styles of group dynamics. Whatever the reason, it impacts upon collaborative work. Technology offers some advantages here, in levelling the playing field. Furthermore, recent research (Michaelson and Pohl, forthcoming) suggests that some students may actually benefit from the asynchronous interaction made possible by the use of technology. Communicating asynchronously takes away time pressures and allows a more reflective approach to making contributions to collaborative work, which seems to suit styles of interaction which are predominant among women. It is well known that face-to-face interaction is framed by interpersonal stereotypes, especially those based on gender, ability and ethnicity, which work against equal collaboration between formal equals. For example, it is well documented that, in face-to-face interactions, men are more likely to ignore their partner's contributions, to interrupt their partner and to try and maintain the focus on their own needs (e.g. Tannen, 1990). In contrast, women seem to be more accommodating and keen to truly collaborate. Such stereotypes are grounded in, and reinforced by, physical differences, as well as by role expectations. In contrast, in asynchronous interaction there is no physical embodiment to reinforce stereotypes and asynchronicity militates against such stereotyped patterns of discourse.

Learning technologies can change the very nature of collaboration. Some people welcome the opportunity to adopt a different style of self-presentation, shielded by the additional psychological distance which computer-mediated working can create (Turkle, 1996). Technology can allow people to present themselves through a new identity, with technology putting a distance between the individual and their apparent persona. This can allow learners to explore a range of 'what if' situations, without jeopardizing their self-esteem. This finds a fruitful place in forums such as electronic bulletin boards and other virtual meeting places, such as multi-user dungeons.

In addition, asynchronous collaboration allows for significant variations in the speed at which students work, which can assist students who have a perceptual or physical disadvantage. For visually handicapped students, we need to ensure that the style of working complements the tools available for students to handle both textual and visual materials. Digital technologies also have the potential to offer students a choice of modality, allowing them to collaborate with colleagues in the medium which most suits their requirements. Curriculum designers benefit from thinking through how to design collaborative tasks in a way which maximizes accessibility.

Technology-mediated collaborative learning can present important options in access for social groups who may otherwise have limitations on their mobility or availability, such as care-givers or those studying in the workplace. Telepresence also allows us to overcome some real limitations posed by health and safety restrictions, in bringing remote learners into laboratory or healthcare environments from which they would otherwise be excluded, for example in surgical teaching.

LIMITATIONS OF COMPUTER-MEDIATED COLLABORATION

In setting out to include technology-supported collaboration within learning situations, it is important to address the question of the appropriateness of our choice. Will the technology do what we need it to do, or are we choosing to do those things which are easy to achieve with the technology? Do these kinds of learning technologies offer equal opportunities to all learners? In planning pedagogical changes, we need to identify the educational aims and check whether our use of technology to support collaborative working will help our students meet these objectives.

When using synchronous collaboration technologies, such as tele- or videoconferencing, there is an increased need for formalisms, such as protocols for turn-taking, hand-raising, leading or summarizing. High cognitive demands can be placed on participants using synchronous technologies, particularly on the co-ordinator or presenter. A level of prior preparation is important, which can reduce the spontaneity of the discussion. However, evaluation of videoconference-mediated foreign-language learning (McAndrew *et al.*, 1996) concluded that videoconferencing emulates working face-to-face sufficiently well for collaborative task-based learning to be supported.

The sense of being protected by the psychological distance that taking on a new identity entails can also lead to a disinhibition in social exchanges, with people adopting more extreme views than they would in a face-to-face context, leading to more emotional discourse styles (e.g. Lea, O'Shea, Fung and Spears, 1992). This has led to more formal statements on online etiquette. Presenting an alternate image also invokes serious issues about trust in collaborative communications. Trust is of particular importance in building up a sense of telepresence, and essential to working closely with distant collaborators. Our perceptions of trustworthiness are based upon many social cues, some of which are unavailable to a distant collaborator using technology to support a shared dialogue.

The fact that technology comes between us and our collaborators means that we must be particularly aware of the act of communication itself, adding a level of meta-communicative awareness which may become unintentionally obtrusive. The converse of this is that the technology can bring to the fore a fruitful awareness of how group interactions are organized.

We should also consider access alongside accessibility, where technology is part of the mix. Do students have equipment which they can use, can they afford the connection charges, and are there services to support their technical needs? There is the potential to inadvertently disadvantage some students and to create collaborative groups which are socially homogeneous. This may affect the quality of both the collaboration and the learning.

COLLABORATIVE TECHNOLOGY AND PEER TUTORING

Having surveyed the broad educational benefits and pitfalls of collaborative technology, let us now turn to its use for peer tutoring. First of all, is peer tutoring actually a collaborative venture? Collaboration is usually seen as involving comparable effort from all participants towards an outcome from which all benefit equally, but this is not characteristic of all forms of peer tutoring. For example, in fixed-role peer tutoring, it may appear that both participants are collaborating to achieve positive learning outcomes for the tutee. However, as we have seen in previous chapters, this style of peer tutoring necessitates a power imbalance in that the tutor and tutee have unequal relationships. In some sense, the tutor is an expert, who is expected to facilitate the tutee's learning, while the tutee is a novice, who depends on the tutor to clarify and explicate the topic under consideration. As we have also seen, tutors often benefit personally from peer tutoring, but a successful outcome depends on the tutee actually acquiring the requisite skills and knowledge on which the peer tutoring is predicated. In other words, in fixed-role tutoring, particularly when it operates cross-level, the enterprise is often biased explicitly towards the tutee. While reciprocal peer tutoring is now widely recognized as the preferred mode in higher education, particularly in same-level learning situations, fixed-role tutoring is still common and often unavoidable. Rather than viewing all peer tutoring as a collaborative venture *per se*, it may be more fruitful to consider collaborative technology as a tool for facilitating a variety of peer-tutoring techniques.

Let us now consider some of the forms of collaborative technology discussed above, and evaluate their suitability for enabling peer tutoring.

Video- or teleconferencing

Video- or teleconferencing, a form of synchronous communication which takes place in specialist suites equipped with high-bandwidth televisual links, is perhaps the technique that can bring peer tutoring participants closest together. Both can see and hear each other in high definition, and can discuss topics actively in real time, referring to copies of the same physical documents. As we argued above, synchronous collaborations benefit from the presence of structured communication within small groups and role taking, all characteristics of well-organized peer tutoring.

There are a number of examples of peer-tutoring techniques (described in Chapter 1) that may operate under teleconferencing conditions, provided that suitable preparatory activities have been completed before the video session. These include:

- Think-pair-share.
- Flashcard tutoring.
- Peer monitoring.
- Dyadic Essay Confrontations.

- The learning cell.
- Reciprocal peer tutoring (mutual testing).
- Reciprocal teaching.
- Scripted Co-operative Dyads.
- Peer-response groups.

In addition, Peer Assisted Study Sessions (PASS) may be organized and conducted to help learners at a distance. Some work has also been done on training peer tutors using conferencing software (e.g. Essid, 1996). Participants used the technology to plan strategies, familiarize themselves with relevant theory and practise ways of dealing with problems that can arise during tutorials. Evaluations indicated that tutors felt that synchronous conferences had improved their tutoring techniques.

In the longer term, the provision of 'web-camera' technology will provide a much cheaper alternative to studio-based teleconferencing. Here, a camera and microphone are mounted on each participant's computer, and Internet technology is used to enable interaction. Web-camera technology will undoubtedly come into its own once higher-speed networks and lower-skill interfaces are available. For example, some writing-based tutoring techniques such as paired annotations might work well using web-camera conferencing interaction.

Text-based interaction

Currently, text-based interaction through computers has considerable advantages over video- or teleconferencing. The vast majority of students now have experience of using text-based systems like word-processors, and the technology is highly mature. Furthermore, in peer tutoring, both participants may work collaboratively on a shared textual dialogue, and record their exchanges for 'off-line' consideration. As noted above, it also has benefits for those organizing peer tutoring in that they may, with the participants' permissions, record and subsequently analyse textual exchanges, enabling a fine level of evaluation of such peer tutoring schemes.

Synchronous text-based peer tutoring is best exemplified by 'chat rooms' where participants respond in real time to each other through typing. Chat rooms might be established via an Internet Service Provider or an institutional server under the control of the person organizing the peer tutoring. As noted above, effective chat-room use for peer tutoring will require a well-defined discipline of turn-taking.

Asynchronous text-based peer tutoring, where tutor and tutee cannot find a mutually agreeable time to co-ordinate, is best effected by e-mail. Here the participants send each other messages, but strict turn-taking is not necessary and a message may contain both questions and answers. As noted above, there is no expectation of immediate response, enabling considerably more reflection than in synchronous interaction. However, e-mail requires a very different discipline of interaction from that required in either face-to-face or technology-supported synchronous interactions. The discussion of peer tutoring in previous chapters has been predicated on the simultaneous physical presence of the participants, usually for an agreed minimum unbroken time period. In asynchronous interaction, it is not clear how to define how long should be spent. Clearly, tutors will not accept any expectation of open-ended service to tutees, but tutees must feel that they are getting reasonable provision from tutors. The peer-tutoring contract should define clearly how long it is reasonable for both tutor and tutee to spend in preparing messages, both participants should record how long they actually spend and there should be unambiguous protocols for ending interactions within a given time period.

Curiously, in contrast to chat rooms, e-mail may make more effective use of the participants' time. In a chat-room interaction, the tutor and tutee are both present simultaneously for the same amount of time. However, each is, on average, only typing for far less than half the time, and spending far more time waiting for the next response than reading, contemplating and responding to the last one. That is, a chat room is at best a poor simulacrum of face-to-face interaction, where responses are usually instantaneous. In e-mail, though, participants can use their time independently. Thus a broken tutor hour (say) interleaved with a broken tutee hour may be more productive than a combined tutor/tutee hour. In e-mail, participants may choose how to pace their interaction time around their other activities, rather than waiting ineffectually for the other to respond.

Paired-learning techniques that involve written work are good examples of peer tutoring that might operate using text-based, rather than face-to-face interaction. These include:

- Collaborative writing.
- Peer criticism.
- Peer review.
- Paired annotations.
- Peer editing.

Such techniques might operate either synchronously or asynchronously.

SUMMARY

Educational institutions are beginning to re-engineer themselves. Some common trends are emerging in bringing together more closely library, computing and learning-technology services. It is within these support services that there is a need for new software tools to support the creation, integration, deployment and maintenance of long-life learning resources. These must necessarily complement the tools which teachers and learners use in creating and updating materials.

An important issue is the articulation between working together in groups online and offline. The seamless integration of technology-supported learning into generic approaches to collaborative learning and peer tutoring is highly dependent on people being able to make the transition between different styles of working

(Baeker, 1993). This allows people to personalize and embed technology-supported collaboration into their everyday learning patterns. Learners need to progress from knowledge, through understanding to becoming empowered. Technology provides a means of achieving this balance for distributed groups of learners, and can improve the quality of distance learning. It can give a broader range of opportunities for constructing the learning dialogues through which understanding is deepened and group identities are developed.

Computing and communications technologies enable, extend, and can also change the nature of collaborative education. In particular, they offer opportunities for assessing the process of collaboration itself and in the development of meta-communication skills. While these technologies are increasingly ubiquitous, they are still to be fully embedded within learning communities, organizational structures and services.

ONLINE INFORMATION SOURCES

Association for Computing Machinery *http://www.acm.org/siggroup/*
A professional association for educational and scientific computing, the ACM provides information on publications, special-interest groups and conferences, including several in the areas of computer-supported co-operative work, technology-supported collaborative work and virtual communities.

The Asynchronous Learning Network *http://www.aln.org*
Provides lists of publications, online discussion and information about conferences and workshops on asynchronous learning. It also gives access to the *Asynchronous Learning Network Journal*.

Disability and Information Systems in Higher Education
http://www.disinhe.ac.uk/
Provides resources and strategic advice on how information systems can be used to support staff and students with disabilities.

Further Education Resources for Learning *http://ferl.becta.org.uk/*
Focuses on learning technology resources and their implementation within the further education sector.

International Forum of Educational Technology and Society
http://ifets.ieee.org/
A subgroup of the IEEE Learning Technology Task Force, this provides resources and scheduled online discussions on a variety of themes related to the design and implementation of educational technologies.

Learning Technology Dissemination Initiative *http://www.ltc.hw.ac.uk/ltdi/*
This provides resources, case studies, evaluations of learning-technology implementations including technology-supported collaborative work.

Mailbase *http://www.mailbase.ac.uk/*
Mailbase provides an entry to a wide range of discussion lists, including many on aspects of teaching, learning and technology.

The Node Learning Technologies Network *http://thenode.org/*
This network promotes the effective uses of technologies in education and

training, through building and fostering online communities, conferences, and online resources on research and development related to learning technologies.

The UK Institute for Learning and Teaching
http://www.ilt.ac.uk/ltsn/index.htm

The Institute provides knowledge brokerage, networking, promotion and sharing of good practice, and advice, both generic, technology-focused and in relation to specific subject disciplines at higher education and further education levels within the UK.

10 Benefiting from hindsight: practitioners reflect on peer tutoring

We may learn a great deal by reflecting on the problems we encounter. Thus, in this chapter, colleagues who are practitioners of peer tutoring, paired learning or co-operative learning or experts in a key field reflect on problems they have encountered, solutions they have tried or on new directions their work is taking. Several focus on a particular issue or problem while others take a more holistic approach. We start with Melissa Highton from Napier University, Edinburgh, UK, who describes how she and her team addressed the 'weak links' in Napier's volunteer tutoring scheme. Next, Jim Wood from the University of Newcastle, UK, considers similar issues relating to quality and funding in the context of their student tutoring for degree credit scheme. Barbara McCombs from Denver Research Institute then reflects on how we might better motivate our students, and Daphne Hampton and Margo Blythman from the London College of Printing describe their study support scheme designed to help combat absenteeism. Ruth Cohen, David Boud and Jane Sampson from the University of Technology, Sydney, discuss the problems of assessing peer-assisted learning. Next, Erin Wilson of LaTrobe University, Melbourne, writes of her experiences of organizing peer learning to support studying at a distance. Dianna Newbern and Donald Dansereau then describe the evolution of their Scripted Co-operative Dyad technique. The penultimate contribution is from Robert Neale and Deborah Laurs from Massey University, New Zealand, who reflect on co-operative learning in the teaching of writing. Finally, Neal Whitman reflects more generally on problems associated with peer tutoring encountered in the medical school at the University of Utah.

STUDENT TUTORING FOR DEGREE COURSE CREDIT

Melissa Highton, Student Tutoring in Schools scheme, Napier University, Edinburgh, UK

At the 1995 and 1997 BP International Student Tutoring and Mentoring conferences in London, Sinclair Goodlad described some of the issues affecting student-tutoring schemes within universities. Using the analogy of a chain, he suggested that people running student-tutoring schemes look carefully at the aims, structure and content, logistics, financing, training, support and evaluation of their schemes. A breakdown in any one of these could be described as a 'weak link'. At Napier the weak links were easily identified as long-term funding, structure and content and logistics (securing numbers of volunteers to meet demand from schools). The aims of the scheme were clear, support processes were in place and evaluation of the scheme was under way.

Weak links

Long-term funding: Long-term funding for the student-tutoring scheme was not guaranteed. The Enterprise in Higher Education (EHE) Initiative funding which had supported student tutoring at Napier ended in 1996.

Structure and content: Graduate employers were communicating clearly to universities that the most desirable graduates were those with a knowledge of the workplace and the ability to reflect on, and articulate, their personal strengths and weaknesses within that environment. The 'transferable skills' and 'employability' agendas pushed strongly for universities to help their students to make the most of their learning through work experience whether paid or unpaid.

Logistics: With regard to securing future volunteers, it seemed likely that numbers could not be assumed. Feedback gathered from students indicated that many were timetabled heavily and had no spare time for volunteering during school hours, while others were reluctant to take on a commitment to student tutoring on top of a full-time course. By 1995, changes in student-funding mechanisms meant many students were using all their spare time to earn money to finance their studies.

Action taken

The decision was made to embed the student-tutoring scheme within the university as a structured development opportunity, with clear learning outcomes for the student. This represented a recognition by the university of the value of student tutoring in terms of transferable skills development and the role which the university plays in the community. Moreover, it addressed directly each of the potentially weak links.

Napier University operates a modular degree structure whereby a total of 120 credits must be achieved each year – normally made up of eight modules, each giving fifteen credits. Over the whole programme, each student has the option to study two elective modules chosen from a wide range on offer. In 1996–97, the Student Tutoring module was passed through university quality and standards procedures and accredited through the Continuing Professional Development Unit as an optional fifteen-credit, level-2 module, available to students on any degree course. The accreditation of part-time term-time volunteering activity was not new at Napier. The Community Volunteering module which gave students a structure through which to reflect on their work within the voluntary sector was already in the elective catalogue and provided a basis for much of the development work on the tutoring module.

The development of student tutoring as a module addressed the 'structure and content' weak link. Designed around a reflective learning log and an oral presentation, it provided a structure through which student tutors describe, analyse, assess and reflect on their experience in the school and the skills they use within that context. The opportunity to become involved in student tutoring was now open to all students, regardless of mode of study or workload. Moreover, students taking the module could now enjoy their experience without having to do it 'on top' of a full load of other modules, thus ensuring more volunteers to the scheme. An additional benefit of embedding the scheme within the university's modular programme was an assurance of quality of training and support for student tutors, as this had been made explicit within the module descriptor, and student work was subject to university marking procedures. Any potential problems which could have arisen due to the module attracting students whose only interest was in gaining credit rather than having a commitment to helping young people learn were avoided by a prerequisite request that students have some experience of supervised work with children before embarking on the module.

The benefits of having an accredited module far outweighed the problems in administration that resulted from this status. The work produced by students on the module is widely considered to be of a high standard and has provided the student-tutoring co-ordinators with a wealth of written evidence to support the benefits of student tutoring as an avenue for personal development among students.

While some students at Napier continue to take part in the student tutoring scheme as unaccredited volunteers, more and more are opting for the accredited option. The module materials are being redeveloped and improved each year. Largely, the potential threats of the weak links have been averted and the scheme continues to grow.

USING NATIONALLY AGREED SKILLS STANDARDS AS DEVELOPMENT TOOLS AND MODULE OUTCOMES

Jim Wood, Project Manager, Tyneside and Northumberland Students into Schools Project, UK

The Tyneside and Northumberland Students into Schools (SIS) Project was established in 1993 as a joint initiative between University of Newcastle, University of Northumbria (UNN), Tyneside Training and Enterprise Council (TEC) and Community Service Volunteers (CSV Learning Together Programme) with the following aims:

- to raise the awareness of higher education among pupils in local schools and colleges;
- to raise the aspirations of young people towards higher levels of attainment leading to further or higher education;
- to broaden the experience of university students.

In 1995, Northumberland TEC became a partner in the Project.

The SIS Project recruits, trains, places, supports and evaluates the work of over 400 student tutors per year from a wide range of undergraduate courses in both universities. During a typical placement, a student will visit a school on one morning or afternoon each week for ten weeks and work alongside the teacher in the role of a classroom assistant. The student is expected to help the pupils with their work and to tell them what it is like to go to university, acting in this capacity in the role of an older brother or sister.

Strategic problems

Three main problems were identified during the early years of the project:

1   Quality assurance in the supply and performance of student tutors.
2   Maintaining contact with large numbers of student tutors.
3   Sustainable funding.

Partial solutions through students tutoring for degree-course credit

Students tutoring for degree-course credit have an explicit interest in how well they perform and assume greater responsibility for ensuring that they have the opportunity to maximize their contribution to the placement. Framing the process by which the assessment is achieved enables learning outcomes and assessment components to be used as development tools to ensure that students know exactly what is expected of them and how they can achieve a high standard. It also provides students with an incentive to maintain contact with the SIS Project staff, and offers the potential for sustainable funding through university internal funding mechanisms.

Outcomes

Since 1997/98, over 300 students each year have gained degree-course credit by choosing optional tutoring modules or units. Each completed a portfolio of prescribed activities which varied according to year/level. In addition, logsheets were completed during the middle period of tutoring. Key skills are used as development tools and measures of outcome. The specific key skills standards used at all levels currently are Qualification and Curriculum Authority (QCA) National Vocational Qualifications (NVQ 4) standards for *Communication* and *Working with Others* and *Self-Management*. At level two, students additionally undertake short assignments based on participant observation and at level three, students undertake an action research project into a topical issue.

Main operational problems in introducing student tutoring for credit, and solutions to date

This section will describe a mixture of generic and specific problems and solutions which required to be interpreted into other local contexts:

1   Satisfying university regulations.
2   Establishing credibility in the universities and persuading courses to allow their students to choose the module.
3   Linking learning outcomes to assessment, i.e. what will be assessed, how, when and by whom?
4   Achieving university internal funding transfer i.e. getting the money.

1. *Satisfying University regulations*

In 1991/92 and 1992/93, engineering foundation-year students in the University of Newcastle had been involved in a student-tutoring pilot programme supported by the British Petroleum (BP) Aiming for a College Education (ACE) initiative. This programme had established a precedent in principle, and also provided a working model in practice, of what to assess. Further development work in 1993/94 which looked at best practice elsewhere in this field (e.g. University of Glamorgan, Manchester Metropolitan University) preceded the introduction in 1994/95 of a free-standing elective, worth ten credits (one-twelfth of a year) at level two, which went through the normal validation process in both universities.

The BP International Tutoring and Mentoring Conferences 1995 and 1997 featured assessment as a substantive item. The Dearing Review of 1997 highlighted the value of key skills development and work experience in general and provided further support for the principle of students tutoring for degree-course credit through an experiential learning framework with explicit use of standards, including key skills within an 'employability and career management' strand. Lifelong learning, widening participation and the use of information and communications technology are all contemporary factors which will influence change more generally within higher education.

2. *Establishing credibility and persuading courses to allow their students to choose the module*

The value of student tutoring to courses is that it will provide valuable personal development for students linked to employability, potentially transferable to their learning performance within the course. In addition, there is an element of direct marketing of their university/course to pupils in local schools. The drawbacks of involvement of students include less time for other studies, and funding transfer out of their course where students tutor for credit.

As is the case for most initiatives in education, positive responses from some course/department/faculty heads were a mixture of enlightenment and expedience. While some heads saw the potential benefit to their students in general terms (or in progression to teaching in particular), others who were experiencing difficulties with recruiting students to their course or where progression to employment was less than satisfactory perceived tutoring as a means of addressing these problems. Over time, the principal recruitment method has been through word of mouth with students telling others about it. However, a cost-effective approach is to speak directly to groups of students at the most appropriate time, that is to say, just before they choose their options.

3. Linking learning outcomes to assessment, i.e. what will be assessed, how, when and by whom?

Theories of experiential learning have been integrated into the assessment process (see e.g. Kolb, 1984), with target setting, action planning and reviewing being consistent features throughout the development. In principle, students should be assessed on how much they contributed to the placement, but in practice this can be very subjective and difficult to measure when working with a large number of students in a large number of very different placements. Ideally, the supervising teacher should have a major input to this process, but schools have been under such increasing administrative pressure since the Education Reform Act of 1988 that it was considered prudent to use a very brief teacher evaluation of the student performance, backed up by visits to the placement by project staff, to verify the students' own self-reporting through logbook and oral and written reports. It is acknowledged that this is a compromise but, on balance, it is thought that this is still the most appropriate approach to take at the present time.

In attempting to answer questions such as, 'What is a good student?', 'What is good student tutoring?' and 'How can it be measured?' through ongoing action research, four performance indicators were identified which could be said to be reasonably effective measures in this context. Therefore, the teacher evaluation referred to above is based on their perception of the student's

- self-management: punctuality and attendance, time management, responsibility, organization;
- communication: ability to listen and speak effectively with pupils and teachers;
- initiative: proactive, self-motivated, capable of independent action;
- teamwork: ability to establish working relationships with teachers and pupils, willingness to compromise.

These skills and qualities have been used as the starting point for developing the criterion-referenced reporting process embodied in the tutoring logbook. There is now sufficient evidence of 'best practice' built up and developed since 1993 within the SIS Project for us to be confident that the assessment criteria now effectively contribute to both the formative and summative aspects of the module.

4. Achieving university internal funding transfer, i.e. getting the money

In both universities involved, some centrally awarded funds per student were negotiated. The net result is that the project budget currently can be sustained by approximately 350 accredited student tutors and managers per year. Student managers are experienced student tutors who are given a group of about six 'new' students to supervise, leading training sessions, holding meetings, leading special projects such as student shadowing and visiting placements. Student managers develop a portfolio of evidence against NVQ Supervisory Management standards which also carries academic credit. A further problem is that there is no guarantee of student numbers prior to the project budget being established. This problem has been partially addressed through both universities underwriting the running costs of the project for the period to August 2001, although there is still a conditional component dependent on the number of students tutoring for credit. The need to recruit quality students from a wide range of courses is an ongoing imperative which involves all of the arguments given above.

Advice to colleagues

(This assumes you know why you want to introduce student tutoring or other peer education initiative for degree-course credit, at what level and with what weighting.)

1 Decide on the scale of operation, now and in the future (potential). This will allow you to fine tune the detail, build in important principles from the start, plan workload (genuinely formative portfolios are not easy things to mark, particularly if you have to generate a percentage mark rather than a grading or simply pass/fail).

2 Decide the most appropriate learning outcomes in relation to the course/s the students are from and the nature of the peer education, and then build these into the assessment process as discrete outcomes. This may sound blindingly obvious but it took me some time to fully make this connection.

3 Be transparent in all procedures with all participants, enabling students to know exactly what is expected of them and how they can go about achieving a good mark, i.e. how to tutor effectively. The use of standards within an experiential self-improvement cycle is strongly recommended. In all cases, highlight how everyone (students, course leaders, school teachers, pupils) can benefit from students tutoring for degree-course credit, stressing the value-added component provided by working for credit.

MOTIVATING STUDENTS IN PEER-LEARNING CONTEXTS: THROUGH THE LEARNER-CENTRED LENS

Barbara L. McCombs, Director of the Human Motivation, Learning and Development Center at the University of Denver Research Institute, USA

When Nancy Falchikov asked me to contribute to this book, my first reaction was to wonder if I had enough background and experience in the topic of peer-mediated learning (and its associated forms such as peer tutoring and co-operative learning) to offer advice to the field about motivating students to be peer tutors and learners in higher education. She was very convincing when I expressed my concerns and we agreed it might be helpful to approach the topic from my more general expertise in human motivation across the age range from the very young to older adult learners in education and training settings.

Beginning in 1991, I have been working with the American Psychological Association (APA) and their education directorate to define and publish research-validated principles that can help educators create the types of schools and classrooms in which students' natural learning and motivation can surface. I am the primary author of the *Learner-Centred Psychological Principles: Guidelines for School Redesign and Reform* – now in its second revision – being disseminated by the American Psychological Association's Task Force on Psychology in Education.

Applying the learner-centred principles to peer learning and tutoring

The fourteen learner-centred principles were developed based on current theories of learning, including constructivism and social constructivism (APA, 1993, 1997). As such, they recognize that individual learners construct their own personally meaningful, goal-directed understandings of any experiences or content to be learned. Each individual constructs different meaning and understanding based on prior experiences, knowledge, and a host of other personal 'filters'. Although the social context and the knowledge imparted by others can have a major influence on what any one person learns and remembers, the information learned and its associated emotional content is uniquely a learner's own.

In the areas of motivation and development, the learner-centred principles focus on the importance of meeting learner needs for belonging. My own research over the past decade has revealed that this need is present in learners of all ages and that college students, in particular, report that classroom practices that create positive relationships between students and their instructors and between students and their peers are highly important for motivation and achievement (McCombs, 1999; McCombs and Lauer, 1998; McCombs and Whisler, 1997). When students perceive that they are in a positive and supportive climate for learning, when they are connected to their instructor and to each other, natural motivation to learn surfaces.

What do the learner-centred principles mean for peer-learning and teaching strategies? I would suggest that peer-mediated learning strategies are potentially very motivational and powerful – but under certain conditions. First, learners need to feel connected and part of the learning community of the classroom. They need to feel comfortable with themselves, each other, and the instructor. They need to feel they can make mistakes as a natural part of learning. They need to feel free from ridicule and put-downs. When these conditions are met, I would contend that natural motivation to learn from and with each other will be present. There are, however, several obstacles inherent in many college environments that need to be addressed.

Table 10.1 The APA learner-centred psychological principles[1]

COGNITIVE AND METACOGNITIVE FACTORS

Principle 1: Nature of the learning process

The learning of complex subject matter is most effective when it is an intentional process of constructing meaning from information and experience.

Principle 2: Goals of the learning process

The successful learner, over time and with support and institutional guidance, can create meaningful, coherent representations of knowledge.

Principle 3: Construction of knowledge

The successful learner can link new information with existing knowledge in meaningful ways.

Principle 4: Strategic thinking

The successful learner can create and use a repertoire of thinking and reasoning strategies to achieve complex goals.

Principle 5: Thinking about thinking

Higher-order strategies for selecting and monitoring mental operations facilitate creative and critical thinking.

Principle 6: Context of learning

Learning is influenced by environmental factors including culture, technology and institutional practices.

MOTIVATIONAL AND AFFECTIVE FACTORS

Principle 7: Motivational and emotional influences on learning

What and how much is learned is influenced by the learner's motivation. Motivation to learn, in turn, is influenced by the individual's emotional states, beliefs, interests and goals, and habits of thinking.

Principle 8: Intrinsic motivation to learn

The learner's creativity, higher-order thinking, and natural curiosity all contribute to motivation to learn. Intrinsic motivation is stimulated by tasks of optimal novelty and difficulty, relevant to personal interests, and providing for personal choice and control.

Principle 9: Effects of motivation on effort

Acquisition of complex knowledge and skills requires extended learner effort and guided practice. Without learners' motivation to learn, the willingness to exert this effort is unlikely without coercion.

DEVELOPMENTAL FACTORS

Principle 10: Developmental influence on learning

As individuals develop, they encounter different opportunities and experience different constraints for learning. Learning is most effective when differential development within and across physical, intellectual, emotional and social domains is taken into account.

Principle 11: Social influences on learning

Learning is influenced by social interactions, interpersonal relations and communication with others.

INDIVIDUAL DIFFERENCES FACTORS

Principle 12: Individual differences in learning

Learners have different strategies, approaches and capabilities for learning that are a function of prior experience and heredity.

Principle 13: Learning and diversity

Learning is most effective when differences in learners' linguistic, cultural and social backgrounds are taken into account.

Principle 14: Standards and assessment

Setting appropriately high and challenging standards and assessing the learner and learning progress – including diagnostic, process, and outcome assessment – are integral parts of the learning process.

Obstacles to motivation to learn with and from each other

Inadequate training

Many times college students are expected to participate in 'learner-centred' practices such as co-operative peer groups with little or no prior experience or training in peer-learning and teaching strategies. Many of these students feel frustrated and angry; many feel their instructors are abdicating their responsibilities as teacher and placing too much responsibility on them. For many college students, the only educational programmes they have known are those in which the instructor does the teaching – the telling and conveying of information – and the students are the passive recipients of this information. The obstacle becomes student 'readiness' for this kind of active learning approach as well as the support available.

Understanding what is meant by 'learner-centred'

A second obstacle to motivation to learn with and from each other, related to the first obstacle, is the misunderstanding of what is meant by 'learner-centred'. Like many terms, the term 'learner-centred' has a host of meanings and definitions. Some researchers and educators equate learner-centred with particular programmes and practices which, too often, involve the implementation of collaborative, co-operative, and peer-tutoring approaches with all learning activities and content in a 'one size fits all' approach. For me, however, learner-centred has a very specific and encompassing definition. It applies to all learners (including teachers and instructors); it is based on research-validated psychological principles of learning, motivation, development, and individual differences; and it adheres to an holistic consideration of these principles as a foundation for systemic educational system design or reform. For a programme or practice to be learner-centred, however, the most important defining characteristic – also based on a host of empirical research – is that it must be perceived as learner-centred from the learner's perspective. What might be perceived as learner-centred by one learner may not be perceived as learner-centred by another learner. This distinction is critical because it calls our attention to the need for a diversity of practices and for caring and supportive teacher qualities to increase the probability that all learners will perceive their learning experiences as learner-centred. Learner-centred is, to a large degree, 'in the eye of the beholder', and does/should not look the same from day to day, classroom to classroom, or school to school.

Understanding students' needs for choice and control

A third obstacle is understanding students' needs for choice and control, and how these needs will differ for students of different ages and stages of development. It has seemed ironic to me that even with the host of research evidence that choice and control support the development of personal responsibility and self-directed learning skills, most educators and educational systems systematically remove choice and control as learners get older. We seem comfortable giving young learners a lot of choice and control, but hesitate to give the same or more levels of choice and control to older learners, and particularly adolescents and young adults. Teachers tell me this is largely because they feel they will lose control, but the fact is that the opposite happens. Teachers willing to take risks, and let students set classroom rules, decide the ways in which they want to learn and be assessed, and determine their own learning schedules and performance evaluation criteria find, in fact, that students are harder on themselves than teachers would be, and that classroom-management problems are reduced, not increased. And most importantly, we own what we create (Wheatley, 1995, 1999; Wheatley and Kellner-Rogers, 1996) and students become more invested in their own learning and more motivated to learn and achieve at high levels.

Putting these things together suggests a number of guidelines to be offered from the learner-centred perspective – a topic I turn to next.

Advice to colleagues: guidelines from a learner-centred perspective

Although peer-learning and teaching strategies have considerable research evidence to support their use in enhancing student motivation and learning (e.g. Boling and Robinson, 1999; King, Staffieri and Adelgais, 1998; O'Donnell, 1999), for the most effective implementation of these strategies, several guidelines can be offered. The following assume that peer-teaching and learning strategies are collaboratively created with learners and that they include the ability to:

1   Diagnose and understand students' unique needs, interests, and goals.
2   Help students define their own personal goals and the relationship of these personal goals to learning goals.
3   Relate learning content and activities to each student's personal needs, interests, and goals.
4   Challenge students to invest effort and energy in taking personal responsibility and to be actively involved in learning activities.
5   Include instructional practices that encourage student initiative, self-expression, excitement, and imagination.
6   Engage in participatory decision making and provide students with opportunities to exercise personal control and choice over selected task variables such as the type of learning activity, ways of demonstrating personal mastery, and skills to master.
7   Create a safe, trusting, and supportive climate by showing real interest, caring, and concern for each student.
8   Attend to classroom goal structures and goal orientations, with an emphasis on co-operative structures and learning goals.
9   Model both self-directed learning skills and personal qualities associated with positive respectful interpersonal relationships.

10 Highlight the value of student accomplishment, the value of students' unique skills and abilities, and the value of the learning process and the learning task; and

11 Reward students' accomplishments and encourage them to reward themselves and develop pride in their accomplishments.

As a 'bottom line' guideline, we need to remember that learner-centred is in the eye of the beholder. That means that whatever instructional method is being used, for maximum motivation and learning, learners need to perceive it as meeting their needs to be supported, cared about, connected to each other and their teacher, and to be successful. Without this, even the best peer-teaching and learning programmes will be less effective than they could be.

INFORMAL PEER TUTORING IN STUDY SUPPORT NETWORKS DESIGNED TO ENCOURAGE ATTENDANCE

Daphne Hampton and Margo Blythman, London College of Printing, UK

Peer tutoring has been used in London College of Printing on a variety of courses including a part-time Higher National Certificate (HNC) course which has run using both daytime and evening modes. Following the success of peer tutoring in this course, it was introduced onto the full-time Higher National Diploma (HND) and Enterprise Management for the Creative Arts courses.

Peer tutoring in the context of study-support networks can be an excellent way of supporting student learning, developing an autonomous approach and helping student retention and achievement. Within study groups, the activities undertaken vary enormously because the decisions over what is useful are taken by the students within the groups. Typical activities might include:

- working on assignments together;
- going through lecture notes and reading together;
- sharing the buying of textbooks;
- picking up information for each other if unable to attend;
- discussing future career or educational pathways with each other;
- supporting and following up students in the group who are dropping by the wayside;
- social activities.

In other words, students within the network provide quite general support for each other which reinforces the idea of autonomous student learning.

Evaluations of the schemes over the years show that study-support networks can be particularly beneficial for part-time students, adult returners and international students. In each of these cases, it can be much harder for students to become familiar with the academic way of life than it is for younger full-time students from the UK. It can also be difficult for these individuals to get to know each other.

Networks help the bonding process with the course, the institution and each other. Many long-term friendships have formed in these groups containing several nationalities and ages. Former student members of such networks meet for social events and visit each other's countries long after the course has finished. There are also other benefits for the institution, as peer tutoring can promote progression from one level to another within the same college. For example, students from several networks of a former part-time HNC course got together to discuss the problems and advantages of moving onto the part-time degree course that we ran. They then all applied for the course and continued using their peer-tutoring arrangements on the new course, gaining support at the new academic level. Some students who would not have considered applying for a new degree course in isolation went on to undertake the course successfully because of their peer-tutoring support.

Problem areas

Study-support networks are not without their difficulties, and a great deal of effort is needed in their initial formation and subsequent development. We shall discuss four problem areas.

1 *Initial setting up of support networks*

The initial setting up of study-support networks when the process of making clear the peer-tutoring arrangements is carried out is the most difficult time. Academic staff play a crucial role here. The induction period must be very interactive. Staff should provide the initial information needed in the first hour of the first meeting and then have a 'jolly' ice-breaker, with everyone moving around to talk to as many people as possible. Academic staff should also join in, but remain watchful, looking for the lonely or lost, or those who see themselves as above such activities. When such people are spotted, subtle (or otherwise) attempts should be made to integrate them. If possible, staff should subsequently monitor attendance of such individuals over the first few days or weeks. It is useful if their personal tutor is kept informed of any concerns. Insecure students do not want to feel that they have been singled out, much as they might value the extra attention at one level. After the initial ice-breaker, there should be further group and paired activities giving people a chance to introduce each other, find out about their backgrounds and learn some names. Towards the end of the first day, working on a case study based around a year in the life of an hypothetical student on this particular course can be very helpful. Groups can discuss how they would have dealt with the problems presented, but can also relate to the good times in the person's life. By now, students are usually working in the same groups, and staff can collect names and reiterate the value and purpose of peer tutoring and support. The students return and work in these groups at their next meeting. Staff should find out if they are happy to stay in these networks for the year. At this stage, some groups agree to 'swap' individuals in an amicable fashion.

2 Dealing with late entrants onto the course

A second problem in the initial stages of study-support networks is how to deal with late entrants to the course. Often, we had five or six people enrol late onto the course. Experience over the years has shown that turning these late entrants into a new peer-tutoring group does not work. They may have nothing in common except late enrolment, and they tend to feel isolated from the rest of the class. All late entrants should be given a chance to mix with the whole class and be introduced to the various peer groups that have already formed. Wide consultation is needed with personal tutors or other staff and with key members of the class who can often give helpful information as to where each person might ideally fit. The late entrants should always be given a warm welcoming introduction at the start of the day/evening and all the peer groups should be asked to mix with them and take them to coffee or lunch.

3 Personality clashes

A third problem is that personality clashes do emerge and arguments do occur occasionally within the peer-tutoring groups. Awareness by staff is again the key. It may be necessary to reorganize two or more networks to accommodate these clashes. Often the networks will achieve this for themselves and 'swap' individuals. Further problems can come when there is an attempt to introduce peer tutoring onto a course where either the course manager or the personal tutor does not believe in the concept. Students soon know if it is only being paid lip service in the course handbook and induction process. They quickly pick up signals if the academic staff do not both actively promote the networks and follow them up.

4 What to do when a key support group member leaves

A fourth possible problem may arise when a key member of a peer-tutoring network leaves midway through a year or course. This has happened rarely and has been the result of such events as pregnancy or promotion at work leading to geographical move. One must be alert to these events, however, and ensure that the peer-tutoring group continues to mesh well together. This should be done without the staff looking too directional – no easy task! If the peer tutoring has been set in motion well from the start, and closely, if sensitively, monitored in its early stages, then all should be well.

Advice to colleagues

On the basis of our experience we suggest the following tips to colleagues.

1   Emphasize the autonomy of each peer-support group. Students respond well to this.
2   Be genuinely committed to the concept yourself. Your enthusiasm will transmit to the groups and they will build on this.

3   Identify people in your institution who already have successful experience of running student networks and talk to them.

4   Make sure that the role of peer tutoring is fully described in all relevant course documentation.

5   Have plenty of interaction in the early stages.

6   Work closely with personal tutors both to acquire information about individual students but also to encourage them to see the benefits of these networks which can be used as one basis for tutorials.

7   Keep a close but discreet eye on the process throughout the year and be prepared to intervene if necessary. Do not assume that the networks are a one-off activity.

8   Remember that late entrants have particular needs.

9   Choose a course team who believe in the concept as well as you, but we realize this may be another problem area!

DEALING WITH PROBLEMS ENCOUNTERED IN ASSESSMENT OF PEER LEARNING

Ruth Cohen, David Boud and Jane Sampson, University of Technology, Sydney, Australia

Our interest and experience have been in the area of reciprocal peer learning, that is students learning with and from each other, normally within the same cohort. The reciprocal nature of the practices we have been developing ensures an essential 'peerness' in all the encounters students have, as students are always both 'teachers' and 'learners' throughout and there is less temptation for them to become surrogate tutors.

Initially, our work on reciprocal peer learning was with our own students. These are mature students, studying undergraduate and postgraduate courses in the area of adult education. We have been using four different approaches: student-led workshops, study groups, learning partnerships and learning exchanges which are described elsewhere (Anderson and Boud, 1996). For example, study groups involve students working in tutorless groups on agreed tasks providing regular written reports to a lecturer; learning partnerships involve students collaborating with a class peer on a one-to-one basis providing each other with a sounding-board for discussing their learning.

More recently we have been working with colleagues in other faculties (business, law, computing and design) on a range of reciprocal peer-learning strategies which suit their particular contexts. The students involved were in classes from all undergraduate and postgraduate years and typically included mixes of recent schoolleavers, mature students and overseas students from non-English-speaking backgrounds.

One of the key features we have focused on has been the interaction between assessment and peer learning (Boud, Cohen and Sampson, 1999). Inappropriate assessment practices in a course can destroy desirable forms of peer learning no matter how well it is otherwise constructed.

Advice to colleagues

Some of the strategies and solutions we have adopted to deal with common problems we have encountered are discussed as follows:

1 *Avoid competition for marks, focus on rich peer feedback, not simple ratings or allocation of grades*

Contradictions between methods of teaching and learning and the ways in which students are assessed will confuse students and undermine well-organized learning activities. For example, if students are in direct competition with each other for grades (as in a norm-referenced assessment system) then it will be difficult to encourage them to co-operate in peer learning. In this context, peer learning among some students may be advantageous to them, but only when they 'beat' others. Fortunately, most post-secondary education institutions have moved towards criterion-based, standards-based or competency-based approaches, or like our own university, banned norm-referencing, so that it is now easier to have an overall approach to assessment which focuses on learning.

However, no matter what the system of assessment, it can still inhibit peer learning. A focus on grading rather than the qualities of the work which students produce can have this effect. Using simple rating scales for peer assessment does not sufficiently assist students to understand how others appreciate their work and therefore help them find ways of improving it.

Assessment activities associated with peer-learning processes can most profitably involve constructive discussion and the giving and receiving of rich feedback which assists students to improve learning outcomes. During times when there are severe limits on the amount and detail of feedback given by staff to students, peer feedback is a process with benefits for both the giver and receiver. The giver of feedback has to identify what constitutes good work in a given subject area and express these ideas in a coherent form, while also communicating effectively with the prospective receivers about their feedback needs. The recipient of feedback benefits from identifying and articulating these needs, from receiving detailed comments from a peer who has faced a similar challenge and from responding appropriately to the feedback. An undoubted benefit is that there are fewer barriers of status and authority between peers than is traditionally the case with students and the givers of feedback.

2 *Don't use one-off activities*

Our experience with a range of groups learning with and from each other is that it often takes at least one round – usually a semester – for students (and staff) to learn to use the opportunities provided by reciprocal peer-learning-assessment activities effectively. It is frequently an unfamiliar learning culture for them and they need time to adjust to new ways of working with each other. The second and subsequent rounds of these activities are likely to be more productive and less anxiety-provoking as students gain experience in negotiating their personal and group goals and clarifying rules of behaviour. Students develop quite sophisticated approaches to using their skills in the group as they become more familiar with the processes involved. When questioned, those students who had engaged in peer learning and assessment over a longer period were clearer about their goals and their gains than other students, and were able to recognize the value of this approach. It seems possible that if students know in advance that this process will be used over a significant period they are more prepared to put an effort into making it effective.

3 Be clear about what you are assessing

The very process of peer learning, including the act of giving and receiving feedback, can promote a number of generic learning outcomes associated with working together. These include valuable work and life skills such as communicating orally and in writing, negotiation skills, group planning and teamwork for which there may be less of an outlet in other parts of the course. Peer assessment may be an appropriate strategy here, particularly if these goals are explicit and students can identify the ways in which they are being promoted through the various activities in which they engage.

A typical structure used after a period of group familiarization and work on more modest activities might lead students through a process of:

a   Clarifying the nature of a given assessment task.
b   Focusing on the learning outcomes which they would expect to demonstrate through management of and the performance of the task.
c   Identifying the possible criteria which might be used to judge the quality of their performance.
d   Selecting criteria appropriate to the nature of the task and context of the task and the outcomes sought.
e   Sharing of draft assignments (one-to-one or in sub-groups) and the giving of structured feedback (Boud, 1995) to each other.
f   Modification of assignments prior to submission.

4 Avoid fragmentation of small tasks

There is a seductive simplicity to breaking up the learning task into small and discrete steps, each denoting a separate value, as a way of determining the tasks to be undertaken as part of assessment. While this may appear on the surface to be equitable and easier for staff and students to control and assess, the seamlessness of learning and assessment, which is a key goal of peer learning, may be diminished. Focusing on an holistic learning approach and defining the generic as well as specific outcomes of the major task is likely to assist students to view learning as a unitary activity rather than isolated events.

5 Involve learners in working with criteria for assessment

Students have traditionally relied on their lecturers to determine what is critical for, and valued in, learning and they have accepted this judgement without critique. Establishing assessment criteria is difficult for many students, as it requires them to focus on how to assess the outcomes of their own learning and provide a language for it in ways they can understand. As students gain experience in developing criteria for assessment they are able to be more specific with the language and clearer in their own mind as to what should be valued. With peer learning, the process of learning collaboratively is highly valued and this needs to be reflected in the assessment process.

6 Make grading allocation transparent

Grading is always contentious because it is important to students. Traditionally, many students self-assess their own efforts by accepting the verdict of an external grade awarded by the lecturer as the sole indicator of their own learning and development. Students may be suspicious of self- or peer assessment and uncertain of their own capacity to use criteria effectively and fairly. Any change to the traditional approach requires clear supportive documentation and full understanding by the student. The documentation presented to students needs to state exactly how grades will be awarded and how criteria are established; it needs to be transparent. Real examples to illustrate the application of the criteria will be helpful, particularly in the cases of criteria for assessing process rather than product. Students will also find practice situations very helpful to help them gain skills and acquire confidence in their own abilities, while at the same time alleviating concerns about using the new approach. In an ungraded system, we have found the process supports the learning needs of most students in a very effective way and students appreciate defining their own goals and criteria and getting feedback on their progress.

7 Be clear about documenting processes to be used

Before students are introduced to these approaches, we have found that it is necessary to produce a document including the following:

- clarification of expectations of the activity;
- methodology to be used for this approach including: how peers are selected or self-selected, time allocated and timing of events, methods for establishing criteria for self- and peer assessment;
- tips about working effectively with others;
- aspects which can be negotiated with staff or peers, compulsory and optional tasks;
- what and how much students are expected to produce individually, in pairs or in groups;
- important dates and roles that need to be undertaken.

8 *Foster critical self-assessment*

Peer learning and assessment enable students to work collaboratively, and in helping their peers they often add significantly to their own learning through a deeper understanding of how to use criteria effectively for assessment of peers. We have found it helpful for students to assess their own learning and development by applying such criteria to assess their own work. Students have indicated that criterion-based self-assessment is a powerful motivator as well as a reality check on their progress. The criteria may be individually developed or the result of peer and/or staff negotiation. Self-assessment may be documented for the student's own eyes only, or in a draft summary form may be presented to one or two peers and a staff member for comments. These comments may then be taken into account for the student's final self-assessment. Our experience indicates that as students are very tough on themselves, the criteria originally set need to be reasonable in relation to normal expectations as governed by the nature and level of the course.

In many formal academic situations assessment is grade-driven. Where this is unavoidable, it may be possible to allocate a portion of the grade to the self-assessment process. The portion allocated needs to be seen as significant and supportive of the learning processes which have featured.

9 *Value contributions to group building and sustenance*

Assessment can easily focus on the normal assessment tasks such as assignments or presentations. However, effective peer learning requires that attention be given to factors such as acknowledging and working with difference in cultural and knowledge approaches, team management skills, recognition of different working styles, speaking, listening and negotiating skills. If these are not acknowledged as part of formal assessment requirements, they can tend to be devalued. Criteria to identify leadership skills as well as skills which cultivate leadership in others can be included, in addition to specific criteria which articulate and acknowledge the provision of academic, social and emotional support to other members of the group. These are important features of useful peer and group activity. Students who are able to apply sensitive, challenging and cohesive group-building ideas, clearly have acquired skills and knowledge worthy of recognition in formal assessment. These matters are difficult to build into simple assessment tasks, but it is possible. Discussing significant incidents in the group may assist in identifying how these group development and maintenance skills have been applied. Students can be encouraged to give and receive feedback about the contributions they make in these areas and to engage in such sessions on, say, two occasions in the life of the group. If this is not done, then it is not possible to make claims that these broader skills are being developed.

10 *Need for involvement of staff*

It is insufficient for the key staff member in a course to commit to engage enthusiastically with notions of peer learning and assessment if the other staff members who have teaching and assessing responsibility for the course are not supportive. We found that meetings with all the staff were needed to provide information, assuage doubts, develop specific solutions to issues arising and provide case studies as examples to support their practice. If the staff members are reluctant or unwilling, the effectiveness of the approach will be in jeopardy.

The above approaches have assisted in embedding reciprocal peer learning as a normal and effective component of a course. We have found students very appreciative of the opportunity for new learning and recognize the generic and specific skills they develop. The more honest and open style of communication inherent in students learning with and from each other serves in sharp contrast to the overly competitive and directive models many staff are more familiar with. The changes in staff and student roles to accommodate peer learning and peer assessment must be acknowledged and the process of developing appropriate task and group-management skills supported. This takes time.

PROBLEMS OF USING PEER LEARNING TO SUPPORT STUDYING AT A DISTANCE

Erin Wilson, LaTrobe University, Melbourne, Australia

This reflection is based on my work as a lecturer in the Aboriginal Community Management and Development Program (ACMDP) of the Centre for Aboriginal Studies at Curtin University in Perth, Western Australia. This programme is offered at both degree and associate degree levels to Indigenous students from remote and urban communities throughout Australia. Students undertake their learning through intensive, one- or two-week residential study blocks held five times per year, as well as through distance-learning strategies which enable them to continue studying in their own communities.

A compulsory component of the course, at all three year levels, is participation in student 'Professional Development Groups' (PDGs). Students are required to form into groups of between three and eight members within their home localities. Groups are to be comprised of peers, that is either fellow-students from across year levels, i.e. a mix of first-, second- and third-year students (which is the most common formation), or professional and community colleagues. Each group must meet twice per semester, and each student must present an issue from work or study to the group for discussion at each meeting. Assessment of student learning in these groups takes place through submission of their presentation notes and a reflective report on the processes and outcomes of the meeting.

The stated aims of the PDGs are threefold:

1   To support student learning (e.g. share ideas, knowledge and experiences relevant to the course, clarify concepts and assessment tasks).
2   To further the professional development of students (e.g. develop professional networks, explore workplace issues, develop strategies to address these issues).

3   To practise group processes (e.g. facilitation, active listening, question posing, feedback and conflict resolution skills).

(ACMDP, 1998)

PDGs are framed as key peer-learning mechanisms whereby students are able to re-teach/learn course concepts through their application to local contexts, via discussion. This enables the translation of course ideas and knowledges into both local languages and local situations. Students also learn from the modelling of group-work processes and analytical skills demonstrated by their peers as part of these meetings. As a group member, each student adopts the role of critical friend, mentor, fellow investigator and tutor to apply course ideas and skills to the student–presenter's issue.

While PDGs provide students with opportunities to focus the learning discussion around their own learning issues, the PDGs also carry a more specific learning agenda. One evolving aspect of this agenda is the notion that PDGs will foster learning in the area of problem identification, analysis and problem solving in group settings; it is this aspect that is mostly unsuccessful and it is this issue which prompts this reflection.

Philosophical base

The course embodies a political or critical understanding of knowledge and of learning. As an Indigenous programme, the course has evolved out of an experience of education as assimilative or colonizing, where Western knowledge is dominant. By contrast, the course opposes this epistemological hegemony by emphasizing the role of students in asserting, producing and maintaining Indigenous knowledges, and in critiquing, co-opting or reinventing non-Indigenous knowledges so as to make them suitable to Indigenous purposes, experiences and cultures (Keefe, 1992; McTaggart, 1988). Pedagogically this requires that the course be structured around strategies for students to 'name' local or Indigenous knowledges, to critique non-Indigenous knowledges and to actively reinvent them (Wilson, unpublished). Associated with this is an understanding of learning or knowledge production which recognizes the many contributors to knowledge construction (Lusted, 1986) including peers, experience, practice, critical self-reflection, and other more traditional learning materials such as written texts and other media (Bagnall, 1989; Evans and Nation, 1989). The learning process then is understood as an active dialogue with this range of contributors. In this context, the PDG is a clear example of a teaching/learning strategy which emphasizes learning through such a dialogue.

Outcomes

Students report positive outcomes of this peer-learning strategy in two major areas: as a general support to their learning as a whole; and as providing specific learning about group skills or problem solving relevant to their own contexts.

As a general support, PDGs reduce the alienation of distance students and provide opportunities to share problems (both personal and professional). The peer-learning groups appear to function as a retention mechanism as many students identify that the support of their peers has prevented their withdrawal from the course. In reports on PDGs, students also comment on specific learning outcomes from these meetings such as an increased critical self-awareness of their own traits and professional practices, learning about alternative strategies and gaining new perspectives on issues discussed. In addition, students commented that the groups directly contributed to development of skills in group work, facilitation and public presentation. These results indicate that the peer-learning strategy is effective as both a learning tool and support mechanism.

However, some students find peer tutoring to be irrelevant and frustrating. Stuck with a group of peers who are unhelpful or uncommitted, these students feel compulsory PDGs to be merely hoop-jumping to meet assessment requirements. For these students, PDGs waste valuable study or work time for no result.

Problems

Like any group activity, especially one that can only be monitored or supported by academic staff from a distance, PDGs suffer a range of problems. While most successfully operate to increase students' learning in the areas of problem solving and strategizing, of key interest to this reflection is the core problem of PDGs failing (in most cases) to increase learning around group-based problem analysis.

That this type of learning doesn't occur is probably due to a range of factors:

- the expected learning (i.e. the learning agenda) of the PDGs is not sufficiently explicit. Students understand that they are to discuss and address issues of relevance to them utilizing course concepts and skills, but are not sufficiently aware that learning should focus on problem *analysis* at least as much as problem *solving*;
- while students have skills to undertake problem analysis as individuals they may lack the additional skills required for group problem analysis and therefore avoid this aspect of their learning, not knowing where to start;
- group analysis, though modelled and employed frequently in class-learning processes, is not a skill explicitly taught in the course. Students are expected to perform this skill in many contexts but little time is given to discussing its components.

It may seem pedantic to identify that learning around problem analysis has not occurred despite learning around problem solution being achieved. However, the distinction is important, as students frequently achieve solutions to a problem without an in-depth analysis of the factors, context and possibilities inherent in the problem.

Action plan

To respond to the issues identified, the following actions need to be taken:

1   Clearly articulate the learning agenda for the peer-learning group, i.e. state that problem analysis is an expected learning outcome of the peer-learning activity. This includes providing more explanation about it in the descriptions of PDGs and more explicit requirements as part of the assessment task. For example, the group could be required to develop and submit a group brainstorm or mind-map of the problem analysis, or a list of critical questions used to analyse the problem.
2   Provide better resourcing/foundational learning for students so as to better equip them to further their own learning around group-based problem analysis through the peer-learning mechanism. This includes prior skilling in facilitation skills required for group-based problem analysis and the provision of some problem-analysis frameworks that could be adopted by the group (such as those often suggested in Problem Based Learning activities – for examples see Crebbin, 1997; Margetson, 1995). In this way, the group has clear resource materials to learn from.
3   Provide supported learning opportunities prior to independent peer-learning opportunities. Explicit discussion about the skills and techniques of group-based problem analysis needs to occur in class-based learning episodes, and practice opportunities (with students as facilitators) need to be provided in situations where lecturer support, modelling and mentoring are directly available. This enables students to develop foundational skills which then provide a starting point of common experience to be further developed in peer-learning groups.

Further reflections

Behind the apparent problems in this case study are some deeper issues. First, the designers of this activity (including myself) appear to have made assumptions about the intuitiveness or 'naturalness' of the peer-learning process, i.e. that learning in these contexts is almost automatic. There has been little analysis of the specific skills or resources required or the difficulties likely to be encountered in a peer-learning activity on the topic of group-based problem analysis.

Second, there is an interesting tension in this task between a pedagogy that emphasizes student-directed learning and the predetermined learning/assessment agenda. Students are very much in control of this peer-learning activity: they are asked to select issues of relevance to them as the context for learning; given autonomy to solve their own problems and assist each other's learning; and they are responsible for forming and managing their own groups. All of these features imply that students also control the learning agenda. In this context, students feel free to identify their learning needs as primarily about support and solutions (and hence the outcomes reported in this area). By contrast, the pre-set learning/ assessment agenda is also interested in learning around problem analysis, an agenda the students don't share, are not aware of, or not skilled appropriately to meet. This is a classic tension between student-directed learning and the institution's agenda of learning, and is inherent in many peer-learning approaches. That is, peer-learning strategies encourage learner autonomy, but may also remain mechanisms of furthering learning within a pre-set learning agenda frequently developed with no, or little, input from students.

Advice to colleagues

For those considering the implementation of similar teaching/learning activities I offer the following 'tips':

1 Identify all the skills involved, particularly identifying those related to performing the learning task as a group/pair rather than as an individual. Distinguish between 'content' skills/knowledge necessary to the learning task and 'process' skills/knowledge necessary to the doing of and learning from the task together.
2 Make sure students have an opportunity to learn and practise these skills in other areas of the course, particularly where there is lecturer support available. Students need models of the process or skill and a level of foundational learning which provides a starting point for further learning, as well as a resource base to fuel it.
3 Clearly name the expectations of the learning task (and the time required to meet these expectations). Reflect on whether or not the peer-learning task is carrying too many expectations which will mean that some will be neglected or insufficiently completed.

Note

It is important to note that this reflection, as my own, reflects but one perspective on the efficacy of this peer-learning strategy. Students and other lecturers offer alternative perspectives and analyses, and this reflection does not seek to synthesize their views. This contribution is published with the permission of the Indigenous management of the programme.

EVOLUTIONS IN SCRIPTED CO-OPERATIVE LEARNING: EMOTIONAL COMPETENCE

Dianna Newbern and Donald F. Dansereau, Texas Christian University

Introduction

There are two goals of this contribution. The first is to briefly overview Scripted Co-operative Dyads (SCD) by reviewing the original purpose in developing scripts, presenting a conceptual framework of SCD, discussing the most current findings, and considering the implications of some late results. Related to this, the second goal is to propose that scripted dyads might be a beneficial strategy to enhance the development of emotional competence (e.g. self-control, sensing another's concerns). Both longitudinal studies and international research in emotional competence indicate growing deficiencies in personal management skills for students (Achenbach, Howell, Quay and Conners, 1991; see Goleman, 1994, 1998). This stream of research suggests a relatively acute need for viable enhancement strategies that could be applied to this domain.

The research programme on SCD was initiated partly to test the impact of imposing more formal interaction activities on learning outcomes (Dansereau, 1988). The use of a script, and the activities included in scripts evolved from cognitive-based, individual learning strategy research (see Dansereau, McDonald, Collins, Garland, Holley, Diekhoff and Evans, 1979). Scripts have been developed and investigated for their potential in increasing the cognitive performance of college dyads in experimental environments (e.g. Dansereau, 1985, 1987b, 1988; Dees, Dansereau, Peel, Boatler and Knight, 1991; Lambiotte, Dansereau, O'Donnell, Young, Skaggs and Hall, 1988; O'Donnell, Dansereau, Hall and Rocklin, 1987; Patterson, Dansereau and Newbern, 1992; Wiegmann, Dansereau and Patterson, 1992). Typically, students are paired in a same-sex dyad and use an assigned script to guide the roles played and the sequence of co-operative activities. In scripted co-operative learning, equal-status dyads interact to enhance their individual knowledge and/or skills. Scripted co-operation can be contrasted with tutoring and team training. Tutoring involves a distinction in status among the participants (expertise) and team training focuses on the enhancement of team or group outcomes rather than individual outcomes.

The history of research in co-operative learning extends over some 90 years and 600 studies (Johnson *et al.*, 1991), although the majority of work has involved mostly schoolchildren and has been conducted as field studies rather than controlled laboratory experiments. The general advantage of co-operative over individual study has been shown in numerous studies with several reviews and annotated bibliographies reporting increases in cognitive outcomes, such as higher academic grades or scores on standardized tests (Dansereau and Johnson, 1994; Johnson and Johnson, 1989). In scripted co-operative dyads (SCD), learners enact an experimenter-provided script that guides their interactions (Dansereau, 1978, 1985, 1988). Empirical results indicate that SCD results in better cognitive performance than non-scripted co-operation and than individual study, as we have seen (see O'Donnell and Dansereau, 1992).

Conceptual framework

A conceptual framework for understanding scripted co-operative dyads has been developed and serves as a way to identify factors and discuss experimental findings that are considered as potential influences on the co-operative interaction (see Figure 10.1).

From the figure, the reader can see that the interaction and its evaluation form the central feature of the model. Influences on the co-operative interaction include individual differences, task characteristics and incentives, and scripts.

Individual differences

The influence of individual differences on co-operative outcomes has been an important area of interest for scripted co-operation (Hall, Dansereau and Skaggs, 1990). Some of the individual differences that have been explored are verbal ability (e.g. Rewey, Dansereau, Skaggs, Hall and Pitre, 1989; Wiegmann *et al.*, 1992) and field-dependence/independence (O'Donnell *et al.*, 1991). Verbal ability (Deignan, 1975) is based on reading vocabulary and generally has a positive correlation with co-operative outcomes (e.g. O'Donnell *et al.*, 1991). Field-dependence/independence can be described as the tendency to have greater or less autonomy in perceptual, social and cognitive domains (Witkin and Goodenough, 1981). It may be that the tendency of field dependants to be aware of context (e.g. notice the partner more) may increase their ability to establish common ground (Schober and Clark, 1989) and/or to construct better shared mental models of the co-operative topic (Resnick, Levine and Teasley, 1991; Salas, Dickinson, Converse and Tannenbaum, 1996; Salomon, 1993). Academic tasks are usually performed better by individuals who are field-independent, although field-dependent persons have greater recall when they can refer to their script or their partner for assistance in scripted co-operation studies (O'Donnell *et al.*, 1991).

Task characteristics and incentives

Task characteristics and incentives in co-operative learning include the nature and difficulty of materials, the goals and duration of the assigned task and the amount of material covered in each interaction. These factors have been examined in non-scripted settings (Johnson *et al.*, 1991) and in scripted co-operation as well (Lambiotte, Dansereau, Rocklin, Fletcher, Hythecker, Larson and O'Donnell, 1987). The results from these studies indicate complicated interactions that are beyond the scope of this contribution.

Scripts

A script is a guide, or role for interaction. Co-operative learning scripts have generally included both metacognition and elaboration roles for interacting dyads, with the result that dyads have shown superior performance over individuals using the same study strategy and over other dyads using self-generated scripts (e.g. Hall *et al.*, 1989; McDonald *et al.*, 1985; Newbern, Dansereau and Patterson, 1994). Role alternations have been experimentally investigated; it appears that the use of these strategies is important although the number of times which partners alternate roles that include metacognitive and elaborative tasks is not particularly important (Lambiotte *et al.*, 1987; Lambiotte *et al.*, 1988).

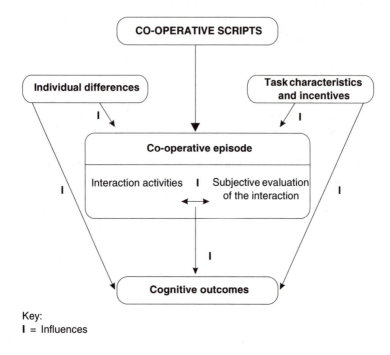

Figure 10.1 Framework for Scripted Co-operation

In earlier work, Larson, Dansereau, O'Donnell, Hythecker, Lambiotte and Rocklin (1985) compared metacognition and elaboration. Their initial study found that metacognition was related to higher scores on the initial learning task while elaboration led to better performance on the individual transfer task. However, not all combinations of script activities were used, so it was unclear which role or role combination might be optimal for general learning situations. Follow-up work subsequently compared each script activity separately, in combination with each other, and with a control group: metacognition, elaboration, metacognition plus elaboration, and un-scripted control (Newbern, 1996). The results were that the metacognitive role was superior alone and in combination with elaboration, with dyads recalling a statistically significantly higher quantity of main ideas, with significantly greater accuracy as well. The two metacognitive groups also recalled in more detail ideas and with greater accuracy, although the group differences for details were not statistically significant.

The interaction and its evaluation

Pragmatically, a script is a behavioural guide that prescribes certain behaviours to engage the partners in speaking, listening, and responding. Conceptually, the script is a cognitive guide that establishes the approach used to apprehend and process the information. Still speaking conceptually, the script is also a social/emotional guide that provides both the limiting boundaries and the enabling scaffold to which the partners adhere for the current interaction. In this regard, participant evaluations of the interaction are likely to be related to not only cognitive outcomes but also motivation to participate in future co-operative episodes. Details on the participant perceptions of the co-operative process may provide diagnostic information about aspects of the interaction that are critical for successful learning. Related findings indicate that dyads engaging in SCD are less anxious than individuals (O'Donnell *et al.*, 1987) and that scripted dyads report more motivation, interest and liking for the partner than un-scripted dyads (Hall *et al.*, 1989; O'Donnell *et al.*, 1987). The effects of script variations on interaction have recently been expanded through assessing subjective ratings from participants, of the interaction itself (Newbern *et al.*, 1994; Newbern, 1996). Four factors have been analysed: synchrony (e.g. 'not choppy', 'make a good team'); stimulating (e.g. 'motivated to help my partner', 'enjoy the interaction'); social concern (e.g. 'concerned with making a good impression'); and spirit of competition (e.g. 'interact with a "spirit of competition"'). Results indicate that dyads using a metacognitive script interact with more social concern and with a spirit of competition (Newbern, 1996).

Conclusion

In conclusion, the focus of our latest work with SCD centres on emotional competence, such as being aware of self, attending to the interaction partner, and appropriate responses based on interaction feedback. It appears that in addition to improving learning, SCD, especially using scripts with a metacognitive component, has the potential to increase emotional competency by providing an arena for exploring intra- and interpersonal strategies for dealing with affect. Additional research is needed to see if emotional skills exhibited in scripted interaction transfer to other settings.

CO-OPERATIVE LEARNING IN THE TEACHING OF WRITING

Robert Neale and Deborah Laurs, Massey University, New Zealand

The course known as '39.106 Writing: Theory and Practice' has run at New Zealand's Massey University for more than 20 years. It is founded upon the belief that the overwhelming bulk of the world's writing is transactional (i.e. a vehicle for informing, entertaining, edifying or persuading an audience), having been developed initially for prosaic purposes like business and administration rather than directly for 'creative' writing, which got into the act much later. The course identifies four major variables (Role, Audience, Format and Topic, usefully abbreviated to RAFT) in the transaction, and for convenience assumes six stages in the writing process – invention, discussion, drafting, revision, proof-reading and publication – while recognizing that in practice these stages overlap and constantly recur[1].

The course is primarily intended for first-year students, but is available to anyone within the university who wishes to enrol. It is offered not only internally (in classes on campus) but also extramurally by correspondence. Its clientele therefore ranges widely both geographically and by age. We introduced 'peer editing' for all students early in the course's history, and 'peer assessment' more recently for internal students only. To assess the problems we encountered and the solutions we tried it is best to take the two groups separately.

The process of peer editing

Internal tutorial groups charactisterically number around twelve to fifteen students, a convenient size for peer editing. This procedure initially tends to prove unfamiliar, and therefore somewhat daunting, to most students, but the vast majority acclimatize to it readily and quickly. Students are set various writing tasks (e.g. a letter to the editor, a children's story, a radio talk), on language-related issues such as mimesis, metaphor, correctness and irony. They bring a succession of drafts to tutorial, and, having grouped students in pairs, we take them through the process by stages.

Peer editing for internal students

1   Introduce yourself to your partner.
2   Exchange scripts and read through your partner's script in silence.
3   Read through again, still in silence, putting **X** in the margin against anything that seems wrong, ✓ against anything that strikes you as good, and **?** against anything you don't understand. Try to use all three symbols.
    Then, when all pairs have finished:
4   Go into conference with each other about what you have noted, consulting a dictionary where necessary and calling on your tutor for any help you need.
    And finally:
5   Redraft what you have written in the light of today's session and bring that new draft for further editing next week.

In a sequence of tutorial sessions we provide students with techniques for analysing structure and indeed for responding to the whole RAFT of variables mentioned above – such procedures as identifying the main idea, evaluating how introduction and conclusion interrelate, editing for 'vigorous verbs' and so on. It is usually not long before the group sets to with a will, so that a tutor arriving a little late may well find proceedings already under way. We normally arrange new partnerships at each weekly tutorial session, so that each piece of writing (which takes three or four weeks to develop) comes under several different scrutinies. Not all pairs, of course, conclude their operations simultaneously, and an experienced tutor can usually tell when earnest discussion of text gives place to earnest discussion of unrelated matters. But these remain minor problems, and vigorous editorial discussion often continues to the very end of the hour or even longer. Indeed the university's regulation 50-minute classes often prove too short, since a profitable class often warrants, but lacks the time for, a general discussion session in which problems and solutions can be aired and shared.

A great many teaching points thus arise from student enquiry rather than having to be initiated by the tutor. And the peer-editing process engenders a firm sense of trust and co-operation. Indeed, students eagerly anticipate the 'next instalment' of their partner's draft, to see what progress has been made. In the long run this is, of course, a university assignment which will be submitted to earn a grade, but before then it is part of a lively collective enterprise, involving the students in intense discussion and feedback, with the intention of helping each other clarify the written expression of their ideas to the best of their ability. One problem we expected – the pairing of students of very different abilities – turned out to be not a problem at all but rather an advantage: the clever and the less clever can learn a lot from each other in different ways.

Dealing with problems

Attendance

This system sees considerable improvements in students' writing and in their awareness of the underlying issues. *But they have to be there.* After a year or two of dealing with only the faithful and conscientious few we decided to make attendance compulsory, docking marks from students absenting themselves without adequate reason. Regular attendance soon becomes a habit, and no further problems of that sort occurred.

Extramural students

Extending this system to extramural students presented problems of a tougher sort. We put pairs of students in touch with each other, linking neighbours as far as possible but having to accept that much, if not all, of the peer editing would happen through the mail.

The comparatively high drop-out rate among such students renders their partnerships fragile, although when two students lose their partners more or less simultaneously we can, of course, link the survivors with each other – so that at any given moment there need be only one student in want of a partner. Nevertheless, difficulties of timing have led us to maintain a system allowing an extramural student to subsist without an editorial partner, perhaps substituting self-editing or a one-way partnership whereby a family member or friend helps out.

And all directions for such editing have of course also to go through the mail. The *Assignments* booklet extramural students receive is accompanied by one on *The Writing and Editing of Assignments*. The rubric for extramural students, in receipt of their partner's draft of a short story, runs:

1   Acknowledge receipt at once. Edit without delay. Return promptly.
2   Read through as usual, and proof-read to 'print readiness'. But remember that short stories in particular may contain deliberate 'mistakes': not everyone, for example, speaks in accordance with the rules of standard grammar. If in doubt, use a footnote in the usual way. Check that the story is *punctuated* and *paragraphed* consistently and effectively, especially when anyone talks.
3   Identify the point about language which the story is meant to illustrate and explore. How far is it integral to the story? How far is it typical of language? Is it convincingly handled? Answer these questions in **blue or black** on a separate sheet of paper, adding any comments and suggestions you think might help the writer.
4   What about narrative point of view? Is the narrator a participant in the story or telling it from the outside? How do you know, and what do you learn about the narrator as you read? Is there more than one point of view within the narrative? Underline in **green** one phrase, clause or sentence where the words convey someone's point of view (not necessarily the narrator's) with particular effectiveness. Explain in **green** why you chose that piece, adding any suggestions that occur to you for handling point of view better. Does the story generate suspense or surprise? If so, underline in **red** one passage that does so, appending your comments and suggestions in **red**.
5   Add in **blue or black** any further comments which you think might be of help to the writer. Think about the story's *structure*: how clearly can you identify its beginning, middle and end? How well does the story suit its juvenile *audience*? Then trace your own reactions during your first reading of the story, and during subsequent readings if they differ. Give reasons for all your findings.

Extramural students may attend a three-day On-Campus course at which they can put into practice the editing skills they have acquired through this correspondence version. They relish the opportunity to work one-on-one, taking a piece of writing (on a topic of their own choice) through three stages of peer editing over the duration of the course, interspersed with discussions of the theory of writing and of the set texts of the course. They are generally even more focused than the internal students, subjecting every word of each other's writing to fine scrutiny, with reference to such precepts as William Strunk's maxim: 'Omit needless words' (Strunk and White, 1979: 23–25). The results are later 'published' in a posting to all extramural students in the paper.

Peer assessment

Peer assessment through the mail we deemed impracticable, but we introduced it among internal students with, we believe, some further benefit to them. Final drafts are circulated at the appropriate tutorial session, and each student is expected to grade at least six (most manage more). They follow a grading system based upon the RAFT mentioned earlier, marking the handling of each variable on a scale of one to five. Although this scale precludes total fence-sitting, we found that the majority tended to award a kindly but cautious 3 out of 5 for each variable, so that twelve out of twenty became the most common score, with the bulk of marks clustering very closely around this. But the benefit to students of having to form a judgement – and particularly of having to write an appreciative or critical comment – remained clear, so without abandoning the system we reintroduced marking by tutors in a way that spread the range of marks a good deal more widely and appropriately. Students seem content with this combined arrangement. The combination of peer editing with peer assessment certainly enables them, over time, to translate their observations about others' work to their own and thus to develop a critical faculty about their own writing.

Most of the problems we encountered therefore seem to have been organizational or incidental rather than systemic. Perhaps it is the nature of writing, but heavy peer involvement, whether for purposes of editing or assessing, seems to us of very high value indeed in the teaching of it. We have, of course, peer edited this account.

PEER TEACHING IN A SCHOOL OF MEDICINE

Neal Whitman, Director of Educational Development in the Office of the Dean and Professor of Family and Preventive Medicine, The University of Utah, USA

While most of my work in academic medicine has been to improve the effectiveness of medical teachers, it would be educational malpractice not to address the students who are doing the learning. Thus, I wrote a handbook in 1995 which is presented annually to our first-year medical students on the first day of medical school (Whitman, 1995). Inspiration, as taught in the first-year physiology course, is an active process. This handbook, of course, makes this assertion in the philosophical sense and adds the premise that inspiration is a two-way process in which students and teachers should be partners in a collaborative teaching–learning process. The suggestion is also made that medical students, themselves, can teach themselves and each other. This can occur informally in study groups or more formally in tutorials conducted by students for students.

Brief description of our peer-teaching programme

In 1991, the Programme for ACademic Enhancement (PACE) was implemented to formalize the informal peer teaching that already was occurring in the school of medicine. The goal of PACE was to enhance medical student academic performance by providing supplemental support in basic science courses during the first two years of medical school. The supplemental sessions were not intended to replace actual classroom time allotted during the medical school schedule. PACE was specifically designed to supplement and enhance material that is taught by the faculty. Participants in the PACE programme were expected to attend their regularly scheduled classes and utilize supplemental support sessions in addition to the normal schedule.

PACE is presented to medical students as a two-way process aimed at students who desire to be tutored and for students who desire to act as tutors. In order to facilitate student access to both parts of this programme, written guidelines have been developed for both tutees and tutors.

Guidelines for participants

Guidelines for students to be tutored

1   Students can come to the Office of Student Advising and Counselling and review the list of tutors available and choose from the list.
2   Some students may be referred by faculty for tutoring, in which case it is up to the student to contact the Assistant Dean for student advising and counselling for a meeting to discuss the referral.
3   Every student who receives a marginal pass or a failure on an exam is required to meet with the Assistant Dean to set up tutoring arrangements.
4   It is up to the student to contact the tutor and set up tutoring sessions, as needed.

Guidelines for students who wish to be tutors

1   Students can contact the course director for the courses they wish to tutor. The course directors must approve tutors.
2   Approved tutors must attend a one-hour orientation conducted by the Director of Educational Development which addresses what is tutoring, benefits of tutoring, what mentors do, the duties of tutors, a game plan for tutoring, and what's in it for them.
3   Tutors are paid $10.00 per hour and must keep a record of their tutoring schedule.

Theoretical and philosophical base for PACE

Medical students are busy with their own learning and helping others may not be a high priority. Nevertheless, they can become peer teachers for reasons other than altruism. The fact is, as their teachers already know, one of the best ways to learn something is to teach it to someone else. This is explained by the cognitive processes that occur when the instructor reviews and organizes the material and seeks out its structure so that it can be explained to others. This premise was adeptly studied in an experiment in which students were asked to study an article on brain functioning; the control group was told that there would be a test and an experimental group was told that instead they would be asked to teach the material to others. That teaching never took place, but both groups were tested, and while there was no difference between groups in rote memory, the experimental group achieved a significantly higher score on conceptual understanding (Benware and Deci, 1984).

Of course, peer teaching would not be feasible if there were not peer learning. Studies of peer teaching support the notion that peers are effective teachers because of their closeness as peers and the individualization that can occur, especially when peer teaching is conducted one-on-one. Medical student tutors are used in many medical schools, including my own, and where systematic studies have been conducted, including the University of Texas Medical Branch at Galveston and the University of Maryland School of Medicine, these programmes have been shown to be effective mechanisms for helping medical students address academic deficiencies (Whitman, 1988).

At times, peer teachers may be more helpful than faculty teachers who are unconsciously competent – faculty may have difficulty teaching medical concepts because their thought processes are automatic and they are too advanced, a problem not likely to be found in student instructors (Whitman, 1999). Common sense tells us that peer teachers can be effective in medical education because, when medical students teach each other, there is mutual understanding and empathy that can facilitate the teaching–learning process. This can occur in study groups where students alternate between the role of teacher and learner, and any 'pimping' (relentless questioning, often of the arcane, until a student is stumped) that occurs is typically good-natured. Peer teaching supports the notion that medicine should be practised as a team sport. Learning is frequently enhanced when it is more like a team effort than a solo race. Good learning, like good work, is collaborative and social, not competitive and isolated, and working with others often increases involvement in learning (Checkering and Gamson, 1987).

Outcomes and experience

In 1991–92, the first year of PACE, three students tutored two students (one student was tutored in two courses). With more publicity, the number of students to be tutored and to tutor increased in 1992–93: thirteen students tutoring eighteen students in nine courses. With the increased interest in tutoring, both group and individual sessions were conducted. Students with the most academic difficulties tended to request one-on-one tutoring, but some participated in both individual and group sessions. For the following six years (1993–94 to 1998–99), the number of students tutored per year ranged from 25 to 60 and the number of tutors per year ranged from 10 to 222. A sizeable number of students participate in the PACE programme. Popular courses tutored in the first year of the curriculum include biochemistry, physiology, and gross anatomy. Second-year courses include short, one- to two-week 'organ system' courses such as endocrinology and cardiovascular organ systems. The growing popularity of the

PACE programme speaks well to the validity of the concept of peer teaching in the first two years of medical school, but also reveals an underlying problem, discussed in the next section.

Problems and lessons

Although peer teaching is predicated on the principle that students benefit from a co-operative and collaborative model of education, underlying the popularity of PACE is the competitive nature of medical school. Students not in academic difficulty sign up for tutorial sessions in hopes of getting supplemental help that will make a difference between a passing grade and an honours grade. In our medical school, there is a pass–fail grading system, with a 'honours' grade assigned to the top students. School policy recommends honours grades for the top 20 per cent. Tutors report that group sessions, swelled with those students, make it difficult to focus on helping students looking for the supplemental instruction that makes the difference between a failing and passing grade. Tutors can meet one-on-one with students having the most academic difficulty, but still report a dilution of group sessions with students not in academic difficulty.

Our medical school continues to offer tutoring on a voluntary basis available to all students. The Assistant Dean for student advising and counselling encourages students in true academic difficulty to arrange individual tutoring and both the Assistant Dean and the Director of Educational Development are hopeful that students of varying ability benefit from group sessions. Students at all levels of achievement report PACE is a positive sign that the school of medicine encourages success for students at all levels.

A lesson learned is that lack of ongoing programme evaluation makes it difficult, if not impossible, to document the difference made to students in academic difficulty. Student failure on medical school courses is rare, two or three per year, and many interventions are in play to remediate and improve performance, including supplemental instruction by faculty. The informal evaluation by students who tutor and who are tutored is that tutoring is a valuable supplement to the curriculum.

Advice to colleagues

1   Ensure that you are directly involved in the recruitment and selection of student tutors so that you have confidence in them.
2   Establish a direct link between what is taught in a course and what is presented in peer-mediated tutorials. This requires periodic meetings of course faculty with peer teachers.
3   Encourage student teachers not to repeat the classroom performance of their teachers. Instead peer teaching should supplement classroom instruction with a fresh look at the old material, presenting it in new and different ways.

NOTES

1 APA Work Group of the Board of Educational Affairs (1997, November) *Learner-centered psychological principles: A framework for school reform and redesign*, Washington, DC: American Psychological Association.
2 The texts currently in use for the course are Mark Twain's *Huckleberry Finn*, Lewis Carroll's *Through the Looking-Glass*, Janet Frame's *The Envoy from Mirror City* and the Neale's *Writers on Writing* anthology which reproduces the comments on writing of writers from Aristotle to New Zealand poet Lauris Edmond.

In the final chapter, I reflect on the development of my own work and identify themes that run through the book. I also speculate about possible ways of developing and extending our knowledge about, and use of, peer tutoring.

11 Reflections and prospects

I shall begin this chapter by describing the development of a major area of my research and practice. Not only will this illustrate some of the differences and similarities between many different ways of involving students more closely in their education, but it will also illustrate, among other things, how theory and research have influenced my work, how important evaluation is to the success of any innovation and how a search for solutions to problems 'drives' much of my work.

A PERSONAL JOURNEY FROM 'PEER ASSESSMENT' TO 'PAIRED LEARNING'

In the mid-1980s, I was fortunate enough to hear John Cowan speak about his experiences of involving students in all aspects of their learning, including the self-assessment of it. His arguments and evidence were persuasive enough to set me on a similar path myself, and very soon I had designed and implemented a scheme of self- and peer assessment of my own. I wished to enable my students to benefit as his appeared to have done. My background as a psychologist proved a sound basis from which to launch such an undertaking. Not only did I have ready access to much theory relevant to learning and teaching with which to inform my questions and hypotheses, I also had experiences as an experimental psychologist which made it natural for me to test new methodologies and to evaluate the effectiveness of what I was attempting. I also found out as much as possible about what others had done before me as a matter of course. It was not until much later that I realized that what I was doing in the classroom and lecture hall was far from standard tertiary teaching practice.

Implementing self- and peer assessment

My initial research into student self- and peer assessment (Falchikov, 1986) addressed a number of questions relating to the degree of agreement between teacher and student ratings. However, I pointed out then, and reiterate now, that teacher ratings themselves may not be as reliable as we would wish. The first step of my study involved a collaboration between first-year undergraduates studying introductory psychology and their teachers to agree a set of criteria of excellence for essay writing. A marking schedule was designed based on the agreed criteria, and tested by a colleague who compared marks generated using the marking scheme with those obtained by the old 'intuitive' grading system. We found a high level of agreement between the two. Students were then required to write their essay and complete the marking schedule, awarding themselves a grade, before handing in their work. A copy of an essay was given to a peer who marked it using the same marking schedule during tutorial time. Teachers marked a further copy of each essay. Teacher, self and peer marks were compared at a later tutorial. All combinations of marks were compared, and between 60 per cent of peer assessments and 74 per cent of self-assessments found to agree with teacher marks to within a less than 10 per cent margin. The scheme was particularly useful in cases where there was unacceptable difference between marks, in that all markers were required to justify their grading. Student evaluations of the scheme suggested that they perceived the process to have conferred benefits in terms of improved learning. Over 90 per cent of the group reported that they found the scheme hard, but that it made them think more and become more critical. Over three-quarters reported that the scheme had helped them become more structured when writing essays.

My keen desire to evaluate the scheme and test the reliability of student marking was instrumental in aiding the dissemination of the results of the study. I now had evidence to show colleagues that a large proportion of students, given a sound preparation, were capable of producing marks for their own work which did not differ significantly from those awarded by teachers themselves. Evidence proved to be a powerful persuader, and my study was not relegated to the bottom of a filing cabinet containing interesting but essentially fringe activities. Colleagues seemed to be interested in what I was doing, and requested copies of my paper in order to learn how to carry out similar studies themselves. I reported my findings in my own institution, and involved new cohorts of students and immediate colleagues in similar studies (some more willingly than others). I continued to collect and read other similar studies and to write up my action research (Falchikov, 1986).

Further investigations of self-assessment

A year later, I entered into correspondence with David Boud (then of the Tertiary Education Research Centre of the University of New South Wales, Sydney, now at the University of Technology, Sydney) whose work was also in the field of student self-assessment, and, in 1988–89, I spent a year working with him in Australia on two projects. We shared many concerns relating to student autonomy and independent learning, and were keen to investigate factors which supported or inhibited successful student self-assessment. Both of the projects we undertook involved an analysis of self-assessment studies in higher education. The first of these was a critical review, and the second a meta-analysis of all quantitative studies we were able to locate (Boud and Falchikov, 1989; Falchikov and Boud, 1989). Both papers focused on the comparison of student-generated marks and those generated by teachers. We were keen to investigate the effects of variables such as ability level, gender and the level of course of which the self-assessment was a part, on the 'accuracy' of self-assessment. In addition, we wished to investigate the effects of practice on students' self-assessment abilities and ascertain whether self-assessments were affected when marks so derived were used for formal assessment.

The analyses suggested that factors which seem to be important with regard to the closeness of correspondence between self and teacher marks included:

- the quality of design of the study, with better-designed studies being associated with closer correspondence between student and teacher than poorly designed ones;
- the level of the course of which the assessment was a part, with students on advanced courses appearing to be the more 'accurate' assessors than those on introductory courses;
- the broad area of study, with studies within the area of science appearing to produce more accurate self-assessment generally than did those from other areas of study.

(Falchikov and Boud, 1989: 395)

While we concluded that we had gone some way towards differentiating among variables that appear to be salient for successful self-assessment, we were also aware that our definition of 'success' was somewhat limited. We asserted that agreement between student and teacher marks may not be the most important aspect of successful self- or peer assessment. Real success should follow from the enhancement of student learning that results from participation in the process.

Self- and peer assessment of group working

During my time in Australia I continued working on two other projects I had started in Edinburgh. The first of these investigated self- and peer assessment of group working (Falchikov, 1991, 1993). By the end of the 1980s, group work was becoming common in many UK higher-education institutions, my own included. This trend was encouraged by both the increase in student numbers entering into higher education, and a growing belief that students needed to practise the skills of self- and peer assessment in order to equip them for work, leisure and lifelong learning (e.g. Cuthbert, 1995; Tate and Thomson, 1994; Green, 1990; Rigg, 1990; Smith, Wolstencroft and Southern, 1989). Group working brought with it many benefits and not a few problems, many of which remain today. For example, student groups sometimes find themselves working in the absence of a teacher, which makes the assessment of group working problematic if student assessments are not used. However, group work can too often give rise to the 'free rider problem'. My psychology background, once again, came to my aid, and I adapted work on Group Process Analysis, originally associated with Robert Bales (1950) to the context of student self- and peer assessment in the context of teacher-less groups. The focus of my interest and student assessments had moved from the product of learning to its processes.

I conducted a small pilot study of assessment of group process skills, differentiating between what Bales (1950) had called 'task' and 'maintenance' skills. Task skills are those which help a group achieve its aims (e.g. solve a problem, prepare a group report), while maintenance skills relate to the working of the group (e.g. resolving conflict, building trust). I designed an assessment checklist using Bales' categories. Students were involved in many decisions regarding the project: they chose what to do and how to do it, they modified the assessment checklist to suit their circumstances and carried out self- and peer assessments. Calculation of the coefficient of concordance (w) showed the degree of agreement between peers. Some differences between task and maintenance functions emerged, in that student ratings tended to be very similar when they were assessing readily observable task skills (e.g. 'asks for facts'; 'pulls together ideas' or 'makes suggestions'), but less so when evaluating some maintenance skills (e.g. 'makes members aware of the direction of the work and reminds group of accepted standards'; 'persuades members to analyse constructively their differences in opinions' and 'tries to reconcile disagreements'). I concluded that more practice in identifying difficult skills was desirable, and allocated more time to this in subsequent implementations of the group process assessment (Falchikov, 1987, 1988).

Same-level peer-tutoring in higher education

The second project on which I worked during my time in Australia was a pilot study of same-level peer tutoring in higher education undertaken in collaboration with Carol Fitz-Gibbon (Durham University, then of the University of Newcastle upon Tyne) (Falchikov, 1990; Falchikov and Fitz-Gibbon, 1989). This study provided the data that were re-analysed in Chapter 4.

The development of peer-assessment schemes: Peer Feedback Marking

As I indicated in the introduction to this book, I developed Peer Feedback Marking as a response to some problematic aspects of peer assessment.

(1) Peer Feedback Marking study I

This study (Falchikov, 1995a, 1995b) differed in one key respect from my previous peer-assessment studies. It emphasized *feedback* to students rather than *grading*. Individuals from a small class of third-year developmental psychology students prepared a short talk which the rest of the group assessed, providing feedback using agreed criteria. In this particular study students also awarded a grade to their peers, but the exercise could equally well omit this. After each presentation, assessment forms were completed by each student and by the lecturer. The audience then told the presenter or group of presenters what they had liked about the presentation.

Next, critical feedback and suggestions for improvement were made. The positive feedback, being pleasurable to presenters, seemed to boost confidence and prepare them for the criticisms.

Comparisons of mean peer and lecturer mark indicated little difference between the two, and evaluation suggested that the benefits of previous systems of peer assessment had been preserved. Feedback to peers reflected the agreed criteria, but more strengths than weaknesses were identified.

(2) Peer Feedback Marking study II

The second PFM study (Falchikov, 1994) involved group presentations of a large first-year class taking a 'Foundations of Social Science' module. Procedures and materials were almost identical to those of PFM study I. Marks awarded by peers and teachers were again found to be similar, supporting the prevailing view that peer assessment is a useful and valid methodology.

After this study was completed, I compared feedback statements by lecturers and students, noting numbers of 'positive' and 'negative' statements. Both lecturers and students provided less helpful critical feedback or suggestions for improvement than positive features, particularly in 'good' presentations, although constructively critical feedback is thought to be more useful. Many similarities were found between the content of student and teacher feedback, but some interesting differences emerged. To a greater extent than lecturers, students focused on practical issues such as preparation and delivery, and on the amount and quality of information. Teachers, on the other hand, emphasized understanding and methodological issues. An 'hierarchy' of feedback was proposed.

By carrying out studies I and II, I was able to investigate the working of PFM within two different cohorts and compare its effectiveness in the contexts of individual and group presentations. However, I was unable to explore longer-term benefits of peer feedback, due to the very short length and limited assessment opportunities of the modules of which they formed a part. Thus, the next study was designed to assess longer-term usefulness of peer feedback by examining modifications to students' written work as a result of a feedback exercise.

(3) Peer critiques

Prompted by continuing problems associated with peer assessment and PFM, and by concerns that students were receiving peer feedback too late for them to benefit immediately, I modified Bruffee's Brooklyn Plan (1978, 1993) which involved the use of peer criticism of student writing. This scheme enabled students to receive critical feedback from, and give critical feedback to, peers before the final version of a piece of written work was to be handed in. My scheme was more modest in scale than Bruffee's original, but involved a greater investment in time than earlier PFM studies I had conducted. Below is a brief account of my peer-critiquing studies (Falchikov, 1994, 1996).

My study took place over an eight-week period and consisted of a number of stages:

1   Essay titles, reading lists and brief notes on essay writing were supplied to students. They were required to choose one topic from the list.
2   Students and teachers agree criteria in the same way as reported in my original scheme of self- and peer assessment.
3   Students prepared first drafts of their essays (out of class).
4   Unevaluative criticism took place in class. This required a peer to make a short description of the main points of each paragraph and of the whole paper.
5   Evaluative criticism took place in class. Using criteria agreed, further criticism was made by a peer, which emphasized ways of improving the paper. Strengths were identified, and hints for improvement supplied.
6   Students reflected on the scheme. All were required to submit a reflective statement on their experiences as reviewers and receivers of feedback which would contribute 20 per cent of the final coursework assessment mark (the remaining 80 per cent being awarded for the essay).
7   Essays and reflective statements were submitted.

On completion of the exercise, student and lecturer feedback statements were subjected to content analysis. The results of the analysis suggested that students (but not lecturers) provided more positive statements than negative. I noted that positive feedback may be very desirable, particularly for female students who lack confidence. This may also apply to male students, but this study involved a very small number of males, none of whom gave any indication of a lack of confidence. However, an over-emphasis on positive feedback may carry disadvantages, as 'negative' criticism and suggestions for improvement are necessary for stimulating reflection and change.

The majority of students reported acting upon some peer advice. Of the very few who did not, most were male.

This study indicated that students are capable of providing useful and timely feedback to their peers. Even though the teacher may supply sound advice, it is often not offered in time for students to benefit immediately, and some reflective statements suggested that advice given by the teacher after submission of a piece of work was not acted upon. Clearly, the study does not provide an unambiguous answer to the question, 'Did the exercise improve the quality of essays written?' However, some self-reports suggested that participation in the exercise had resulted in a better product, and several female students expressed an intention to use peer feedback and review in the future.

Changing approaches to student assessment: the ASSHE project

The Assessment Strategies in Scottish Higher Education (ASSHE) project, a joint venture between the University of Edinburgh and Napier University, Edinburgh, began in September 1994 and ended in December 1996. It aimed to survey all

Scottish universities and other tertiary education institutions, to map all recent changes to assessment practice and to disseminate the results of the survey. We found many examples of changes to assessment practice involving self-assessment, peer assessment, feedback provision, self or peer testing and negotiation or collaboration with teachers concerning some aspect of the process. The most frequently encountered of these forms was peer assessment, often in the context of group work (Falchikov, 2000).

We attempted to find out which factors were influential in getting the initiative off the ground. Nearly a third of respondents mentioned colleagues within their department or university as a key factor. Heads of department, heads of school, departmental steering committees, curriculum development committees and 'individual senior managers' or university policy were also mentioned. However, a fifth of respondents identified personal factors such as their own commitment, enthusiasm, expertise or knowledge as the most important. This information has wider application and may relate to the introduction of any non-traditional educational practice.

Teachers reported benefits to themselves in the areas of professional practice and teaching quality, improved relationships with students and clearer insights into what it is to be a student today. Lecturers also appreciated seeing improvements to students' learning and intellectual development. Some reported increased job satisfaction and others particularly liked the change of role which student involvement in assessment had entailed. A few reported reduced workloads and time saved. However, a larger number of teachers found that their initiative demanded more of them in terms of organization and resources.

Problems encountered when involving students in assessment affected both students and teachers. The main problem for students and staff was seen as student lack of experience and reluctance to participate in schemes together. These problems appear to be short lived.

> Initially students were **suspicious** ...
> Initial **apprehension**, which soon evaporates ...
> Initially there was some **resistance to change**, but there are no problems now.
> Student **uncertainty** in the early stages ...

Once again, some students reported disliking assessing or judging their peers. Group dynamics also appeared to contribute to student reluctance to participate. Both students and staff reported that peer assessment can be time consuming. However, the majority of teachers felt the time was well spent.

We concluded that students are likely to continue to be involved in assessment and advised colleagues wishing to introduce student self- or peer assessment to

1   Build on existing practice which lends itself to student involvement.
2   Address problems and any factors which may hinder development of the scheme.
3   Spend more time preparing students for the task/reassure them.

4   Increase attendance at staff-development events, etc.
5   Evaluate studies.
6   Disseminate results of studies and publicize the evidence relating to reliability.

This advice might equally apply to the introduction of any innovation.

Reliability and bias in summative peer assessment

Dissemination of the ASSHE findings took me back to Australia where I also seized the opportunity to work with Doug Magin of the University of New South Wales on the extent of bias, in particular gender bias, in the peer assessment of group presentations (Falchikov and Magin, 1997).

We described a technique for detecting gender bias in cases where student raters have awarded marks to same- and opposite-sex peers, and illustrated its use by data from two case studies. Our analysis found that effect sizes were very small, which we took as an indication that no gender bias was operating in these two cases. However, we concluded that it would be premature to conclude that gender bias does not exist, as behaviour, performance and results may vary in relation to task and other contextual variables. In any case,

> ... it is quite possible for gender bias of this kind to operate in situations where virtually no gender differences in outcomes are found. Such situations could arise where marker gender bias is in the opposite direction to that of a substantiated gender difference in performance skills.
>
> (Falchikov and Magin, 1997: 387)

Nonetheless, we concluded that the technique described can contribute to the good practice necessary to ensure the success of peer assessment in terms of pedagogical benefits and reliable and fair marking outcomes. In this paper, we also discussed the benefits of the use of multiple ratings in peer assessment.

My concern with gender issues is now translated into a routine investigation of gender difference and similarity in every educational investigation I carry out.

A meta-analysis of peer assessment studies

Some details of this recently completed study were mentioned in the introduction to this book. Results of this meta-analysis (Falchikov and Goldfinch, 2000) suggested that peer assessments more closely resemble teacher assessments when students are required to make global judgements based on clear and explicit criteria and have some ownership of these criteria, rather than when grading involves assessing several individual dimensions. We also found that assessment of professional practice seems to be more difficult than assessment of academic products and processes. We were not surprised to find that peer–teacher similarities were greater in well-designed studies than in poorly designed ones.

Encouraging co-operative learning and student autonomy

In 1997, I returned to the research area of co-operative learning, being constantly reminded of the problems experienced by students caused by increasing numbers and large class sizes, and the reduction in resources for higher education. Students require social as well as academic support if they are to succeed in higher education (e.g. Tinto, 1975). They need to develop an institutional and course identity, but can no longer rely on being able to achieve these in one-to-one or very small group tutorials or on being able to find their tutor on demand. Students can, however, be helped to support themselves. Thus, I introduced paired learning into the module on life-span development I taught to second-year social science and health studies students.

I encountered problems in my first implementation of this paired-learning scheme. Students resented the methods of partner choice, whether they had been allowed to choose their own partner or whether pairs had been constituted randomly. Some resented having to work with anyone. In spite of what I regarded as careful preparation on my part, some students felt insufficiently prepared for the exercise. The following year I made some changes and spent more time introducing the exercise and elaborating the benefits of learning with a peer. In the first year, I had given over some time to in-class paired learning, but the bulk of paired-learning exercises were designed for students working together out of class times. In the second year of operation, I included more paired-learning exercises to be carried out in tutorial times. I also conducted an in-class 'experiment' to test the effectiveness of some varieties of paired learning compared with independent study. As we saw in Chapter 5 (Table 5.1.9), results supported the superiority of paired learning, and students appeared to take note of this. The end-of-semester module evaluation suggested that paired learning had been enjoyed on this occasion and that students perceived themselves to have benefited from it.

REFLECTIONS

This chapter has described an educational journey which brought me to the starting point for writing this book. The journey I have described has taken me from what appears to be a somewhat narrow focus on one element of the learning environment, assessment, albeit a very important element, to a wider concern with 'the whole student' and her/his modes of learning. My work may now be characterized by more diversity, but the elements are united by the same concerns which drove my first experimental study: to increase student autonomy, facilitate intellectual development and improve the quality of learning. This book allows me to share my experiences with a wider audience, who, I hope, may find something useful contained within it on their own pedagogic travels. The latest phase of my journey is now almost completed. What do I see as significant signposts on the way?

SIGNIFICANT SIGNPOSTS

Enthusiasm and commitment

I hope that my enthusiasm for improving student learning through peer tutoring has provided a clear signal to readers. Enthusiasm is vital. The importance of engaging the commitment of colleagues and students features in several contributions to the book, particularly in Chapter 10. It is stressed by Hampton and Blythman, and Cohen *et al.* also emphasize the benefits of involving all participants in peer learning. Similarly, Wood reiterates many of the arguments that feature prominently in Chapter 5 about the importance of persuading and motivating one's colleagues at the start of a scheme. Whitman (Chapter 10) argues that maintaining contact with colleagues throughout the initiative is vital.

Supporting and improving student learning

Contributors to the book share my concerns for improving student learning and many see the main aim of their work as providing support for students. In Chapter 9, Tomes describes a model which conceptualizes learning as a dialogue between teacher and learner, and among learners, and identifies where technology can support the key learning processes. Similarly, support for student learning is the first stated aim of the Professional Development Groups that Wilson describes in Chapter 10. Hampton and Blythman (also Chapter 10) have found that their student-support networks succeed in helping attendance and retention as well as improving learning and achievement. In addition, evaluations of their scheme suggest that it helps students bond with each other, with the course and with the institution. McCombs also argues that, without positive relationships between learners and teachers, learner motivation and achievement may be compromised.

The importance of a theoretical and research base

Looking back to Chapter 1, many of the great variety of techniques available are designed with the clear aim of improving some aspect of student learning and have clear theoretical roots. It is interesting to note that, although contributors to Chapter 10 are writing about different types of peer tutoring, paired or peer learning in a variety of contexts, a number draw attention to the philosophical, theoretical or research base to their work. McCombs, for example, sees social constructionism and 'research-validated psychological principles of learning, motivation, development and individual differences' as informing her work. Wood, on the other hand, identifies experiential learning as having guided the Newcastle peer-tutoring scheme, while Wilson's work with Aboriginal students is founded in theories of knowledge. Other contributors such as Cohen *et al.* and Whitman situate their work within robust research frameworks. I believe that the benefits of developing any innovation from a sound theoretical or research basis cannot be overstated and hope that the frameworks discussed in Chapter 3 prove useful in the design and implementation of new peer-tutoring studies.

The work of Dansereau and colleagues (see Chapter 1) provides an excellent example of how a well-designed programme of research can contribute to both an increase in understanding and improved practice. Newbern and Dansereau's account of the evolution of scripted dyadic learning (Chapter 10) reports an exciting new development in this line of research.

Organization and preparation

Many other themes run through the chapters. The importance of good organization and thorough preparation is stressed throughout the book. There is no doubt that organization and preparation really can influence outcomes for success or failure. This concern is aired, not only by myself, but also in contributions from several colleagues. Sinclair Goodlad's seven golden rules in Chapter 5 constitute one such example, and organizational and operational issues also emerge as features in many contributions to Chapter 10. Highton, for example, describes in some detail the organization and preparation which enable students to gain credit for tutoring. Neale and Laurs conclude that most of the problems they encountered seem to have been organizational or incidental rather than systemic. Similarly, Hampton and Blythman stress the importance of the initial meeting with students and vigilant monitoring of study groups to prevent organizational chaos developing as students join and leave groups.

The importance of transparency

Several contributors to Chapter 10 stress the importance of transparency. Wood advocates it 'in all procedures with all participants'. Cohen *et al.* stress the importance of making procedures and decision making explicit in the context of assessment and advocate involving students in the generation of criteria. They also emphasize that we should make it clear to students what we are intending to assess and ensure that the grading allocation is transparent. Neale and Laurs provide a practical example of transparency with the inclusion in their contribution of detailed instructions for peer editing in both face-to-face and distance modes. Similarly, Whitman includes examples of instructions to students which again illustrate the importance of making procedures explicit.

Issues relating to assessment

Assessment is an influential element in the learning environment. It can affect the type of learning that takes place and the approach to studying employed by the learner. It is not surprising, therefore, that issues relating to assessment are mentioned by several contributors. Cohen *et al.* (Chapter 10) devote the whole of their contribution to this topic. They emphasize the important role that assessment has in facilitating learning, arguing that inappropriate assessment practices in a course can destroy desirable forms of peer learning no matter how well they are otherwise constructed. They also remind us to be quite clear and explicit about why and what we are assessing, and stress that feedback is more desirable than competition for marks. I also arrived at this conclusion when I developed the PFM schemes briefly outlined above. Cohen *et al.* also argue that assessment mechanisms should value contributions to group building and group sustenance. The relationship between module or course objectives and assessment practices too often seems to be unclear. Assessing generic skills may not be as straightforward as assessing increase in knowledge or understanding, but this is no reason not to attempt to do so. Assessment of the achievement of Bloom's (1956) higher cognitive skills, such as analysis and synthesis, or of Perry's (1970) stages of intellectual development, may be more familiar to teachers, and, therefore, may seem easier, than assessing the development of skills such as the ability to reflect and benefit from the reflection. Several contributors stress the importance of both matching assessment to peer-tutoring learning outcomes and making this relationship explicit. Wood (Chapter 10), for example, reports that performance indicators derived from theories of experiential learning were identified and used as 'reasonably effective measures' in the assessment of tutors in the Newcastle tutoring project. The benefits of peer assessment are mentioned by several contributors.

The importance of evaluation

Another theme that runs through the book is the importance of evaluation. Chapter 7 deals with this topic exclusively. Inadequate evaluation, or absence of evaluation altogether, may not affect the outcomes of an initial peer-tutoring study, but lack of knowledge of what did and did not work, and the reasons for this, are likely to impede future developments. Evaluation which is limited to qualitative self-report measures may prove less useful than quantitative data, though qualitative data can supply us with rich insights into processes. Self-reports also provide us with information about student attitudes to the experience. However, we may be less convinced when students tell us that their learning has improved as a result of peer tutoring than when we have hard evidence to support the claim.

I hope that the information contained within the book will make its way into new studies and implementations to benefit new generations of students. I trust, too, that any such studies will be evaluated. Quality and standards are issues addressed by several contributors and appear to be particularly salient when peer tutoring is carried out for academic credit. In Chapter 10, Highton and Wood, for example, both emphasize the importance of demonstrating quality, satisfying university regulations and maintaining standards. The act of reflection itself shows concern with improving the quality of student learning.

Peer learning in non-traditional settings

With an increase in commitment to lifelong learning and plans for virtual universities, problems of learning in non-traditional settings are likely to become more prominent and pressing. In Chapter 9, Tomes reviews some of the important issues and likely ways in which peer tutoring and co-operative learning may be supported by technology. Two contributions to Chapter 10 also reflect on problems of peer learning at a distance: Neale and Laurs in the context of peer editing and Wilson in that of peer learning of Indigenous students from remote communities. Too often, enthusiasts of distance learning forget the important role in learning played by the peer group. However, the rapid development of technologies to support learning is already enabling learners to co-operate with each other even when partners are geographically and temporally separate. It is to be hoped that increasing use of, and familiarity with, visual aspects of technology to support learning will go some way towards providing a more human face to collaboration at a distance.

The importance of reciprocity

There is ample advice in the book for us to be able to argue that the concept of reciprocity is particularly relevant to successful peer tutoring and paired learning. In same-level peer tutoring in higher education, equal relationships between learners seem to lead to success while unequal ones are more likely associated with problems, as we saw in Chapter 4. Taking turns and role reversals within a tutoring relationship are both more stimulating and educationally beneficial than fixed roles. Such concerns are less relevant in cross-level situations, though it is good to remember that even the lowliest tutee has something to bring to the relationship that cannot be provided by the tutor.

Problems of peer tutoring

Finally, we should consider the problems that have been identified which can interfere with successful peer tutoring. Poor planning and organization, as we have learned from a variety of sources, can compromise the activity. The composition of pairs and groups seems to be another area of difficulty in peer learning. I have encountered such problems in my own work on peer tutoring, and in Chapter 8, we learn from the work of Feichtner and Davis about students' negative and positive experiences of group work. Also in Chapter 8, Felder and Brent supply advice on how best to constitute learning groups. Lack of willingness to participate may also be problematic. Individual differences are likely to play a significant part in variations in the degree of willingness to try something new. This applies to both students and teachers. Maybe this does not matter where individual teachers are concerned, as long as students are given the opportunity to experience a variety of ways of learning across their programmes. Students, however, may lose out if they choose not to participate in paired or co-operative learning, as ample research studies have indicated. My own research suggests that there may be a gender dimension here also. In my experience, female students seem to be more willing to work together and benefit from sharing another point of view than their male counterparts. However, I must report that my implementations have generally involved more female students than male, so generalization from my results would be unwise. However, further investigation is desirable.

PROSPECTS

To return again to the theme of a journey, and believing, as I do, that it is better to travel hopefully than to arrive, new avenues now present themselves for future expeditions. In what direction might these avenues take us? There are still problems associated with group work that would benefit from further study. There appears to be a gap between our knowledge of what might or might not work and the ways in which group work is set up and conducted. The encouragement of students to learn co-operatively in settings which too readily advocate competition needs further investigation. As I have indicated, I think it important to explore the gender differences I encountered in attitudes to paired learning and peer review. I am happy to collaborate with any colleague who wishes to explore any of these routes with me. Let us use the technology to support this co-operation!

References

Abercrombie, M. L. J. (1983) 'The state of play in the management of peer-group learning', in G. Collier (ed.) *The management of peer-group learning. Syndicate methods in higher education*, Guildford: Society for Research into Higher Education.

Achenbach, T. M., Howell, C. T., Quay, H. C. and Conners, C. K. (1991) 'National survey of problems and competencies among four-to-sixteen-year-olds', monographs of the Society for Research in Child Development, 56, 3, Serial No. 225.

Ackerman, M. S. and McDonald, D. W. (1996) 'Answer Garden 2: Merging Organizational Memory with Collaborative Help', proceedings of the ACM Conference on Computer-Supported Cooperative Work (CSCW '96), November, 97–105.

ACMDP (1998) 2nd year course outline and assessment pack, semester one, 1998, Perth: Centre for Aboriginal Studies, Curtin University.

Adams, D. and Hamm, M. (with the collaboration of Drobnak, M. and Lazar, A.) (1996) *Cooperative learning. Critical thinking and collaboration across the curriculum* (2nd edn.), Springfield, Illinois: Charles Thomas Publishers.

Adams, S. (1953) 'Status congruency as a variable in small group performance', *Social Forces*, 32: 16–22.

Al-Hilawani, Y. A., Marchant, G. J. and Poteet, J. A. (1993) 'Implementing reciprocal teaching: was it effective?', paper presented at the 23rd annual meeting of Midwest Association of Teachers of Educational Psychology, Anderson, Indiana, October.

Allen, V. L. (ed.) (1976) *Children as teachers*, London: Academic Press.

Allen, V. L. and Feldman, R. (1973) 'Learning through tutoring: low achieving children as tutors', *Journal of Experimental Education*, 42: 1–5.

Anderson, G. and Boud, D. (1996) 'Extending the role of peer learning in university courses', *Research and Development in Higher Education*, 19: 15–19.

Annis, L. F. (1983a) 'The processes and effects of peer tutoring', *Human Learning*, 2: 39–47.

Annis, L. F. (1983b) 'The processes and effects of peer tutoring', paper presented at the Annual Meeting of the American Educational Research Association, Montreal, Canada, April.

APA Task Force on Psychology in Education (1993, January) *Learner-centered psychological principles: guidelines for school redesign and reform*, Washington, DC: American Psychological Association and Mid-Continent Regional Educational Laboratory.

APA Work Group of the Board of Educational Affairs (1997, November) *Learner-centered psychological principles: a framework for school reform and redesign*, Washington, DC: American Psychological Association.

Arfken, D. (1982) 'A peer tutor staff: four crucial aspects', in M. Harris, *Tutoring writing. A sourcebook for writing labs*, Glenview, Illinois: Scott, Foresman & Company.

Aronson, E. with Blaney, N., Sikes, J., Stephan, C. and Snapp, M. (1975) 'The Jigsaw route to learning and liking', *Psychology Today*, February: 43–50.

Aronson, E., Blaney, N., Stephan, C., Sikes, J. and Snapp, M. (1978) *The Jigsaw Classroom*, Beverly Hills, California: Sage.

Baeker, R. M. (1993) *GroupWare and computer-supported cooperative work: assisting human–human collaboration*, San Mateo, California: Morgan Kaufmann Publishers.

Bagnall, R. G. (1989) 'Educational distance from the perspective of self-direction: an analysis', *Open Learning*, 4, 1: 21–26.

Bales, R. F. (1950) *Interaction process analysis: a method for the study of small groups*, Cambridge, Massachusetts: Addison-Wesley.

Bandura, A. (1982) 'Self-efficacy mechanisms in human agency', *American Psychologist*, 37: 122–47.

Bangemann Report (1995) 'Europe and the global information society', European Commission, Brussels.

Bannister, D. and Fransella, F. (1980) *Inquiring man. The psychology of personal constructs* (2nd edn), Harmondsworth: Penguin Books.

Bard, T. B. (1996) 'Co-operative activities in interactive distance learning', *Journal of Education for Library and Information Science*, Winter, 37, 1: 1–10.

Bargh, J. A. and Schul, Y. (1980) 'On the cognitive benefits of teaching', *Journal of Educational Psychology*, 72, 5: 593–604.

Barron, A.-M. and Foot, H. (1991) 'Peer tutoring and tutor training', *Educational Research*, 33, 3: 174–95.

Baty, P. (1997) '"Elitism" hinders learners', *Times Higher Education Supplement*, November 14: 4.

Baty, P. (1998) 'Learners are born, says report', *Times Higher Education Supplement*, January 16: 5.

Beard, R. and Hartley, J. (1984) *Teaching and learning in higher education*, London: Harper & Row.

Beardon, L. A. (1998) 'Casting the net: peer assisted learning on the Internet', in S. Goodlad (ed.) *Mentoring and tutoring by students*, London: Kogan Page.

Bell, J. H. (1991) 'Using peer response groups in ESL writing classes', *TESL Canada Journal/ Revue TESL du Canada*, March, 8, 2: 65–71.

Bellamy, L., Evans, D. L., Linder, D. E., McNeill, B. W. and Raupp, G. (1994) 'Teams in Engineering Education', report to the National Science Foundation on Grant Number USE9156176, Tempe, Arizona, Arizona State University.

Benware, C. A. and Deci, E. L. (1984) 'Quality of learning with an active versus passive motivational set', *American Educational Research Journal*, 21, 4: 755–65.

Bierman, K. L. and Furman, W. (1981) 'Effects of role and assignment rationale on attitudes formed during peer tutoring', *Journal of Educational Psychology*, 73, 1: 33–40.

Bloom, B. S. (1956) *Taxonomy of educational objectives. Handbook I: Cognitive domain*, New York: Longmans Green.

Bloom, S. (1976) *Peer and cross-age tutoring in the schools*, Chicago: Chicago Board of Education, District 10.

Bohlmeyer, E. M. and Burke, J. P. (1987) 'Selecting cooperative learning techniques: a consultative strategy guide', *School Psychology Review*, 16, 1: 36–49.

Boling, N. C. and Robinson, D. H. (1999) 'Individual study, interactive multimedia, or cooperative learning: which activity best supplements lecture-based distance education?', *Journal of Educational Psychology*, 91, 1: 169–74.

Bossert, S. T. (1988) 'Cooperative activities in the classroom', *Review of Research in Education*, 15: 225–50.

Boud, D. (1995) 'How can peers be used in self assessment?', in D. Boud, *Enhancing learning through self assessment*, London: Kogan Page.

Boud, D. and Falchikov, N. (1989) 'Quantitative studies of student self-assessment in higher education: a critical analysis of findings', *Higher Education*, 18, 5: 529–49.

Boud, D. and Feletti, G. (eds) (1991) *The challenge of problem based learning*, London: Kogan Page.

Boud, D., Cohen, R. and Sampson, J. (1999) 'Peer learning and assessment', *Assessment and Evaluation in Higher Education*, 413–26.

Brannon, L. (1982) 'On becoming an effective tutor', in M. Harris, *Tutoring writing. A sourcebook for writing labs*, Glenview, Illinois: Scott, Foresman & Company.

Brehm, S. S. and Kassin, S. M. (1993) *Social psychology* (2nd edn), Boston: Houghton Mifflin Company.

Brehm, S. S. and Kassin, S. M. (1996) *Social psychology* (3rd edn), Boston and Toronto: Houghton Mifflin Company.

Brown, G. (2000) Department of Psychology, University of Nottingham, personal communication.

Brown, J. S., Collins, A. and Duguid, P. (1989) 'Situated cognition and the culture of learning', *Educational Researcher*, Jan.–Feb., 18, 1: 32–42.

Bruffee, K. A. (1978) 'The Brooklyn Plan: attaining intellectual growth through peer-group tutoring', *Liberal Education*, 64, 4: 447–68.

Bruffee, K. A. (1980) 'Two related issues in peer tutoring: program structure and tutor training', *College Composition and Communication*, 31: 76–80.

Bruffee, K. A. (1993) *Collaborative learning. Higher education, interdependence, and the authority of knowledge*, Baltimore and London: The Johns Hopkins University Press.

Burke, C. (1998) 'The academic discussion list as a space for learning and research', paper for the twentieth International Standing Conference for the History of Education Conference; History and new media session, Kortrijk, July 1998 (http://www.mailbase.ac.uk/lists/history-child-family/files/ische-paper.html)

Carroll, D. W. (1986) 'Use of the Jigsaw Technique in laboratory and discussion classes', *Teaching of Psychology*, 13, 4: 208–10.

Carroll, M. (1996) 'Peer tutoring: can medical students teach biochemistry?', *Biochemical Education*, 24, 1: 13–15.

Cate, R. M., Lloyd, S. A. and Long, E. (1988) 'The role of rewards and fairness in developing premarital relationships', *Journal of Marriage and the Family*, 50: 443–52.

CBI (1997/8) *Times Higher Education Supplement*, Nov. 7: 7.

Checkering, A. W. and Gamson, Z. F. (1987) 'Seven principles for good practice in undergraduate education', *American Association of Higher Education Bulletin*, 39, 7: 3–7.

Chou, C. and Sun, C.-T. (1996) 'Constructing a cooperative distance learning system: the CORAL experience', *Educational Technologies Research and Development*, 44, 4: 71–84.

Cicirelli, V. G. (1972) 'The effect of sibling relationships on concept learning of young children taught by child-teachers', *Child Development*, 43: 282–87.

Clark, M. S., Gotay, C. C. and Mills, J. (1974) 'Acceptance of help as a function of similarity of the potential helper and opportunity to repay', *Journal of Applied Social Psychology*, 4, 3: 224–29.

Cloward, R. A. (1967) 'Studies in tutoring', *Journal of Experimental Education*, 36, 1: 14–25.

Collier, K. G. (1969) 'Syndicate methods: further evidence and comment', *University Quarterly*, Autumn, 23, 4: 431–36.

Collier, K. G. (ed.) (1983) *The management of peer-group learning. Syndicate methods in higher education*, Guildford: Society for Research into Higher Education.

Collins English Dictionary (1991) (3rd edn), Glasgow: HarperCollins Publishers.

Collins, A., Brown, J. S. and Newman, S. E. (1989) 'Cognitive apprenticeship: teaching the crafts of reading, writing and mathematics', in L. B. Resnick (ed.) *Knowing, learning and instruction. Essays in honor of Robert Glaser*, Hillsdale, New Jersey: Lawrence Erlbaum Associates, Publishers.

Committee on Science, Engineering and Public Policy (1999) http://www.peer.ca/mentor.html

Condravy, J. (1995) 'Tutors learning about learning and assessment', *Research and Teaching in Developmental Education*, 11, 2: 43–56.

Congos, D. H. and Schoeps, N. (1997) 'A model for evaluating retention programs', *Journal of Developmental Education*, 21, 2: 2–4, 6, 8, 24.

Conrad, E. E. (1975) 'The effects of tutor achievement level, reinforcement training, and expectancy on peer tutoring', unpublished PhD Thesis, University of Arizona. University Microfilms No. 76, 1407.

Cornwall, M. G. (1979) *Students as teachers: peer teaching in higher education*, Centrum voor Onderzoek van het Wetenschappelijk Onderwijs (C.O.W.O.), University of Amsterdam, publication 7906-01.

Crebbin, W. (1997) 'Teaching for lifelong learning', in R. Ballantyne, J. Bain and J. Packer (eds) *Reflecting on university teaching: academics' stories*, Canberra: AGPS.

Cross, K. P. (1976) *Accent on learning*, San Francisco: Jossey-Bass.

Cross, K. P. (1981) *Adults as learners*, San Francisco: Jossey-Bass.

Cross, K. P. (1999) http://tip.psychology.org/cross.html

Cuthbert, K. (1995) 'An innovative approach to teaching undergraduate psychology: rationale for a major final year project and some evaluative evidence', *Psychology Teaching Review*, 4, 1: 52–64.

Dansereau, D. F. (1978) 'The development of a learning strategies curriculum', in H. F. O'Neil, Jr (ed.) *Learning strategies*, New York: Academic Press.

Dansereau, D. F. (1985) 'Learning strategy research', in J. Segal and S. Chipman (eds) *Thinking and learning skills*, Hillsdale, New Jersey: Lawrence Erlbaum.

Dansereau, D. F. (1987a) 'Transfer from cooperative to individual studying', *Journal of Reading*, April: 614–18.

Dansereau, D. F. (1987b) 'Technical learning strategies', *Engineering Education*, 77, 5: 280–84.

Dansereau, D. F. (1988) 'Cooperative learning strategies', in C. E. Weinstein, E. T. Goetz and P. A. Alexander (eds) *Learning and study strategies. Issues in assessment, instruction, and evaluation*, New York and San Diego: Academic Press, Inc.

Dansereau, D. F. and Johnson, D. W. (1994) 'Cooperative learning', in D. Druckman and R. A. Bjork (eds) *Learning, remembering, believing: enhancing human performance*, Washington, DC: National Academy Press.

Dansereau, D. F., McDonald, B. A., Collins, K. W., Garland, J., Holley, D. D., Diekhoff, G. M. and Evans, S. H. (1979) *Cognitive and affective learning strategies*, New York: Academic Press.

Dart, B. C. and Clarke, J. A. (1991) 'Helping students become better learners: a case study in teacher education', *Higher Education*, 22: 317–35.

Davies, J. and Johnston, S. (1994) 'The institutional implementation of Supplemental Instruction', in C. Rust and J. Wallace (eds) *Helping students to learn from each other: Supplemental Instruction*, Birmingham, UK: Staff and Educational Development Association.

Davis, A. and Rose, D. (2000) 'The experimental method in psychology', in G. M.

Breakwell, S. Hammond and C. Fife-Schaw (eds) *Research methods in psychology*, London: Sage Publications.

Dearing, R. (1997) 'Higher education in the learning society. National Committee of Inquiry into Higher Education (Great Britain)', London: HMSO.

Dees, S. M., Dansereau, D. F., Peel, J. L., Boatler, J. G. and Knight, K. (1991) 'Using conceptual matrices, knowledge maps, and scripted cooperation to improve personal management strategies', *Journal of Drug Education*, 21, 3: 211–30.

Deignan, G. M. (1975) *The Delta Reading Vocabulary Test*, Air Force Human Resources Laboratory, Lowry Air Force Base, Aurora, Colorado.

Dennis, G. (1993) Office of Research Education Consumer Guide No. 7, October 1993, http://www.ed.gov/pubs/OR/ConsumerGuides/mentor.html

Denzin, N. K. and Lincoln, Y. S. (eds) (1994) *Handbook of qualitative research*, Thousand Oaks, California and London: Sage Publications.

De Stephano, J. S., Miller, E., Clegg, L. B., Vanderhoof, B. and Soldner, L. B. (1992) 'Open to suggestion', *Journal of Reading*, October, 36, 2: 132–35.

DfEE (1997) *Learning and working together for the future. A strategic framework for the work of the Department for Education and Employment and partners*. http://www.open.gov.uk/dfee/lwt/aims.htm

The Directory of Mentor Arts and Mentorship (1999) http://www.peer.ca/mentor.html

Donaldson, M. (1978) *Children's minds*, Glasgow: Fontana/ Collins.

Dong, Y. R. (1997) 'Collective reflection: using peer response to dialogue journals in teacher education', *TESOL Journal*, 7, 2: 26–31.

Doolittle, P. E. (1995) 'Understanding cooperative learning through Vygotsky's zone of proximal development', paper presented at the Lilly National Conference on Excellence in College Teaching, Columbia, South Carolina, June 2–4.

Dörnyei, Z. and Malderez, A. (1997) 'Group dynamics and foreign language teaching', *System*, 25, 1: 65–81.

Duffy, C., Arnold, S. and Henderson, F. (1995) 'NetSem – electrifying undergraduate seminars', *Active Learning*, 2: 42–8.

Dunn, D. S. (1996) 'Collaborative writing in a statistics and research methods course', *Teaching of Psychology*, February, 23, 1: 38–40.

Ellson, D. G. (1976) 'Tutoring', in N. L. Gage (ed.) *The psychology of teaching methods, part 1. The seventy-fifth yearbook of the National Society for the Study of Education*, Chicago: The University of Chicago Press.

Ellson, D. G. (1986) 'Improving productivity in teaching', *Phi Delta Kappa*, October: 111–24.

Ellson, D. G. and Harris, P. L. (1970) 'Project evaluation report: programmed tutoring on beginning reading, New Albany public school system 1969–70', mimeo, Illinois: Department of Psychology, University of Indiana.

Ellson, D. G., Barber, L. W. and Harris, P. L. (1969) 'A nation-wide evaluation of programmed tutoring', Illinois: Department of Psychology, University of Indiana.

Ellson, D. G., Barber, L., Engle, T. L., and Kampwerth, L. (1965) 'Programmed tutoring: a teaching aid and a research tool', *Reading Research Quarterly*, Fall, 1: 77–127.

Ellson, D. G., Harris, P. L. and Barber, L. (1968) 'A field test of programmed and directed tutoring', *Reading Research Quarterly*, Spring, 3, 3: 307–67.

Elmes, D. G., Kantowitz, B. H. and Roediger, H. I. III (1992) *Research methods in psychology* (4th edn), St Paul: West Publishing.

Entwistle, N. J. (1997) 'Contrasting perspectives on learning', in F. Marton, D. Hounsell and N. J. Entwistle (eds) *The experience of learning* (2nd edn), Edinburgh: The Scottish Academic Press.

Entwistle, N. J. and Tait, H. (1990) 'Approaches to learning, evaluations of teaching, and preferences for contrasting academic environments', *Higher Education*, 19: 169–94.

Essid, J. J. (1996) 'Training peer tutors with conferencing software: practicing collaboration and planning for difficult tutorials', *Research and Teaching in Developmental Education*, 13, 1: 45–55.

European Commission DGXIII (1998) 'Review of research and development in technologies for education and training 1994–98: supporting the lifelong learning society through the development of telematics-based tools for learners, educators, trainers and trainees', September 1998, European Commission DGXIII, Brussels.

Evans, T. and Nation, D. (1989) 'Dialogue in practice, research and theory in distance education', *Open Learning*, 4, 2: 59–71.

Falchikov, N. (1986) 'Product comparisons and process benefits of collaborative self and peer group assessments', *Assessment and Evaluation in Higher Education*, 11, 2: 146–66.

Falchikov, N. (1987) 'Collaborative peer group and self assessment of essays: correspondence with tutor assessment and possible learning benefits', in F. Percival, D. Craig and D. Buglass (eds) *Aspects of educational technology*, London: Kogan Page.

Falchikov, N. (1988) 'Self and peer assessment of a group project designed to promote the skills of capability', *Programmed Learning and Educational Technology*, 25, 4: 327–39.

Falchikov, N. (1990) 'An experiment in same-age peer tutoring in higher education', in S. Goodlad and B. Hirst (eds) *Explorations in peer tutoring*, Oxford: Basil Blackwell.

Falchikov, N. (1991) 'Group process analysis: self and peer assessment of working together in a group', in S. Brown and P. Dove (eds) *Self and peer assessment*, SCED Paper 63, Birmingham: Standing Conference on Educational Development.

Falchikov, N. (1993) 'Group process analysis: self and peer assessment of working together in a group', *Educational Technology and Training International*, 30: 275–84.

Falchikov, N. (1994) 'Learning from peer feedback marking: student and teacher perspectives', in H. C. Foote, C. J. Howe, A. Anderson, A. K. Tolmie and D. A. Warden (eds) *Group and interactive learning*, Southampton and Boston: Computational Mechanics Publications.

Falchikov, N. (1995a) 'Improving feedback to and from students', in Peter Knight (ed.) *Towards better learning: assessment for learning in higher education*, London: Kogan Page.

Falchikov, N. (1995b) 'Peer feedback marking: developing peer assessment', *Innovations in Education and Training International*, 32, 2: 175–87.

Falchikov, N. (1996) 'Improving learning through critical peer feedback and reflection', *Higher Education Research and Development*, 19: 214–18.

Falchikov, N. (2000) 'Peer assessment: what's in it for staff and students?', in D. Hunter and M. Russ, *Peer learning in music*, University of Ulster.

Falchikov, N. and Boud, D. (1989) 'Student self-assessment in higher education: a meta-analysis', *Review of Educational Research*, 59, 4: 395–430.

Falchikov, N. and Fitz-Gibbon, C. (1989) 'Peer tutoring in higher education: an experiment', in C. Bell, J. Davies and R. Winders (eds) *Promoted learning: aspects of educational and training technology XXII*, London: Kogan Page.

Falchikov, N. and Goldfinch, J. (2000) 'Student peer assessment in higher education: a meta-analysis comparing peer and teacher marks', *Review of Educational Research*, 70, 3: 35–70.

Falchikov, N. and Magin, D. (1997) 'Detecting gender bias in peer marking of students' group process work', *Assessment and Evaluation in Higher Education*, 22, 4: 385–396.

Fantuzzo, J. W., Dimeff, L. A. and Fox, S. L. (1989a) 'Reciprocal peer tutoring: a multimodal assessment of effectiveness with college students', *Teaching of Psychology*, 16, 3: 133–35.

Fantuzzo, J. W., Riggio, R. E., Connelly, S. and Dimeff, L. A. (1989b) 'Effects of reciprocal peer tutoring on academic achievement and psychological adjustment: a component analysis', *Journal of Educational Psychology*, 81, 2: 173–77.

Feichtner, S. B. and Davis, E. A. (1985) 'Why some groups fail: a survey of students' experiences with learning groups', *The Organizational Behavior Teaching Review*, 9, 4: 58–73.

Felder, R. M., Felder, G. N., Mauney, M., Hamrin, C. E. Jr and Dietz, E. J. (1994) 'A longitudinal study of engineering student performance and retention: gender differences in student performance and attitudes', ERIC Document Reproduction Service Report ED 368 553.

Fisher, J. D., Nadler, A. and Whitcher-Alagna, S. (1982) 'Recipient reactions to aid', *Psychological Bulletin*, 91, 1: 27–54.

Fitz-Gibbon, C. T. (1978) 'A survey of tutoring projects', CSE Report on Tutoring No. 118, University of California, Los Angeles: Center for the Study of Evaluation.

Flannagan, K. and Miles, I. (1999) 'The multimedia melting pot: from moulding products to shaping frameworks', in R. S. Slack, J. K. Stewart and R. A. Williams, 'The social shaping of multimedia: proceedings from a COST (Co-ordination in the Field of Scientific and Technological Research) A4 Workshop held in Edinburgh, Scotland, June 27–29, 1997', Luxembourg, European Commission (DGXII).

Foot, H. and Barron, A.-M. (1990) 'Friendship and task management in children's peer tutoring', *Educational Studies*, 16, 3: 237–50.

Forman, E. A. and Cazden, C. B. (1985) 'Exploring Vygotskian perspectives in education: the cognitive value of peer interaction', in J. V. Wertsch (ed.) *Culture, communication and cognition: Vygotskian perspectives*, Cambridge: Cambridge University Press.

Forsyth, D. R. and McMillan, J. H. (1991) 'Practical proposals for motivating students', in R. J. Menges and M. D. Svinicki, *College teaching: from theory to practice. New directions for teaching and learning*, Number 5, Spring 1991, Jossey-Bass Inc. Publishers.

Fraser, S. C., Beaman, A. L., Diener, E. and Kelem, R. T. (1977) 'Two, three, or four heads are better than one: modification of college performance by peer monitoring', *Journal of Educational Psychology*, 69, 2: 101–08.

Frasson, C. and Aimeur, E. (1996) 'A comparison of three learning strategies in intelligent tutoring systems', *Journal of Educational Computing Research*, 14, 4: 371–83.

Freedman, M. (1995) 'From friendly visiting to mentoring: a tale of two movements', in S. Goodlad (ed.) *Students as tutors and mentors*, London: Kogan Page.

Fresko, B. (1988) 'Reward salience, assessment of success and critical attitudes among tutors', *Journal of Educational Research*, 81, 6: 341–46.

Fresko, B. (1996) 'Effects of tutor–tutee intimacy, tutoring conditions and tutor background on college student tutor satisfaction', *Educational Studies*, 22, 2: 147–64.

Fuchs, L. S., Fuchs, D., Bentz, J., Phillips, N. B. and Hamlett, C. L. (1994) 'The nature of student interactions during peer tutoring with and without prior training and experience', *American Educational Research Journal*, Spring, 31, 1: 75–103.

Garrett, M. P. (1982) 'Toward a delicate balance: the importance of role playing and peer criticism in peer tutoring training', in M. Harris, *Tutoring writing. A sourcebook for writing labs*, Glenview, IL: Scott, Foresman & Company.

Gillam, A., Callaway, S. and Wikoff, K. H. (1994) 'The role of authority and the authority of roles in peer writing tutorials', *Journal of Teaching Writing*, 12, 2: 161–98.

Ginsburg-Block, M. and Fantuzzo, J. W. (1997) 'Reciprocal peer tutoring: an analysis of "teacher" and "student" interactions as a function of training and experience', *School Psychology Quarterly*, 12, 2: 134–49.

Glassman, S. (1982) 'Tutor training on a shoestring', in M. Harris, *Tutoring writing. A sourcebook for writing labs*, Glenview, IL: Scott, Foresman & Company.

Gnagey, W. J. and Potter, K. I. (1996) 'The effects on learning, course evaluation and team evaluation of changing STAD teams at midterm', EDRS Report ED 401 812.

Goffman, E. (1956) *The presentation of self in everyday life*, Edinburgh: Edinburgh University Press.

Goldberg, D. (1978) *Manual of the General Health Questionnaire*, Windsor: NFER-Nelson.

Goldberg, D. and Williams, P. (1988) *A user's guide to the General Health Questionnaire*, Windsor: NFER-Nelson.

Goldfinch, J. and Raeside, R. (1990) 'Development of a peer assessment technique for obtaining individual marks on a group project', *Assessment and Evaluation in Higher Education*, 15, 3: 210–25.

Goldschmid, B. and Goldschmid, M. L. (1976) 'Peer teaching in higher education: a review', *Higher Education*, 5: 9–33.

Goldschmid, M. L. and Shore, B. M. (1974) 'The learning cell: a field test of an educational innovation', in W. A. Verreck (ed.) *Methodological problems in research and development in higher education*, Amsterdam: Swets & Zeitlinger, B.C.

Goleman, D. (1994) *Emotional intelligence*, New York: Bantam.

Goleman, D. (1998) *Working with emotional intelligence*, New York: Bantam.

Goodlad, S. (1979) *Learning by teaching*, London: Community Service Volunteers.

Goodlad, S. (1985) 'Putting science into context', *Research*, 27, 1: 61–67.

Goodlad, S. (ed.) (1995a) *Students as tutors and mentors*, London: Kogan Page.

Goodlad, S. (1995b) *The quest for quality: sixteen forms of heresy in higher education*, Buckingham: Society for Research into Higher Education and Open University Press.

Goodlad, S. (1997a) 'Responding to the perceived training needs of graduate teaching assistants', *Studies in Higher Education*, 22, 1: 83–92.

Goodlad, S. (1997b) 'Simulating laboratory teaching for graduate teaching assistants', in P. Saunders and B. Cox (eds) *Research into simulations in education: the international simulation and gaming yearbook volume 5*, London: Kogan Page.

Goodlad, S. (ed.) (1998) *Mentoring and tutoring by students*, London: Kogan Page in conjunction with BP.

Goodlad, S. and Hirst, B. (1989) *Peer tutoring: a guide to learning by teaching*, London: Kogan Page.

Goodlad, S. and Hughes, J. (1992) 'Reflection through action: peer tutoring as service learning', in R. Barnett (ed.) *Learning to effect*, Milton Keynes: SRHE and Open University Press.

Goodlad, S. and McIvor, S. (1998) *Museum volunteers*, London: Routledge.

Grasha, A. F. (1972) 'Observations on relating teaching goals to student response styles and classroom methods', *American Psychologist*, 27, 2: 144–47.

Green, S. (1990) 'Analysis of transferable personal skills requested by employers in graduate recruitment advertisements in June 1989', Occasional Paper, University of Sheffield, Personal Skills Unit.

Griffin, M. M. and Griffin, B. W. (1998) 'An investigation of the effects of Reciprocal Peer Tutoring on achievement, self-efficacy, and test anxiety', *Contemporary Educational Psychology*, 23: 298–311.

Groccia, J. E. and Miller, J. E. (1996) 'Collegiality in the classroom: the use of peer learning assistants in cooperative learning in introductory biology', *Innovative Higher Education*, Winter, 21, 2: 87–100.

Gross, E. and Stone, G. P. (1964) 'Embarrassment and the analysis of role requirements', in M. Argyle (ed.) (1973) *Social encounters. Readings in social interaction*, Harmondsworth: Penguin.

Habeshaw, T. (1999) isl (improving student learning, a mailbase list) electronic discussion list, 8 March.

Hall, D. T. (1972) 'A model of coping with role conflict: the role behavior of college educated women', *Administrative Science Quarterly*, 17: 471–86.

Hall, R. H., Dansereau, D. F., O'Donnell, A. M. and Skaggs, L. P. (1989) 'The effect of textual errors on dyadic and individual learning', *Journal of Reading Behavior*, 21, 2: 127–40.

Hall, R. H., Dansereau, D. F. and Skaggs, L. P. (1990) 'The cooperative learner', *Learning and Individual Differences*, 2, 3: 327–36.

Hammond, S. (2000) 'Using psychometric tests', in G. M. Breakwell, S. Hammond and C. Fife-Schaw (eds) *Research methods in psychology*, London: Sage Publications.

Harrap's Concise French and English Dictionary (1978), London: Harrap.

Harris, M. (1982) *Tutoring writing. A sourcebook for writing labs*, Glenview, Illinois: Scott, Foresman & Company.

Harrison, G. V. (1969) 'The effects of trained and untrained tutors on criterion performance of disadvantaged first graders', ERIC No. ED 031 449, Los Angeles: University of California.

Harrison, G. V. (1971a) 'Structured tutoring', ERIC No. 053 080, Provo, Utah: Department of Instructional Research and Development, Brigham Young University.

Harrison, G. V. (1971b) *How to organise an inter-grade tutoring program in an elementary school*, Provo, Utah: Brigham Young University Printing Service.

Harrison, G. V. (1972a) *Supervisors' guide for the structured tutorial reading program*, Provo, Utah: Brigham Young University Press.

Harrison, G. V. (1972b) 'Tutoring: a remedy reconsidered', *Improving Human Performance*, 1, 4: 1–7.

Hawkins, T. (1978) 'Training peer tutors in the art of teaching', *College English*, 40, 4: 440–43.

Hawkins, T. (1982) 'Intimacy and audience: the relationship between revision and the social dimension of peer tutoring', in M. Harris, *Tutoring writing. A sourcebook for writing labs*, Glenview, Illinois: Scott, Foresman & Company.

Healy, D. (1991) 'Tutorial role conflict in the writing center', *Writing Center Journal*, Spr/Sum, 11, 2: 41–50.

Heider, F. (1958) *The psychology of interpersonal relations*, London: Wiley.

Heller, P. and Hollabaugh, M. (1992) 'Teaching problem solving through cooperative grouping. Part 2: Designing problems and structuring groups', *American Journal of Physics*, 60, 7: 637–44.

Hertz-Lazarowitz, R. and Miller, N. (eds) (1992) *Interaction in cooperative groups*, Cambridge: Cambridge University Press.

Highton, M. (1999) Module information for the Student Volunteering in Schools project, Napier University, Edinburgh.

Highton, M. and Goss, S. (1997) 'Perceptions of benefits to students of volunteering activity in schools', paper presented at the Conference on the Student Experience in the 1990s, Napier University, May 26.

Homans, G. C. (1961) *Social behavior. Its elementary forms*, New York: Harcourt, Brace & World, Inc.

Homans, G. C. (1976) 'Commentary', in L. Berkowitz and E. Walster (eds) *Advances in experimental social psychology, vol. 9. Equity theory: toward a general theory of social interaction*, New York: Academic Press.

Houston, J. P., Bee, H., Hatfield, E. and Rimm, D. C. (1979) *Invitation to psychology*, New York: Academic Press.

Houston, K. and Lazenbatt, A. (1996) 'A peer-tutoring scheme to support independent learning and group project work in mathematics', *Assessment and Evaluation in Higher Education*, 21, 3: 251–66.

Inhelder, B. and Piaget, J. (1958) *The growth of logical thinking from childhood to adolescence*, trans. A. Parsons and S. Milgram, London: Routledge & Kegan Paul.

Isley, G. (1994) 'Introducing college-wide Supplemental Instruction', in C. Rust and J. Wallace (eds) *Helping students learn from each other: Supplemental Instruction*, Birmingham, UK: Staff and Educational Development Association (SEDA).

Jackson, E. F. (1962) 'Status consistency and symptoms of stress', *American Sociological Review*, August, 27, 4: 469–80.

Johnson, D. W. and Johnson, R. T. (1985) 'The internal dynamics of cooperative learning groups', in R. Slavin, S. Sharan, S. Kagan, R. Hertz-Lazarowitz, C. Webb and R. Schmuck (eds) *Learning to cooperate, cooperating to learn*, New York and London: Plenum Press.

Johnson, D. W. and Johnson, R. T. (1989) *Cooperation and competition: theory and research*, Edina, MN: Interaction Book Co.

Johnson, D. W., Johnson, R. T. and Smith, K. A. (1991) 'Cooperative learning. Increasing college faculty instructional productivity', ASHE-ERIC Higher Education Report No. 4, Washington, DC.: Association for the Study of Higher Education/The George Washington University, School of Education and Human Development.

Kagan, J. (1985) Chapter 3, 'Dimensions of cooperative classroom structures', in R. Slavin, S. Sharan, S. Kagan, R. Hertz-Lazarowitz, C. Webb and R. Schmuck (eds) *Learning to cooperate, cooperating to learn*, New York and London: Plenum Press.

Kahn, R. L., Wolfe, D. M., Quinn, R. P., Snoek, J. D. in collaboration with Rosenthal, R. A. (1981) *Organisational stress: studies in role conflict and ambiguity*, Malabar, Florida: Robert E. Krieger Publishing Company.

Kaplan, P. S. (1998) *The human odyssey: life-span development* (3rd edn), Pacific Grove, California: Brooks/Cole.

Keefe, K. (1992) *From the centre to the city. Aboriginal education, culture and power*, Canberra: Aboriginal Studies Press.

Kelley, H. H. (1967) 'Attribution theory in social psychology', in D. Levine (ed.) *Nebraska symposium on motivation, vol. 15*, Lincoln: University of Nebraska Press.

Kelly, G. A. (1955) *The psychology of personal constructs, vols 1 and 2*, New York: Norton.

Kennedy, M. (1990) 'Controlled evaluation of the effects of peer tutoring on the tutors: are the "learning by teaching" theories viable?', in S. Goodlad and B. Hirst (eds) *Explorations in peer tutoring*, Oxford: Basil Blackwell.

Kerka, S. (1998) 'New perspectives on mentoring', ERIC Digest No. 194, http:// www.peer.ca/mentor.html

King, A. (1991) 'A strategy for enhancing peer interaction and learning during teacher training sessions', *Teacher Education Quarterly*, Winter, 18, 1: 15–28.

King, A. (1993) 'From sage on the stage to guide on the side', *College Teaching*, Winter, 41, 1: 30–35.

King, A., Staffieri, A. and Adelgais, A. (1998) 'Mutual peer tutoring: effects of structuring tutorial interaction to scaffold peer learning', *Journal of Educational Psychology*, 90, 1: 134–52.

Knowles, M. (1984) *The adult learner: a neglected species* (3rd ed), Houston, Texas: Gulf Publishing.

Koch, L. C. (1992) 'Revisiting mathematics', *Journal of Developmental Education*, Autumn, 16, 1: 12–18.

Kolb, D. A. (1984) *Experiential learning: experience as the source of learning and development*, Englewood Cliffs, New Jersey: Prentice-Hall.

Lambiotte, J. G., Dansereau, D. F., O'Donnell, A. M., Young, M. D., Skaggs, L. P. and Hall,

R. H. (1988) 'Effects of cooperative script manipulations on initial learning and transfer', *Cognition and Instruction*, 5, 2: 103–21.

Lambiotte, J. G., Dansereau, D. F., Rocklin, T. R., Fletcher, B., Hythecker, V. I., Larson, C. O. and O'Donnell, A. M. (1987) 'Cooperative learning and test-taking: transfer of skills', *Contemporary Educational Psychology*, 12, 1: 52–61.

Larson, C. O. and Dansereau, D. F. (1986) 'Cooperative learning in dyads', *Journal of Reading*, 29: 16–20.

Larson, C. O., Dansereau, D. F., O'Donnell, A. M., Hythecker, V. I., Lambiotte, J. G., and Rocklin, T. R. (1985) 'Effects of metacognitive and elaborative activity on cooperative learning and transfer', *Contemporary Educational Psychology*, 10, 4: 342–48.

Laurillard, D. (1993) *Rethinking university teaching: a framework for the effective use of educational technology*, London: Routledge.

Lave, J. (1999) http://tip.psychology.org.lave.html

Lave, J. and Wenger, E. (1990) *Situated learning: legitimate peripheral participation*, Cambridge: Cambridge University Press, UK.

Lea, M., O'Shea, T., Fung, P., and Spears, R. (1992) 'Flaming in computer mediated communication', in M. Lea (ed.) *Contexts of computer-mediated communication*, London: Harvester Wheatsheaf.

Learning theories web site (2000) http://www.gwu.edu/~tip **OR** http://tip.psychology.org

Levene, L.-A. and Frank, P. (1993) 'Peer coaching: professional growth and development for instruction librarians', *Reference Services Review*, 21, 3: 35–42.

Levin, P. (1998) *Times Higher Education Supplement*, Teaching Supplement, February 6: viii.

Lewin, K. (1935) *A dynamic theory of personality*, New York: McGraw-Hill.

Lewin, K. (1948) *Resolving social conflicts*, New York: Harper.

Lippitt, R. (1947) 'Adventures in the exploration of interdependence', *Sociometry*, 10, 1: 87–97.

Littlejohn, A. H. and Stefani, L. A. (1999) 'Effective use of communication and information technology: bridging the skills gap', *ALT-J*, 7, 2: 66–76.

Lusted, D. (1986) 'Why pedagogy?', *Screen*, 27, 5: 2–14.

Lyons, E. (2000) 'Qualitative data analysis: data display model', in G. M. Breakwell, S. Hammond and C. Fife-Schaw (eds) *Research methods in psychology*, London: Sage Publications.

Mainiero, J., Gillogly, B., Nease, B., Sheretz, O. and Wilkinson, P. (1971) 'A cross-age teaching resource manual', California: Ontario-Montclair School District, Ontario.

Mann, A. F. (1994) 'College peer tutoring journals: maps of development', *Journal of College Student Development*, May, 35: 164–69.

Margetson, D. (1995) 'Introducing problem-focused education in a context of reaching more students', in L. Conrad and L. Phillips (eds) *Reaching more students*, Queensland: Griffith Institute for Higher Education.

Martin, D. C. and Arendale, D. R. and associates (1992) 'Supplemental Instruction: improving first-year student success in high-risk courses', The Freshman Year Experience Monograph Series Number 7, ED 354 839, South Carolina University.

Marton, F. and Säljö, R. (1976a) 'On qualitative differences in learning: outcome and process', *British Journal of Educational Psychology*, 46: 4–11.

Marton, F. and Säljö, R. (1976b) 'On qualitative differences in learning: II. Outcomes as a function of the learner's conception of the task', *British Journal of Educational Psychology*, 46: 115–27.

Marton, F. and Säljö, R. (1997) 'Approaches to learning', in F. Marton, D. Hounsell and N. Entwistle (eds) *The experience of learning* (2nd edn), Edinburgh: Scottish Academic Press.

Maslow, A. H. (1954) *Motivation and personality*, New York: Harper Row.

May, M. A. and Doob, L. W. (1937) 'Competition and cooperation', Bulletin No. 25, April, Social Science Research Council, New York.

Mayes, T., Coventry, L., Thomson, A. and Mason, R. (1994) 'Learning through telematics', report to British Telecom, Institute for Computer Based Learning, Heriot-Watt University, Edinburgh.

McAndrew, P., Desmulliez, M., Flockhart, S., Schnurr, C., Tomes, N., Martins Ferriera, J. M., Simoes Santiago, M. A., Ra, O., Strom, T., Smith, S., Gracie, M., Rorvik, R., Johnsen, S. and Mayes, T. (1998) 'Advanced software for the teaching and analysis of processes: analysis of user needs', report to the European Commission, ASTEP (Advanced Software for Teaching Electronics Processing) Consortium, Heriot-Watt University.

McAndrew, P., Foubister, S. P. and Mayes, T. (1996) 'Videoconferencing in a language learning application', Research and development in Advanced Communications technologies in Europe (RACE) Report, European Commission, Brussels.

McClelland, D. C., Atkinson, J. W., Clark, R. A. and Lowell, E. L. (1953) *The achievement motive*, New York: Appleton-Century-Crofts.

McCombs, B. L. (1999) 'What role does perceptual psychology play in educational reform today?', in H. J. Freiberg (ed.) *Perceiving, behaving, becoming: lessons learned*, Alexandria, VA: Association for Supervision and Curriculum Development.

McCombs, B. L. and Lauer, P. A. (1998, July) 'The learner-centered model of seamless professional development: implications for practice and policy changes in higher education', paper presented at the 23rd International Conference on Improving University Teaching, Dublin.

McCombs, B. L. and Pope, J. E. (1994) *Motivating hard to reach students*, Washington, DC: American Psychological Association.

McCombs, B. L. and Whisler, J. S. (1997) *The learner-centered classroom and school: strategies for enhancing student motivation and achievement*, San Francisco: Jossey-Bass Publishers.

McCormick, C. B. and Pressley, M. (1997) *Educational psychology: learning, instruction and assessment*, New York: Longman.

McDonald, B. A., Larson, C. O., Dansereau, D. F. and Spurlin, J. I. (1985) 'Cooperative dyads: impact on text learning and transfer', *Contemporary Educational Psychology*, 10: 369–77.

McGroarty, M. E. and Zhu, W. (1997) 'Triangulation in classroom research: a study of peer revision', *Language Learning*, March, 47, 1: 1–43.

McKendree, J., Stenning, K., Mayes, T., Lee, J. and Cox, R. (1998) 'Why observing a dialogue may benefit learning: the vicarious learner', *Journal of Computer Assisted Learning*, 14, 2: 110–19.

McMillan, J. H. and Forsyth, D. R. (1991) 'What theories of motivation say about why learners learn', in R. J. Menges and M. D. Svinicki, *College teaching: from theory to practice. New Directions for teaching and learning*, Number 5, Spring 1991, Jossey-Bass Inc. Publishers.

McTaggart, R. (1988) 'Aboriginal pedagogy versus colonization of the mind', *Curriculum Perspectives*, 8, 2: 83–92.

Medway, F. J. (1991) 'A social psychological analysis of peer tutoring', *Journal of Developmental Education*, 15, 1: 20–26, 32.

Metcalfe, R. (1992) 'The assessment of proctoring', in D. Saunders and P. Race (eds) *Developing and measuring competence, Aspects of Educational and Training Technology Vol. XXV*, London: Kogan Page.

Metheny, D. and Metheny, W. (1997) 'Enriching technical courses with learning teams', *College Teaching*, 45, 1: 32–35.

Mevarech, R. (1985) 'The effects of co-operative mastery learning strategies on mathematical achievement', *Journal of Educational Research*, 78, 6: 372–77.

Michaelson, G. and Pohl, M. (forthcoming) 'Gender in email based co-operative problem solving', in A. Adams and E. Green (eds) *Virtual Gender*, London: Routledge.

Millis, B. J. and Cottell, P. G. Jr (1998) *Cooperative learning for higher education faculty*, Phoenix, Arizona: American Council on Education and Oryx Press.

Millis, B. J., Cottell, P. and Sherman, L. (1993, Spring) 'Stacking the DEC to promote critical thinking: applications in three disciplines', *Cooperative Learning and College Teaching*, 3, 3: 12–14.

Moore, W. (1987) *Learning environment preferences*, Olympia, Washington: Center for the Study of Intellectual Development.

Morris, S. and Hudson, W. (1995) 'International education and innovative approaches to university teaching', *Australian Universities Review*, 2: 70–74.

Nadler, A. and Fisher, J. D. (1986) 'The role of self esteem and perceived control in recipient reaction to help: theory development and empirical validation', in L. Berkowitz (ed.) *Advances in Experimental Social Psychology*, 19: 81–122.

Nadler, A. and Porat, I. (1978) 'Names do not help: effects of anonymity and locus of need attribution on help-seeking behavior', *Personality and Social Psychology Bulletin*, 4: 624–26.

Nattiv, A., Winitzky, N. and Drickey, R. (1991) 'Using cooperative learning with preservice elementary and secondary education students', *Journal of Teacher Education*, May–June, 42, 3: 216–25.

Neimark, E. D. (1975) 'Intellectual development during adolescence', in F. D. Horowitz (ed.) *Review of child development research (vol. 4)*, Chicago: University of Chicago Press.

Newbern, D. (1996) 'Cooperative learning: a closer look at interaction scripts', unpublished doctoral dissertation, Texas Christian University, Fort Worth, Texas.

Newbern, D., Dansereau, D. F., and Patterson, M. E. (1994) 'Toward a science of cooperation', presentation at American Educational Research Association Annual Meeting, New Orleans, Louisiana.

Newcomb, T. M. and Hartley, E. L. (eds) (1952) *Readings in social psychology* (2nd edn), New York: Holt.

Newcomb, T. M. and Wilson, E. K. (eds) (1966) *College peer groups: problems and prospects for research*, Chicago: Aldine.

Ney, J. W. (1991) 'Collaborative learning in university grammar courses', *Innovative Higher Education*, 15, 2: 153–65.

Niedermeyer, F. C. (1970) 'Effects of training on the instructional behaviors of student tutors', *Journal of Educational Research*, 64, 3: 119–23.

O'Donnell, A. M. (ed.) (1999) *Cognitive perspectives on peer learning*, Mahwah, New Jersey: Lawrence Erlbaum Associates, Publishers.

O'Donnell, A. M. and Dansereau, D. F. (1992) 'Scripted cooperation in student dyads: a method for analyzing and enhancing academic learning and performance', in R. Hertz-Lazarowitz and N. Miller (eds) *Interaction in cooperative groups*, Cambridge: Cambridge University Press.

O'Donnell, A. M., Dansereau, D. F. and Rocklin, T. R. (1991) 'Individual differences in the cooperative learning of concrete procedures', *Learning and Individual Differences*, 3, 2: 149–62.

O'Donnell, A. M., Dansereau, D. F., Rocklin, T. R., Hythecker, V. I., Lambiotte, J. G., Larson, C. O. and Young, M. D. (1985) 'Effects of elaboration frequency on cooperative learning', *Journal of Educational Psychology*, 77, 5: 572–80.

O'Donnell, A. M., Dansereau, D. F., Hall, R. H. and Rocklin, T. R. (1987) 'Cognitive, social/affective, and metacognitive outcomes of scripted cooperative learning', *Journal of Educational Psychology*, 79, 4: 431–37.

Okawa, G. Y., Fox, T., Chang, L. J. Y., Windsor, S. R., Bella Chavez, F. Jr and Hayes, LaGuan (1991) 'Multi-cultural voices: peer tutoring and critical reflection in the writing center', *The Writing Center Journal*, Fall, 12, 1: 11–33.

Oldfield, K. A. and Macalpine, M. K. (1995) 'Peer and self-assessment at tertiary level – an experimental report', *Assessment and Evaluation in Higher Education*, 20, 1:125–31.

Owen, G. (1983) 'The tutor's role', in G. Collier (ed.) *The management of peer group learning*, Guildford: Society for Research into Higher Education.

Palincsar, A. S. and Brown, A. L. (1984) 'Reciprocal teaching of comprehension-fostering and comprehension-monitoring activities', *Cognition and Instruction*, 1, 2: 117–75.

Pask, G. (1975) *Conversation, cognition, and learning*, New York: Elsevier.

Pask, G. (1976) 'Styles and strategies of learning', *British Journal of Educational Psychology*, 46: 128–48.

Patterson, M. E., Dansereau, D. F. and Newbern, D. (1992) 'Effects of communication aids and strategies on cooperative teaching', *Journal of Educational Psychology*, 84, 4: 453–61.

Perry, W. G. Jr (1970) *Forms of intellectual and ethical development in the college years*, New York: Holt, Rinehart & Winston, Inc.

Piaget, J. (1971) *Science of education and the psychology of the child*, trans. D. Coltman, London: Longman.

Posen, B. (1983) 'Peer tutoring among young offenders: two experiments', MEd. Thesis, University of Newcastle upon Tyne.

Price, M. and Rust, C. (1995) 'Laying firm foundations: the long-term benefits of Supplemental Instruction for students on large introductory courses', *Innovations in Education and Training International*, 32, 3: 123–30.

Proctor, R., Williams, R. and Cashin, L. (1999) 'Social learning and new strategies for the management of innovation in multimedia: a case study of desktop videoconferencing', in R. S. Slack, J. K. Stewart and R. A. Williams, 'The social shaping of multimedia: proceedings from a COST [Coordination in the Field of Scientific and Technological Research] A4 Workshop held in Edinburgh, Scotland, June 27-29, 1997', Luxembourg, European Commission (DGXII).

Qualtrough, A. J. E. (1996) 'Student operator-assistant pairs', *Journal of Dental Education*, 60, 6: 527–32.

Randels, J., Carse, W. and Lease, J. E. (1992) 'Peer-tutoring training. A model for business schools', *Journal of Business and Technical Communication*, July, 6, 3: 337–53.

Reid, B. (1999) 'Building an online community with Mailbase', *Vine*, 109, April 1999.

Resnick, L. B., Levine, J. M. and Teasley, S. D. (eds) (1991) *Perspectives on socially shared cognition*, Washington, DC: American Psychological Association.

Rewey, K. L., Dansereau, D. F., Skaggs, L. P., Hall, R. H. and Pitre, U. (1989) 'Effects of scripted cooperation and knowledge maps on the processing of technical material', *Journal of Educational Psychology*, 81, 4: 604–09.

Rhodes, J. (1993) 'How pupils and staff experienced a peer tutoring project involving paired reading', *Reading,* 27, 3:14–19.

Richardson, S. (1994) 'How Supplemental Instruction came to Britain', in C. Rust and J. Wallace (eds) *Helping students to learn from each other: Supplemental Instruction*, Birmingham, UK: Staff and Educational Development Association (SEDA).

Rigg, M. (1990) *An overview of the demand for graduates*, London: HMSO.

Rings, S. and Sheets, R. A. (1991) 'Student development and metacognition: foundations for tutor training', *Journal of Developmental Education*, Fall, 15, 1: 30–32.

Ritter, L. (1997) 'An educreational approach to the teaching of history in an Australian College of Advanced Education', in P. Ritter, *Educreation and feedback: Education for creation, growth and change*, Oxford: Pergamon Press.

Roberts, V. C. (1994) 'Tutor resource manual: tutoring students in the community college', Arrowhead Community Colleges, Virginia, Minnesota, ED document 304 227.

Roethlisberger, F. J. and Dickson, W. J. (1939) *Management and the worker*, Cambridge, Massachusetts: Harvard University Press.

Rogers, C. R. (1969) *Freedom to learn*, Columbus, Ohio: Charles E. Merrill Publishing Company.

Rosen, S., Powell, E. R. and Schubot, D. B. (1977) 'Peer-tutoring outcomes as influenced by the equity and type of role assignment', *Journal of Educational Psychology*, 69, 3: 244–52.

Rosenshine, B. and Meister, C. (1991) 'Reciprocal teaching: a review of nineteen experimental studies', paper presented at the annual meeting of the American Educational Research Association, Chicago, April 3–7.

Rubin, L. and Herbert, C. (1998) 'Model for active learning: collaborative peer teaching', *College Teaching*, 46, 1: 26–30.

Salas, E., Dickinson, T. L., Converse, S.A. and Tannenbaum, S. I. (1996) 'Toward an understanding of team performance and training', in R.W. Swezey and E. Salas (eds) *Teams: their training and performance*, Norwood, New Jersey: ABLEX.

Salomon, G. (1993) *Distributed cognitions*, New York: Cambridge University Press.

Saunders, D. and Gibbon, M. (1998) 'Peer tutoring and peer assisted student support: five models within a new university', *Mentoring and Tutoring*, 5, 3: 3–13.

Saunders, D. and Kingdon, R. (1998) 'Establishing student tutoring within a higher education curriculum through the theme of personal and professional development', in S. Goodlad (ed.) *Mentoring and tutoring by students*, London: Kogan Page.

Schallert, D. L., Alexander, P. A. and Goetz, E. T. (1988) 'Implicit instruction of strategies for learning from text', in C. E. Weinstein, E. T. Goetz and P. A. Alexander (eds) *Learning and study strategies: issues in assessment, instruction and evaluation*, San Diego: Academic Press.

Schmuck, R. A. and Schmuck, P. A. (1975) *Group processes in the classroom* (2nd edn.) Dubuque, Iowa: Wm. C. Brown Company Publishers.

Schober, M. F. and Clark, H. H. (1989) 'Understanding by addressees and overhearers', *Cognitive Psychology*, 21: 211–32.

Scott, A. M. (1995) 'Collaborative projects in technical communication classes: a survey of student attitudes and perceptions', *Journal of Technical Writing and Communication*, 25, 2: 181–200.

Sharan, S. (1980) 'Cooperative learning in small groups: recent methods and effects on achievement, attitudes and ethnic relations', *Review of Educational Research*, 50, 2: 241–71.

Sherman, L. W. (1988) 'A pedagogical strategy for teaching human development: Dyadic Essay Confrontations through writing and discussion', paper presented at 8th annual Lilly Conference on College Teaching, November 5–6, Oxford, Ohio.

Sherman, L. W. (1991) 'Cooperative learning in post secondary education: implications from social psychology for active learning experiences', paper presented to the annual meeting of the American Educational Research Association, Chicago, April 3–7.

Sherwood, P. (1982) 'What should tutors know?', in M. Harris, *Tutoring writing. A sourcebook for writing labs*, Glenview, Illinois: Scott, Foresman & Company.

Shore, M. (1995) 'Students as tutors in early childhood settings: the acquisition and transmission of problem-solving skills', in S. Goodlad (ed.) *Students as tutors and mentors*, London and Philadelphia: Kogan Page.

Simon, J. G. and Feather, N. T. (1973) 'Causal attributions for success and failure at university examinations', *Journal of Educational Psychology*, 64, 1: 46–56.

Singh-Gupta, V. and Troutt-Ervin, E. (1996) 'Preparing students for teamwork through collaborative writing and peer review techniques', *Teaching English in the Two Year College*, 23, 2: 127–36.

Skinner, B. F. (1961) 'Why we need teaching machines', *Harvard Educational Review*, 31: 377–98.

Slaughter, J. P., Blaukopf, H. and Toohy, K. (1991) 'Tips for tutoring: improving reading abilities. A guidebook for the peer tutor', ERIC teaching guide 052.

Slavin, R. E. (1980) 'Effects of student teams and peer tutoring on academic achievement and time on-task', *The Journal of Experimental Education*, Summer, 48: 252–57.

Slavin, R. E. (1985) 'An introduction to cooperative learning research', in R. Slavin, S. Sharan, S. Kagan, R. Hertz-Lazarowitz, C. Webb and R. Schmuck (eds) *Learning to cooperate, cooperating to learn*, New York and London: Plenum Press.

Slavin, R. E. (1990) Cooperative learning. Theory, research and practice, Eaglewood Cliffs, NJ: Prentice Hall.

Smith, D., Wolstencroft, T. and Southern, J. (1989) 'Personal transferable skills and the job demands on graduates', *Journal of European Industrial Training*, 13, 8: 25–31.

Sobral, D. T. (1997) 'Improving learning skills: a self-help group approach', *Higher Education*, 33: 39–50.

Sobral, D. T. (1998) 'Productive small groups in medical studies: training for cooperative learning', *Medical Teacher*, 20, 2: 118–21.

Soven, M. (1993) 'Curriculum-based peer tutoring programs: a survey', *Writing Program Administration*, F/W, 17, 1-2: 58–74.

Spurlin, J. E., Dansereau, D. F., Larson, C. O. and Brooks, L. W. (1984) 'Cooperative learning strategies in processing descriptive text: effects of role and activity level of the learner', *Cognition and Instruction*, 1, 4: 451–63.

Starr, B. C. (1991) 'Linking students and classes: strategies for improving learning and thinking', *Community/Junior College*, Oct.-Dec., 15, 4: 427–38.

Sternberg, R. J. (1986) *Intelligence Applied*, New York: Harcourt Brace Jovanovich.

Strunk, W. and White, E. B. (1979) *The elements of style* (3rd ed.), New York: Macmillan.

Svinicki, M. D. (1991) 'Practical implications of cognitive theories', in R. J. Menges and M. D. Svinicki, *College teaching: from theory to practice. New directions for teaching and learning*, Number 5, Spring 1991, Jossey-Bass Inc. Publishers.

Tait, H. and Entwistle, N. J. (1996) 'Identifying students at risk through ineffective study strategies', *Higher Education*, 31: 91–116.

Tajfel, H. and Fraser, C. (1978) *Introducing social psychology*, Harmondsworth: Penguin Books.

Tang, J. C. (1991) 'Findings from observational studies of collaborative work', *International Journal of Man-Machine Studies*, 34: 143–60.

Tannen, D. (1990) *You just don't understand*, London: Virago Press.

Tate, A. and Thomson, J. E. (1994) 'The application of enterprise skills in the workplace', in S. Haselgrove (ed.) *The student experience*, Milton Keynes: The Society for Research into Higher Education and Open University Press.

Taylor, N. K. (1998) 'Survey of paid employment undertaken by full-time undergraduates at an established Scottish university', *Journal of Further and Higher Education*, 22, 1: 33–40.

Thibaut, J. W. and Kelley, H. H. (1959) *The social psychology of groups*, New York: John Wiley & Sons Inc.

Tinto, V. (1975) 'Dropouts from higher education: a theoretical synthesis of recent research', *Review of Educational Research*, 45: 89–125.

TIP (1999) http://www.gwu.edu/~tip **OR** http:tip.psychology.org

Tooley, J. with Darby, D. (1998) 'Educational research: a critique', report to Office for Standards in Education (OFSTED), London: OFSTED.

Topping, K. J. (1988) *The peer tutoring handbook*, Cambridge, Massachusetts: Brookline Books.

Topping, K. J. (1996a) 'Effective peer tutoring in further and higher education: a typology and review of the literature', *Higher Education*, 32: 321–45.

Topping, K. J. (1996b) 'Effective peer tutoring in further and higher education', SEDA Paper 95, Birmingham: Staff and Educational Development Association.

Topping, K. J. (1997) 'Peer tutoring for flexible and effective adult learning', in P. Sutherland (ed.) *Adult learning*, London and Stirling (USA): Kogan Page.

Topping, K. J. (1998) 'The effectiveness of peer tutoring in further and higher education: a typology and review of the literature', in S. Goodlad (ed.) *Mentoring and tutoring by students*, London: Kogan Page.

Topping, K. J. and Whiteley, M. (1993) 'Sex differences in the effectiveness of peer tutoring', *School Psychology International*, 14: 57–67.

Topping, K. J., Simpson, G., Thompson, L. and Hill, S. (1997) 'Faculty-wide accredited cross-year student supported learning', *Higher Education Review*, 29, 3: 41–64.

Trombulak, S. C. (1995) 'Merging inquiry-based learning with near-peer teaching', *BioScience*, 45, 6: 412–16.

Turkle, S. (1996) *Life on the screen: identity in the age of the Internet*, London: Phoenix Paperback.

Vaile, E. O. (1881) 'The Lancastrian System. A chapter in the evolution of common-school education', *Education* VI, January: 265–75.

Vygotsky, L. S. (1962) *Thought and language*, Cambridge, MA: MIT Press.

Vygotsky, L. S. (1978) *Mind in society*, Cambridge, MA: Harvard University Press.

Wall, G. (1997) 'Teach yourself autonomy does not work', *Times Higher Education Supplement*, January 31: 12.

Wallace, J. (1996) 'Peer tutoring: a collaborative approach', in S. Wolfendale and J. Corbett (eds) *Opening doors: learning support in higher education*, London: Cassell Publishers.

Wallace, J. and Rye, P. D. (1994) 'What is Supplemental Instruction?', SI University of Missouri-Kansas City Homepage. http://www.umkc.edu/cad/SI/SIPublications.htm

Walster, E., Berscheid, E. and Walster, G. W. (1973) 'New directions in equity research', *Journal of Personality and Social Psychology*, 25, 2: 151–76.

Watson, J. (1999) Research in progress, School of Economics, University of New South Wales, Sydney, j.watson@unsw.edu.au

Watters, J. J. and Ginns, I. S. (1997) 'Peer assisted learning: impact on self-efficacy and achievement', paper presented at annual meeting of the American Educational Research Association, 24–28 March, Chicago, IL.

Webb, N. (1985) 'Student interaction and learning in small groups', in R. Slavin, S. Sharan, S. Kagan, R. Hertz-Lazarowitz, C. Webb and R. Schmuck (eds) *Learning to cooperate, cooperating to learn*, New York: Plenum Press.

Webb, N. M. (1992) 'Testing a theoretical model of student interaction and learning in small groups', in R. Hertz-Lazarowitz and N. Miller (eds) *Interaction in cooperative groups*, Cambridge: Cambridge University Press.

Wedman, J. M., Kuhlman, W. I. and Guenther, S. J. (1996) 'The effect of Jigsaw on preservice teachers' knowledge of reading pedagogy and concerns about group learning in a reading methods course', *Reading Improvement*, Summer, 33, 2: 111–23.

Weinstein, C. E. and Meyer, D. K. (1991) 'Cognitive learning strategies and college teaching', in R. J. Menges and M. D. Svinicki, *College teaching: from theory to practice. New Directions for Teaching and Learning*, Number 5, Spring 1991, Jossey-Bass Inc. Publishers.

Wertsch, J. V. (1985) *Cultural communication, and cognition: Vygotskian perspectives*, Cambridge: Cambridge University Press.

Wheatley, M. J. (1995) 'Leadership and the new science', presentation transcribed as Professional Development Brief No. 3, September, California State Development Council.

Wheatley, M. J. (1999) 'Reclaiming hope: the new story is ours to tell', Summer Institute, July, University of Utah.

Wheatley, M. J. and Kellner-Rogers, M. (1996) *A simpler way*, San Francisco: Berrett-Koehler Publishers, Inc.

Wheldall, K. and Mettem, P. (1985) 'Behavioural peer tutoring: training 16-year-old tutors to employ the "pause, prompt and praise" method with 12-year-old remedial readers', *Educational Psychology*, 5, 1: 27–44.

Whimbey, A. and Lochhead, J. (1982) *Problem solving and comprehension: a short course in analytical reasoning*, Philadelphia: Franklin Institute Press.

Whitman, N. (1988) *Peer teaching. To teach is to learn twice*, ASHE-ERIC Higher Education Report No. 4. Washington, DC: Association for the Study of Higher Education.

Whitman, N. (1995) 'Inspiration is an active process: taking charge of your own learning in Medical School', Salt Lake City, Utah: Whitman Associates.

Whitman, N. (1999) 'Not only for the left-brained', in Notes of a Medical Educator, Salt Lake City, Utah: University of Utah School of Medicine.

Wiegmann, D. A., Dansereau, D. F. and Patterson, M. E. (1992) 'Cooperative learning: effects of role playing and ability on performance', *Journal of Experimental Education*, 60, 2: 109–16.

Willson, V. L. (1988) 'Evaluation of learning strategies research methods and techniques', in C. E. Weinstein, E. T. Goetz and P. A. Alexander (eds) *Learning and study strategies: issues in assessment, instruction and evaluation*, San Diego: Academic Press.

Wilson, E. K. (unpublished work) 'Knowledge in production: constructing worlds of difference. An exploration of post colonial agency in indigenous education', PhD in progress, Perth: University of Western Australia.

Winter, S. J. (1997) 'Cooperative learning in teacher education: a South-East Asian case study', unpublished study, Department of Education, Pokfulam Road, University of Hong Kong, sjwinter@hkusua.hku.hk

Witherby, A. (1997) 'Peer mentoring through Peer-Assisted Study Sessions (PASS)', in R. Hudson, S. Maslin-Prothero and I. Oates (eds) *Flexible learning in action. Case studies in higher education*, London: Kogan Page Staff and Educational Development Series.

Witkin, H. and Goodenough, D. R. (1981) *Cognitive styles: essence and origins. Field dependence and field independence*, New York: International Universities Press.

Wizer, D. R. and Beck, S. S. (1996) 'Studying diversity issues in teacher education using online discussions', *Journal of Computing in Teacher Education*, 13, 1: 6–11.

Wood, J. (1998) 'Quality assurance through the accreditation of student tutoring and student management of tutoring', in S. Goodlad (ed.) *Mentoring and tutoring by students*, London: Kogan Page.

Wyatt, S. A. and Medway, F. J. (1984) 'Causal attributions of students and student-proctors for performance on a university examination', *Contemporary Educational Psychology*, 9: 25–37.

Zajonc, R. B. (1960) 'The process of cognitive tuning in communication', *Journal of Abnormal and Social Psychology*, 61: 159–67.

Author index

Subject index